LITHUANIA

RICHARD BUTTERWICK

Lithuania

A History

HURST & COMPANY, LONDON

First published in the United Kingdom in 2025 by
C. Hurst & Co. (Publishers) Ltd.,
New Wing, Somerset House, Strand, London, WC2R 1LA
© Richard Butterwick, 2025
All rights reserved.

The right of Richard Butterwick to be identified as the author of this publication is asserted by him in accordance with the Copyright, Designs and Patents Act, 1988.

A Cataloguing-in-Publication data record for this book is available from the British Library.

ISBN: 9781911723608

This book is printed using paper from registered sustainable and managed sources.

EU GPSR Authorised Representative
Easy Access System Europe Oü, 16879218
Address: Mustamäe tee 50, 10621, Tallinn, Estonia
Contact Details: gpsr.requests@easproject.com, +358 40 500 3575

www.hurstpublishers.com

Every effort has been made to trace the provenance of Figure 26. The author and the publisher would be grateful for any information relating to this image or its rights.

For Februaries in Vilnius

CONTENTS

Note on Transliteration	ix
Introduction	1
1. The Rise of an Empire (to 1386)	15
i. From the Ice Age to the Iron Age	15
ii. Pagans and Christians	23
iii. Dynastic Empire	33
2. Forging a Union (1386–1569)	49
i. Jogaila and Vytautas	51
ii. The Political Nation of the Grand Duchy of Lithuania	68
iii. Reformation, Reform, and Union	80
3. A Commonwealth of Two Nations? (1569–1795)	97
i. Defining and Defending the Union	98
ii. Consolidation and Counter-Reformation	107
iii. Crisis of the Commonwealth	124
iv. Christians and Jews in Town and Country	142
v. Sarmatians and Revolutionaries	150
4. Under Imperial Rule (1795–1914)	179
i. Romantic Lithuania	182
ii. Risings and Reprisals	196

iii. Temperance and Literacy	208
iv. Modern Lithuanian Nationalism and its Rivals	225
5. Breaking Empires, Making Nations? (1914–1940)	245
i. From Occupation to Independence	247
ii. Between Democracy and Autocracy	271
iii. Independence Lost	289
6. Hammer, Swastika, and Sickle (1940–1991)	299
i. Soviet and Nazi Occupations and the Holocaust	301
ii. Diplomats and Diasporas	314
iii. Sovietisation and Lithuanisation	318
iv. Independence Regained	342
7. A Country in Europe (1991–2024)	361
i. A Democratic Republic	363
ii. Social Transformations	384
iii. 26 May 2024	393
Family Tree of the Gediminid–Jagiellonian Dynasty	397
Acknowledgements	399
List of Maps and Illustrations	401
Notes	405
Further Reading	421
Index	443

NOTE ON TRANSLITERATION

Transliterations from the Cyrillic alphabet have been made according to a slightly modified version of the Library of Congress system. The letter Г/г has been transliterated as H/h for words in Belarusian or Ukrainian and as G/g for words in Russian. The initial Latin letter Y/y has been used where this corresponds to familiar and intuitive renditions in English, such as in Yuri or Yurii, rather than Iuri or Iurii (for Юрі or Юрий), or as in Yeltsin, rather than El′tsin (for Ельцин). As in this case, some diacritics for 'soft' and 'hard' sounds have also been omitted for the same reason, but most diacritics, as in Rus′ (Русь), have been retained.

INTRODUCTION

The first landmark when flying into Vilnius is the Television Tower. This slender needle pierces a revolving restaurant just over half-way up. The tower was intended to symbolise the thrust of the Lithuanian Soviet Socialist Republic towards the radiant future—like others elsewhere in the Soviet bloc. Instead, it became a symbol of national sacrifice. On 13 January 1991, Soviet forces killed fourteen people: eleven were shot, two were crushed to death by Soviet tanks, and one man suffered a fatal heart attack. These people and thousands of others had been trying to prevent a violent reversal of the declaration, made almost a year earlier, that Lithuania was once again a sovereign and independent state. The defenders succeeded. The spectacle of the coffins outside Vilnius Cathedral, attended by tens of thousands of mourners, persuaded Mikhail Gorbachev to back down. Seven months later, the world recognised the independence of Lithuania, Latvia, and Estonia.

Three 'Singing Revolutions' catalysed the downfall of the USSR. On 23 August 1989, fifty years to the day after the Molotov–Ribbentrop pact carved up Eastern Europe, hundreds of thousands of Estonians, Latvians, and Lithuanians linked hands in a line of protest that stretched from Tallinn via Riga to Vilnius. It was a spectacular display of Baltic solidarity. For most of the outside world, 'the Baltics' form a convenient package, not least because their territories and populations are small, even by the standards of the European sub-continent. Some excellent guidebooks and histories treat them together, and for good reasons. The three countries won their independence at the end of the First World War, lost it in 1939–40, and regained it in 1990–91. Their shared experience of Soviet rule; their common path into NATO and the EU; and the consequent resentment in the Kremlin, all encourage joint treatment.

But the three countries are very different. Especially Lithuania. One joke asks: what do Estonia and Lithuania have in common? Latvia. On the one hand, Estonian, an Ugro–Finnic tongue, differs profoundly from Lithuanian and Latvian, which belong to the Baltic group of languages. On the other hand, the lands which now make up Estonia and northern Latvia shared most of their history up until 1918. Moreover, the standard stories of the Estonians and Latvians fit a model familiar to students of nations and nationalism: nineteenth-century intellectuals took an interest in the language and folklore of a long-oppressed native peasantry; activists promoted a 'national awakening' among the populace; the movement grew in numbers and radicalism, before finally achieving independence and creating an ethnically defined nation-state. They are stories of underdogs' victories, won against the odds of history.

These elements are also crucial to the Lithuanian national story. Like its two northern companions, the modern Lithuanian nation identifies itself chiefly by ethnicity and language. However, Lithuania's restored statehood is grounded in many centuries of complex and entangled history. The pattern holds at the local level as well. Lithuania's five ethnographic regions are distinguished by their dialects, songs, dances, costumes, cooking, and homesteads, but only Žemaitija (Latinised as Samogitia) claims a distinct political identity, and it has it for strong histori-

INTRODUCTION

cal reasons. On the other hand, the neighbouring region of Mažoji Lietuva (Lithuania minor) has practically ceased to exist—taken by the flood of history, as it were.

Although all three Baltic states face a common threat from neo-imperial Russia, today's Lithuanians' geopolitical outlook necessarily differs from that of their northern neighbours. According to another saying, there is only one truly Baltic state. Again, it is Latvia. The metropolis of Riga looks across the Baltic Sea towards Stockholm (Riga was once the richer city of the two). Picturesque Tallinn is a short ferry crossing across the Gulf of Finland from Helsinki (with a tunnel planned) and Estonians often claim a 'Nordic' rather than a 'Baltic' identity. Lithuania has a much shorter coastline. Its capital city is in the south-eastern corner of the country, close to the frontier with Belarus and not far from the Schengen-zone border with Poland. Like it or not, Lithuania is inseparable from East-Central Europe. To understand why, we need to leave the Television Tower and the surrounding Soviet-era suburbs (spruced up, these days). We take our bearings at Cathedral Square, the heart of Vilnius.

The Roman Catholic cathedral rises up in front of us like a Greek temple. The statues atop the Doric portico, taken down in 1950 by the Soviet authorities, were re-mounted in 1997. St Stanislaus—the patron of Poland—and St Casimir—the patron of Lithuania—flank the Emperor Constantine's mother, St Helena, venerated as the finder of the True Cross. Most of the cathedral was rebuilt at the end of the eighteenth century, but it incorporates much older structures. The earliest date back to the bishopric's foundation in the late fourteenth century. This belonged to a crucial turn in Lithuania's path.

Elsewhere in the eastern Baltic region, Catholic Christianity was forcibly imported. Two orders of monk-knights conquered and ruled the lands that became Estonia, Latvia, and East Prussia. During these 'northern crusades', the indigenous inhabitants died, fled, or became unfree subjects of the Teutonic Knights. In the sixteenth century, the Protestant Reformation ended the orders' rule, but the peasantry remained subjected to mostly German-speaking noble lords. Lutheranism, often lapsed, remains the default religion of Estonians and most Latvians to this day—if they profess a religion at all. The mostly Catholic exception that proves the rule is Latgale (Latgola), the southeastern part of Latvia, whose historical trajectory before 1918 was closer to that of Lithuania, as we shall see.

In contrast, the less accessible and better led Lithuanians withstood the crusaders' onslaught. In 1385–87, their ruler decided to accept Catholic baptism and convert his pagan subjects by explanation and example. The new faith soon put down deep roots in receptive soil, which in turn prepared the ground for the swift spread of the Protestant Reformation in the sixteenth century, as well as its slower retreat in the seventeenth. The default religion of most Lithuanians remains Roman Catholicism, although many are now irreligious and some profess neo-paganism.

Unlike the obscure leaders of other Baltic and Ugro–Finnic tribes, the medieval monarchs of Lithuania made decisive political choices. Their sway extended over vast areas of eastern and central Europe. Even as the Teutonic Knights were advancing, Lithuania's pagan warriors were subjecting Slavic lands that are now in Belarus, Ukraine, and the western reaches of Russia.

To the left (or north) of the cathedral portico is a statue of the first and, so far, only King of Lithuania enthroned and crowned. Mindaugas gained his royal status from a Roman pope as a reward for converting to Catholic Christianity; he may or may not have kept his baptismal promises. Within a few years of his violent death in 1263, pagans were back in charge. Nevertheless, Mindaugas's coronation in 1253 merits an annual holiday— Statehood Day—on 6 July. A visitor can sometimes see young

INTRODUCTION

soldiers, performing national service, brought in groups to this statue, whose significance is impressed upon them.

To the right of the cathedral is the striking statue of a stern, ironclad warrior leading his horse. This is Grand Duke Gediminas. Legend has it that in 1322 he dreamed of a howling iron wolf on a wooded hill where he had hunted down an aurochs. On this hill he built his castle, and at its feet grew a city. From Vilnius in 1323, in a series of letters written by his scribes in Latin, the Grand Duke invited German merchants, artisans, and knights to settle in Lithuania, and Catholic friars to minister to them. While remaining a pagan, Gediminas negotiated skilfully with popes, and with Catholic and Orthodox rulers. Many of his subjects, and much of his growing family, were Orthodox Christians. Carved on the high plinth are the profiles of two of his sons—Algirdas and Kęstutis—and two of his grandsons.

It was these grandsons, Jogaila and Vytautas, who made the momentous decision to accept Christian baptism from Rome, rather from Constantinople, via Kraków. For in 1386, Jogaila married the young heiress of the Kingdom of Poland, inaugurating a union which, for better or worse, would shape Lithuania's destiny for centuries to come. For worse, according to modern Lithuanian tradition. But before the long 'decline' set in, Vytautas the Great supposedly seized the reins of the Grand Duchy of Lithuania from his treacherous cousin Jogaila and led the state to its dazzling zenith. His authority briefly spanned the shores of the Baltic and Black Seas.

Many Lithuanian boys are called Vytautas, Gediminas, or Mindaugas. Almost none are named Jogaila.

High above Cathedral Square, the Lithuanian flag—a horizontal tricolour in yellow, green, and red—flutters proudly from the tower of the Upper Castle begun by Gediminas. This castle perches precariously on its steep mound which erodes with every downpour. In better condition is the Lower Castle which adjoins the cathedral. This building bears the name, when literally translated, of the National Museum of the Palace of the Sovereigns of the Grand Duchy of Lithuania. It is in the Renaissance style, with an Italianate arcaded courtyard. Despite appearances, it was only begun in 2002, partly opened on 6 July 2009, and completed in 2018. Although the costs have provoked taxpayers' complaints, most visitors find the result impressive. The reconstructed upper floors stage conferences, concerts, ceremonies, and temporary exhibitions under their coffered ceilings. Below are the foundations uncovered by archaeologists. The original palace was erected in the mid-sixteenth century, but later fell into disrepair. A few years after the third and final partition of the joint Polish–Lithuanian Commonwealth in 1795, the city's new Russian rulers ordered the Lower Castle's demolition.

The symbolism of the two castles is subtly different. Gediminas's Upper Castle stands for Lithuania's venerable and defiant statehood, created by the pagan grand dukes, and defended by Vytautas the Great. It became the emblem of interwar Lithuanians' desire to retake their historic capital city from the Poles who had seized it in 1920. The Lower Castle evokes the sophistication of a cosmopolitan city at the heart of a European great power. It is also romantically associated with star-crossed lovers: the cultured Grand Duke and King Sigismund Augustus, and his beautiful queen who died tragically young. One of the streets bordering Cathedral Square is named after her: Barbora Radvilaitė. She is also known as Barbara Radziwiłł. The story of Sigismund and Barbara can have an anti-Polish flavour, as Polish lords impugned her reputation and were reluctant to accept her as their queen. Nevertheless, she also became a heroine to generations of Poles, and Lithuania and Poland issued a joint stamp featuring the couple in 2020. The emphasis placed on the splendour of the sixteenth-century Renaissance requires a less one-

INTRODUCTION

sided interpretation of Lithuania's long union with Poland. This is reflected in the measured tone of the permanent exhibition on the history of the Grand Duchy of Lithuania, which is located on walkways above the excavated foundations of the original Lower Castle.

Behind the Upper Castle rises another, larger hill. Close to the summit, three large white crosses stand out from the trees. They date from 1989. Their predecessors were blown up by the Soviet authorities in 1950. The original monument was fashioned in concrete in 1916, replacing the wooden crosses which had been periodically renewed since the seventeenth century. These commemorated Franciscan friars believed to have been martyred here, about a generation before Jogaila's Catholic baptism changed the course of Lithuanian history.

The view is worth the steep climb. The hill falls precipitously and unstably to the banks of the Vilnia (or Vilnelė). This effervescent river swerves around the 'transfluvial suburb' of Užupis. At the turn of the 1980s and 1990s, artists set up studios in this picturesque, run-down district and established a 'republic' with a 'constitution', celebrated on April Fools' Day. For three decades, Užupis has been in the throes of gentrification; on some plots developers wait for historic buildings to fall down, preferring new-builds to costlier renovation. The Vilnia darts along the short distance to the statelier River Neris, beyond which soar the skyscrapers of the commercial centre. Further away, prefabricated apartment blocks march drearily to the horizon. Rising westwards from Cathedral Square, the oft-renamed Gediminas Avenue (*Gedimino prospektas*) cuts straight through the districts laid out for nineteenth-century Russian imperial officials and professionals, until it reaches the nondescript late Soviet-era parliament building. This was defended from behind barricades in January 1991, after the restoration of Lithuanian independence was proclaimed within. Beyond two bridges over the winding

LITHUANIA

Neris stretches the great green lung of the Vingis Park. Its open-air amphitheatre hosts an annual folksong festival. This was the venue for one of the great events of the 'Singing Revolutions'. On 23 August 1988, a quarter of a million people gathered here to protest against the Molotov–Ribbentrop Pact.

The enveloping hills and the two rivers create a much larger natural amphitheatre. The effect is enchanting. From Cathedral Square, the Old Town rises southwards—red-tiled roofs enlivened by ecclesiastical domes, belfries, and spires. Scudding clouds echo the rhythms of the architecture. Despite some notable gothic churches, and the austere classicism of the cathedral, the old City Hall, and the presidential palace, the quintessential Vilnan style is baroque—going on rococo. Finely wrought iron crosses top tapering towers and rippling facades. One major edifice is missing, though. The ruins of the Great Synagogue, the pride of the 'Jerusalem of the North', were cleared away after the Second World War. Archaeologists have to dig around the kindergarten that now occupies the site.

As investment pours into the Old Town, it is becoming harder to see or smell the suffocating squalor that for centuries seeped into the ecclesiastical, academic, and aristocratic splendour. But traces remain in ramshackle, almost rural courtyards reached through dark gateways off side-streets and alleys. Like fishbones, they can be found either side of the crowded 'royal route' with its hotels, restaurants, cafés, and shops selling amber. This route leads up Castle Street (*Pilies gatvė*), through Great Street (*Didžioji gatvė*), past the old City Hall, to the southern portal known to Lithuanians as the 'Gates of Dawn' (*Aušros vartai*) and to Poles and Belarusians as the 'Sharp Gate' (*Ostra Brama*, *Vostraia Brama*). The street narrows in front of the wonder-working image of the Madonna and Child, venerated in a chapel directly above the gate. This space is considered an open-air church. Once we have passed its praying pilgrims and clicking

INTRODUCTION

tourists, and exited the Old Town, we enter a different world. Here, beside the railway tracks, poverty is as evident as in the huge flea market north of the Neris. Further south lie the historic cemetery of Rasos (or Rossa)—the site of many a battle for memory between Lithuanians and Poles—the airport, and the road to Minsk.

South and east of Vilnius, in an extended band that traverses the EU's now strictly guarded frontier with Belarus, most of the population identifies as Polish or 'local Polish'. They, or their parents, grandparents, or great-grandparents, were not deported after the Second World War—unlike most Poles in the city itself. For more than a century, Lithuanian nationalists have asserted that these people are the descendants of 'Polonised' local peasants who should be reclaimed for the Lithuanian nation. The main battlefields have been language—in officially documented personal names, place names, and schools—and landownership. The Polish population's loyalty has also been questioned, mainly because its local Communist leaders placed their bets on the USSR in 1989–91. Fears of a 'fifth column' have never entirely been dispelled, despite the great improvement in relations between Vilnius and Warsaw after a rocky start in the early 1990s.

Lithuania's national demography provides a further contrast with Latvia and Estonia. There, the scale of migration from the rest of the Soviet Union was almost overwhelming. Shortly before they recovered their independence, ethnic Latvians constituted just 52 per cent of their country's population, and ethnic Estonians 62 per cent of theirs. Native speakers of Russian constituted nearly all of the rest (although not all Russian speakers were ethnic Russians). Hence the controversial decisions to restrict citizenship to descendants of the pre-war populations and to those able to pass examinations in the Latvian or Estonian languages respectively. In Lithuania, however, ethnic Lithuanians comprised 80 per cent of the population in the 1989 census.

Most of the remaining fifth was divided between persons declaring Russian or Polish nationality, with smaller proportions identifying as Belarusian or Ukrainian. All inhabitants of Lithuania in 1991 received Lithuanian citizenship.

During the passing of a generation, during which hundreds of thousands of Lithuanian citizens have emigrated and many Polish, Russian, and Belarusian speakers have assimilated, these demographic proportions have altered slightly in favour of those identifying as Lithuanian. At the south-eastern margins of Lithuania, literary Polish is taught at school and practised in church, whereas the lilting everyday speech still tends to be blended locally from Polish, Belarusian, and Russian. Larger concentrations of native speakers of Russian are still located in Visaginas, next to the decommissioned nuclear power plant of Ignalina in the north-east, and in the port city of Klaipėda in the west. It was once better known as Memel. The pattern reflects Soviet-era migration. In the city of Vilnius, denuded of nearly all of its Jewish and most of its Polish inhabitants through genocide and deportation during and after the Second World War, native speakers of Lithuanian have since the 1980s constituted the clear majority. Many Vilnans of Polish, Belarusian, or Russian descent speak the Lithuanian language fluently. Nonetheless, Vilnius remains far more diverse than most of the country.

Elsewhere, homogeneity is a relatively new phenomenon. Take Kėdainiai, in the centre of the Republic of Lithuania. This now thoroughly Lithuanian town draws visitors to the traces of its polyglot past, when a cacophony in Yiddish, German, Scots, Polish, Ruthenian, and Lithuanian echoed through its streets, markets, and alleys. The monuments include a former synagogue and a Jewish cemetery—the 3,000-strong community was annihilated in 1941. The crypt of the spacious Calvinist church houses the coffins of its Radziwiłł patrons. A seventeenth-century representative of this famous aristocratic family is honoured by a

INTRODUCTION

statue in the market square. Jonušas II Radvila is celebrated as a Lithuanian patriot, while Janusz II Radziwiłł is still regarded as a traitor to Poland. To understand why is to understand the difference between modern and pre-modern ideas of the nation.

Concise as this book must be, it cannot confine itself to the story of the modern, ethno-linguistic Lithuanian nation. This is partly because Lithuanian hackles are sometimes raised by foreigners who presume to tell them 'their history'. They can—and do—tell it themselves.[1] Nor is this book a lofty exercise in debunking ethno-linguistic Lithuanian national narratives. They need to be understood, but in the context of rival national narratives. The term 'nationalism', essentially meaning the conviction held by a community that considers itself a 'nation' that it should form its own state on the territory it claims as its own, will be used neutrally, and not as a pejorative term akin to chauvinism and xenophobia. My main aim is to explain to visitors the history of a country once much larger than it is now, inhabited by many peoples that developed and interacted in concord and discord. Lithuania's history is particularly entangled with the histories of Belarus, Estonia, Germany, Latvia, Poland, Sweden, Russia, and Ukraine. Long after the vast empire of Vytautas the Great had contracted, and for about a century after the destruction of the Grand Duchy of Lithuania in 1795, the current territories of Lithuania and Belarus, and the northeastern corner of Poland, were known as 'Lithuania'. The habit endured until the establishment of the modern republic in 1918. So this book will chart the changing meanings of 'Lithuania' and 'Lithuanian'.[2]

For this reason, the names of many persons who considered themselves Lithuanian in various senses will be rendered in the languages that seem to me to be the most appropriate. Inevitably, many of my choices will not do justice to the complex, multilingual environments in which these people communicated.

LITHUANIA

Lithuanian versions of personal names will rarely be encountered between the sixteenth and eighteenth centuries (mostly as alternatives on first mention). However, the dissatisfaction that some readers will feel is preferable to a rigid policy of assigning Lithuanian names to people who wrote in other languages, but not in Lithuanian. Ideally, place names would also be provided in all their bewildering variety of forms, so that the same place would appear in different languages at different places in the text. However, the book is intended for travellers who need to be able to find places on a map or the internet. Except in those rare cases when acceptable English versions exist, I have adopted the widely employed solution of naming places in the official language of the state in which they are currently located. Occasionally alternatives are provided in the text when the context demands it. Others are in the index. But I refuse to call Königsberg 'Kaliningrad' before 1945.

Even a short history of Lithuania must have a different chronological balance from those of its companion volumes about Latvia and Estonia, which focus chiefly on the nineteenth and twentieth centuries. Much of what follows is devoted to the centuries—from the thirteenth to the eighteenth—when the Grand Dukes of Lithuania reigned over vast swathes of Europe. Those times were full of the events—successions, parliaments, confrontations, wars, alliances, and reforms—that constitute political history. They were equally enriched by the ideas—such as loyalty, community, solidarity, consent, liberty, equality, and trust—that endow political events with meaning. Last but not least, a rich cast of characters have made their mark on Lithuania, Europe, and beyond. They range from the unsuccessful apostle St Bruno of Querfurt, via monarchs, magnates, educators, and writers, to Lithuania's own 'Iron Lady'—President Dalia Grybauskaitė. Many of these people have streets named after them, and visitors may wish to understand their places in this

INTRODUCTION

story. In sum, I hope readers will find it easier to understand why this long and complex history mattered, and why it matters still—not only in Lithuania.

Map 1: Lithuania, its neighbours, and the five ethnographic regions—Aukštaitija, Dzūkija, Suvalkija, Mažoji Lietuva, and Žemaitija

1

THE RISE OF AN EMPIRE

(TO 1386)

i. *From the Ice Age to the Iron Age*

The Earth was cold, windy, dry, and dusty. So much seawater was locked up in ice that sea shores were more than 120 metres below their present level. Glaciers slowly, slowly flowed down from the Scandinavian mountains into the Baltic basin. They merged into a continental ice cap that extended from Ireland to the Arctic—itself covered in sea ice more than 3 kilometres thick. One icy tentacle crept beyond Lithuania's current junction with Belarus and Poland. Then, about 20,000 years ago, Earth began to warm up again. Gradually the great Scandinavian Ice Sheet shrank. By about 12,000 BCE, all of the present territory of Lithuania and Latvia was ice-free.

As this huge ice sheet retreated from lower terrain depressed by its mass, it gouged out countless lakes, and left residues of heavy moraine in steep-sloped drumlins. Over several thousand years, the post-glacial, perma-frosted tundra thawed out, and trees began to grow. The taiga or boreal forest advanced. First came evergreens—pine, spruce, larch, and fir. Birch, maple,

LITHUANIA

alder, and willow followed, with oak in favoured spots. Meltwater created a Baltic lake, fed from the south and east by the Rivers Vistula, Nemunas, and Daugava. This lake later drained into the rising Atlantic Ocean before a post-glacial 'rebound' (part of the process called isostatic adjustment) briefly shut it in again. Around 6,000 BCE, Atlantic saltwater once more began to flow through the Danish Straits. Even today, the Baltic Sea remains low in salinity and has negligible tides.

Humans followed herds of reindeer into the tundra and taiga. Their first traces in the south-eastern Baltic region date from around 10,000 BCE. Two or three thousand years later, the climate had warmed up further. Rivers and lakes full of fish and fowl, and forests teeming with aurochs, beavers, bears, bison, boars, deer, elk, and wolves, with abundant berries, nuts, mushrooms, and honey, were beginning to support larger groups of hunter-gatherers. These people made weapons and implements from flint, horn, and bone. Some were buried with amulets—to invoke or placate spirits. By the third millennium BCE there is evidence of settlements, domesticated animals, and two-field agriculture. The people of these parts fired ceramics and carved jewellery. They hoarded and bartered amber. This natural treasure of fossilised resin is washed up on the Baltic shores in rare quality and quantity. Humans have coveted it for thousands of years.

'Lithuanian history is deeper and wider than the scant and late documentary evidence would indicate,' a leading Lithuanian medievalist reminds non-Lithuanians. She refers to archaeological evidence reaching as far back as the Neolithic period.[1] But were these people and their culture in any meaningful sense Lithuanian? The temptation to associate similarities in material cultures (usually worked out from excavated potsherds) with group identities or even common biological descent has often been overwhelming. Many of the consequences of racial assumptions have been deadly. Nonetheless, it is natural for people to

THE RISE OF AN EMPIRE

ask: 'who are we?' and 'where are we from?'. From this point in the region's prehistory, archaeology has to work hand in hand with philology. Just such a synthesis was promoted by Marija Gimbutas (originally Gimbutienė), a staunchly Lithuanian archaeologist and linguist who escaped the advancing Red Army in 1944. She did her best work at Harvard in the 1950s and early 1960s, before moving to California.[2]

Since classical antiquity, scholars have recognised families of languages, investigated the processes by which they diverge and evolve, and searched for evidence of common ancestral tongues. Most of the languages spoken between the River Ganges and the Atlantic Ocean are related to one another in an 'Indo–European' family. By the later nineteenth century, the proto-Indo–European language had been largely reconstructed using comparative methods. Gimbutas's greatest contribution was to locate the original homeland of proto-Indo–European speakers in the Pontic steppes north of the Black and Caspian Seas. She called it her 'Kurgan hypothesis' after the Russian word for the characteristic burial mounds first found in the region. It has largely withstood the test of time. As the proto-Indo–European language spread, its north-western thrust morphed into proto-Baltic–Slavic, from which proto-Slavic and proto-Baltic are thought to have branched off sometime after 1500 BCE. Among the Slavic languages are Polish, Belarusian, Ukrainian, and Russian.

Among the extinct Baltic languages, the best recorded is Old Prussian, whose last native speakers probably succumbed to the plague shortly after 1700. Others are known in fragments, with the rest surmised from linguistic theory. The two living Baltic languages are Lithuanian and Latvian, both codified from regional dialects in the later nineteenth century. While closely related, they are not mutually intelligible. Moreover, some Samogitians and Latgalians consider their tongues languages in their own right, rather than dialects of Lithuanian and Latvian respectively. Lithuanian is usually considered to have preserved more of the proto-Indo–European spoken 5,000 years ago than any other living language. Its similarities to ancient Sanskrit, Greek, and Latin have been noticed for centuries.

The evidence of hydronyms—the names of rivers, lakes, and other bodies of water—led Gimbutas to stake out a vast area in which proto-Baltic or Baltic languages were once spoken. It spread from the mouth of the River Oder in the west to the headwaters of the Volga in the east, and from the marshy Prypiats' in the south to some point beyond the Daugava in the north. Linguistic analysis does not in itself prove that this was the ancestral homeland of the Baltic peoples. Many scholars have, however, made the connection, and none was more important than the German author Johann Gottfried Herder, who straddled the Enlightenment and Romanticism. Herder studied the folklore of the local peasants while he taught in Riga during the 1760s. He concluded that each people of common descent had its own language. This language, especially when sung, expressed that people's unique spirit: its *Volksgeist*. Many have since taken his point; Mara Kalnins, the Latvian author of the eloquent companion volume to this book, endorses it wholeheartedly.[3] When Lithuanians, Latvians, and Estonians sang their way back to freedom in 1988–91, they made a powerful case for Herder's idea. Sceptical outsiders, taught at university to consider nations as 'modern' communities 'imagined' or even 'invented' in the nineteenth and twentieth centuries, should not dismiss such convictions lightly. If nations are indeed 'imagined communities', it follows that some have been imagined by more people, more intensely, and for longer than others. Many theorists of nation-building would concede that some of the necessary components of 'modern nations' are very old indeed.

In Herder's wake, for most of the nineteenth and twentieth centuries scholars tended to assume that migrations of 'barbarians' in prehistoric, ancient, and early medieval times essentially involved movements of discrete 'tribes': extended kin-groups with their own languages and customs. Such movements of peoples tended to imply conquests, flights, and displacements. In recent decades, this view of migration has become unfashionable, and ideas of group identity have become more complex. 'Migrations' have typically become 'régime changes' in which low numbers of migrants can impose far-reaching changes in ideologies, rituals, and languages. Perhaps the pendulum is now swinging back towards the view that substantial numbers of people were on the move for millennia, even if they did not bring their nineteenth-century folk dances and costumes with them. The ongoing debates between 'movers' and 'shakers' are passionate and politicised.

Gimbutas and her reputation cast light on these trends. In her controversial last works, she argued that relatively pacific and egalitarian cultures, featuring prominent 'goddesses', were common across 'Old Europe', before they were replaced by those of the more warlike and masculine Bronze Age. Her critics caricatured her ideas as the violent suppression of a matriarchal Utopia by cruel, semi-nomadic 'Kurgan' horsemen.[4] Cue hyper-masculine pagan Lithuanian warriors rampaging through eastern Europe thousands of years later...

For our purposes, these debates boil down to an argument over the proportions among the (proto-)Baltic speakers: between the descendants of Pontic steppe-dwellers, and the descendants of subjected and assimilated peoples. Did the earlier inhabitants bequeath a peaceable and feminine streak to the progeny of their fusion with the semi-nomadic newcomers? Many have found the idea attractive. The most likely candidates for the earlier arrivals are speakers of non-Indo–European, Ugro–Finnic languages. These are the forebears of Finnish, Estonian, and Livonian (the latter has been revived; the last native speaker, Grizelda Marija Kristiņa, died in Canada in 2013, aged 103).

LITHUANIA

The evidence of chromosomes is difficult for non-specialists to fathom, but for what it is worth, both excavated and contemporary eastern Baltic populations reveal some distinctive genetic characteristics. Particularly striking is the low proportion of genomes from the Neolithic farmers found across much of Europe. This finding may support the idea of a substantial direct migration of pastoralist proto-Indo–Europeans from the Pontic steppes to the Baltic shores. It may also correspond with the appearance of characteristic 'corded ware' pottery in the late Neolithic archaeological record, in the middle of the third millennium BCE. But a case has also been made for 'Uralic' genomes from the east arriving later than 'Baltic' ones from the south.

Closer to the surface, the archaeological evidence thickens. Excavations of grave mounds and hillforts dating from the middle of the second millennium BCE have brought forth bronze jewellery, weapons, and other implements. Sites from a thousand years later yield objects of iron. Preserved remains of human and animal waste show that fishing, hunting, livestock-raising, and agriculture co-existed. Nevertheless, as average temperatures rose and fell cyclically, most of the south-eastern Baltic region remained fastnesses of forest and bog.

In the fifth century BCE, the first written source irrupts into the arguments of geologists, dendrologists, archaeologists, philologists, and geneticists. The Histories of Herodotus mention the 'Neuri' who lived north of the Scythians. Modern scholars have speculated over whether these people were 'Balts' (a name only invented in the nineteenth century, in connection with their languages). Much, much later, in CE 77, Pliny the Younger described the legendary voyage of Pytheas to the 'Amber Isles', whose name—Glaesaria—derived from the local barbarians' word for amber: *'glesum'*. As it happens, the word for amber in Latgalian is *glēze*. Pliny also described the 'amber route' from the Baltic Sea across central Europe to the Romans' Danubian frontier in Pannonia. Many Roman coins have been found on the Baltic shores.

Trade in amber (*glesum*) also features in Tacitus' *Germania* (CE 98). The northern barbarians fascinated this otherwise sceptical historian. He ascribed to them that fierce love of freedom which he feared the Romans had lost. Tacitus devoted a few lines to the inhabitants of the 'right-hand' shores of the Baltic, beyond the lands of the Goths. These Aestii—as he called them—were supposedly patient farmers who worshipped the 'mother of gods' and whose language most resembled that of the Britons. Whatever its etymology, the name stuck; half a century later the Aestii appeared in Claudius Ptolemy's *Geographia*, which described the south-eastern Baltic coast—'the last known country'—reasonably accurately. The Aestii (spellings varied) also turn up in, for example, works of the sixth-century Gothic historian Jordanes and in the ninth-century biography of Charlemagne by Einhard. Wulfstan, an Anglo-Saxon merchant sent east by King Alfred the Great, reported that when the greatest among these people died, the feasts and games could last for months before the pyre was finally lit. The corpse had to be kept cold by ancient lore. By this time, however, another name had begun to circulate: the Prussians (first recorded as Bruzi). According to Adam of Bremen, who wrote his chronicles in the eleventh century, these pagans were kind to seafarers—usually. Besides amber, these faraway lands were rich sources of commodities acquired by violence: furs and slaves.[5]

In contrast to the coast-dwellers, the peoples of the interior remained unknown to the 'civilised world' throughout the first Christian millennium. It is risky (to say the least) to project the names of tribes known from much later written sources back into the distant past. Archaeology and philology supply almost all we know. For example, over hundreds of years, the practice of cremation, rather than burial, spread from the south-east to the north-west of the region—but what was the significance of this shift? Changing patterns in the graves, ceramics, and even skull-types excavated by archaeologists may—or may not—be related to the branching out of the Baltic languages which philologists conclude must have taken place at this time. One intriguing suggestion is that the splendid attire and jewellery with which prematurely deceased girls were equipped by their high-status families in the third century CE was intended to assure, by the payment of their dowries, their favourable reception into the world of their ancestors.[6] In general, over several hundred years, the evidence of farming and livestock-rearing becomes richer, while traces of buildings indicate increasingly sophisticated structures. Jewellery and weapons become more ornate, requiring specialist skills. It seems logical to associate this evidence with the development of more hierarchical tribal structures.

These hierarchical tendencies partly coincide with what used to be called the 'barbarian invasions' blamed (but sometimes credited) for the fall of the western Roman Empire and the onset of the 'Dark Ages'. Most scholars now use less cataclysmic language: the transformations of 'late antiquity'. For all that, many people were on the move, often fleeing west in terror of the Huns. Most of this movement would have occurred south of the River Prypiats´. But repercussions were felt in the less accessible lands inhabited by Baltic speakers. Arrows of the types used by steppe nomads have been excavated at fortified sites in today's Lithuania.

Of crucial importance to our story are the Slavs. 'Sclaveni' enter eastern Roman (Byzantine) historical records in the sixth century CE. They seem to have come from the steppes north of the Black Sea and the Carpathian Mountains. They moved south into the Balkans, west towards the River Elbe, and north into the forested zone. Over several hundred years, the eastern branches of Slavic languages spread over a wide area, with a corresponding retreat of Baltic tongues. The Slavic and Baltic linguistic groups,

THE RISE OF AN EMPIRE

according to philologists, had separated about two millennia earlier. During their later interactions, words were borrowed, but the languages remained distinct. The extent to which this process reflected either a physical displacement of genetically different populations, or changes in group identities, is largely a matter of speculation. Some violence is suggested by the traces of burnt settlements excavated and dated by archaeologists, while one group of Slavic newcomers, the Krivichi, bequeathed the Latvian word for 'Russians'—'Krievi'. It has long been supposed, however, that much mixing of peoples took place. Such conjectures gave rise in the twentieth century to the conviction, convenient to advocates of a 'Greater Lithuania', that Belarusians were 'really' slavicised Balts.

ii. *Pagans and Christians*

Profound changes affected much of north-eastern Europe in the ninth and tenth centuries CE. Some transformations were catalysed by Norse raiders and traders, popularly known as 'Vikings' ('viking' being a predatory activity). It has become fashionable to emphasise their less terrifying side, but reiving, raiding, and trading overlapped, not least from the luckless slaves' perspective. Some of these Scandinavians visited the south-eastern shores of the Baltic. These parts offered leaner pickings than defenceless Christian monasteries across the North Sea, but perhaps more 'reputation'. For the seafaring Curonians were not passive victims: the plea 'O Mighty God, protect us against the Curonians' echoed through eleventh-century Danish churches.[7] There is archaeological evidence of flourishing emporia, including at the site of what is now Lithuania's liveliest seaside resort—Palanga. Among the diverse merchants who traded here, some were Christians. Other Scandinavians penetrated the river systems between the Baltic and Black Seas, beginning with the Daugava.

LITHUANIA

They established strongholds and trading posts, some of which would grow into cities, such as Novgorod and Kyiv.

These chieftains and warriors appear in later Byzantine sources as 'Varangians' but became known locally as the 'Rus''. The name probably derived from the old Norse for 'rowers' and is corroborated by the Finnish and Estonian names for Sweden: *Ruotsi* and *Rootsi*. In migratory terms, these people were 'shakers' rather than 'movers'. In time, the name Rus' came to denote the lands they dominated, while the east Slavic tongue they learned from the native population came to be called *ruski*. When a descendant of the semi-legendary Norse leader Riurik accepted baptism from Constantinople in 988 CE, Kyivan Rus' joined Christendom. This man was Volodymyr the Great (called Vladimir in Russian, Uladzimir in Belarusian, and Valdamarr in the Norse sagas). He and his son, Yaroslav the Wise, established a huge, rich, and powerful realm. Despite the tendency to political fragmentation as the generations passed, Rus' prospered until the early thirteenth century. Beyond the great river networks, the Riurikid princes and their followers collected tribute over vast, sparsely settled areas, including some of those still inhabited by speakers of Baltic languages. There are sporadic mentions in Rus'ian annals of punitive expeditions against troublesome pagans, but no evidence of any sustained attempt to Christianise them.[8]

It was the Western, or Latin, Church that first sent missions to the south-eastern Baltic region. First Bohemia, then Poland, and finally Hungary emerged as Christian realms by the end of the millennium: the new faith underpinned the idea and institutions of monarchy. In 997 CE, the Polish duke, Bolesław the Valiant, supported the risky mission of the bishop of Prague Adalbert (Vojtěch, Wojciech) to convert the pagan Prussian tribes east of the Vistula estuary. Some of the people he encountered seem to have feared and resented Adalbert's harangues (reading may have been construed as hostile magic), and he was

THE RISE OF AN EMPIRE

soon killed. Duke Bolesław bought his body from the Prussians for its weight in gold. Within three years the duke had used the swiftly canonised martyr to found an archbishopric at Gniezno, with the support of the Holy Roman Emperor Otto III. This metropolitan province, independent of any German see, helped the idea of 'Poland' to congeal and endure.

Bruno of Querfurt, who had been Otto's court chaplain, not only wrote a saint's life (hagiography) of Adalbert, but followed in his footsteps as a missionary. He seems to have been warmly received by Volodymyr the Great in Kyiv in 1008 CE, who may have hoped for a mission to the Pechenegs, pagan semi-nomads who inhabited the steppes further south. Be that as it may, Bruno was intent on resuming Adalbert's mission to the Prussians. According to an account written about a generation later, Bruno baptised a pagan ruler called Nethimer, whose angry brother then had the apostle beheaded. Although Bruno is venerated as a saint in both the Eastern and Western Churches, neither Volodymyr nor Bolesław the Valiant were able to capitalise on his martyrdom. His cult never rivalled that of Adalbert, perhaps because his mission entered a space between and beyond the two Christian traditions. A brief entry in the near-contemporary annals of Quedlinburg Abbey dates Bruno's death to 9 March 1009 and locates it '*in confinio Rusciae et Lituae*'—'at the frontier of Rus' and Lithuania'. Bruno met his maker just beyond the sway of the Kyivan ruler.[9]

This first known mention of Lithuania has intrigued historians and philologists alike. Much and more was made of it during the millennium celebrations of 2009. The Latin *Litua* evidently comes from the Slavic *Litva* (Литва or Литьва in Cyrillic). *Lit′va* in turn derives from a compressed pronunciation of *Lietuva*—Lithuania in Lithuanian. To explain this word, at least three theories compete. The popular one associates *Lietuva* with *lietus*—rain. It does rain in Lithuania, but only about as much as

25

in the east of England. Moreover, *Lietuva* has a suffix like a hydronym. The second theory derives *Lietuva* from the River Lietava or Lietauka (the verb *lieti* means to spill, and the Lietava is known to spill over). Although this rivulet is all of eleven kilometres long and thirty kilometres away from the ancient stronghold at Kernavė, mighty nations have been named for less. A third and perhaps more likely idea is that the name Lietuva (or Leituva) derives from *leitis*, an archaic word for a Lithuanian (plural: *leičiai*). Much later, this term is attested to for military servitors of the grand dukes, used alongside the derivative of Lietuva—*lietuvis*, which still connotes a Lithuanian. Taking the theory one stage further, the word *leitis* has been linked to the Rivers Leitė and Leita (which derive their name from clay). The suffix 'ava' or 'uva' then gives a collective noun. Beginning with a late eleventh-century inscription on birch-bark, Rus′ian chroniclers long referred interchangeably both to the land and the people as *Litva* (usually in the context of fighting). Lithuania may ultimately mean the land of those who dwell by the clayey river. Or possibly—by the overflowing river.[10]

Leaving the philologists to their disputations over patterns of stress and intonation, we return to 1009 CE. The Lithuanians—irrespective of exactly who they were, how many there were of them, and where they lived—evidently had a militarised political structure. Their leader was attracted by the message preached by Bruno, but he lacked his warriors' consent to emulate the Slav rulers and become a Christian prince. This outcome would set a pattern for almost two centuries. The various pagan tribes of the region sporadically raided their Christian neighbours and were raided by them in turn. Conflict was endemic, for example, with the principality of Polatsk (in what is now Belarus). The archaeological record points to growing trade, skilful crafts, deadlier weapons, and stronger hillforts—all markers of a more hierarchical society. Neither the closeness of Slav Christian principalities,

THE RISE OF AN EMPIRE

nor the presence of small Christian communities along the south-eastern Baltic coast entailed successful missions to the interior. The old ways and beliefs maintained their grip.

Further changes came at the turn of the twelfth century. In 1186, a missionary bishopric was established for Livonia. This name comes from the Ugro–Finnic-speaking Livs, who then inhabited much of the coastline of the Gulf of Riga. Not unlike Jesuits in sixteenth-century South America, some of the early missionaries were concerned for the temporal welfare as well as the eternal souls of the local population, but misunderstandings were inevitable. Tensions between Christians and pagans at the mouth of the River Daugava prompted the mightiest of all the medieval popes, Innocent III, to proclaim a crusade in defence of the Church there in 1199. The energetic new bishop, Albert, moved the see to the newly founded city of Riga in 1201 and then pushed upriver. His lobbying in Rome on behalf of 'the Land of Mary' (*Terra Mariana*) produced results: Baltic crusades were deemed as pleasing to God as those to the Holy Land. This was part of a general shift in the idea of crusading, from campaigns for Jerusalem to sanctified slaughter of pagans, heretics, and sundry enemies of the Roman pontiff. This meant that the pope and the Holy Roman Emperor, the two patrons of the northern crusades, were usually at odds with each other. The Sword-Brothers, modelled on the Templars and other crusading orders, were founded in 1202. The bishop initially sent these monk-knights northwards, the better to keep the lucrative Daugava trade under his own control. Merchants from northern German cities—the nucleus of the Hanseatic League—soon supplanted the Scandinavians and Slavs who had hitherto predominated.

After the Sword-Brothers had subjugated most of the northern tribes, exploiting their divisions, they moved against those of Semigallia and Curonia (in the south of today's Latvia). The

Knights ignored the Curonian ruler's treaty with the pope, involving his baptism and recognition as king, and seized the coastal lands. However, they soon overreached themselves. In 1236, they suffered a shattering defeat at a place called Saulė at the hands of the combined tribes (including those called *Littowen*) led by a Samogitian ruler called Vykintas. The official site of the 'Battle of the Sun', near the village of Jauniūnai north of Šiauliai, now features a twenty-nine-metre-high sundial and a grove of oaks. Since 2000, the battle's anniversary on 22 September has been jointly celebrated by Lithuania and Latvia as 'Baltic Unity Day'.

In 1237, the battered remnants of the Sword-Brothers merged into the Teutonic Knights. The Order of Brothers of the German House of Saint Mary in Jerusalem, commonly known as the Teutonic Order, founded in 1190, had recently begun its own crusade against the pagan Prussians. They did so at the invitation of a Polish duke, Conrad, whose Duchy of Mazovia had long suffered Prussian raids. From 1231, the Teutonic Knights swiftly conquered land for themselves on the east bank of the Vistula. As the decades passed, they took more land, first from the Prussians, and then from the related Yotvingian tribes who lived further east. The Knights discovered that winter, when the lakes and bogs froze over, was the best campaigning season. The Order settled burghers, farmers, and secular knights, mostly from the German lands. A similar, but less intensive process took place in Livonia, where more of the autochthonous population survived. The continual and often vicious fighting pushed the pagan tribes towards political and ethnic consolidation. Refugees and rebels from Livonia, Prussia, and Yotvingia were absorbed into Samogitian and Lithuanian tribes.

The leaders of warbands recruited warriors over a wide area. Their ability to act collectively is evident from a peace treaty concluded in 1219. The parties were the Riurikid prince of

THE RISE OF AN EMPIRE

Halych and Volhynia and no less than twenty-one Lithuanian leaders, called *kniazi*—the east Slavic word for dukes or princes. One was a widow, and several Samogitian clans were represented. Five senior dukes from Aukštaitija—the Lithuanian 'high country'—were given precedence. This quintet included Mindaugas, who would emerge over the next quarter-century as the Lithuanians' sole ruler.[11] Little is certain about the process of political unification. Tomas Baranauskas has projected the process of 'state-formation' back into the eleventh century. Admittedly, he does not include Samogitia, but only the territory called 'Lithuania propria' in later sources, which straddled what is now the eastern half of Lithuania and the north-western half of Belarus.[12] The leading families, who could summon many warriors and were provisioned by numerous farmsteads and villages, experienced the vicissitudes of war and fertility. They made alliances, quarrelled, and rose or fell in significance. As elsewhere in 'barbarian' Europe, political success depended on a leader's ability to capture treasure and slaves, reward his followers with loot, and protect their families. One of the ducal élite may well have exercised a supremacy over the others, but to suppose this does not entail the stable existence of an office of 'Grand Duke of Lithuania', let alone a state called 'the Grand Duchy of Lithuania'.

Rus'ian chroniclers told blood-curdling tales of how Mindaugas killed or expelled his kinsmen. But it is clear that other 'dukes' accepted his overlordship, in some cases by marrying his sisters. By the mid-1240s, Mindaugas's sway transcended his own ducal domain located between the Rivers Nemunas and Neris. To the south-east, it extended well beyond Hrodna, Navahrudak, and Minsk into what was known as 'Black Rus''. This made him lord of many Orthodox Christian Slavs. In the west it approached the Baltic shore. Hostile foreign sources referred to him as the Lithuanians' 'high king'.

LITHUANIA

The road to becoming a king recognised by Christendom was rocky. Mindaugas first sent his old rival Vykintas and their shared nephews on an expedition against the Rus′ian principalities to the east. Their campaign failed. The two nephews fled for their lives to the realm of their Christian brother-in-law, Danylo of Halych and Volhynia, who mounted a coalition against the Lithuanian ruler. The Teutonic Order penetrated deep into Mindaugas's lands, discontented Samogitians and Yotvingians rose up against him, and his rebel nephew Tautvilas accepted baptism from the bishop of Riga. In 1251, Mindaugas agreed to be baptised himself, through the offices of the Livonian branch of the Order. He exploited the tensions between the Knights and the bishop of Riga, and outmanoeuvred and defeated his remaining enemies. He began negotiations for a royal crown with Pope Innocent IV. It helped that the pope was trying to mount a crusade against the fearsome Mongols (also called Tatars) who had irrupted into Christendom during the previous decade and a half. The coronation took place in the summer of 1253, at an unknown location. The date supported by most historians, 6 July, is now a national holiday in Lithuania: Statehood Day. Very enjoyable it is too.

Mindaugas also wanted a Lithuanian bishopric. The man he wanted was Brother Christian of the Livonian Order, who had instructed and baptised him. The pope agreed. Better still, the new missionary diocese of Lithuania would be subject only to the Holy See. Mindaugas had now joined the exclusive club of Christian kings. How seriously did he treat his new faith? His wife Morta seems to have been an enthusiastic Christian. A clutch of Franciscan and Dominican friars, mostly from Livonia, tried to evangelise beyond the King's entourage. It is hard to say how many they baptised. The adjacent lands of the Yotvingian tribes saw rival missionary efforts, because religious and political allegiances overlapped. One of the contenders for regional supremacy, Danylo of Halych and Volhynia, obtained his own royal crown from Innocent IV in the same year as Mindaugas, having dangled the prospect of church unity before the pontiff.

King Mindaugas found it much harder to provide for the Catholic clergy. There is no convincing evidence that the promised cathedral was ever built—its 'discovery' in Vilnius in 1986 proved to be wishful thinking. Rather than alienate his supporters in central and eastern Lithuania, Mindaugas decided to grant the Church land and tithes in parts of Samogitia where his authority was weak or non-existent. Bishop Christian, unable to collect his revenues, handed over his rights to the Order and left for Germany. This effectively meant the cession to the Knights of the lands assigned to the bishop, and more besides. They demonstrated their intent by building a castle and port on the Curonian coast at Memel (now Klaipėda). This secured the land bridge between the two branches and provided a springboard into Samogitia. The Samogitians responded ferociously, and in 1260 crushed the Knights on the shores of Lake Durbė (ten miles inland from Liepāja in Latvia). This victory sparked a massive revolt against the Order in Prussia that lasted fourteen years.

This widespread pagan resistance to the Teutonic Knights damaged the Christian cause in Lithuania. To most warriors, the old gods had proved themselves. Under intense internal and external pressure, Mindaugas abandoned his alliance with the Order in 1261. Historians dispute whether or not he also reverted to paganism. Later it would suit both the Order and the Rus'ian chroniclers to allege his apostasy, but in Rome he was regarded as having died a Christian. Either way, Mindaugas and his sons were killed in 1263. One of those responsible for their murder was Daumantas, Duke of Nalšia, whose wife had been abducted by Mindaugas, following the death the previous year of her sister, Queen Morta. During the ensuing power struggle, Daumantas fled to Pskov, where in 1266 the people chose him as their prince, under his baptismal name of Timofei. He enjoyed a long and successful reign of thirty-three years, and an enduring, if local, cult as a saint.

Although he was probably no great warrior, Mindaugas's political achievements were remarkable. For three decades he eliminated or manipulated his rivals, and skilfully switched alliances within the Catholic, Orthodox, and pagan worlds. However, he did not found a stable Christian realm. He even seems to have been forgotten in his own people's oral tradition—until he was reintroduced via histories written by foreigners.

Mindaugas's estranged nephew Treniota seized power, only to be murdered himself a year later. Mindaugas's last surviving son then returned from exile. Vaišvilkas (also known as Vaišelga) had an extraordinary life, partly shrouded in conflicting stories. It is agreed that he converted to Orthodox Christianity and helped his father make peace and a marriage alliance with Danylo of Halych and Volhynia in 1254. At some point in the next few years, he became a monk and went on pilgrimage to Mount Athos. After his father's murder he fled to Pinsk. He returned with supporters after Treniota's death, and with the support of the Teutonic Order and his Rus'ian allies massacred his opponents. In 1267, Vaišvilkas handed over the ducal throne to his brother-in-law Shvarno (a son of King Danylo) and resumed his monastic vocation. Within months, however, he had been killed by another brother-in-law, Prince Lev of Halych. Shvarno, the only Riurikid ruler of Lithuania, was unable to cling to power. Another cycle of bloodletting ended with the supremacy of the unquestionably pagan Traidenis (c. 1268–c. 1282).

Traidenis was a formidable warrior. In the winter of 1269–70, he responded to the Livonian Order's incursion into Semigallia by leading an expedition far to the north. He crossed the frozen Väinameri Sea (recorded in the sole source, the Livonian Rhymed Chronicle, as the Moon Sound) on to the island of Saaremaa

THE RISE OF AN EMPIRE

(Ösel in German). He could have been cut off, but in an epic battle on the ice he defeated the army fielded by the Order, the Livonian bishoprics, and their allies from Danish-ruled Estonia. Many charging Knights were entangled in the Lithuanian sleighs and then speared to death. Among those slain was the Master, Otto von Lutterberg, who is buried in the local church. No one has yet created a cinematic masterpiece to match Sergei Eisenstein's majestic depiction of the battle on Lake Peipus in 1242 in *Aleksandr Nevskii*, so the Battle of Karuse remains little known, although it has aroused some interest among wargaming geeks. Traidenis continued to wage war on the Order and the principality of Halych, sometimes winning, sometimes losing, never yielding. He found a Catholic ally in the nearest of the Polish duchies, Mazovia, to whose duke he wed his daughter, Gaudemunda. Nevertheless, the first sustained attempt to create a Christian realm—whether Catholic or Orthodox—was over. Lithuania would remain a pagan empire for a further century.

Traidenis had been Duke of Kernavė, which remained his principal residence. It is first recorded as the object of an attack by the Teutonic Order in 1279. Abandoned after the Knights burned down the town in 1390, the site has been excavated since the nineteenth century. The archaeological digs, conducted more systematically in the last three decades, have revealed that Kernavė was inhabited and fortified for thousands of years. No place in today's Lithuania is more evocative of the pagan era. Every summer, crowds flock to this complex of five steep mounds on the winding banks of the River Neris, to enjoy medieval reconstructions, folk festivals, and neo-pagan ceremonies.

iii. *Dynastic Empire*

The years that followed Traidenis's death c. 1282 are obscure, even by the standards of the thirteenth century. His presumed successor, another Daumantas, is known only from his death in 1285, on campaign in north-eastern Rus'. Within a few years a new dynasty emerged, which would reign over the Grand Duchy of Lithuania until 1572. Its first undoubted member was Pukuveras, also known as Butvydas. Not much is known of him either, but, around 1295, Pukuveras was succeeded by his eldest surviving son, Vytenis. After about two decades at the helm, Vytenis was succeeded by his younger brother (or possibly his cousin) Gediminas, who reigned for a quarter of a century. Before we follow the breathtaking expansion of his rule across Rus', let us take stock of the Lithuanian empire, focusing first on the 'high country' or Aukštaitija.

Vytenis and Gediminas exercised great, but not unlimited power over their subjects. They assigned and revoked rights to inherit lordship and property, issued permissions to foreign merchants and settlers, including arrangements for their Christian worship, ordered the construction of fortifications, and demanded and received military service and provisions. As the ruler's court progressed between the towns and castles of the expanding empire, it collected contributions in kind. Agriculture flourished in the more secure regions. Trade routes traversed the proverbially dark—but not impassable—forests. Under Gediminas, his chosen capital of Vilnius (first mentioned in the letters he despatched in 1323) grew into a thriving commercial centre. The town had a cosmopolitan flavour from the start. Catholic and Orthodox churches served congregations which settled in 'German' and 'Ruthenian' quarters. That division is still evident in the street layout today. It is possible that Jews came to Vilnius as well. Gediminas is sometimes imagined as a kind of high priest (a *pontifex maximus*, even) presiding over pagan ceremonies, but the archaeological and written evidence permit no more than speculation on the subject.

That said, a concentration of temporal and sacral authority was reflected in the exalted style Gediminas assumed when corre-

THE RISE OF AN EMPIRE

sponding with foreign rulers and their representatives: a typical rendition in Latin was *Gedeminne Dei Gratia Letwinorum et multorum Ruthenorum Rex*, that is to say 'Gediminas, by grace of God, King of the Lithuanians and many Ruthenians' (Rus´ians).* Even popes sometimes addressed him as *rex*, despite not acknowledging the royal title formally. Gediminas employed a team of scribes able to produce documents in Latin, German, Ruthenian, and Byzantine Greek. Papal diplomats recalled him *cum consiliariis in aula sedentem* ('sitting with [his] councillors in a hall').[13] For when they took important decisions, both Vytenis and Gediminas made a point of consulting not only their brothers and cousins, but also a wider group of boyars or nobles. The latter were obliged to provide military service at the head of their warriors. Vytenis and Gediminas controlled redoubtable military forces but faced a formidable enemy in the Teutonic Order.

Before the thirteenth century had ended, the two branches of the Order had subdued the remaining Baltic tribes. Their names have come down to us as Prussians, Yotvingians, Selonians, Lettgallians, Semigallians, Curonians, and Skalvians. The conquered peoples either accepted the fate of an unfree rural undercaste or left their ancestral lands. The 'hard-necked' Lithuanians were next in line. Marshalling its resources, the Order attracted immigrants from north-western Europe, settled colonists on

---

* The name *Ruthenia* comes from the medieval dog-Latin for *Rus´* (alongside the older Latin translation, *Russia*, which later became associated with Moscow's stubborn claim to supremacy over 'all of Rus´'). 'Ruthenian' will henceforth be used for *ruski*, the east Slavic language spoken in the Grand Duchy of Lithuania, and 'Ruthenians' will denote its east Slavic population. *Rus´* became *Rhossia* in Byzantine Greek, whence it became *Rossiia* in the Muscovite dialect of *ruski* that evolved into the modern Russian language. 'Russia' will be reserved for the *Rossiiskaia imperiia* proclaimed by Peter I in 1721 and its post-1991 successor-state.

farms, founded and fortified towns, built castles, gradually took control of the bishoprics and chapters of the province of Riga, and cultivated its diplomatic contacts. In 1309, the grand master of the Order moved from Venice to the huge 'fortress of Mary', the Marienburg (now Malbork in northern Poland). This became the heart of a disciplined *Ordensstaat* (whose name may well be the first use of the term 'state' in something like its modern sense). From the 1320s, the Order regularly organised destructive raids deep into Lithuania, in which a growing number of foreign knights rode and fought as crusaders for a season or two. The most famous were John, King of Bohemia, who went blind while in Lithuania in 1336 and was slain at the battle of Crécy a decade later, and the Earl of Bolingbroke, the future King Henry IV of England, who joined expeditions in 1390 and 1392. Archaeological evidence confirms hostile Teutonic accounts of the ferocious violence involved in the Lithuanian counter-attacks.

From the perspective of western Christendom, the lands of the Lithuanians were the least accessible in the Baltic region. The Lithuanians had more time than their neighbours to prepare themselves for the Knights' onslaught, match their opponents' standard of arms and armour, and hone their own techniques of reconnaissance, diversion, and ambush amidst the dense, but not impenetrable forests and bogs. They took in diverse Balts, including experienced warriors, who found the harsh rule of the Order unendurable. We can be sceptical about the idea that any of the Baltic peoples were fanatically attached to their pagan 'religion' and chose martyrdom for their 'faith'. Rather, a traditional way of life was at stake, and the alternative was unattractive. The two-pronged pressure from the Order also helped to consolidate the refugees and the hitherto divided tribes of Samogitia and Aukštaitija around a leadership with powerbases in what is now eastern Lithuania. However, this pressure could sometimes work against unity, as those discontented with the

THE RISE OF AN EMPIRE

ruler could find a ready ally in the crusaders. Compared to Aukštaitija, Samogitia had a more dispersed distribution of political power and economic resources. It was more exposed to aggression and would be contested between the Grand Dukes of Lithuania and the Order until 1422.

To some extent these geographical factors also worked to protect the Lithuanians from invaders from the south-east. Rus´ian chroniclers were as likely as Teutonic ones to lament the difficulties of campaigning in the wilderness. Crucially, the forested zone was less accessible and less attractive to the mounted archers of the great Mongol or Tatar armies that swept across Kyivan Rus´ from 1237 onwards. True, a major raid penetrated into Lithuanian lands during the winter of 1258–59. It may have contributed to the crisis that finally engulfed Mindaugas. Nevertheless, the devastation of most of the Rus´ian principalities and their subsequent transformation into tributaries of the Tatar Golden Horde ensured that Lithuania could not only hold its own against its Orthodox neighbours to the east and south-east, but expand into them.

A further consequence of the 'Tatar yoke' imposed on most of Rus´ was the emergence of the less damaged south-western realm of Halych and Volhynia as a key player between eastern and western Christendom. However, its branch of the Riurikid dynasty become extinct in 1322–33. Its last two princes (sometimes called kings) had allied themselves with King Władysław I, ruler of the recently restored Polish kingdom. Although a compromise solution was agreed between the rival Lithuanian and Polish claimants, the death in 1340 of Prince Bolesław (called Yuri by his Orthodox subjects) inaugurated half a century of continual, but not continuous warfare. The Kingdom of Hungary, which then extended as far as the Carpathian Mountains, also played a major part in these struggles: its monarchs had styled themselves *Rex Galicie et Lodomerie* since the early thirteenth century. In the end, the southern part—Halych—became part of Poland, and most of the northern, Volhynian, part went to Lithuania. The Lithuanian claimant was Liubartas, youngest son of Gediminas and son-in-law to one of the last Riurikid rulers. For more than sixty years he ruled part or all of Volhynia from his imposing castle in Luts'k, until his death at a ripe old age around 1385.

This strategy of dynastic marriage, negotiation, and if necessary, war, reproduced itself elsewhere in Rus', encountering less resistance. The lesser Riurikid princes found themselves caught between the khans of the Tatar Golden Horde and their principal enforcers, the princes of Moscow, who demanded irksome tributes, and the Grand Dukes of Lithuania. This style (*Velikii Kniaz' Litovskii* in Ruthenian) was adopted, possibly in response to Muscovite pretensions to primacy among the princes of Rus', by Gediminas's formidable son and successor. Algirdas exemplified the family strategy: in 1318 he became prince of Vitsebsk through marriage to its heiress. During his reign as Grand Duke (1345–77), territorial expansion accelerated. The process was neither wholly peaceful nor entirely violent. Much was 'brokered with the Tatars', who kept a share of the spoils and still expected tributes from the Ruthenian lands. The famous victory at the 'Blue Waters' (Synia Voda) of 1362 has, on closer inspection, turned out to be a retrospective myth.[14]

Beyond doubt is Algirdas's virility. He sired at least twenty children from his two marriages. His sons, grandsons, and nephews ruled far-flung principalities including from the 1360s, the symbolically resonant, albeit devastated Kyiv. Most of these dukes converted to Orthodox Christianity, took Slavic baptismal names, and governed according to their subjects' traditional laws, customs, and language. These junior Gediminids delivered soldiers and revenues to the dynastic patriarch—vital for the defence of the ethnic Lithuanian and Samogitian heartlands in the north-west. The Grand Duke of Lithuania did not rule a

THE RISE OF AN EMPIRE

unitary state: his authority was much more direct in Lithuania propria (including much of modern Belarus and fringes of modern Poland) than it was in Samogitia, or in the Ruthenian principalities which extended in a great arc from Polatsk, through Vitsebsk, Briansk, Novhorod-Siverskyi, Kyiv, lower Podolia, Volhynia, and Pinsk. As Darius Baronas and S. C. Rowell put it, 'in pagan times the Grand Duchy of Lithuania represented a conglomerate of lands that, except for the ruling dynasty, had very little in common.'[15]

Did these lands constitute, as sometimes suggested, an 'empire'?[16] In medieval Europe, claims to imperial status implied either legitimate succession to the Roman Empire, or equality of status with those who claimed that succession. On one known occasion in 1371, sending a missive in Greek to the Patriarch of Constantinople, Algirdas styled himself *Basileus*, thereby claiming equal status with the Emperor of the Romans. By this time Byzantium's imperial rank was out of joint with its diminished power and territory. In common and academic parlance, the term 'empire' has long been used more loosely, acquiring first positive, and then negative connotations. Most recently, some continental empires, notably Austria–Hungary, have been cautiously rehabilitated as multicultural alternatives to conflicted nation-states. Besides the expansive dynamic, and the ethnic and religious diversity that provide the lowest common denominator of empires, the dominions of Gediminas and Algirdas were also structured into a 'metropolitan' part— Lithuania propria, centred on Vilnius, where the pagan supreme ruler headed a pagan military elite, and more or less distant peripheries. These were acquired by more or less hostile takeovers and had varying political, legal, and religious arrangements under subordinate dukes drawn from the ruling family. Nevertheless, this immense space remained an 'empire-light'; it even had some elements of a union, for the Gediminids had to bargain with their subjects. As an empire, it was not in the same league as the much larger one established far more violently by Genghis Khan and his descendants.

The family strategy required more than one delicate balancing act. Gediminas was loyally supported by his two remaining brothers. In the next generation Kęstutis provided sterling support to Algirdas. After they had overthrown their ineffectual brother Jaunutis in 1345, Grand Duke Algirdas concentrated on the diplomatic and military challenges in Rus´, while Duke Kęstutis of Trakai co-ordinated the resistance to the Teutonic Knights in the west. Their partnership was not a form of joint rule, but the supreme example of the 'family firm' in action. However, towards the end of Algirdas's long reign, the limits of expansion were apparent. Thrice came the Grand Duke to Muscovy; thrice he saw; thrice he failed to conquer. Novgorod, Tver´, and Smolensk all swithered between Vilnius and Moscow. Under Grand Duke Dmitrii Donskoi (1359–89), Muscovy was becoming an awkward rival, not least because of the support it enjoyed from some Orthodox hierarchs. Many Gediminid princes did accept Orthodox baptism, and their children were raised as Christians. Both Gediminas and Algirdas established Orthodox metropolitan archbishoprics beyond Moscow's reach. Nevertheless, they themselves remained pagans. Their choice encouraged Muscovite subversion of Lithuanian subjects.

Why did the grand dukes not convert to Orthodoxy? Let us briefly follow the 'road not taken'. Had the grand dukes converted early enough, they might just have pre-empted the Muscovite princes in gathering all of Rus´ under their sway. Or then again, they might not have won the contest, and could have ended up as ordinary princes struggling to preserve their autonomy. Did they think in such terms? Perhaps not, but had they thus gambled, they may well have lost the support of the dukes and boyars of the Lithuanian heartlands and Samogitia, who held fast to the old

THE RISE OF AN EMPIRE

ways (if not necessarily to the old gods). Traditional, orally transmitted Lithuanian culture and language would probably have been reduced to rural insignificance, had the grand ducal court in Vilnius become a centre of Orthodox Christianity and Ruthenian literary and legal culture. The Gediminid empire contained many more Orthodox Slavs than pagan Balts, but at least in Lithuania propria, the leading clans among the latter wished to keep the pecking order intact. Moreover, the Teutonic Order could have easily continued its crusades if pagan Lithuania became a 'schismatic' Orthodox realm.

Algirdas was succeeded in 1377 by his eldest son of his second marriage to Yuliana of Tver´. Jogaila was probably born in 1351 or 1352. His inheritance was as problematic as it was vast. The opportunities for a pagan-led empire to expand and flourish in the space between eastern and western Christendom were vanishing. The Teutonic Order basked in the zenith of its power under Grand Master Winrich von Kniprode. Almost annual crusades slashed and burned deep into the Lithuanian heartlands. The flower of western chivalry came to kill and rob the pagans in the name of God. To the south, Halych and Volhynia had long been contested with Poland and Hungary. Now King Louis the Great of Hungary also held the Polish throne, and a joint Hungarian and Polish army invaded Volhynia from the south. Jogaila's uncle, Duke Liubartas, prudently swore allegiance to Louis. Jogaila also encountered opposition from the Orthodox sons of his father's first marriage. He tried to assert himself by replacing his eldest half-brother Andrei as Duke of Polatsk with his younger full-brother Skirgaila. Andrei was joined by his own full-brother Dmitrii, Duke of Briansk, and the two found shelter in Moscow. They returned with their Muscovite protector, Dmitrii Donskoi, to raid Lithuanian lands. Meanwhile the burghers of Polatsk expelled the pagan newcomer, and not even conversion to Orthodoxy could enable Skirgaila to take back the city. Jogaila had to send significant forces east, just when they were needed in the west.

Jogaila's trickiest problem proved to be Kęstutis. Their clash is sometimes represented in strategic and ideological terms: the uncle is cast as the indomitable pagan foe of the Teutonic Order, while the nephew intrigued in Rus' and Poland. Inter-generational tensions cannot have helped. The Teutonic Order sowed mistrust between them, and Jogaila concluded a treaty with the Order behind his uncle's back. In 1381, Kęstutis surprised and captured Jogaila in Vilnius. He forced his nephew to resign the grand ducal throne but left him his hereditary duchies of Kreva and Vitsebsk. Jogaila's younger brother Kaributas, Duke of Novhorod Siverskyi, then rose up against Kęstutis. The merchants of Vilnius, fearful of the Teutonic Knights, helped Jogaila to retake the capital. He allied with the Order and laid siege to Trakai. Kęstutis hurried back from the south-east. His son Vytautas brought the remnants of a force that had been beaten outside Vilnius. On 3 August 1382, two unequal armies squared up outside Trakai.

Jogaila invited his uncle and cousin to peace talks, then took them captive. Within five days, Kęstutis was found dead in Kreva Castle. One contemporary account suggested suicide, but rumour had it he had been murdered by Skirgaila, the failed Duke of Polatsk. True or not, Skirgaila received the Duchy of Trakai. Jogaila dutifully burned his uncle's corpse and horses on a great pyre with all the pagan trimmings. Kęstutis has long been one of the most popular of Lithuanian national heroes, but Baronas and Rowell are less complimentary: 'Duke Kęstutis would perhaps have found much appreciation in Viking-Age Scandinavia or in the world of the Nibelungs, but even in the pagan Lithuania of his time he was a man from another age.'[17]

His son was cast in a different mould. Vytautas slipped past his guards, dressed as a female servant. Jogaila may have con-

THE RISE OF AN EMPIRE

nived in the escape: the two cousins were apparently close in their youth. Vytautas fled to the Order which then dictated eye-watering peace terms. Jogaila would have to ally Lithuania with the Order against its enemies, cede the western half of Samogitia, and accept Catholic baptism for himself and his pagan subjects. Having at first reluctantly agreed, in the end he preferred to resume the war in the summer of 1383. The following year, the Order burnt down Kaunas, and Jogaila invited his cousin to come home. Vytautas left Prussia, was baptised in the Orthodox Greek rite, and regained part of his patrimony.

The conflict in the east was also unresolved, but the price of peace with Moscow would have been equally unpalatable: to accept Orthodox baptism and acknowledge Muscovite seniority in Rus'. However, the Tatars had avenged their defeat on the field of Kulikovo in 1380 by burning down Moscow two years later. Muscovy remained hostile, but for the moment could not mount an invasion of Lithuania. The notion that Jogaila seriously negotiated with Dmitrii Donskoi for his daughter and Orthodox baptism has recently been exposed as based on documents forged in Moscow in the seventeenth century.[18]

The third option was an arrangement with Catholic Poland. Starting with Traidenis, Lithuanian rulers had given daughters in marriage to various Polish dukes; Gediminas's daughter Aldona (baptised as Anna) wed Casimir, heir to the throne of Poland, and became his first queen. Unfortunately, both their two daughters died young. Most Lithuanian rulers had at some time played the possibility of conversion as a diplomatic card—only to remain pagan. Gediminas had refused baptism from the papal envoys who came to Vilnius at his invitation in 1324. Algirdas had similar opportunities to gain a Christian royal crown. Surely the fact that they were winning their wars showed that the old gods were strong? But even after suffering setbacks, Algirdas and Kęstutis refused to convert. Perhaps they preferred the pleasures of the pagan lifestyle to the self-restraint and mortifications urged by nagging priests.

These pagan grand dukes valued Catholic and Orthodox priests for their clerical skills and knowledge of the world beyond Lithuania. Christian clergy were welcome to minister to merchants in Vilnius, but they risked execution if they openly proselytised among the pagan population and denounced the old ways. Two Franciscan friars who would not curb their tongues were martyred in 1341; five more followed in 1369. Three grand ducal servants who had converted to Orthodoxy and refused to eat meat at feasts held on Christian fast days suffered a similar fate around 1347. Although Algirdas took two Orthodox wives and many of his children and grandchildren became Christians in his lifetime, he would not tolerate public defiance. By the same token, a growing number of Algirdas's entourage practised Christian worship discreetly. The faith was spreading among the lower strata as well.

Jogaila, whose mother was a Ruthenian princess, would have been familiar with Christianity long before his formal baptism. He certainly appreciated Byzantine religious art, as is evident from his later commissions in both Lithuania and Poland. But he may have been still more influenced by Catholicism: as a young man he became friendly with a Franciscan missionary, Petros Philargis—the future pope (or antipope) Alexander V. Almost from the start of his reign he explored the possibility of a marriage to a Christian princess. It was a question of finding the right moment—and the right girl.

Skirgaila had journeyed via the Marienburg to the Mazovian and Hungarian courts in 1379–80. He was probably sounding out his elder brother's marital prospects. Louis the Great, King of Hungary since 1342, had succeeded his maternal uncle Casimir the Great as King of Poland in 1370. This was a purely personal union of the crowns. Louis died in September 1382,

THE RISE OF AN EMPIRE

leaving two young daughters. The elder, Mary, succeeded in Hungary. It took lengthy negotiations between the dowager Queen Elizabeth and the Polish lords before the younger daughter, Hedwig (Jadwiga in Polish), came to Kraków and was crowned queen regnant of Poland in Wawel Cathedral on 16 October 1384. In January 1385, Skirgaila arrived at the head of a Lithuanian delegation to press Jogaila's suit. The main obstacle was Hedwig's betrothal to William, son of the Duke of Austria. Their undoubted attachment has generated many a romantic yarn, including the story that she used an axe to hack her way out of her chamber in an effort to reach her fiancé. At twelve years old, she was deemed nubile. The hard-headed (and perhaps hard-hearted) elite in Kraków insisted that the reluctant maiden wed Jogaila. The Polish lords wanted an adult king, an end to the conflict at the kingdom's eastern border, an ally against the Teutonic Order, and the prestige accruing from bringing a pagan empire into the Latin Christian fold.

The pre-nuptial agreement was sealed at Kreva on 14 August 1385. The castle is now an evocative ruin, just inside Belarus's border with Lithuania. Grand Duke Jogaila, along with three of his brothers and his cousin Vytautas, sealed a three-way treaty with Queen Elizabeth and envoys from Poland. Jogaila would marry Hedwig, pay 200,000 florins in compensation to William (who showed his spirit by rejecting it), accept baptism for himself and his pagan relatives and subjects, recover lost lands, and 'join in perpetuity his Lithuanian and Ruthenian lands to the Crown of the Kingdom of Poland' (*Terras suas Litvanie et Rusie Corone Regis Polonie perpetuo applicare*).[19]

The exact meaning of this phrase, especially the verb *applicare*, is still disputed, but the short-term consequences were clear enough. A few weeks into 1386, an assembly of Polish nobles and clerics gathered at Lublin and accepted Jogaila as their king. He proceeded to Kraków, where on 15 February 1386, he was

LITHUANIA

baptised with the name Władysław (Ladislaus or Vladislaus in Latin). Three days later he married Hedwig, and on 4 March was crowned King of Poland. However, the nature of the bond thus established was not precisely defined. The Polish–Lithuanian union would evolve for centuries to come.

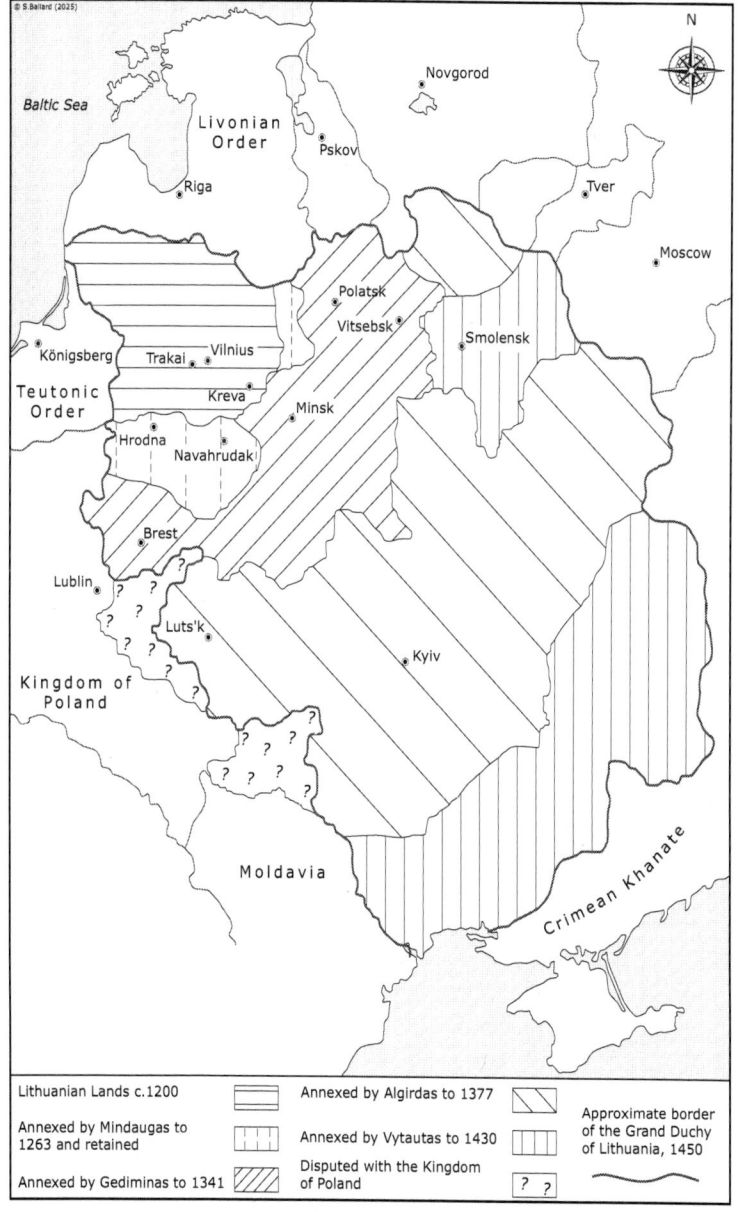

Map 2: Lithuanian expansion from the thirteenth to the fifteenth centuries

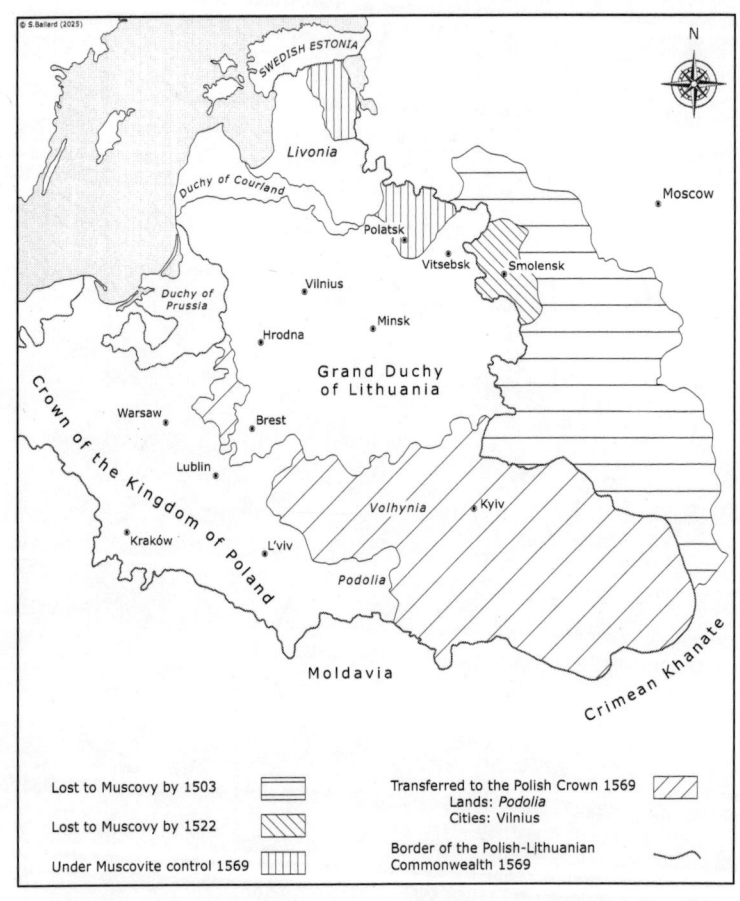

Map 3: The contraction of the Grand Duchy of Lithuania, 1487–1569

2

FORGING A UNION

(1386–1569)

We view the past with hindsight. Historians, educators, and politicians have long projected later ideas of states and nations back on to medieval rulers and communities. Modern Lithuania is no exception to the rule, making it hard to judge the Grand Duchy of Lithuania's long union with the Kingdom of Poland dispassionately. In the standard Lithuanian verdict, after the triumphant reign of Vytautas the Great (1392–1430), the lop-sided union dominated by Poland failed. Utterly. For their part, Poles have often held Lithuanians in ignorant contempt. Catholic Poland supposedly converted and civilised pagan Lithuania, only to become entangled in the barbarous east. In recent decades, many Polish historians have jettisoned such prejudice. Working in Lithuanian archives and libraries, they study the Grand Duchy of Lithuania on its own terms. A few have even learned Lithuanian. At the same time, prominent Lithuanian historians (most of whom have excellent Polish) have reinterpreted the union with Poland as Lithuania's necessary 'road to Europe'.[1] Most, but not all of the legal, institutional, and social models adopted and adapted in the Grand Duchy of Lithuania came from or via Poland. Two decades ago, the historian Darius Staliūnas noted the shift away from ethnocentric concerns among his professional colleagues, but he cautioned, 'Lithuanians are still unwilling in their mass consciousness to share the historical heritage with other nations. Events from the past belong either to "us" or to "them."'[2] Since then, a shared vulnerability to neo-imperial Russia has encouraged rethinking of the common past beyond academe, but this road still runs uphill.

Anachronistic assumptions about the Polish–Lithuanian union have contributed to the relative neglect of the third partner: Rus′ and the Ruthenians. In Belarusian and Ukrainian narratives, Orthodox Christian Slavs contributed high culture and political know-how to the Grand Duchy of Lithuania. However, until very recently, the centuries when the Grand Dukes of Lithuania ruled southern Rus′ have been eclipsed in Ukrainian memories by the era after 1569, when Zaporizhian Cossacks violently contested Ukraïna with the Polish Crown, Muscovy, the Crimean Khanate, and the Ottoman Empire. On the other hand, the present Belarusian lands remained part of the Grand Duchy of Lithuania until the partitions of 1772, 1793, and 1795. Unsurprisingly, the Belarusian claim to the Grand Duchy's legacy is better developed than the Ukrainian one. It posits the crucial role of the principalities of north-western Rus′ in a largely peaceful and consensual formation of a shared state, whose official language was 'Old Belarusian'. Lithuanian historians have often decried this Belarusian narrative, although recently Rūstis Kamuntavičius has explained it to his compatriots.[3] These polemics have been overshadowed by Aleksandr Lukashenko's regime's pursuit of historical legitimacy in Belarusians' contribution to Soviet victory in 'the Great Patriotic War of 1941–45'. This policy dovetails with Russian imperial narratives that all of Rus′ belongs by right to Moscow. This worldview can only explain divergences among the eastern Slavs by blaming malign Polish and Catholic interference.

Appreciating the Ruthenian role in the Polish–Lithuanian union does not imply an equilateral triangular partnership. On the contrary, Jogaila and Vytautas shaped the union by privileging Catholicism over Orthodoxy. This asymmetry long affected the political, social, and cultural dynamics of the Grand Duchy of Lithuania. It was not until the 1560s that Catholic, Orthodox, and Protestant nobles of the Grand Duchy shared equal political rights, shortly before the Polish-Lithuanian union was tightened at Lublin. Even then, much remained unsettled. As the Scottish historian Robert Frost has argued, the union was a continuously evolving relationship between political partners. The deal made in 1385–86 was between a political community—the Crown of the Kingdom of Poland—and a monarch—Jogaila. But by the end of Vytautas's reign in 1430, a Lithuanian political community was beginning to make its voice heard. Over the next century and a half this community grew into a Lithuanian 'political nation'. These shifting relationships are far more interesting than bland categorisations of a 'dynastic union' between 1386 and 1569 and a 'real union' from then until the partitions of the Polish-Lithuanian Commonwealth at the end of the eighteenth century.[4]

i. *Jogaila and Vytautas*

Jogaila—Jagiełło in Polish—had to learn the laws, customs, and values of his new realm, which had long since ceased to be the patrimony of its princes and kings. The Christian Polish monarchy had thrust itself into history during the 960s, but Poland fractured after 1138. The fourteenth-century reunification of the realm was incomplete: in the west, the Silesian and Pomeranian duchies were lost, while in the north-east, the duchy of Mazovia remained a feudal vassal until 1529. Nonetheless, the idea of a

Polish kingdom had been kept alive. Crucially, the archbishopric of Gniezno was not part of the Church in the Holy Roman (or German) Empire, but was directly subordinated to the papacy.

In medieval Poland, as elsewhere in Latin Christendom, the idea of the community of the realm (*communitas regni*) put down deep roots. The process was facilitated by ongoing Christianisation, accompanied by grants and privileges for the Catholic Church, as well as the issue of charters to towns. Migrants settled, and more land was cultivated. Polish dukes granted estates to their warriors, shrinking their own domains. However, in contrast to the spread of feudal tenures of land in western Europe, held in return for obligations of military service, in Poland the outright hereditary possession of land became common. Clan groups, based on kinship, gradually transformed themselves into families who constituted the nobility (*szlachta*). Uncertain successions to the throne led kings to negotiate with assemblies of their chief subjects. In 1374, King Louis replaced the irregular taxation of noble lands with a moderate, annual land tax of two groats per hide, whose value would shrink through inflation. Any further taxes on nobles' lands would require their explicit consent. This crucial privilege also underlined the unity of the realm and its nobility.

Polish monarchs were expected to govern, heeding the advice of their chief subjects, for the common good. The notion of the community of the realm was expressed in the term we have already encountered: the Crown of the Kingdom of Poland (*Corona regni Poloniae*), a concept distinct from the office of kingship. 'The Polish Crown' came to be associated with its territories too, but unlike in Hungary, it did not mean that the kingdom was embodied in the royal headgear. In and after 1386, the lords spiritual and temporal of the Polish Crown felt their own importance vis-à-vis their young Hungarian queen and freshly baptised Lithuanian king. In the lords' view, Jogaila had incorporated his Lithuanian and Ruthenian lands into the Polish Crown; he saw things differently. Hedwig and Jogaila were co-monarchs in Poland—they jointly issued charters and even went on campaign together, taking back Red Ruthenia from Hungary. Within a few years of their marriage, she would have cut a more imposing figure than her husband. Analyses of her remains revealed she was about 175 centimetres tall, with excellent teeth, nobly proportioned features, and blonde hair. Hedwig probably never visited Lithuania, but she was famed for her ascetic piety and practical charity. At the end of the twentieth century, Pope John Paul II first beatified and then canonised her as Patron of Poland and Apostle of Lithuania. At the time, Lithuanians had fewer reasons to venerate her: the maturing queen's court attracted Poles who wished to implement the incorporation promised in 1385. Much might have turned out differently had she lived longer, but she died after giving birth to a daughter in 1399, and Jogaila had to renegotiate his position in Poland. He and his descendants would repeatedly play a trump card in their negotiations with the Polish nobility—their patrimonial inheritance in Lithuania and Rus´.

Games of thrones were at the heart of the complex relations between Jogaila and Vytautas. The former faced daunting challenges while the latter refused to be marginalised. Jogaila soon discovered just how difficult it was to govern the vast Lithuanian empire from Kraków. Initially, he asked his younger brother Skirgaila to hold the fort in Vilnius. However, Skirgaila's Orthodox faith went down badly in the freshly Catholicised Lithuanian heartlands, while Vytautas resisted Jogaila's attempt to deprive him of his patrimonial duchy of Trakai in favour of Skirgaila. In 1390, Jogaila's angry reaction on hearing of a plot pushed Vytautas into promising Hrodna to the Teutonic Order in return for support. With neighbouring monarchs also girding their loins for battle, Jogaila compromised.

LITHUANIA

The events of 4–5 August 1392 at Astrava are often portrayed as the moment when the vindicated Vytautas restored Lithuania's sovereign statehood. But the surviving sources indicate that Jogaila received his cousin's oath of loyalty to himself, to Hedwig, and to the 'Crown of the Kingdom of Poland'. In return he restored Vytautas's patrimony of Trakai and Luts'k and recognised him—ambiguously—as *dux Lithuaniae*.* Only after Skirgaila died in 1394 did Jogaila acknowledge Vytautas's unchallenged rule over the Lithuanian and Ruthenian lands. Vytautas skilfully and swiftly exploited discord among the surviving Gediminids to gain the appanage duchies of Polatsk, Vitsebsk, Novhorod Siverskyi, and Kyiv. Their revenues, lands, and offices vastly increased the rewards he could offer his followers.

Vytautas pushed his hegemony eastwards, taking Smolensk in 1395, before moving south against the Tatars of the Golden Horde. At first, the results were spectacular. Together with his ally, the deposed Khan Tokhtamish, he reached the Black Sea coast in 1397 and again in 1398. There, he had forts built 1,000 kilometres from Vilnius. Even now, a tower survives at Kherson. Vytautas marched into the Crimea where he captured the port of Caffa (now Feodosiia). This Genoese colony, protected by the Crimean Khan, was a major slave market. During these campaigns Vytautas recruited disaffected Crimean Tatar warriors, whom he settled on privileged terms in Lithuania propria and Podlachia. This 600-year-old Muslim community has produced many distinguished soldiers and public servants of both Lithuania and Poland.

Vytautas also settled Karaites, a people from the northern shores of the Black Sea, who followed a form of Judaism shorn of

---

* The absence of the definite and indefinite article in Latin (as in Baltic and Slavic languages) make it unclear whether Vytautas was to be 'a' duke of Lithuania (one among several family members) or 'the' Duke of Lithuania (its ruler). There is no such ambiguity in *magnus dux Lithuaniae*.

the Talmud (the wider body of the Law). A small community still lives in Trakai, where tourists gorge themselves on the Karaites' traditional *kibinai*. These are rather better than the Cornish pasties which they superficially resemble. Jews had long been settled in parts of Rus', but in 1388–89 Vytautas issued the first charters to Jewish communities in Trakai, Brest, and Luts'k. The terms, modelled on a privilege issued by a Polish duke in 1264, assured Jews communal authority and legal protections. Although subject to the same tolls as others, it stated: 'wherever a Jew travels through our realm, no one shall place any barrier in his way nor cause him trouble or harm'. Protection covered the notorious 'blood libel': 'we strictly forbid that Jews settled in our realms should hereafter be singled out and accused of using human blood' (allegedly for ritual purposes). The level of proof for accusations of Jews murdering Christian children was set high.[5]

During the 1399 campaign, Vytautas overreached himself. The Golden Horde surrounded his forces—Lithuanians, Ruthenians, Tatars, Poles, and a detachment from the Teutonic Order—on the banks of the River Vorskla. Vytautas was lucky to escape the carnage alive. In political terms, however, he suffered a setback, rather than a disaster. Within a decade, he re-established his dominant position in northern and north-eastern Rus', and by the 1420s he was again an arbiter in Crimean politics. To achieve all this, he reset his relations with Jogaila.

Vytautas had been styling himself Grand Duke and even Supreme Duke of Lithuania. In 1398 he was reportedly toasted by his followers as King (*rex*). However, by an agreement sealed at Vilnius in January 1401, Vytautas recognised Jogaila as Supreme Duke of Lithuania and Lord of Rus' (*supremus dux Lithuaniae ac heres Russiae*). He received in return, for his lifetime, but not for his heirs, all the grand ducal rights and revenues as Duke of Lithuania. Ten years elapsed before Jogaila recognised Vytautas's style of *magnus dux Lithuaniae*. Jogaila's delegation of power to Vytautas was personal and patrimonial; he did not do so as King of Poland. At the same time, the union was declared perpetual and irrevocable. After Vytautas's death, his lordships were to go to Jogaila as his overlord, but also to the Crown of the Kingdom of Poland. Lip service was thus paid to Poles' idea of incorporation, but in practice Vytautas would rule Lithuania, which suited Jogaila. Moreover, the Poles, who ratified the treaty in March 1401, undertook not to elect a new king, in the event of Jogaila dying without an heir, without reference to Vytautas and the Lithuanians. Inclusion in the community of the realm brought rights as well as obligations.

As the fifteenth century dawned, Jogaila and Vytautas were approaching fifty years of age. The winnowing of the Gediminids drew attention to the fact that neither cousin had a son. Vytautas sought recognition as Jogaila's heir in Poland. Such a solution would strengthen the king against the Polish lords, who wished to decide the succession themselves. For similar reasons, Jogaila needed to safeguard his own reversionary rights in Lithuania. He probably connived at Vytautas's manifestations of status because they strengthened his own hand vis-à-vis his Polish subjects. So Jogaila needed Vytautas in Vilnius, just as Vytautas needed Jogaila in Kraków. Moreover, they each faced foreign enemies. Throughout tensions and tempests, the cousins maintained mutual understanding and respect. From 1409, Jogaila came to Lithuania to consult with Vytautas every year. Sometimes they conversed in Lithuanian, frustrating most eavesdroppers. There would be compelling reasons why Vytautas became a national hero to modern Lithuanians, while Jogaila was vilified, but both were medieval dynasts, not modern nationalists. They were also committed Christians.

After his marriage and coronation in Kraków, Jogaila spent several months acquainting himself with his new kingdom, receiving oaths of loyalty and service, before returning to Vilnius in the autumn of 1386. The traditional account of what happened the following year is based on the chronicle written eight decades later by an opiniated Cracovian clergyman. Jan Długosz tells us that Jogaila personally urged his subjects to embrace the true faith. Seeing their reluctance, he ordered his Polish retinue to fell the sacred groves, kill the holy vipers, destroy the pagan temple, and extinguish the eternal fire. As the high- and low-born folk then presented themselves for baptism, their ruler taught them the Lord's Prayer and the Creed in their own tongue. Darius Baronas and S. C. Rowell treat this tale sceptically. There is scant evidence for any pagan temples or priests prior to 1386. 'Lithuanian paganism', they argue, was no unitary faith, still less an organised religion, but 'a way of life', featuring magic, divination, spirits, and nature, all of which varied between warriors, farmers, and traders.[6]

The incentives to convert announced by Jogaila on 22 February 1387 included written confirmation of boyars' rights to dispose of their property and womenfolk without obtaining the ruler's permission. He also assured widows' rights. But these privileges did not encompass Orthodox Christians. In the long term, these measures may have helped to prevent ethnic Lithuanians' absorption into eastern Slavdom, although we should be cautious about reading such intentions back into the Middle Ages. Formal restrictions against 'schismatics' derived from the canon law of the Catholic Church were invoked sporadically and implemented rarely. In the Ruthenian lands, they had negligible impact. Nevertheless, in Lithuania propria, with its mixed population, the privileging of freshly baptised Catholics must have rankled with Orthodox boyars. Their assumption of cultural superiority was harder to sustain when their ruler (*hospodar* in Ruthenian) was no longer neutral between Rome and Constantinople.

Baptism probably did not traumatise most pagan Lithuanians. Orthodox Christianity was already familiar to higher-status persons and to inhabitants of mixed areas. Jogaila, Vytautas, and lesser patrons still commissioned murals in the Byzantine style. Catholic Franciscans had long been present in Vilnius and elsewhere. The building of their former church was the obvious choice for the cathedral. A cathedral needed a city. On 22 March 1387, Jogaila granted the *civitas* of Vilnius a charter, providing for self-government according to Magdeburg Law—as practised in many other towns across central Europe. A charter dated 17 February 1387 founded, privileged, and endowed the new bishopric, three or four years before the pope formally erected the see.[7] The cathedral was soon supplied with holy relics.

Initially the Catholic Church in Lithuania needed clergy from Poland. Among the Polish Franciscans was the first bishop of Vilnius, Andrzej Jastrzębiec. In 1397 Jogaila and Vytautas recognised his evangelising labours with an annual revenue of 200 silver marks from the grand ducal treasury, plus ten barrels of mead. Many Franciscans, including Jakub Plichta, the second bishop of Vilnius (1398–1407), learned the Lithuanian and Ruthenian languages. Following Lithuanian communities who had moved along trade routes, the Franciscans established friaries as far east as Vitsebsk. The instructions given by Jogaila and Vytautas to the lords for the welcome of the bishop and missionaries may help to explain how the word *kunigas* came to denote a priest. It derives from the old Lithuanian word for the ruler, itself descended from the proto-Germanic *kuningaz*, whence comes 'king'. Other religious orders and secular clergy followed. Vilnius Cathedral acquired a chapter of prelates and canons, as well as a school. Jogaila and Vytautas founded a dozen parishes within the first dozen years. By 1430, the huge diocese of Vilnius had twenty-nine parishes. Vytautas's most famous foundation was a votive offering for his deliverance at the River Vorskla. The delightful red-brick gothic Church of the Assumption of the Blessed Virgin Mary perches on the banks of the flood-prone River Nemunas in Kaunas. The number of parishes grew through the fifteenth century as lay and ecclesiastical patrons invested in the spiritual and material benefits offered by the Catholic Church.

The coming of Catholic Christianity changed the rhythm of the calendar. Fasts were observed and feasts celebrated. The use of Christian names alongside older ones of pagan origin was another marker. Jogaila used his Latin baptismal name of Wladislaus in official documents issued from Kraków (objecting to the Teutonic Order's use of 'Jagyelo' or variants thereon), while his cousin styled himself 'Allexander alias Wytowdus'.[8] One change concerned the dead. Previously cremated well away from settlements, they were henceforth buried close to the living, with prayers and masses to speed their eternal souls to Paradise. Pilgrimages, as well as donations and bequests, were rewarded with indulgences. Incidents of sacrilege were liable to severe punishment, often at the instance of outraged locals. The growing number of requests for papal dispensations from observances and vows, and marital barriers of consanguinity, indicates respect for the Holy See.

The new religious order gained visual expression in the sign of the chasing knight with a double-barred apostolic cross on his shield. Adopted by Jogaila on his great seal as King of Poland in 1388, it later became the coat of arms of the Grand Duchy of Lithuania. Today this is the state emblem of Lithuania (the Vytis), while in a slightly different form it symbolises the cause of Belarusian freedom (the Pahonia). The first silver coins minted by a Grand Duke of Lithuania date from 1386–87. They variously feature Jogaila's crowned head, an apostolic cross, fishes, a lion, an eagle, and the chasing knight. Another mark of his—and Hedwig's—commitment to Christianisation was the establishment of the theological faculty in Kraków in 1397 and the endowment and re-establishment of the university in 1400. Lithuanians would train for the priesthood there.

LITHUANIA

By the first decade of the fifteenth century, the evident success of Christianisation, especially among the elite, made it harder for the Teutonic Knights to justify their crusade against Lithuania. Not that they stopped trying, but fewer recruits came east. Vytautas was not reconciled to the price he had paid for peace in 1398—Samogitia. He stoked the fires of revolt in 1401 but was unable to regain control of the territory. The price of the next peace treaty he concluded in 1404 was assisting the Knights to suppress another rebellion in 1405. The Poles had kept their own peace treaty with the Order since 1343. As the reckoning approached, Polish ire was stirred by the Knights' chicanery towards merchants and their appetite for territory.

After Samogitians rose up again in 1409, once again encouraged by Vytautas, the Teutonic Order foolishly declared war on Poland as well as on Lithuania. On 15 July 1410, the combined Polish and Lithuanian forces met the Order's army between the villages of Grunwald (Grünfelde) and Stębark (better known as Tannenberg, which gave the battle its German name). Even the most conservative estimates of 16,500 Poles and Lithuanians, and 11,000 on the Order's side, are high by medieval standards. Many of those fighting were heavily armoured knights and men-at-arms, comparable to those who fought at Agincourt five years later. Recollections varied. On the right flank, the Lithuanians, composed mainly of lighter cavalry, including Tatars, attacked first, while Jogaila, who may still have been hoping for negotiations, held back the Poles in the centre and on the left. The Lithuanians were driven back after suffering heavy casualties. Długosz claimed that they fled the field. Earlier sources, however, indicate that the retreat was, at least in part, a feint. Certainly Vytautas (whose bravery Długosz lauded) led many Lithuanian horsemen back into the fray. By then the Poles were fully engaged, and after further fierce fighting, the Order's army was destroyed. Those killed included the grand master, almost all the senior officers, and three quarters of the knight-brothers present.[9]

After the joint victory, Vytautas led his bloodied Lithuanian forces home. The exhausted Poles could not reach the Marienburg before it was reinforced. The peace made in 1411 returned Samogitia to Lithuania, but only for the lifetimes of Jogaila and Vytautas. One reason for this modest outcome was that the shock result of the battle had rallied the kings of Hungary and Bohemia to the Order's side against 'schismatics', 'infidels', and 'pagans'. For the psychological impact of Grunwald–Tannenberg not only shattered the Teutonic Knights' prestige; it announced to Europe the immense potential of Poland and Lithuania acting together.

In the 1870s, the Cracovian painter Jan Matejko created the definitive image of the battle. Slightly to the left of the 10-metre-long canvas, two sturdy Lithuanian foot-soldiers fell the grand master, while just to the right of centre, Vytautas rides straight towards the beholder, arms aloft in a gesture of triumph. He wears the grand ducal mitre rather than a helmet. Jogaila is depicted in the top-right corner, his life having been saved, with some celestial assistance, by the cleric Zbigniew Oleśnicki (of whom we shall hear more). This tumultuous picture has become as popular in Lithuania as it is in Poland. The Lithuanian translation of Grunwald is Žalgiris.

Three years after the battle, Lithuania and Poland manifested their unity before Catholic Christendom. Negotiations between Jogaila, Vytautas, and their leading subjects culminated in the sealing of an act at Horodło on the Polish bank of the River Bug on 2 October 1413. The first clause attributed the union between Lithuania and Poland both to the hostility of the Teutonic Order and to the Holy Spirit, which had brought the Catholic Faith to Lithuania via the Crown of the Kingdom of Poland. On the one hand, the act described Lithuanian and Ruthenian lands as incorporated into the Polish realm. On the other hand, the vision of how this relationship might work emphasised conjugation rather than subjection. There were provisions for mutual consultation, not least over future choices of a King of Poland and Grand Duke of Lithuania. Following the Polish model, the offices of palatine and castellan were established for the core Lithuanian territories of Vilnius and Trakai. The act extended the privileges and rights already granted to the Catholic Church and Catholic nobles in Lithuania to match those enjoyed by the Church and nobles in Poland. The creative ambiguities of the act thus heralded a union between two political communities. The Lithuanian elite, predominantly descended from the forty-seven families selected by Vytautas for 'adoption' at Horodło by forty-seven Polish families and their heraldic clans, would repeatedly demand the keeping of the promises made in 1413. On the other hand, the marginalisation of the Orthodox would store up problems for the future. For the moment, the act justified their exclusion from the grand ducal council by the danger of discord, which would imperil secrets.[10]

Lithuania and Poland confronted the Teutonic Order at the Council of Constance. This met in 1414–18 to end the Western Schism. Since 1378, two lines of popes, in Rome and Avignon (and from 1409 a third line in Pisa) had contested the papacy. The scandal stimulated the Conciliarist movement, which drew on the belief that Christ had delegated his authority to all the apostles and their episcopal successors, rather than to Peter and his papal successors alone. It followed that general councils, guided by the Holy Spirit, exercised supreme authority in the Church. Its political corollary was that the force of law-making was conferred by citizens or the people, either directly at an assembly, or indirectly, via elections. These and other ideas were absorbed by a brilliant Cracovian canon lawyer who had also studied at Padua and Prague. At Constance, Paweł Włodkowic denounced the Order's violent, rapacious, and avaricious subjugation of pagan Prussians, Lithuanians, and Samogitians. He contended that as created, rational beings, pagans had freedom of conscience. They had the right to self-defence in their own state, while Christians might aid them in good cause. Part of the Polish–Lithuanian case against the Order was that according to the law of nations and the law of nature, princes could not dispose of territory without the consent of the people concerned. This far-reaching argument conveniently invalidated the cessions of Samogitia to the Order by Vytautas and Jogaila.

In a theatrical thunderclap, a delegation of sixty Samogitians told the Council of their peaceful conversion by Jogaila and Vytautas. Długosz spins a yarn of how in 1413 Jogaila sailed up the Samogitian rivers in order to evangelise and translate in person, before extinguishing another eternal flame. Baronas and Rowell consider this an embellishment of events that actually occurred in 1417. The conversion of Samogitia, they argue, proceeded as smoothly as that of Lithuania propria in 1387. They ascribe the delay not to the Samogitians' supposedly intense attachment to their old gods and shrines, but to the need to gain the Council's assent for ecclesiastical structures in territories that had been part of the archdiocese of Riga.[11] Jogaila and Vytautas's endeavours for church unity also aided their cause at Constance. Their connections in beleaguered Constantinople (where Vytautas's granddaughter Anna married the heir to the imperial throne), bolstered their credentials to reconcile the Orthodox Church to papal authority. In 1417, the cousins founded and endowed the Samogitian bishopric at Medininkai (Varniai), together with at least seven parishes. Tellingly, the Order had not established a single parish during its rule over Samogitia. In 1422, the Order unconditionally ceded all of Samogitia to Lithuania, as well as a strip of coastline. When delineated, this border lasted for almost five centuries.

Vytautas again turned his gaze eastwards. After the death of his son-in-law, Grand Duke Vasilii I of Moscow in 1425, he became guardian to his grandson Vasilii II. He also asserted his influence in Pskov and Novgorod, backed by Jogaila. The dynamics of their relationship were changed by the birth in 1424 of a son—christened Władysław—to the septuagenarian Jogaila and his twenty-year-old fourth queen: Sonka Halshanska. Vytautas had suggested the match: she was a granddaughter of his trusty brother-in-law, Ivan Halshanski. Sonka gave birth to two more boys, of whom the younger—Casimir—would survive infancy. Jogaila's efforts to assure his sons' hereditary rights collided with the conviction of his leading Polish subjects that Poland was an elective kingdom. He therefore accepted that the Polish Crown could decide which of his sons would succeed him. Among the privileges he conceded to the Polish nobility was freedom from arbitrary arrest and incarceration without trial. This pillar of individual liberty would later underpin the legal order of the Polish–Lithuanian Commonwealth.

Jogaila would need Vytautas to look after his infant sons, while Vytautas would have expected one of the boys to succeed him in Lithuania. So Jogaila initially supported the idea of Vytautas becoming King of Lithuania. Sigismund, King of Hungary, Germany, and Bohemia, made this proposal during a regional summit at Luts'k in January 1429, doubtless anticipating dissension. Vytautas prematurely informed the Polish council of Jogaila's acceptance of the idea. Zbigniew Oleśnicki, by now bishop of Kraków, bluntly responded that Lithuania had been 'incorporated into Poland and subjected to it', and most of the Polish councillors present supported him. Jogaila withdrew his assent. Emotions ran high as Vytautas rhetorically asked an assembly of Lithuanian lords and nobles if they wished to be subjects and tributaries of the Poles. Of course not. But even at this point, the Lithuanians demanded equal status within the union, not its rupture.[12]

Vytautas planned his coronation for August 1430. However, neither King Sigismund nor the promised crown arrived in

FORGING A UNION

Vilnius. Although the story that the Poles stole the crown has been debunked, Polish forces did intercept Sigismund's envoys, seizing documents which proposed an anti-Polish alliance, hereditary succession for Vytautas's heirs, and a consequent end to the union. As the dying Vytautas realised he could not prevail, Jogaila came to see his cousin. They made their peace with each other before Vytautas died at Trakai on 27 October 1430. Their partnership worked so well for so long, despite the tensions, because it maintained appearances by upholding Jogaila's hereditary status as Supreme Duke of Lithuania while not explicitly denying the Polish position that Lithuania had been incorporated into a single elective realm. In practice Vytautas could rule the Grand Duchy as he thought best.

Vytautas's long reign brought profound changes to vast territories—about a million square kilometres, unevenly inhabited in 1430 by about 3.5 million people. To put this into perspective, in the 1990s, a similar number of people inhabited the 65,000 square kilometres of the Republic of Lithuania, while the combined population of Lithuania, Belarus, and Ukraine peaked around 65 million. Claims that over 90 per cent of the Grand Duchy of Lithuania were eastern Slavic in character are exaggerated. The area inhabited by Lithuanian speakers was larger in the fifteenth century than it is now, although bi- and multilingualism, intermarriage, and religious conversions, as well as premodern markers of identity and loyalty, all blurred distinctions between Lithuanians and Ruthenians. Very roughly, Lithuanian-speakers constituted up to a fifth of the population and predominated in about a sixth of the territory. Gradually cultural barriers eroded from the top down. Ruthenian, refined by the grand ducal scribes, was the shared language of law and letters.

Gediminids, their numbers already depleted by civil wars, were mostly replaced in their ducal appanages by trusted governors appointed by Vytautas. Most of these men were first-generation

LITHUANIA

Catholics from Lithuania propria. The exception was Vytautas's brother-in-law Ivan Halshanski, the son of a convert to Orthodoxy, who became governor of Kyiv. Granted tracts of land as well as perquisites of office, these men began to be called 'lords' (borrowing the word *pany* from Polish) rather than boyars (*bajorai* in Lithuanian). The wide dispersal of aristocratic lands bound their recipients to the ruler. Vytautas also appealed to less wealthy boyars, promising them security of life, liberty, and property. He rewarded those who did him military or political service. Some non-Catholics benefited too: besides the martial Tatars settled by the Grand Duke, he honoured and enriched loyal Orthodox princes of Riurikid or Gediminid descent.

The spread of hereditary landholding among nobles, together with continued grants of lands and privileges for military service, increased pressures on peasants to provide dues in labour and kind. The Samogitian rebellion of 1418 may have been driven more by social and economic tensions than by attachment to paganism. Free peasants resisted subjection to nobles, while the poorest boyars struggled to meet their obligations to their ruler, and thereby to distinguish themselves from peasants. Nobles' gradual subjugation of peasants would continue through several generations. It eventually gave rise to a condition conventionally called serfdom, often misunderstood as akin to chattel slavery. Serfdom is best conceived of as an overlapping set of dependencies between a peasant and landowner, who was most often a noble, but might be the monarch, an ecclesiastical institution, or a town. Personal servitude or subjection to a lord was reinforced by the jurisdiction of the manorial court, and the obligation to render labour, produce, or money in exchange for the use of a plot of land.

The origins of the Lithuanian nobility lie deep in the fourteenth century. As Rimvydas Petrauskas has shown, Vytautas did not raise up 'new men' from obscurity; he chose from among the high-born. As an itinerant monarch, Vytautas intervened in local affairs directly, but when he moved on, he relied on local elites. 'Horizontal' kinship between cousins and brothers-in-law traditionally held these elites together in clans, which held lands collectively. As time passed, however, wealthier nobles began to hold their land personally, and to pass it on to their children. The emergence of the patrilineal idea of noble ancestry can also be traced in personal names. For the pagan era, genealogies are almost unknowable (hence the elaborate pedigrees invented during the Renaissance). Baptismal names appear in sources generated in Lithuania in the first years after conversion. They often took the form of an alias joined to a pagan name, such as *Michael alias Keszgal* (Kęsgaila), *Andreas alias Gastold* (Goštautas), and *Cristinus alias Ostyk* (Astikas). From the early fifteenth century, many pagan names survive as patronymics, such as *Petrus Montigerdowicz* (Petras Mangirdaitis). A few were used in their own right. The best known of these was Astikas's son *Radivil Ostikowicz* (Radvila Astikaitis), a key player in the middle decades of the fifteenth century. Nicknames or diminutives such as Olekhno (for Alexander) also became patronymics in the next generation. These patronymics would transmute into surnames, but ancestral names also returned as family surnames, such as Kęsgaila, Goštautas, or Radvila (which became Radziwiłł in Polish). Even among elite families, this process took over a century, but it began under Vytautas.[13]

Polish ideas and culture spread widely in the wake of Catholic Christianisation. Vytautas took many pen- and sword-wielding Poles into his service, and cultivated his network in Poland. Elite Lithuanians became acquainted with their Polish counterparts during joint diplomatic missions and assemblies. Encouraged by Vytautas, they learned to articulate their legal rights and liberties, and to cite Polish political principles in the Lithuanian cause. These ideas spread through the complex relations with the Polish community of the realm, but increasingly served to forge a collective Lithuanian identity that transcended personal loyalty. The Grand Duchy's nobles were becoming a political community in their own right: the genie could not be re-bottled. In sum, Vytautas the Great transformed the Gediminids' empire into the Grand Duchy of Lithuania; tellingly, the first recorded use of the term to designate all the territories ruled by the Grand Duke dates from 1430. Vytautas's Grand Duchy was far from a modern, unitary state, but it was more than a dynastic, patrimonial enterprise.

ii. *The Political Nation of the Grand Duchy of Lithuania*

The sense of community bequeathed by Vytautas's long reign helped the Grand Duchy of Lithuania survive the turbulence that followed. Jogaila's youngest surviving brother, Švitrigaila, was an incorrigible rebel. Jogaila, pressed by the Polish lords to incorporate Lithuania into Poland, but anxious to safeguard his sons' patrimony, did not trust his brother to govern the Grand Duchy as he had trusted his cousin. However, while Jogaila was preoccupied with Vytautas's funeral in Vilnius, Švitrigaila's supporters took control of the city and castle. Švitrigaila had Jogaila placed under house arrest, but did not depose him. While the Grand Duchy's elites expected to choose their own Grand Duke, rather than be governed from Kraków, they did not desire a complete rupture. Jogaila swiftly recognised his brother as Grand Duke, retaining his own status as Supreme Duke, and so regained his liberty.

A long-simmering dispute flared up when Polish territorial claims on Volhynia and Podolia led Švitrigaila to reject the Polish council's offer, made in May 1432, to recognise him as Grand Duke of Lithuania on the same terms as Vytautas. But he was over-reliant on Orthodox supporters. A plot was hatched among a group of mostly Catholic nobles. At Ashmiany, during the night of 31 August–1 September 1432, they ambushed and defeated Švitrigaila, who escaped. Žygimantas, Vytautas's surviving younger brother, was proclaimed Grand Duke with Polish support—essentially on the same terms as Vytautas, but without talk of incorporation. Although Žygimantas quickly established his rule over Lithuania propria, most of the duchies further east still recognised Švitrigaila. This forced Žygimantas's concession in 1432 of most of the rights enjoyed by Catholics to 'Ruthenian' nobles, although offices in the palatinates of Vilnius and Trakai were still closed to the Orthodox. The civil war reached its culmination in the battle of Pabaiskas on 1 September 1435, when Švitrigaila and the Livonian Knights were crushed by Žygimantas and his Polish allies. Švitrigaila was again lucky to escape alive, and the war dragged on until he was finally forced out of the Grand Duchy towards the end of 1438.

The resolution of the conflict was delayed by Jogaila's death, aged about eighty-two, on 1 June 1434. Without reference to Lithuania, the Polish lords elected and crowned his elder son, the nine-year-old Władysław, as King of Poland. Bishop Oleśnicki, a hardliner towards the Grand Duchy of Lithuania, dominated the Polish political scene, although the still youthful Queen Mother Sonka built up a rival party. The septuagenarian Žygimantas would not defer to the boy king as he had done to Jogaila, and took back Luts'k from the Poles in 1439. Within the Grand Duchy he acquired a reputation as a tyrant. Fearing a purge, on 20 March 1440, plotters murdered Žygimantas as he heard mass in his chambers at Trakai Castle.

The Polish council could not respond effectively. It had just negotiated the terms of Władysław's election to the vacant throne of Hungary. Despite the arrival in Kraków of a Lithuanian delegation, the fifteen-year-old monarch crossed the Carpathian Mountains, escorted by Polish knights, to take possession of his

LITHUANIA

new realm. Full of hubris, the Polish council sent the twelve-year-old Prince Casimir to Vilnius, but only as Władysław's deputy, not to govern the Grand Duchy as Vytautas had done. This was an insulting novelty. Just as they had done in 1430, the strongest group among the Lithuanian elites, denied an election according to the terms of Horodło, took matters into its own hands. Early in the morning of 29 June 1440, it elected Casimir as Grand Duke of Lithuania. This group of lords, led by Jonas Goštautas, did not intend to break the union; they had earlier invited Władysław to come to Vilnius and they did not question his title of Supreme Duke.

Within three years, the precociously shrewd Casimir emerged from his tutelage. Together with Goštautas, he pacified the Grand Duchy, wielding carrot and stick. Orthodox Ruthenian princes were now among the favoured elite. Neither Poland's council nor its absent king recognised Casimir as Grand Duke of Lithuania. Nevertheless, the costs of establishing Władysław (known to the Hungarians as I. Ulászló) on his new throne, and trying to stop the advance of the Ottoman Empire, emptied the Polish treasury. On 10 November 1444 disaster struck: Władysław charged an Ottoman host and was slain. The battlefield of Varna (now in Bulgaria) gave him his sobriquet. His body was never found.

The news reached first Kraków, then Vilnius, and finally Polatsk, where Casimir was campaigning against Muscovy. In April 1445, an assembly of Polish nobles invited him to come to Poland to be elected King. But he refused to confirm Lithuania's incorporation into Poland. He insisted on his patrimony as Supreme Duke of Lithuania, while the Lithuanian lords—in the spirit of Horodło—demanded a say in the arrangements. The stand-off continued for over a year before Casimir gained his election on his own terms. His earlier election as Grand Duke of Lithuania was recognised, while the union was declared to be one of love, with no mention of incorporation. The monarch could have Lithuanians at his Polish court, and travel between his two realms as he pleased. Having held his nerve and seen off all potential rivals to his two thrones, Casimir was crowned in Kraków on 24 June 1447. He was not yet twenty.

From this point until 1569, most historians have defined the union as a mere dynastic bond. Yet Lithuania and Poland were linked by more than hereditary happenstance. On 2 May 1447, Casimir issued a charter to his Lithuanian, Ruthenian, and Samogitian lords, nobles, boyars, clergy, and burghers, which promised them similar rights to those of their Polish counterparts. Yet this privilege was distinctly Lithuanian. Local offices and estates were to be reserved for local nobles, while the monarch promised to consult the lords on all the most important questions affecting the Grand Duchy. This was, according to Jūratė Kiaupienė, 'perhaps the most important event in the creation of the Lithuanian political nation and the political life of the state'.[14] Four joint assemblies between 1447 and 1454 helped to hammer out the *modus vivendi* between the two political communities and their shared monarch. No new treaty was agreed: in effect, the Poles and Lithuanians agreed to differ about the nature of their union. Exploiting divisions between the Polish nobles, Casimir at last settled the territorial dispute between Lithuania and Poland in 1453. The Grand Duchy would keep almost all of Volhynia and the eastern half of Podolia. After the deaths of Švitrigaila and Žygimantas's son Mykolas in 1452, Casimir could pursue his own dynastic agenda. The day of the Gediminids was over; the Jagiellonian era had begun.

In February 1454, Casimir Jagiellon married Elizabeth Habsburg, daughter of the late Albert II, King of Germany. She was no beauty, but the austere Casimir proved an uxorious husband. Between her nineteenth and forty-seventh birthdays she bore him thirteen surviving children. Every remaining royal house in Europe descends from them. Five of their seven daugh-

LITHUANIA

ters married a Wittelsbach, a Hohenzollern, a Pomeranian Piast, a Silesian Piast, and a Wettin. Italian Renaissance humanism shaped the children's education. The eldest son Władysław was elected King of Bohemia in 1471 and King of Hungary in 1490. He was therefore Vladislav I of Bohemia and II. Ulászló of Hungary. The second son, the promising Casimir, was intended to become King of Poland, but he died of tuberculosis in Hrodna in 1484 and was buried in Vilnius Cathedral. Noted for his piety, he became the dynastic saint in 1521. Because the bull of canonisation was lost in Rome, his sainthood was confirmed by a new bull in 1602, whereupon his damp tomb was opened, and his body reputedly found uncorrupted. The feast of Lithuania's patron saint—his diminutive is Kaziukas—on 4 March has long been celebrated by a great fair in Vilnius, with further festivities elsewhere. It is a perfect opportunity to enjoy hearty street food as the long Baltic winter nears its end. The martial but sybaritic third son, John Albert, would be elected to succeed his father on the Polish throne in 1492. Alexander, the fourth son, was destined to follow Casimir as Grand Duke of Lithuania. Sigismund, the fifth, deputised for the King of Bohemia in Silesia, but would ultimately rule both Poland and Lithuania for four decades. Not to be outdone by his five elder brothers, Frederick managed to hold the bishopric of Kraków simultaneously with the archbishopric of Gniezno, and to gain a cardinal's hat before his early death, blamed on syphilis, in 1503.

These were glittering dynastic successes. When Columbus sailed westwards in search of the Indies, Jagiellons reigned over almost a third of Europe. But 'Jagiellonian Europe' was fragile and short-lived; only recently have scholars sought to excavate and recast its memory. Although the King of Bohemia and Hungary sometimes reminded his brothers that their shared Lithuanian patrimony should be subject to collective decision-making, coordinated political and military action was the exception, rather

FORGING A UNION

than the rule. The dynasty lost Hungary and Bohemia in 1526. The Jagiellons are remembered in those countries—when they are recalled at all—as feckless and weak. Perhaps unjustly: the decades around 1500 brought the flourishing of Hungarian and Bohemian parliamentarianism and jurisprudence, as well as Renaissance art, architecture, and literature.

When the usual caveats about medieval dynastic priorities, rather than modern nationalist ones, have been made, the Grand Duchy of Lithuania still paid a heavy price for the Jagiellonian turn southwards. It was not that Casimir neglected Lithuania after 1447. He probably provoked more grumbling in Poland for favouring Lithuania than vice versa. Until almost the end of his long reign, he divided his time fairly evenly between the two realms. His ceremonial entries into Vilnius, proceeding down the hill along Great Street and Castle Street to the cathedral, deployed the full panoply of medieval monarchy and underlined the reciprocal bonds between ruler and subjects. When in Lithuania, he kept a splendid court; when abroad, he delegated authority to his Lithuanian councillors. From 1468, the council's powers in the ruler's absence were defined in written law. During Casimir's lifetime, the council remained a consultative body comprising the principal office holders and hereditary princes. In practice, many important decisions were taken by an inner group: the bishop of Vilnius, and the palatines and castellans of Vilnius and Trakai. The two palatines were usually the chancellor and marshal respectively. Stable governance was assured by the long tenure of the chancellorship, between 1444 and 1476, by Mykolas Kęsgailaitis ('Kyensgalowicz' in written sources). He headed an institution based in Vilnius, which prepared, registered, and stored important documents: the grand ducal chancellery. Copies of these documents were beginning to be collected into books which would in time become the Lithuanian Metrica—in effect the state archive of the Grand Duchy of Lithuania. Grand duke and great lords usually acted in harmony.

LITHUANIA

Nevertheless, Casimir had other priorities. Poland fought the Thirteen Years' War against the Teutonic Order. Provoked into revolt by the Knights' onerous rule, a league of Prussian nobles and cities swore loyalty to Casimir and joined the Polish Crown on 15 April 1454. Polish nobles extracted concessions from their hard-pressed king. Casimir would henceforth have to negotiate all extraordinary levies and taxes with the local assemblies of the nobility, called sejmiks in Polish. This enshrined the practice of consensual politics in written law. Unfortunately, the chance of an early victory was lost on the battlefield of Chojnice (Konitz) in September 1454. The days of calling out the banners of mounted knights were passing; what counted now were funds to raise trained mercenaries and the know-how to conduct sieges. In the long war of attrition, the *Ordensstaat* could tap fewer resources than the Prussian cities and Poland. Its strongholds fell one by one. In 1466, the Order ceded its richer, western half to Poland (henceforth known as Royal Prussia) and acknowledged feudal vassalage for the poorer eastern part. The Grand Duchy of Lithuania did not formally enter the war, although it did prevent the Livonian Order from aiding the Prussian branch, and some Lithuanians fought for their monarch.

Casimir could not prevent the erosion of his suzerainty over the principality of Moldavia. For decades the Moldavian ruler (*hospodar*) Stephen the Great (reigned 1457–1504) manoeuvred between Poland, Hungary, and the Ottoman Empire—which had captured Constantinople in 1453. Ottoman influence finally prevailed in Moldavia and also grew over Crimea. Lithuanian claims to the Black Sea coastline became nominal, while the traditional strategy of playing the Crimean Khanate off against Muscovy became harder to implement. Instead, the Tatars would raid the Grand Duke's Ruthenian lands. They burned Kyiv in 1482.

Western readers of textbook accounts of 'the rise of Russia' should beware generalisations inspired by Muscovite pretensions to 'gather the lands of Rus''. An exalted imperial ideology did not foreordain the eighteenth-century expansion of the Russian Empire. Muscovy's attractions for the Grand Duchy of Lithuania's Orthodox Ruthenian princes and bishops have been exaggerated, while numerous defections in the other direction have been underplayed. Although the cause of church unity faltered, from 1458 the Grand Duchy had its own Orthodox metropolitan archbishop of Kyiv and all Rus', independent of Moscow.

For all these caveats, the Jagiellons squandered their early advantages. Muscovy had been afflicted by civil war and Tatar raids for most of the first half of the fifteenth century. The palmy days when Vytautas could hold his son-in-law Vasilii I and grandson Vasilii II in his tutelage bred a complacency in Vilnius that ignored changing realities in the east. In the middle decades of the century, Vasilii II overcame his enemies and matured into a hard-bitten—indeed, hideously blinded—politician. Riazan', Pskov, Tver', and the city-republic of Novgorod, with its vastness of taiga and tundra, all came under the sway of Vasilii II's son Ivan III (reigned 1462–1505). In 1478, the Novgorodians rose up against Muscovy, but Casimir failed to come to their aid. Ivan suppressed the revolt and removed the great bell which had summoned the citizens' assemblies. Imperial autocracy, not republican liberty, would shape first Muscovy, and then Russia.

Ivan III expressed his imperial pretensions through his marriage to Sophia Paleologue, the niece of the last Byzantine emperor, and his adoption of the double-headed eagle. As so often, territorial annexations enabled the distribution of lands to followers on condition of military service, further enhancing the ruler's capacity to wage war. In the 1480s, Ivan induced several minor princes in the borderlands to transfer their allegiance from Casimir to himself. On learning of Casimir's death in 1492, he ordered his army westwards. The following year he claimed to be 'ruler of all Rus'' (*gosudar' vseia Rusi*) in official communication

LITHUANIA

with Vilnius. The cycle of wars, punctuated by truces, continued under his son Vasilii III (reigned 1505–33). The Grand Duchy of Lithuania lost about a third of its territory and a fifth of its population. Only with Polish aid could this Muscovite onslaught be reversed. It has been argued that the loss of indirectly ruled and thinly populated peripheral territories helped to consolidate the Grand Duchy of Lithuania internally. The problem was that these lands strengthened the viscerally hostile rulers of Muscovy.

Casimir Jagiellon died, aged sixty-four, in Hrodna on 7 June 1492. His widow, Queen Elizabeth, commissioned Veit Stoss, the finest sculptor north of the Alps, to create a stunning monument in Kraków Cathedral. The cares of ruling seem to trouble the sleep of the wizened monarch, recumbent on his sarcophagus under a baldachin supported by eight columns. The sophisticated iconography emphasises divinely sanctioned majesty. The carved mourners represent the estates of the Polish Crown—clergy, nobility, burghers, and peasants—but prominent among the heraldic signs is the mounted knight of the Grand Duchy of Lithuania. The monument is situated in a chapel decorated with murals in the Byzantine style by Ruthenian masters. Casimir's mostly peaceful reign brought the rapid development of the Lithuanian political community. Its leaders would now have to show their mettle.

Before expiring, Casimir made known his wish for Alexander to be the next Grand Duke of Lithuania, and John Albert the next King of Poland. They were respectively elected by Lithuanian and Polish assemblies on 30 July and 27 August 1492. In principle, the system of Jogaila—dynastic Supreme Duke—and Vytautas—elected Grand Duke—was restored. Indeed, Alexander presented himself as the heir of Vytautas (whose baptismal name he shared). At Alexander's enthronement in Vilnius Cathedral, the palatine of Trakai impressed upon him the need to rule according to the example of Vytautas and Lithuanian customs.

FORGING A UNION

What this meant in practice was that the council's advice and assent would be required for grants of land, appointment to and removal from office, and much else. Although Alexander was far from supine, he faced overwhelming challenges. Fiscal plight and pressures from high-born debtors probably explain why he expelled the Jews from the Grand Duchy in 1495. The economic consequences were predictably baleful, and the ruler invited them back in 1503.

Poland, beleaguered in the south-east by the Tatars, Moldavians, and Ottomans, would help Lithuania against Muscovy only in exchange for a tighter union. In contrast to the Poles' pursuit of incorporation, the negotiations and projects of the 1490s reveal a Lithuanian concept of a union of two equal realms and communities, each of which could, in consultation with the other, elect its ruler. The acts finally agreed by the two councils and approved by more broadly based parliamentary assemblies in Kraków and Vilnius in 1499 largely confirmed the Horodło act. There was by now a sense that the Lithuanian *res publica* or commonwealth had become a fully-fledged partner for its Polish counterpart.

To end the first phase of the war against Muscovy in 1494, Alexander agreed to marry Ivan III's daughter Helena, who would remain an Orthodox Christian. Alexander's confirmation of the privileges of the Orthodox Church in 1499 did not prevent a new Muscovite invasion the following year. Catastrophic defeat on the banks of the River Vedrosha led to the loss of swathes of territory. At this critical juncture, King John Albert died on 17 June 1501. Although leadership was required in Lithuania, the Lithuanian council recognised the paramountcy of Polish assistance and backed Alexander's candidacy for the vacant throne. The Polish council, which was fast evolving into the senate of a bicameral parliament, or sejm, made it clear that Alexander would govern in accordance with its wishes, or not at all. The Poles also proposed a new treaty incorporating Lithuania into a

LITHUANIA

single body politic, people, and council, with one jointly elected monarch. The king-elect felt obliged to accept, despite the implied threat to the dynasty's patrimonial rights to the Grand Duchy. In the end, however, references to incorporation were dropped, and the treaty of Mielnik (in Podlachia) spoke of two nations 'united and combined into one indivisible body'.[15]

Once crowned, Alexander avoided implementing his promises with the help of a talented Polish cleric. Jan Łaski, who was engaged in a compilation of Polish laws published in 1506, took the spirit of *res publica*—the commonwealth—from the Mielnik articles, but encompassed within it a much wider political community. It comprised the nobility as a whole, as well as the principal royal towns. The Polish sejm of 1505 passed the statute known as *Nihil Novi*. King Alexander accepted that:

> nothing new [*nihil novi*] should be decreed by us or our successors that is to the prejudice or inconvenience of the commonwealth [*res publica*], or to the injury or detriment of whatsoever private interest, or that alters the common law or public liberties, without the common agreement of our councillors and envoys of the lands.

In effect, new laws and taxes would require the express consent of both houses of parliament. 'Envoys of the lands' were the elected delegates of their noble brethren gathered at sejmiks. Much power, revenue, and influence were still left to the King, but the principle of a parliamentary monarchy being part of the commonwealth or republic was now firmly established in the Polish Crown. The example would attract ordinary nobles in the Grand Duchy of Lithuania.[16]

Alexander suffered six strokes during 1505. Having been absent from the Grand Duchy for most of his Polish reign, he died in Vilnius on 19 August 1506. The Lithuanian council had the deceased monarch buried in Vilnius Cathedral, before electing his younger brother, the thirty-nine-year-old Sigismund, as Grand

FORGING A UNION

Duke of Lithuania on 20 October. It also noted Sigismund's hereditary rights. Pre-empted, the Polish sejm elected Sigismund as King on 6 December, making no new attempt to incorporate the Grand Duchy. Lithuania's priority remained the threat from Muscovy. War was renewed in 1507, and after a truce in 1508, broke out again in 1512. The Muscovites took Smolensk in July 1514. The city could not be recovered, despite the spectacular victory won at Orsha on 8 September 1514 by a Lithuanian and Polish army commanded by Kostiantyn Ostroz'kyi. This triumph scotched a Habsburg–Muscovite alliance against Poland–Lithuania and stemmed the haemorrhage of territory.

Ostroz'kyi, the hetman (highest military commander) of Lithuania and castellan of Vilnius, blazed a trail into the heart of the political elite for Orthodox Ruthenes. Having already founded one splendid Orthodox church in Vilnius (with Sigismund's permission), following his victory he had two more churches constructed in the capital. However, his further advance to palatine of Trakai in 1522 sparked protests from the chancellor and palatine of Vilnius, Albertas Goštautas. Ostroz'kyi is now the patron of LITPOLUKRBRIG, the Lithuano–Polish–Ukrainian brigade formed in 2015.[17]

The war sputtered on until the truce of 1522. The Grand Duchy regained Homel' (now in south-eastern Belarus) during the next round in 1534–37, during the minority of Ivan IV. But if wars, rather than mere battles, were to be won, many more men and much more money would be needed. Across Europe, nothing has been more conducive to the development of parliamentary assemblies than monarchs' need of men and money to fight wars. The Grand Duchy of Lithuania was no exception. Its parliament (*seimas* in Lithuanian, *sejm* in Polish, *soim* in Ruthenian—the language of the records) emerged gradually over several decades. Under Alexander assemblies were held almost annually, and their importance grew further under his successor. At the soim summoned by Sigismund to Vilnius in 1507, representatives of all parts of the Grand Duchy—albeit nominated by lords and officials—consented to taxes, registers, and levies. In 1514 another soim agreed a poll tax. Parliamentary gatherings became frequent even in the monarch's absence. This gave rise to a system of dialogue and negotiation via envoys, written messages, petitions, and decisions. The long soim of 1528–29—at which Sigismund was present—introduced more systematic registration of landed estates and military obligations. Neither the Lithuanian nor the Polish parliament evolved procedures whereby decisions were routinely taken by majority vote. Matters of state were either resolved by consensus, or their resolution was postponed pending consensus. In hammering out solutions, opinions were not counted, but weighed according to their merit and the status of the person who articulated them. Much later, this mode of proceeding would harden into a legalistically interpreted requirement of unanimity—the notorious *liberum veto*—but the pursuit of broad-based consensus helped to keep the body politic together.

Despite widening political participation, the key players all came from a few staggeringly wealthy families. The names at the head of the 1528 register were Kęsgaila, Radvila, Goštautas, Okelkovych, and Ostroz´kyi. During his long stays in Poland, Sigismund relied on the council to look after Lithuania, but it was riven by fierce, occasionally violent rivalry. Nevertheless, Muscovite pressure and Polish challenges (and examples) encouraged an ethnically and religiously diverse, yet politically Lithuanian nation to cohere and mature.

iii. *Reformation, Reform, and Union*

The 1520s left multiple watersheds in the history of the Jagiellonian dynasty, the union, and the Grand Duchy of Lithuania. The Teutonic *Ordensstaat* fought one last war against

FORGING A UNION

Poland 1519–21, before succumbing to the Reformation. In 1525, Grand Master Albrecht von Hohenzollern became Duke of Prussia at the head of Europe's first Lutheran state. He paid feudal homage to his uncle, King Sigismund, in a ceremony on Kraków's market square. At this time much of the Duchy of Prussia was still inhabited by people who spoke Baltic tongues. Four years later, following the deaths of the last dukes from the Piast dynasty, their Duchy of Mazovia was fully incorporated into the Polish Crown. Given Lithuania's losses to Muscovy, Poland was becoming much the stronger partner in the union. Meanwhile, another of Sigismund's nephews, Louis, King of Hungary and Bohemia, died while fleeing from the Ottoman Turks after losing the battle of Mohács in 1526. That tragedy passed the mission of resisting Ottoman expansion to the Habsburgs with whom the Jagiellons had made a marital pact in 1515. Prince Sigismund Augustus, born in 1520 to Sigismund and his second queen, Bona Sforza, was now the last hope of the dynasty in the male line.

The efforts of Sigismund and Bona to assure their son's succession offered a *quid pro quo* to the Lithuanian council. The participants in the soim held in Vilnius in 1522 declared that they desired no other successor as grand duke than Sigismund Augustus. His mother hoped for more. Chancellor Albertas Goštautas saw a linked opportunity in demands from the nobility for a codification of Lithuanian law. This well-travelled, polyglot aristocrat, polished by the humanist learning of the Renaissance, developed a vision of a union of equal partners, articulated through history and secured by law. He sponsored and contributed to the writing and rewriting (in Ruthenian) of the *Chronicle of the Grand Duchy of Lithuania and Samogitia*. This history claimed, probably adapting older oral traditions, that the leading Lithuanian and Samogitian families descended from Roman patricians, led by the legendary Palemon. Arriving in Lithuania, they conquered the local population. This story, also adopted by some of the principal Orthodox Ruthenian families, served the lords' claims to head the Lithuanian 'nation' and govern the Grand Duchy alongside the Grand Duke. Crucially, in the third redaction of the *Chronicle*, much was made of Horodło as a union of equals. Evoking the glories of Vytautas the Great, the *Chronicle* also dwelt on the 'Coronation Tempest' of 1429–30, dovetailing with Goštautas's 1526 proposal for the coronation of the young Sigismund Augustus. A kingdom of Lithuania, he believed, could not be incorporated into Poland.

The elder Sigismund would take no such risks. The soim of 1528–29 elected Sigismund Augustus as Grand Duke of Lithuania alongside his father. There followed the young grand duke's enthronement and an oath taken by both monarchs to uphold their subjects' privileges and laws. Besides the military reform discussed above, this soim accepted the First Lithuanian Statute. This drew on the customary law of the various parts of the Grand Duchy, the privileges issued by the grand dukes, and the principles and solutions of Roman law. A true codification, as opposed to a mere compilation, the First Statute brought order to the criminal and civil law, for example in enhancing noblewomen's rights of inheritance and their security in widowhood. The legal system was, however, skewed in favour of the great lords. There would be no Polish-style land courts with elected judges. The ruler's ability to legislate depended on the consent of the council, not of the broader-based soim, which was not even mentioned in the text. The original of 1529, written in Ruthenian, was soon translated into Polish and Latin. Sigismund's acceptance of the Statute was a powerful statement of the right of the Grand Duchy of Lithuania to make and remake its own laws. The Polish sejm, bounced by its Lithuanian counterpart, elected Sigismund Augustus to the Polish throne. However, the backlash that followed the 'young king's' coronation in 1530 served notice on the 'old king' and his queen that never again could they violate the principle of a freely and fully elective monarchy.

By this time, a spirit of *reformatio* was challenging the Catholic Church across Europe. The rapid spread of the Reformation in the Grand Duchy of Lithuania has coloured later views of its earlier Christianisation. S. C. Rowell has persuasively argued that sixteenth-century Protestant and Catholic polemicists, zealous for their respective causes of 'True Religion', shared an interest in caricaturing the Catholic religion practised in fifteenth-century Lithuania as superficial and superstitious. He points to a piety, stimulated by religious diversity and debate, as rich and varied as any in the late medieval West. By the early sixteenth century, ecclesiastical structures and foundations—including dioceses, parishes, consistory courts, fraternities, almshouses, indulgences, monasteries, convents, and friaries—were thriving. The statutes of the cathedral chapter of Vilnius, granted by Bishop Albertas Radvila in 1515 and subsequently expanded to meet new challenges, expressed a reforming impulse from above. Much, perhaps most, of the clergy was, in one sense or another, Lithuanian. Even at the cosmopolitan top of the hierarchy, scions of the most prominent Catholic Lithuanian aristocratic families were becoming canons, prelates, and bishops. Some bishops sought to control popular religious practices, but lay people's expectations of the clergy were rising. Baronas and Rowell conclude: 'Failure on the part of the ecclesiastical hierarchy to meet the increasing spiritual demands of the faithful would result as elsewhere in revolt and reformation.'[18]

Sigismund I issued edicts against the dissemination of writings by the 'heretic' Martin Luther in Vilnius in 1521 and Hrodna in 1522. It is not clear, however, whether they were reactive—against a movement that had already reached Lithuania—or preventive. Perhaps they were intended to humour the papal nuncio, for this mild-tempered monarch was disinclined to enforce his stern decrees. During the 1520s and 1530s it was unclear that Christendom had been irrevocably riven. 'Correct doctrine' had yet to acquire its later importance in defining confessional identities. Nevertheless, the reformers' message that the Catholic Church's teaching on Heaven, Hell, and Purgatory was spurious meant that its ordained clergy was not only corrupt, but fundamentally useless.

The first known Lutheran activists in the Grand Duchy of Lithuania were Jonas Batakietis in Samogitia and Abraomas Kulvietis in Vilnius. Both had to flee to the neighbouring Duchy of Prussia, where they joined others, notably a Samogitian student at Königsberg's Lutheran university—the Albertina—called Martynas Mažvydas. His Lutheran Catechism of 1547 was the first published book in the Lithuanian language. Of a print run of 300 copies, only two are known today: one in Toruń in Poland, and one in Vilnius (having been rediscovered in Odesa in 1957). Mažvydas is now the patron of Lithuania's National Library. During the second half of the sixteenth century, Königsberg's presses produced prayer books, hymnals, psalters, and postils in Lithuanian. The first complete translation of the Bible into Lithuanian was by another graduate of the Albertina, Johannes Bretke (known to Lithuanians as Jonas Bretkūnas), a pastor of mixed German and old-Prussian stock, who could preach in the Prussian and Lithuanian languages. However, after completing the work in 1590, he was unable to find anyone prepared to pay for the publication of the Lithuanian Bible, whose manuscript remains in the Prussian Secret State Archives in Berlin.

Harassment of religious reformers within the Grand Duchy of Lithuania ended when the intellectually curious Sigismund Augustus moved to Vilnius in 1544, after his aged father finally entrusted him with power. The young grand duke welcomed heterodox scholars and preachers at his cosmopolitan court. By

FORGING A UNION

the middle of the century, while Lutheranism consolidated itself among German-speaking burghers, the second, more radical wave of the Reformation was advancing among the Grand Duchy's nobility. One attraction of Calvinism to them was clear and challenging doctrine, another was governance by laymen. During the 1550s and 1560s, the Reformed (Calvinist) Church expanded its congregations, held synods, and won over a majority of the Lithuanian aristocracy.

The foremost patron of the Reformation was the cerebral Mikołaj Radziwiłł (Mikalojus Radvila) known as 'the Black'. He founded Evangelical Reformed churches, corresponded with Jean Calvin personally, and polemicised in print with the papal nuncio Luigi Lippomano. His interest in anti-Trinitarian theology and patronage of radical preachers might well have taken the Reformed Church in Lithuania further down that road. After his death, his cousin, Mikołaj Radziwiłł, known as 'the Red', became the Reformed Church's chief protector and remained a Trinitarian Calvinist.* The crowning religious achievement of Radziwiłł the Black was to sponsor the translation of the Bible and its publication in Brest in 1563. Significantly, the language of the translation was Polish. Mikołaj the Black could not speak Lithuanian, had poor Latin, and no more than adequate Ruthenian, but having been brought up in Poland, he was fluent in Polish. He married a Pole, as did his cousin, Mikołaj the Red, whose mother was Polish too. Hence the Polish spelling of the name used in this book for this and subsequent generations of their family. Several Lithuanian and Polish aristocratic families intermarried during the sixteenth century.

A little further down the social scale, many Poles settled in the Grand Duchy, not least Reformed Protestant and Roman

---

* The sobriquet *Rudy/Rudasis* referred to the reddish colour of his hair (before it turned grey). Other translations such as 'the Brown', 'the Ginger', 'the Ruddy', or 'the Rusty' seem unacceptable.

LITHUANIA

Catholic clergy (between whom the boundaries remained blurred until the last quarter of the sixteenth century). Over half of the seventy-five canons and prelates of Vilnius Cathedral during the second half of the century were born in the Polish Crown, with less than a third born in the Grand Duchy of Lithuania (including Podlachia). Others hailed from afar: the noted poet and lawyer Petrus Roysius (Pedro Ruiz de Moros) came from Aragón. He drafted the statute of the Samogitian cathedral chapter and contributed to the drafting of the Second Lithuanian Statute.[19] Evidence of the spread of the Polish language at the expense of Ruthenian includes a demand made by the soim held in Vilnius in 1566 that the grand ducal chancellery provide documents in Latin or Polish, 'as they cannot read Ruthenian script here'.[20] The growing attractions of Polish families and language did not, however, erode Lithuanian political identity among the Grand Duchy's elite, which was steeped in the culture and learning of the Renaissance. No doubt this sophistication enhanced the attraction for newcomers: political Lithuanisation proceeded simultaneously with cultural Polonisation. Indeed, Lithuanian aristocrats' very closeness to Poland would enable them to express their opposition to an incorporative union in Ciceronian rhetoric.

The influence of the Radziwiłł cousins reached its zenith in the mid-sixteenth century. Mikołaj the Red's younger sister, Barbara, married Stanislovas Goštautas, the last of his line. When, in 1542, she was widowed after five years of marriage, the monarch claimed the vast Goštautas fortune. Even Barbara's own dowry remained precarious until she caught the roving eye of Sigismund Augustus the following year. The young Jagiellon was keen to escape his domineering mother Bona and his unhappy marriage to his cousin Elizabeth of Austria. After moving to Vilnius in 1544, Sigismund Augustus had the Lower Castle, already partly rebuilt in the Renaissance style by his parents, transformed into the grand palace that was reconstructed early in the twenty-first century. Exactly when he and Barbara became lovers is unknown; it may have been as early as the autumn of 1543, but perhaps not until after the epileptic Elizabeth's death. By then, in the summer of 1545, the Radziwiłłs enjoyed his firm favour and friendship. Mikołaj the Black had earlier been the prince's companion and mentor. The cousins seized their opportunity to break the hold on Lithuania of Bona Sforza, who had been auditing and expanding the grand ducal domain. Her abrasive legal proceedings antagonised other lords. Against this background, Sigismund Augustus's affair with Barbara presented the cousins with an opportunity that was too good to miss. The story that they surprised the enamoured couple in bed and forced them to wed on the spot sounds fanciful, but they did all they could to encourage the royal marriage, which took place during 1547.

The scandal broke at the end of that year. Barbara's reputation was shredded. The political storm did not abate after the 'young king' succeeded his father on 1 April 1548. At the next Polish sejm, held in the autumn, speaker after speaker implored Sigismund Augustus to put aside Barbara and marry again. He was, they reminded him, an elective monarch who should heed their counsel in so weighty a matter of state as his marriage. The monarch was adamant. He brought Barbara to Kraków and had her crowned queen in December 1550. She was already dying. Cancer—perhaps of the ovary or the cervix—caused her to putrefy from within. Only her husband stayed devotedly at her bedside to the end, which came on 8 May 1551. Sigismund Augustus was heartbroken, but his bond with the Radziwiłłs endured. Until the early 1560s they dominated his grand ducal council. Mikołaj the Black became palatine of Vilnius and chancellor, while Mikołaj the Red became palatine of Trakai and hetman.

The same decades also brought transformations to the countryside. Bona Sforza, besides reclaiming vast domains for the monarch, purchased huge estates for herself, multiplying their revenues through sound management and investment. She redistributed farms and holdings, introducing linear villages and the rotating three-field hide or *voloka* system, as practised in Poland. Following her example, Sigismund Augustus had all remaining grand ducal estates converted to the new system. Ultimately, most private landowners did likewise, and the earlier, more dispersed pattern of settlement and cultivation gradually yielded to the new one. Manorial farming increased, but (contrary to Marxist–Leninist assumptions about an oppressive 'feudal' economy) there is no evidence of significant peasant resistance to these changes. The redistribution may well have reduced inequalities among peasants and been perceived as fair. Labour rents remained moderate, even for top-quality land. A by-product of the reform was the gradual disappearance of slavery (not to be confused with serfdom). As in many ancient and early medieval societies, this unfree condition had once been the lot of many people captured in wars; it had been inherited by their descendants.

Polish-style liberty attracted Lithuanian nobles. By the mid-sixteenth century, middling Polish noblemen were asserting themselves against the grandees. Faced by royal demands for taxes and military service, demands intensified for the reclamation of the royal domain lands which kings had for generations 'illegally' granted to magnates. This movement 'for the execution of the laws' gathered strength until, at the Polish sejm held in the winter of 1562–63, Sigismund Augustus accepted some of its demands. Not coincidentally, Muscovite armies were again devastating the Grand Duchy of Lithuania, and the price demanded for Polish aid would be closer union.

This decisive cycle of wars had been triggered by the death agonies of the Livonian branch of the Teutonic Order, fatally weakened by the Reformation. Sigismund Augustus was still trying to negotiate a solution when, at the start of 1558, Tsar

FORGING A UNION

Ivan IV ('the Terrible') invaded Livonia. Blood-curdling tales of Muscovite atrocities were not always exaggerated. The tsar's army overwhelmed the Livonian Knights, and King Erik XIV of Sweden seized the port of Tallinn (then known as Reval), before the Polish–Lithuanian monarch acted decisively. Late in 1561, Sigismund Augustus accepted the homage of the Livonian Estates, the archbishop of Riga, and the last Teutonic landmaster in Livonia. The latter, Gotthard von Kettler, received the south-western wedge of Livonia as the vassal Duchy of Courland and Semigallia. Tsar Ivan then invaded the Grand Duchy of Lithuania. In February 1563, he celebrated the fall of Polatsk by having the city's Jews drowned in the icy River Dzvina.

Facing the Muscovite surge, Sigismund Augustus had sought taxes and levies from the Lithuanian nobility at Vitsebsk in September 1562. He got less than he wished. The assembly presented him with a petition whose first demand was for a joint sejm with the 'Polish lords', so that 'a union be formed in the closest of unity for two reasons: to choose a common ruler, and for common defence; and that there be one common sejm and one common law.' These startling words have provoked controversy, but Frost convincingly argues that ordinary nobles' resentment of the lords had long been evident in petitions to the Grand Duke. He also points to nobles' growing familiarity with Poland and the appeal of equality before the law. What this closer acquaintance and even admiration did not entail, however, was a desire to incorporate Lithuania into Poland. The union demanded was one between equal partners.[21]

With closer union in prospect, the Polish sejm agreed to substantial taxes and levies. The reinforcements helped the Lithuanian army, led by Radziwiłł the Red, to crush a larger Muscovite force near Chashniki on the banks of the River Ula in 1564. However, despite further successes and the chaos wreaked in Muscovy by Tsar Ivan's establishment of his infamous separate realm (the *Oprichnina*), a decisive breakthrough eluded the Lithuanian and Polish forces. Pestilence and famine ravaged the Grand Duchy. The truce agreed in 1570 left Polatsk and eastern Livonia in Muscovite hands.

The victory of Chashniki stiffened Lithuanian resistance to Polish demands for incorporation. The Grand Duchy's delegation to the Polish sejm held in Warsaw in 1563–64, skilfully led by Radziwiłł the Black, but including lesser noble and urban representatives, insisted on the union under a common monarch of separate and equal Lithuanian and Polish nations. In the Lithuanian vision, the two communities would make some decisions jointly, although meetings of the common sejm would be reserved for the most important matters concerning both realms. Legal systems, treasuries, and offices would remain separate. In contrast, the prevailing view among the Polish parliamentarians was that the union already existed and only needed to be implemented (despite difficulties in finding the relevant acts). Lithuania should become a province of Poland—one insulting suggestion was to call this province 'New Poland', alongside Greater Poland and Lesser Poland. Even the monarch—the great-great-great-grandson of Gediminas—accepted the principle of an incorporative union. On 13 March 1564, he bequeathed his hereditary rights to the Grand Duchy of Lithuania, not to the Lithuanian Estates, but to the Crown of the Kingdom of Poland. No agreement was reached, either in Warsaw or at the Lithuanian soim held later in 1564, leading to mutual recrimination.

As the push for closer union stalled, the pace of internal reform quickened. In 1563, Sigismund Augustus opened up all remaining offices in the Grand Duchy to Orthodox nobles, abolishing the restrictions in the 1413 Horodło Act, which had long been tacitly ignored. The lords of the council endorsed the monarch's decree. The council included four Catholic bishops, but at this time none were zealots. Indeed, the monarch's nominee for the far-flung bishopric of Kyiv, Mikołaj Pac never took priestly orders. Instead, he embraced the Reformed faith and a wife. Yet he maintained his claim to the see and continued to sit on the council.

In 1564, judicial powers devolved from the Grand Duke's representatives to judges elected by nobles, as land courts were established on the Polish model. The soim held in Vilnius in 1565–66 implemented a territorial division of almost all of the Grand Duchy into palatinates, sub-divided into districts. Some of the palatinates were newly created; they joined the existing ones, which had evolved out of older duchies. The districts corresponded to the territories pertaining to offices, courts, sejmiks, other assemblies, and military recruitment, on a more regular and logical basis than that which had arisen piecemeal in Poland. The sole exception to the pattern remained the duchy of Samogitia, which retained a unique territorial, judicial, and administrative structure.

Taken together, these reforms might—given time—have brought Lithuania propria and the Ruthenian lands closer together. Part of the reason was that the additional offices of palatine and castellan created in 1566 widened the 'charmed circle'. Moreover, after Radziwiłł the Black's death in 1565, the monarch redistributed the offices of marshal and hetman to the rival Chodkiewicz family, and created the new office of vice-chancellor. These changes left the new chancellor, Radziwiłł the Red, with less power than his late cousin had wielded. The reforms were consolidated in the revision of the Grand Duchy's legal code accepted by the soim in 1566. Compared to its predecessor of 1529, the Second Lithuanian Statute strengthened the position of ordinary nobles. Magnates would henceforth have to work harder to keep their supporters. Rapid economic, social, political, and institutional developments necessitated the integration of the many decisions taken by the grand dukes and the soim into the law. The Second Statute also marked the maturation of the state by differentiating between public and private law, in the Roman tradition. It did not, however, endorse the imperial Roman principle that the ruler was 'absolved' from the law.

In January 1569, the Lithuanian and Polish parliaments met in Lublin. Except for a few joint sessions, they deliberated separately, negotiating via deputations. They would only merge into a joint sejm the day after the union was agreed. Many Poles demanded incorporation, while the Lithuanians offered less than they had been prepared to concede five years earlier. Most of the Grand Duchy's representatives at Lublin were moderately wealthy nobles, often with some association with the royal court. Their dependency on the magnates was questionable, but initially, the leadership of Radziwiłł the Red held firm. After being ordered by the monarch to attend a joint session on 1 March, he led most of the Lithuanian delegates back into the Grand Duchy. The Polish sejm responded by resurrecting old territorial disputes, whereupon Sigismund Augustus made a decisive choice. He declared Podlachia and Volhynia to be part of the Polish Crown and demanded oaths of fidelity from those lands' officials and nobles as King of Poland. Most Podlachian nobles readily complied. The Volhynians, taking their lead from their princely families, followed suit when reassured that their laws, language, and customs, as well as the Orthodox Church, would be respected. At the same time, delegates from Royal Prussia also took their seats in the Polish sejm. They too joined the Crown as equal citizens.

While these incorporations took effect, divisions widened among the Lithuanian elite. As Lithuanian lords with property in Podlachia and Volhynia began to swear loyalty to Sigismund Augustus as King of Poland, and to return to Lublin, the monarch struck a further blow. He ordained the incorporation into the Polish Crown of the vast palatinate of Kyiv. He probably did so at the Volhynians' request, for few Poles desired an expansion this far eastwards. Kyiv and Luts'k would be reunited with L'viv.

FORGING A UNION

The terms of these unions, including the retention of the 1566 Lithuanian statute, were negotiated between Polish and southern Ruthenian parliamentarians and their monarch. Contrary to older Lithuanian and Ukrainian assumptions, the elites of most of southern Rus´ consented to their transfer from Lithuania to Poland 'as the free to the free, the equal to the equal'. South of the Prypiats´, Vilnius was distant. As the Grand Duchy's fiscal and military position worsened, the Lithuanian elites had to strike a bargain swiftly.[22]

A deal was there for the taking, but even Radziwiłł's rival Jan Chodkiewicz, favoured by the monarch, found the terms on offer hard to swallow. 'We declare before God and men that you are proceeding with us not as brothers but violently', he told Polish senators on 6 June 1569.[23] The entire Lithuanian delegation knelt before Sigismund Augustus on 20 June, imploring him to change his mind. He did not. Nevertheless, the conditions of the union between the Polish Crown and the Grand Duchy of Lithuania, agreed by both sejms on 1 July, were less unfavourable to Lithuania than the drama of the previous six months might suggest. The act itself was made in two copies—one given by the Poles to the Lithuanians, the other given by the Lithuanians to the Poles. When the monarch confirmed the union in an identically worded privilege issued on 4 July, he used both seals—of the Kingdom of Poland and of the Grand Duchy of Lithuania.

The Lublin treaty does not speak of incorporation. Instead, its key clause states that 'that the Kingdom of Poland and the Grand Duchy of Lithuania is one indivisible and uniform body, and also one uniform and shared commonwealth which has already joined and united two states and two nations in one people.' In contrast to previous acts of union, written in Latin, this text is in Polish. The keywords are 'commonwealth' (the Polish *rzeczpospolita* being a translation of the Latin *respublica*), 'state' (*państwo* being derived from the Latin *dominium*), 'nation' (*naród* for *natio*), and

LITHUANIA

'people' (*lud* for *populus*, a word that evoked the citizenry of ancient Rome, rather than the inhabitants of the country as a whole).[24] This ambiguous clause, full of overlapping meanings, managed to square the circle. Neither side was wholly satisfied, but Poles gained an acknowledgement that the two communities were already united, while Lithuanians had their Grand Duchy recognised as a separate realm and nation within the joint political community. This shared commonwealth or republic would have a single monarch, council (or senate), parliament, and currency. The jointly elected monarch would be crowned only once, in Kraków, but he would use the title of Grand Duke of Lithuania alongside that of King of Poland. The Grand Duchy of Lithuania would retain its own seals, legal system, army, treasury, and hierarchy of offices. Much and more remained to be worked out in practice. Once the tide of anger at the loss of southern Rus´ had ebbed, the terms of the Lublin act would enable Lithuanian statesmen to argue that they had joined a union of free and equal partners.

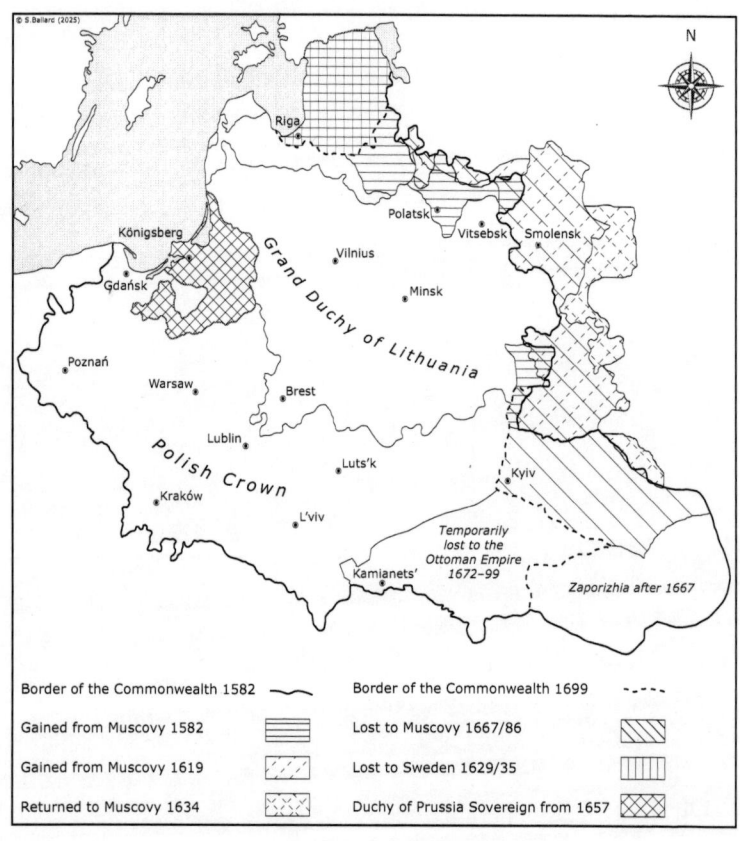

Map 4: The Commonwealth's territorial gains and losses, 1582–1699

3

A COMMONWEALTH OF TWO NATIONS?

(1569–1795)

The histories of Lithuania and Poland become even more entwined between 1569 and 1795. The historian's challenge is to identify and explain the things that distinguished the Grand Duchy of Lithuania from the Polish Crown, without losing sight of all they had in common. For eight or nine generations, institutions and political culture converged—bumpily. The union was still evolving in the 1790s, during the conflagration that brilliantly illuminated and finally consumed the Polish–Lithuanian Commonwealth.

The inescapable fact of the three partitions of 1772, 1793, and 1795 has encouraged views of the Commonwealth as a 'warning from history': behold the fatal consequences of too much power in the hands of an anarchic, fanatical, and oppressive nobility! Even before the final dismemberment, the Founding Fathers of the United States of America treated 'Poland' as a lesson in how not to build a republic. Many Lithuanian, Belarusian, Ukrainian, and even Polish historians and opinion-formers have echoed the apologists of the partitioning powers. Yet the harsh glare of hindsight can distort past reality just as much as the heat generated by the polemics of the time. The Commonwealth flourished until the 1640s, then endured seven torrid decades. Converging crises involved continual warfare on home soil, global cooling, plagues, economic and demographic regression, chronically malfunctioning politics, and intellectual and cultural introspection.

The exhausted Commonwealth's loss of effectual sovereignty to Peter the Great's Russian Empire during the first quarter of the eighteenth century made later attempts at reform a daunting task. These efforts have often been dismissed as 'too little, too late'. Yet the near impossibility of implementing political and constitutional reforms against the will of successive Russian rulers makes the renewal more impressive. Economic, cultural, and intellectual revivals began in the 1730s, before the Commonwealth demonstrated its political vitality during a window of recovered sovereignty in 1788–92. If we could set hindsight aside, we could appreciate the remarkable, and for many decades remarkably successful, practice of consensual and participatory government in a shared political community. Besides, the alternative model—Muscovite autocracy—is today less appealing than ever.

i. *Defining and Defending the Union*

The last three years of Sigismund Augustus's reign brought neither the love and concord for which he appealed in Lublin, nor the tying up of the loose ends in the Act of Union. On 7 July 1572, he died in his favourite residence at Knyszyn in Podlachia. The surrounding forest teemed with bison, elk, deer, and other beasts worthy of a royal hunter. He granted the town self-government in 1568. Two centuries later, fire destroyed the palace. Little remains of that transient splendour, but in the late summer of 1572 Knyszyn hosted negotiations between Lithuanian and Polish senators. Besides relations with Muscovy, they dis-

A COMMONWEALTH OF TWO NATIONS?

cussed arrangements for the forthcoming royal election. During the next four years, when the throne was twice vacant, Lithuanian senators, attended by representatives of the wider nobility, met separately from the Poles on nine occasions. They decided on military, fiscal, and diplomatic matters reserved by the 1569 treaty for the joint sejm. In doing so they responded pragmatically to delays in joint decision-making and asserted the status of the Grand Duchy of Lithuania. Lithuanian delegates also participated in some of the joint sejms and electoral assemblies held at this time. As usual, at stake were the terms of the union, not the fact of it.

It may now seem extraordinary that in 1572–73 the Grand Duchy's elite offered the Lithuanian throne to a son of Tsar Ivan the Terrible. But they needed to extend the truce with Muscovy. The tsar countered by putting himself forward for the joint Polish–Lithuanian throne. Ivan's terms were unpalatable, but the Lithuanian side kept negotiations going over the winter, helped by the slowness of travel over great distances, while quietly promoting the candidacy of Archduke Ernest, younger son of the Holy Roman Emperor Maximilian II, and a great-great-grandson of Casimir Jagiellon. They hoped the Habsburg would restore the Grand Duchy's lost lands and its parliament, but the first joint royal election took another course.

The electoral process that emerged in 1573 was unwelcome to the Lithuanian magnates, but it had considerable potential for the wider nobility of the Grand Duchy. For any nobleman might participate in person. The location of the election field just outside Warsaw favoured the numerous and mostly impoverished nobles of surrounding Mazovia. These staunch Catholics were usually inclined to defer to their king, but not to 'heretical' grandees. Yet the assembly that met in Warsaw in January 1573 to prepare the election (albeit with only two Lithuanian delegates present) agreed a formula for lasting religious peace. Noting tur-

LITHUANIA

moil elsewhere in Europe, those present foreswore persecution and violence because of differences in religion. Contrary to the myth of the Polish–Lithuanian Commonwealth as an oasis of religious 'tolerance', this pact was conceived in terms of peace, not of 'tolerance', liberty, or equality. It did however imply mutual toleration, or sufferance, between citizens already possessed of more or less equal political rights, for the public good. It formed part of the Act of the General Confederation of Warsaw. Confederations were leagues of the nobility, formed in emergencies for the common good. They abbreviated procedures to expedite decision-making. They could be formed either 'around' the king, or against a king deemed to have broken his oath, or else to ensure that a king was elected. The royal election of 1573, like all subsequent ones, was held under the auspices of a confederation. For between reigns, the realm had to carry on.

Most of the Polish nobles who came in their thousands to the election field feared entanglement in an Austro–Ottoman war and so opposed the Habsburg candidate. Meanwhile, Lithuanian leaders cut their own deal with the French ambassador. On 16 May 1573, the throng elected as monarch the younger brother of King Charles IX of France: Henri Valois. The electoral assembly set stringent limits to royal power. Henceforth, the king could not work for the election of a successor in his own lifetime. Every two years he would have to call a sejm, which should deliberate for six weeks. Between sejms, he would be advised by a council of resident senators whose assent he needed for important decisions, such as sending embassies to foreign courts. He would also have to swear to maintain peace between those divided by religion. Should the king default on these and other promises, his citizen-subjects could refuse him obedience. These 'Henrician Articles' were incorporated into the *pacta conventa*—effectively contracts of employment—made with all subsequent elected monarchs.

A COMMONWEALTH OF TWO NATIONS?

During the negotiations with the Commonwealth's delegation to France, the king-elect, implicated in the recent St Bartholomew's Day massacres of Huguenots, reluctantly agreed to swear to uphold the religious provisions of the Confederation of Warsaw. During his coronation in Kraków Cathedral on 21 February 1574, he swore in general terms to maintain religious peace. But at the sejm that followed the coronation (which for the first time had a marshal—or speaker—from Lithuania), he merely confirmed old laws and privileges, casting doubt on the settlement hammered out since 1569. Sensing an opportunity, Lithuanian lords and nobles sought to convey the status of the Grand Duchy to their monarch. A convention held in Vilnius in October 1573 even established a confederation in the name of '*Nos Senatus populusque Lithuanus*'.[1] This Latin formula adapted the famous acronym SPQR—the senate and people of Rome—and thus acknowledged the role of lesser nobles as citizens of a *res publica*.

The delegation that came to Poland to campaign for Henry's election included a translator called Jean Bodin who was intrigued by the Commonwealth's mixed form of government. Three years later, he published the first edition of his *Six livres de la république* (whose 1606 English translation was titled *The Six Bookes of a Commonweale*). Faced with the problem of political and religious division, Bodin advocated a hereditary monarch wielding the absolute sovereignty of 'the republic', although not in an arbitrary fashion. He regarded the sharing of sovereignty in Poland–Lithuania as unnatural. Henry doubtless held similar convictions intuitively. He does, however, seem to have learned from his time in Kraków. No later French monarch matched his efforts to reach consensus among his leading subjects through the Estates-General.

In June 1574, King Henry suddenly left Poland, having inherited the French throne on the death of his elder brother. Many Polish nobles believed that he should be deposed for desertion.

LITHUANIA

The Lithuanian elite, used to running the Grand Duchy in monarchs' absence, showed more understanding of Henry's position. Convening in Vilnius, they declared Lithuania's continued recognition of its grand duke and supplicated his return. Nevertheless, they were already planning another Habsburg candidature. Henry stayed in France, so an assembly of Polish nobles announced his forfeiture of the throne on 12 May 1575. Seven months later, a high-ranking Lithuanian delegation participated in the election of the Holy Roman Emperor Maximilian II as King of Poland and Grand Duke of Lithuania. But thousands of ordinary Polish nobles refused to accept the Habsburg. Instead, they acclaimed as their monarchs Anna Jagiellon, the unmarried sister of Sigismund Augustus, and their choice of husband for her, Stephen (István) Báthory, the elective prince of Transylvania. Báthory rapidly agreed the terms, promising to observe the Henrician Articles and the Confederation of Warsaw. An assembly of Polish nobles confirmed his election in February. Having marched into Poland in early April, on 1 May 1576 in Kraków he married Anna, and the pair were crowned together. A Lithuanian delegation arrived in Kraków three days after the coronation. Báthory graciously listened to them and met many of their demands. A mutual exchange of oaths on 29 June 1576 in Warsaw confirmed him as Grand Duke of Lithuania. Emperor Maximilian helpfully died the same year.

Báthory, the unwanted Transylvanian hard man, would prove himself one of the greatest ever Grand Dukes of Lithuania. Following another Muscovite incursion into Livonia, in 1578 King Stephen and Lithuanian leaders persuaded the Commonwealth's sejm to vote taxes for the war. During three hard-fought campaigns the Lithuanian and Polish forces recaptured Polatsk and took the war deep into enemy territory. Making peace in 1582, the tsar yielded Livonia to the Commonwealth. The Swedish conquest of Estonia completed his humiliation. Ivan's

A COMMONWEALTH OF TWO NATIONS?

capricious rule, which demoralised his subjects, contributed to the result, but much and more can be attributed to Báthory's grasp of logistics and strategy, his military reforms, and his choice of lieutenants, such as the talented son of Mikołaj Radziwiłł the Red, Krzysztof 'the Thunderbolt'.

The Polish–Lithuanian armies of the later sixteenth and seventeenth centuries were far from the stereotype of a 'medieval' cavalry force untouched by the 'Military Revolution'. This theory posits a transformation of warfare in western Europe between about 1550 and about 1715, largely driven by technological advances in firearms and fortifications. The Commonwealth had plenty of soldiers with theoretical knowledge of the art of war and practical experience of campaigning in Italy or the Low Countries, which they adapted to the sparse population, thick forests and marshes, and harsh winters of northeastern Europe. Poland–Lithuania relied overwhelmingly not on 'feudal' levies, but on professional soldiers on annual contracts. The size of the forces raised by the monarch depended on the taxes voted by the sejmsejm and monies raised by sejmiks. Individual magnates also contributed contingents. In the east of the Commonwealth, many lesser boyars or military servitors, whose fortunes were meagre and whose status as noble citizens was fragile, had few alternatives to serving a lord. After peace was made in 1582, some impoverished nobles plied their soldierly trade where they could, causing trouble beyond the Commonwealth's borders.

Although foreign mercenaries formed units of light cavalry, infantry, and artillery familiar to western Europeans, the justly famous components of the Commonwealth's armies were the hussars. Originating early in the sixteenth century, and reformed during Stephen's reign, these were not quasi-medieval knights lumbering into battle in full plate armour on destriers, but medium-weight cavalry who combined the advantages of manoeuvrability, speed, and impact. Depending on the theatre of war, they were equipped with hollowed-out lances that were longer than pikes, straight swords, curved sabres, and bows and arrows. Their famous feathered 'wings' were not—yet—the towering twin-framed apparatus known from preserved eighteenth-century parade examples. But even more modest constructions attached to saddles would have looked and sounded disconcerting in the field, as they hummed in the wind. The costs of warhorses, armour, and weapons were eye-watering. Noble 'companions', often motivated by their families' military traditions, and attended by their 'posts' of poorer nobles, effectively subsidised the Polish–Lithuanian armies. Their decisive say in many matters, via regimental assemblies called 'circles', echoed the Commonwealth's social and political life. Cavalrymen often served on foot, especially during sieges. But they also covered long distances on horseback to raid and forage, guard supply trains, and disrupt and defeat enemy relief forces. Radziwiłł the Thunderbolt excelled in leading cavalry forces into the Muscovite rear.

The collective effort was enormous. Each year between 1579 and 1581, the Lithuanians raised between 14,500 and 26,000 soldiers, while the Crown raised between 19,000 and 24,000.[2] Most of these men served on horseback, especially in the Lithuanian army, which was more dependent on noble volunteers. The mobilisation of the Commonwealth's resources and King Stephen's leadership delivered on the basic premises of the union—victory and security. That alone would earn Báthory, who spent much time in the Grand Duchy, Lithuanians' respect, even if his austere personality did not invite affection.

Stephen's ten-year reign also brought internal reforms. One tangible change was the decision of the 1582 sejm to introduce the Gregorian calendar, thereby 'losing' ten days. The Orthodox Church did not follow suit for liturgical purposes, so major feasts were henceforth celebrated on different days by Catholics and Protestants on the one hand, and by eastern Christians on the other. Diverse cities such as Vilnius experienced overlapping rhythms of fasting and feasting for centuries to come. The custom of celebrating Christmas and Easter twice is still often observed in the borderlands of Lithuania, Belarus, and Poland.

Monarchs were traditionally considered the founts of justice, but the pressures on their time clogged up the appeal system, frustrating the litigious nobility. In return for substantial taxes, King Stephen agreed to a Supreme Tribunal for the Polish Crown in 1578. Lithuania would not be left behind. Agreed at the sejm of 1581, the Supreme Tribunal of the Grand Duchy of Lithuania began its work the following year, following the election of judges at the Candlemas sejmiks.

The drafting of the Third Lithuanian Statute also began in earnest in 1581. At stake was the separate legal system. But questions of jurisdiction, taxes, military service, and liabilities in kind also created tensions, not least between Roman Catholic clergy and Protestant nobles. On the other hand, the Catholic leaders Mikołaj Radziwiłł the Orphan and his younger brother Cardinal Jerzy had to cooperate with their Calvinist cousins. They also had to reckon with sejmiks that demanded assured peace between Christians divided by religion. These provisions of the Confederation of Warsaw, given teeth by punishments specified for attacks on Christian churches and meeting houses, entered the draft Statute. So did the prohibition on 'foreigners' (including Poles from the Crown) holding land and office within the Grand Duchy, which had been lifted by the Union of Lublin. Indeed, the Statute did not mention the Lublin act at all. The role of the ruler—usually called the *hospodar*—was drafted so that the Grand Duchy of Lithuania could function with or without the union with Poland. It remained to have the Third Statute confirmed by the monarch.

Stephen Báthory died at Hrodna on 12 December 1586. The Lithuanian elite, together with some Polish magnates, again

LITHUANIA

favoured a Habsburg candidate: the Archduke Maximilian (a younger son of the late Emperor Maximilian II). The bulk of the Polish nobility again preferred Jagiellonian lineage, this time in the person of Sigismund Vasa, the twenty-one-year-old son of Sigismund Augustus's sister Catherine and King John III of Sweden. Lithuanian nobles took no part either in Sigismund Vasa's election on 19 August 1587, or the rival election of Maximilian three days later. The issue was settled by the defeat and capture of the Habsburg by Báthory's right-hand man in the Polish Crown, Jan Zamoyski. The Grand Duchy of Lithuania accepted Sigismund III at the coronation sejm in January 1588.*
In return, the monarch confirmed the Third Lithuanian Statute on his own authority. This codification inspired much pride and one-upmanship. Lithuanian parliamentarians would rather pass laws correcting its chapters and articles than agree to a new codification for the entire Commonwealth. Judges in the Polish Crown, faced with a thicket of statutes and customs, often consulted the Third Statute (which was published in Ruthenian, Polish, and Latin). Much of the Statute would remain in force in the annexed territories of the Russian Empire until 1840.

During the two decades that followed the 1569 union, the Grand Duchy of Lithuania defended and consolidated its own institutions, laws, and status. The Third Statute finally abolished formal and legal divisions within the nobility. On the other hand, nobles from Podlachia and southern Rus´ showed negligible interest in returning to the Lithuanian fold. In terms of territory, population, taxable wealth, and military potential, the Polish Crown was the senior partner in the Union. Structural inequality was reflected in the fact that not all members of the grand ducal council became senators of the Commonwealth. Only twenty-six

---

* He might be considered Grand Duke Sigismund IV, given the reign of Žygimantas in 1432–1440, but this style never caught on.

A COMMONWEALTH OF TWO NATIONS?

Lithuanians made the cut, compared to 114 senators from the expanded Crown. Perhaps, however, the territorial shrinkage from the end of the fifteenth century onwards helped to integrate the Lithuanian political nation. The Grand Duchy's heartlands, approximating to Lithuania and Belarus today, remained intact. The challenges of defending the southern lands, and of managing their distinctive social, economic, and religious dynamics, fell to the Crown. Ukraine would follow its own path.

ii. *Consolidation and Counter-Reformation*

The Polish–Lithuanian union bedded down between the Grand Duchy of Lithuania's acceptance of Sigismund III in 1588 and the death of his eldest son Władysław IV in 1648. New generations of Lithuanian statesmen and generals played important roles for the Commonwealth as a whole. Processes of cultural Polonisation encompassed middling nobles and wealthier burghers, but they did not weaken Lithuanian political identity or its expression via parliamentary institutions. The principle that every third marshal of the joint sejm should be from the Grand Duchy of Lithuania was well observed. Of the 173 sejms held between 1569 and 1793, fifty-six had Lithuanian marshals. The Grand Duchy's parliamentarians would coordinate their stances at general sejmiks before each sejm, and at provincial sessions during sejms. Consequently, many of the laws and resolutions passed by the sejm applied either to the Grand Duchy of Lithuania or to the Polish Crown. Monarchs still called Lithuanian convocations, especially when they needed troops.[3] Despite the Commonwealth's wars against Sweden, Muscovy, and the Ottoman Empire, the Lithuanian heartlands enjoyed six decades of relative peace and prosperity.

Sigismund III inherited the Swedish throne in 1592, but his Lutheran subjects could not trust a Catholic king, and his uncle Charles seized power. Following a civil war the Swedish parliament deposed Sigismund in 1599. The latter responded by formally incorporating Estonia into the Commonwealth, having previously promised this part of his patrimony to help secure his election in 1587. The monarch thus involved Poland–Lithuania in a territorial conflict with Sweden, which became a long war (albeit broken by truces) in defence of Livonia.

Diverted by civil strife and wars with Muscovy and the Ottoman Empire, the Commonwealth repeatedly failed to follow up its victories over the Swedes. Its greatest triumph was at Kircholm (now Salaspils in Latvia) in 1605, when a perfectly timed charge by the Grand Duchy of Lithuania's hussars, led by Hetman Jan Karol Chodkiewicz, shattered a much larger Swedish force. Lightly garrisoned Livonian towns and castles frequently changed hands, but the pattern changed when the city of Riga, with its population of 30,000, fell to the Swedes after a month-long siege on 25 September 1621. The previous day Hetman Chodkiewicz had died far away to the south in an encampment at Khotyn. He commanded a 45,000-strong force, including 20,000 Ukrainian Cossacks, that would successfully hold off an even larger Ottoman army. The Commonwealth mobilised a record 86,000 soldiers that year, but few of them were in Livonia.[4] By this time, King Gustavus Adolphus (the son of the usurper Charles IX) had learned lessons from earlier defeats. He reformed the Swedish army into a more mobile force, which won its first victories in the field against the Lithuanian and Crown armies in 1626. Although Polish–Lithuanian forces inflicted reverses on the Swedes during the last phase of the war, Sweden retained most of Livonia by the truce agreed in 1629 and the peace treaty concluded in 1635. Only south-eastern Livonia remained with the Commonwealth.

Gains from Muscovy partly recompensed these losses. Ivan IV's tyrannous rule and wars had exhausted his lands and peoples. The tsar had also all but extinguished his dynasty by killing his

A COMMONWEALTH OF TWO NATIONS?

heir Ivan in a fit of rage. On the death of his feeble remaining son Fedor in 1598, Muscovy plunged into chaos, later known as the 'Time of Troubles'. The vacuum of authority sucked in foreign adventurers. At least three impostors claimed to be Dmitrii, a younger son of Ivan IV, who had died in a suspicious accident in 1591. The first two 'false Dmitriis' attracted significant support within Muscovite society, whose ranks were out of joint. Most senators and nobles of the Grand Duchy of Lithuania had little appetite for a new war against Muscovy. The Polish–Lithuanian intervention emerged from a group of ambitious magnates and their under-employed military retinues. Hopes for the spread of the Catholic faith also played a part, especially after the first 'Dmitrii' was crowned tsar in Moscow in 1605. 'Dmitrii's' marriage to Maryna Mniszech, the daughter of a Polish magnate, helped spark a revolt that placed Vasilii Shuiskii on the throne. The victors literally blasted the pretender westwards from a cannon, and killed or imprisoned many Poles and Lithuanians in Moscow. But a second 'Dmitrii' soon appeared, and it suited some of the Lithuanian and Polish elites—including Maryna—to recognise him.

The havoc wrought by an unlicensed, 10,000-strong Polish, Lithuanian, and Cossack force supporting the second 'Dmitrii' contributed to Shuiskii's decision early in 1609 to yield Muscovy's last foothold on the Baltic coast to Sweden in return for a military alliance. Full-scale war between the Commonwealth and Muscovy followed. At Klushino on 4 July 1610 the Polish–Lithuanian cavalry crushed a much larger Muscovite and Swedish army. Later that year it rode into Moscow. Muscovite boyars opposed to the second 'Dmitrii' deposed Shuiskii and offered the throne to Sigismund's son Władysław, but they demanded the prince's conversion to Orthodoxy and the retention for Muscovy of the besieged city of Smolensk. Despite widespread oath-taking to Władysław, Sigismund's prevarication, and rumours that he wanted to become tsar himself, allowed rival Muscovite boyars to regroup and revolt. Cut off from relief, the starving Polish-Lithuanian garrison in the Moscow Kremlin surrendered to the insurgents on 7 November 1612. Many soldiers were butchered anyway. The following March, a broad-based assembly of Muscovites chose the sixteen-year-old Mikhail Romanov as tsar.

The events of 1605–13 still resonate in Russian historical memory as the moment when 'the Poles' threatened Russia's very existence. For Russians and Poles alike, generations of myth-making have overshadowed the crucial Lithuanian dimension of the story. It was the chancellery of the Grand Duchy of Lithuania that managed relations with Muscovy. Once the war had started, the crucial Lithuanian goal was the recovery of Smolensk. The city fell to Sigismund III after a twenty-month siege in June 1611. Two years later, the palatinate of Smolensk became part of the Grand Duchy of Lithuania. The war sputtered on until a truce took effect at the start of 1619. For a few years the total area of the Commonwealth exceeded a million square kilometres. Twenty-first-century Lithuania has recultivated the memory. The 400th anniversary of King Sigismund's triumphant entry into Vilnius on 24 July 1611, having regained Smolensk, was marked by the publication and exhibition of the manuscript commemorating the event.[5] The showing at the Palace of the Grand Dukes of Lithuania in Vilnius in 2019–21 of the surviving smaller version of Tommaso Dolabella's depiction of the oath of homage sworn by Vasilii Shuiskii and his brothers to Sigismund III at the sejm in Warsaw impressed the Lithuanian public. Peter the Great probably had the huge original canvas destroyed when he occupied Warsaw in the early eighteenth century.

The interregnum after Sigismund III's death in 1632 prompted a Muscovite war of revenge. A large army, partially reformed on western European lines, besieged Smolensk. However, the smaller, but more mobile Lithuanian army ably led by Krzysztof

A COMMONWEALTH OF TWO NATIONS?

II Radziwiłł (the younger son of the Thunderbolt), disrupted Muscovite supply lines and got vital supplies into the city. In September 1633, King Władysław IV reached Smolensk at the head of a large army of his own. As Frost argues, the crucial factor was the ability of the Commonwealth's cavalry to control the surrounding territory and deter a relief army. A prisoner-of-war admitted 'that the Muscovites feared nothing more than [...] the hussars'.[6] Outmanoeuvred, they were blockaded and bombarded into surrender in March 1634. Their commanders prostrated themselves before the Polish–Lithuanian monarch, whose horse trampled their standards. By the subsequent treaty of 'eternal peace', Władysław resigned his claim to the Muscovite throne, and the Commonwealth gave up some of the lands it had reclaimed since 1611. Nonetheless, Tsar Mikhail formally ceded Smolensk and much territory further east.

In the years 1632–34, the consensus-based political system of the Commonwealth met the simultaneous challenges of Muscovy, the Ottoman Empire, and the Tatars. In 1634 it mobilised 53,000 soldiers, many of whom were Ukrainian Cossacks.[7] The tax burden multiplied during the first third of the seventeenth century. Although most historians have judged the fiscal system severely (especially that of the Grand Duchy of Lithuania), the Commonwealth could not have matched the Dutch Republic's sophisticated public debt-financing to pay for sustained warfare, decades before England took that path to global pre-eminence. The 1630s and 1640s saw improvements in artillery, firearms, and fortifications as the Commonwealth's military reputation climaxed. Later calamities should not be projected back on to an era of success.

The public spirit manifest in 1632–34 contrasted with the acrimonious first half of Sigismund III's reign. The young king's negotiations for an alliance with the Habsburgs were exposed. Sigismund's critics in the Polish Crown, led by Jan Zamoyski, who sought political dominance for himself, demanded greater parliamentary accountability. Lithuanian grievances were more concerned with disorder, especially the problems created by unpaid soldiers. But the uproar vitiated the monarch's efforts to expand and fund the standing army, and several sejms dispersed without agreeing new legislation and taxes. Across the Commonwealth, many Catholic nobles agreed with their Protestant and Orthodox fellow-citizens that the Catholic clergy was encroaching on secular matters, encouraging the monarch to subvert their liberties, enlarging its wealth at their expense, and failing to contribute its fair share in taxes.

In 1606–07 the King and his opponents called out their supporters to rival assemblies, and the Commonwealth slid towards civil war. The rebels accused the monarch of seeking absolute rule and withdrew their obedience to him. The marshal of the first rebel assemblies was the richest magnate of the Grand Duchy of Lithuania, Janusz I Radziwiłł, who headed the Calvinist branch of the family after the death of his father Krzysztof the Thunderbolt. His personal rival, Jan Karol Chodkiewicz, was the principal Lithuanian royalist. However, most Lithuanian magnates and nobles avoided taking sides. At the same time, they objected to any solutions concerning Lithuania without its participation. Despite the King's victory on the battlefield, this crisis of the Commonwealth ended in stalemate. In 1609, Sigismund III forgave the rebels, but fiscal, military, parliamentary, and judicial challenges remained unresolved. This civil war is often seen as a turning point, after which neither royal nor republican remedies could cure the Commonwealth's malady. If so, the problem was not immediately apparent: only one sejm failed to reach a conclusion during the second half of Sigismund's long reign. The ageing monarch won respect as he dourly carried out his duties.

Some Polish historians have long since argued that Lithuanian and Ruthenian magnates pursued their own oligarchic interests

A COMMONWEALTH OF TWO NATIONS?

at the expense of the common good, and so corrupted Polish civic republican traditions. Since the fall of the Soviet Union, some Lithuanian and Belarusian historians have re-cast the principal Radziwiłłs, Chodkiewiczes, Sapiehas, and others as exemplary patriots, but most have agreed that ordinary nobles remained subordinated to great lords. At any one time, a dozen or so families enjoyed a disproportionate share of the Grand Duchy's land, wealth, prestige, and offices, while two or three families stood out from the rest. The Crown's elite was more numerous, diverse, and fluid. Nonetheless, Lithuanian aristocratic clans were also prone to decline and extinction. The lotteries of fertility and mortality affected everyone, while much depended on royal grace and favour.

Members of the Calvinist line of the Radziwiłłs often waited longer for the highest offices and plumpest Crown estates. They redressed their disadvantage by marrying into the family of the Hohenzollern Electors of Brandenburg, inflating their pretensions to trans-national princely status. That heightened expectations of good lordship to the inhabitants of their latifundia, including privately owned towns. The self-interest of the lord and that of the Christian and Jewish burghers could, and often did, coincide with each other, and with the public good as well. The last of this line, Janusz I's late-born son Bogusław Radziwiłł, exemplifies the trend. As governor of the Duchy of Prussia he imposed order on behalf of his cousin, Frederick William the Great Elector. Yet as Karin Friedrich has demonstrated, at sejmiks he could equally convincingly campaign for the liberties of the Lithuanian nobility, not least its religious freedoms.[8] Even Radziwiłłs had to work hard to maintain their support. Shared parliamentary, judicial, and military experiences bound patrons and clients together into a political culture that prized the common good. Artūras Vasiliauskas has revealed successive generations of politically active, moderately wealthy families as the pillars of district sejmiks. Such nobles expected much of their patrons, and, if repeatedly disappointed, they switched loyalties. For the first half of the seventeenth century at least, the pejorative label of 'magnate oligarchy' is unwarranted.[9]

The rise of the Sapiehas was as spectacular as any. Despite claiming princely status, this family of Ruthenian origin remained fairly obscure until Lew Sapieha excelled as a secretary to Stephen Báthory. He served as marshal of the 1582 sejm, negotiated an extension of the truce with Muscovy after Ivan the Terrible's death in 1584, and became the Grand Duchy's vice-chancellor in 1585 and its chancellor in 1589. He crowned his long career as grand hetman from 1625. Sapieha's religious path, from his Orthodox upbringing through Calvinism (during his studies in Leipzig in the early 1570s) to Catholicism (in 1586), was characteristic of his era. The church he founded in Vilnius, dedicated to the Archangel Michael, contains the huge monument he commissioned for himself and his two wives. After tsarist, Nazi, and Soviet closures, this fine church now houses a museum of sacral art.

The first seeds of the resurgence of the Catholic Church in Lithuania were planted after the Council of Trent (1545–63). Tridentine definitions of Catholic doctrine and prescriptions for liturgy distinguished them from Protestant teaching and worship, disappointing hopes for the restoration of the unity of western Christendom. In its later sessions, however, the council addressed many abuses and shortcomings identified by Reformers. Higher standards of observance and learning among the clergy would raise its standing with the laity. Bishops were expected to visit their dioceses regularly, to check that the parish clergy administered the sacraments, taught their flocks the essentials of Catholic belief and practice, and did not cause scandal through unbecoming lifestyles.

As elsewhere in the Catholic world, the Polish–Lithuanian reception of the Tridentine reforms proved a long-drawn-out,

A COMMONWEALTH OF TWO NATIONS?

uneven process. Objections ranged from jurisdiction to practicality. Sigismund Augustus accepted the council's decrees in 1564, but the ecclesiastical province of Gniezno only did so at a synod in 1577, to which the bishop of Vilnius sent a representative. Gaps in the Commonwealth's ecclesiastical structures impeded implementation of pastoral changes. The distances between Catholic parishes were greatest in the east. Most of the Catholic dioceses of Vilnius and Lut´sk, and all of those of Kyiv and Smolensk (founded in 1636) were predominantly inhabited by Orthodox Christians.

Even in the relatively compact diocese of Samogitia, residual 'pagan' practices and the spread of 'heresy' among the nobility and clergy had combined to make the rural populace ripe for re-evangelisation. That, at least, was what the long-serving bishop, Melchior Giedroyć (Merkelis Giedraitis), wrote in his reports to Rome. When asking the pope to confirm Giedroyć's nomination in 1575, the cathedral chapter of Samogitia stressed that his knowledge of the language of the flock would help to combat ignorance and superstition. He patronised the first books in the Lithuanian language printed in the Grand Duchy of Lithuania, rather than in Protestant Prussia. However, because Giedroyć had flirted with the Reformation during his studies at four German universities, including Königsberg, he had an interest in criticising the laxity of his predecessors and manifesting his own zeal.

Giedroyć continued to spend much time in Vilnius, both as a bishop-senator engaged in the Grand Duchy's public life and as a prelate of the cathedral. This was not unusual. As Wioletta Pawlikowska has written, the Vilnius chapter, long plagued by scandals of heterodoxy, concubinage, and even alcohol-fuelled violence and arson, gradually mended its ways, but it still contributed to the problem of non-residence. Besides bishops of other dioceses, the Vilnius chapter also included scholars and medics who spent much time at the court of their royal patron. But even when canons and prelates resided in Vilnius, they were not ministering to their parishes. The chapter and its individual members possessed some of the best endowed parishes in the Grand Duchy, so services could be provided by assistant clergy, but the Tridentine ideal of residence fell short of reality.[10]

Following the long tenure of the bishopric of Vilnius by the peaceable Walerian Protasewicz, his more militant successor Jerzy Radziwiłł ordered the burning of 'heretical' books in 1581. Thereafter, not least because of his Calvinist cousins, he was usually more circumspect. He founded a seminary in Vilnius, but he earned most of his reputation for Counter-Reformation zealotry after 1591 as bishop of Kraków. The grumbling among Crown nobles about Sigismund III's appointment of a Lithuanian to one of the richest bishoprics in Europe subsided, but the protests of the Lithuanian Estates against the corresponding nomination to Vilnius of a Crown Pole did not. After a stand-off of nine years, Radziwiłł's death in 1600 allowed the King to translate his nominee for Vilnius, Bishop Bernard Maciejowski, to Kraków. All the remaining bishops of Vilnius until the partitions of the Commonwealth were born in the Grand Duchy of Lithuania. This conflict over the bishopric of Vilnius is usually cast as a tale of Lithuanian patriotism (or obduracy), but as Pawlikowska has noted, the cathedral chapter, which declined to elect the bishop, was in dispute with the nominee over money. During the vacancy, it used episcopal revenue to repair the crumbling fabric of the cathedral. The next bishop of Vilnius was Benedykt Woyna, the prelate who had administered the diocese for most of the previous decade.[11] A stern foe of Protestantism, he used his position to ensure the perpetrators of confessional violence got off scot-free. Most of these hooligans were students of the Jesuit Academy.

The first six Jesuits came to Vilnius on the invitation of Bishop Protasewicz, who founded their college in 1569. Ten years later, King Stephen Báthory elevated the college to the status of an academy, or university. By this time the Society of Jesus, founded by St Ignatius Loyola in 1534, had become as focused on the Counter-Reformation in Europe as on global evangelisation. Jesuits distinguished themselves by their additional vow of fidelity to the pope, the length and rigour of their studies, the importance they attached to pedagogy, and their flexibility in pursuing the greater glory of God. The curriculum in Jesuit schools, colleges, and academies, standardised by the 1599 *ratio studiorum*, offered structured schooling in seven stages: three classes in grammar before proceeding to poetry and rhetoric, thence to philosophy, and finally to theology. Teaching began in Latin, before Greek was added, and finally Hebrew. Auxiliary teaching was provided in history, geography, mathematics, modern languages, and other subjects as required. Didactic theatrical performances by pupils were an integral part of Jesuit education, thereby initiating the history of the theatre in the Grand Duchy of Lithuania. Few students stayed for the final two classes of philosophy and theology, offered in select colleges or academies, but of these young men, many became Jesuits themselves. Completing the first five classes equipped a nobleman to cut a figure in the public life of the Commonwealth.

The excellence of this education encouraged Protestant and Orthodox families to enrol their sons in Jesuit colleges. Predictably, many pupils converted to Catholicism. Jesuits engaged in confessional polemics against 'heresy' and 'schism' via sermons, some of which were published, but also through published correspondence with Reformed and Orthodox theologians. They operated their own press in Vilnius from 1576. Jesuits also had a knack for attaching themselves to monarchs and magnates as spiritual advisors, which brought them prosperity and influence, but also made enemies. Their foes included other religious orders that might otherwise have benefited from the legacies and vocations that went to the Jesuits.

LITHUANIA

Among the Jesuits' most generous patrons was Albrycht Stanisław Radziwiłł, head of the Catholic line based at Niasvizh, now in central Belarus. Educated by the Jesuits in Vilnius, he founded their college at Pinsk. As learned as he was pious, Radziwiłł succeeded Lew Sapieha as chancellor of the Grand Duchy of Lithuania in 1623 and remained at the helm for more than three decades. His detailed memoirs are an outstanding source for historians. Despite his manifest hostility to 'heretics', this fervent Catholic kept open lines of communication between the royal court and his Calvinist cousins.

The first rector of Vilnius University was Piotr Skarga. This son of a Mazovian miller graduated from Kraków Academy, covered up his plebeian origins, tutored magnates' children, was ordained a priest, and joined the Society of Jesus in Rome. After returning to Kraków, he distinguished himself in pastoral and pedagogical work. Besides his five years as rector in Vilnius, he set up Jesuit colleges at the north-eastern extremities of the Commonwealth: in Polatsk, Riga, and Tartu (Dorpat). Although he spent twenty-four years as court preacher to King Sigismund III, he never actually preached his sermons to the sejm (*Kazania sejmowe*) from a pulpit. These texts began to be celebrated a century later, when the parlous condition of the Commonwealth seemed to bear out his doom-laden prophecies. In his lifetime, Skarga was a divisive figure who hurled abuse at 'heresy' and 'schism'. He denounced the religious liberty and equality implied by the 1573 Confederation of Warsaw and incited the Commonwealth's bishops to oppose its 'execution'. That term meant salutary punishment of those engaged in 'tumults'—the riotous destruction of the churches, schools, and property of rival confessions. Because the perpetrators were often students, academic and ecclesiastical authorities could usually prevent justice from being done. Skarga could barely countenance a strictly limited toleration as a temporarily conceded lesser evil, pending the achievement of religious

A COMMONWEALTH OF TWO NATIONS?

unity in the True Church. His critique of nobles' licence brought him an exaggerated reputation as a supporter of absolute monarchy. The 1606–09 civil war was a chastening experience for the Society of Jesus. Afterwards, Jesuits accommodated themselves to nobles' republican values, emphasising that freedom could only flourish when founded on patriotic virtue, which in turn depended on the True Religion.

The Catholic Church's gradual marginalisation of its rivals ultimately bred complacency. When combined with nobly born clergymen's near-monopoly of positions of authority and wealth, this ensured that nobles' assumptions and prejudices shaped the clergy more than vice versa. The less numerous female orders were still more populated and governed by the nobly born than their male equivalents. Abbesses and prioresses were often influential local figures, not least because of the economic resources at their disposal. Some female orders ran schools for nobly born girls, notably the Poor Clares, established by Lew Sapieha in Vilnius in 1596, and the nuns of the Visitation of the Blessed Virgin Mary, who arrived in Vilnius in 1694.

In the Grand Duchy of Lithuania, intellectual and educational decline set in later, and proceeded more slowly than in the Polish Crown. Partly this was because Vilnius University continued to form the brightest talents. Among them was Konstantinas Širvydas (Konstanty Szyrwid), schooled by the Vilnan Jesuits, to whom he returned after study in Riga, Niasvizh, and Tartu. Lithuanian may have been his native tongue. In the last years of his life, he published a Latin–Polish–Lithuanian dictionary, a grammar (*Clavis linguae lituanicae*), which is probably lost, and a collection of sermons in Lithuanian with a Polish translation. Maciej Kazimierz Sarbiewski, known internationally as Sarbievius, was probably seventeenth-century Europe's most important neo-Latin poet. This Mazovian noble, educated in Vilnius, Polatsk, and Rome, where he immersed himself in classical poetry, returned to Vilnius as a professor. Such was his fame, especially for his *Lyrics*, that before the century had ended, not only had Latin editions multiplied, but works of his were translated into languages including German, Flemish, English, French, Italian, and of course Polish. Among the academy's rectors was Albertas Kojelavičius-Vijūkas (Wojciech Wijuk Kojałowicz), a prolific historian and genealogist, born to a minor Lithuanian noble family in what was later called the House of Perkūnas in Kaunas. His *History of Lithuania*, written in classical Latin and published in two volumes in 1650 and 1669, was triply polemical: about previous historians; Crown Poles, concerning the rights and status of the Grand Duchy of Lithuania; and foes of the Catholic Church. His association of the *natio* with a community shaped by shared history and a shared religion would prove influential for centuries to come.

The Roman Catholic Church in Lithuania long faced competition from the Reformed Church. Its network of parishes and schools expanded, not least because of the patronage of the Calvinist Radziwiłłs. At the Reformed Church's zenith early in the seventeenth century, about 200 parishes were organised into six districts. Graduates of the Calvinist grammar school in Vilnius often studied at Protestant universities in northern Europe. Grammar schools also functioned in the Radziwiłłs' towns of Kėdainiai and Slutsk. Among the books that rolled off the presses at the turn of the sixteenth century were the first Lithuanian-language catechism and postil printed in the Grand Duchy of Lithuania, rather than in Ducal Prussia. The Reformed Church thus held its own: pastorally, educationally, and intellectually. Its leading theologian, Andreas Volanus, conducted polemical correspondences not only with Jesuits such as Skarga and the papal legate Antonio Possevino, but also with the anti-Trinitarian Fausto Sozzini. His political tracts linked law and liberty.

Despite their differences regarding belief, worship, and authority, Protestant and Orthodox nobles came together to defend

A COMMONWEALTH OF TWO NATIONS?

religious liberty. Orthodoxy fell into crisis during the second half of the sixteenth century, as many leading Ruthenian families converted to either Protestantism or Catholicism. The Orthodox bishops' negotiations in Rome concluded at the end of 1595 with the papal proclamation of the Eastern Rite of the Catholic Church. This Uniate Church would follow its own liturgical and clerical traditions insofar as they did not contradict Catholic doctrine (so in the Creed, the Holy Spirit would henceforth proceed from both the Father and the Son, rather than the Father alone, as in the Orthodox tradition). In October 1596, a synod held at Brest established the Union in the Grand Duchy of Lithuania and the Polish Crown. However, far from achieving harmony, this step split the Eastern Church in acrimony. The Uniates, led by most of the bishops, confronted the pejoratively named 'disuniates': those Orthodox clergy and laity who rejected the Union of Brest. The latter included most monasteries and confraternities, which remained the liveliest centres of religious life, as well as the foremost Orthodox magnate, Konstanty Wasyl Ostrogski (Kostiantyn Vasyl' Ostroz'kyi). One reason for the widespread rejection of the Union of Brest was that Sigismund III, the Holy See, and the Jesuits evidently had no interest in uniting equal Eastern and Western Churches: they saw the Uniates as a vehicle for the conversion of the Orthodox. The Uniate bishops hoped for seats in the Commonwealth's senate, but did not get them.

The monarch refused to nominate Orthodox clergymen to vacant bishoprics, but the Orthodox contested handovers of their churches to the Uniates in the law courts.[12] Many sejmiks in the Lithuanian and Ruthenian lands called for the settlement of the grievances of 'the Greek religion'. A step towards reconsolidation came in 1620, when the Patriarch of Jerusalem secretly consecrated a new Orthodox episcopal hierarchy while travelling through the Commonwealth. It was not a secret for long, and confrontations continued. An enraged Orthodox crowd killed the zealous Uniate archbishop of Polatsk, Yosaphat Kuntsevych. The Uniates venerated him as a martyr, leading to his beatification in 1637 and canonisation in 1867. His Orthodox rival for the see of Polatsk, Meletii Smotryts'kyi, subsequently accepted and promoted the Union himself. His work on the grammar and syntax of Church Slavonic had a lasting impact on Eastern Slavdom.

The Muscovite attack on Smolensk in 1632 prompted the Commonwealth to recognise the restored Orthodox hierarchy. This brought a measure of stability, although some bishoprics were in Orthodox hands, others in Uniate, while still others had rival heads. Hopes for the renegotiation of a more equitable union largely rested on an exiled Moldavian prince named Petru Movilă. As Petro Mohyla, he proved an inspirational Orthodox metropolitan archbishop of Kyiv who revitalised learning, publishing, worship, and practical charity. Besides refreshing the study of the Greek Church Fathers, he took the best of the pedagogical and philosophical ideas of the Latin West, not least from Jesuit colleges in the Commonwealth. The college he founded in Kyiv became the leading seat of learning in the Orthodox world. The Mohylan reform also galvanised the schools and colleges run by Orthodox monks and brotherhoods in the Grand Duchy of Lithuania. In the long term, this impulse would bring even Muscovy (whose elites suspected anything novel of being tainted by 'heresy' and 'schism') into an outer orbit of Latin civilisation. The Basilian monk Simeon of Polatsk, often claimed as the first Russian poet and playwright, learned his sophisticated art at the blurred educational, cultural, linguistic, and confessional boundaries of his native Grand Duchy of Lithuania, before he entered the service of Tsar Aleksei Mikhailovich.[13]

Hopes of confessional reconciliation ended with the massive revolt of the Zaporizhian Cossacks and much of the peasantry of Ukraine in the spring of 1648. Social, religious, cultural, and political factors combined to ignite this explosion. The Cossacks'

A COMMONWEALTH OF TWO NATIONS?

charismatic leader, Bohdan Khmel'nyts'kyi, made a game-changing alliance with the Crimean Tatars. Together they defeated the Crown army and overran the south-eastern reaches of the Commonwealth. The rebels slaughtered tens of thousands of Jews and nobles; others fled. King Władysław IV, the one person who might just have calmed the storm, died during a hunting expedition at Merkinė on the banks of the River Nemunas. The third and last joint monarch to die in the Grand Duchy of Lithuania, Władysław had begun his reign as a military victor and confessional conciliator, but he squandered his credit of trust among the *szlachta*.

The Commonwealth plunged into an interregnum at the worst possible juncture. It endured further military and political humiliations, before the new king led a recovery of sorts. The chequered career of Sigismund III's second son John Casimir Vasa had seen him held captive in France and become a Jesuit and cardinal in Rome. Having changed his vocation, he married his elder half-brother's Franco–Italian widow, the formidable Louise-Marie Gonzaga. Theirs was a tempestuous political and amorous partnership.

The revolt spread into the south-eastern margins of the Grand Duchy of Lithuania. In 1651, Janusz II Radziwiłł, son of Krzysztof II, led a Lithuanian army into Kyiv, briefly re-establishing the Commonwealth's control of the ancient capital of Rus', but neither side could turn battlefield successes into final victory. Khmel'nyts'kyi made a fateful choice. Negotiating with the tsar's legation at Pereiaslav in January 1654, he believed that he was gaining a powerful ally, rather than a despotic master. The Cossack hetman had been shaped by a political culture of liberty, law, and binding contracts, but Aleksei Mikhailovich saw things differently. The deal emboldened the tsar to invade the Grand Duchy of Lithuania.

LITHUANIA

iii. *Crisis of the Commonwealth*

On 12 August 1654, the Muscovite vanguard forded the River Dniapro near Shkloŭ. Janusz II Radziwiłł, commanding the outnumbered Lithuanian army, created a diversion to the flank before timing the attack of his cavalry to shattering perfection. The panicked Muscovites lost ten times as many men as the Lithuanians. Nature marked the event with an eclipse of the sun.

Alas, nothing else went right that year. Muscovy's armies were better equipped and trained than twenty years earlier. Within a fortnight, Radziwiłł was beaten by a larger Muscovite force that had earlier butchered the mostly Orthodox burghers of Mstsislaŭ for having refused to surrender. Terror worked, and elsewhere rituals of submission saved lives. Smolensk fell after a siege of just three months on 3 October 1654, and the Muscovites reached the River Biarezina before an epidemic of plague halted their advance.

1655 brought even direr calamities. Radziwiłł lacked the resources to defend the Grand Duchy's heartlands from renewed Muscovite attack. Minsk yielded on 11 July, and on 7 August the tsar's host defeated Radziwiłł's much smaller army before Vilnius. Mass slaughter and rapine followed, and the city reputedly burned for seventeen days. The loot carted off to Moscow included copper roofs, architectural features in marble, church bells, furniture, tapestries, pictures, and entire libraries—all of which stimulated the cultural ambitions of the tsar and his court. So did the abducted craftsmen. Many nobles, clergy, and burghers fled, often to Ducal Prussia. Kaunas surrendered on 16 August.

With the Grand Duchy of Lithuania facing annihilation, Radziwiłł negotiated with the Swedes. In 1654, King Charles X had succeeded his unconventional cousin Queen Christina, who abdicated, converted to Catholicism, and went into exile. An experienced soldier, Charles saw war as an opportunity to heal political

A COMMONWEALTH OF TWO NATIONS?

divisions and solve the problem of paying and provisioning his army. With the Commonwealth unable to offer serious assistance against Muscovy, he would invade Poland–Lithuania himself and head off potential Muscovite gains there. The main Swedish army terrified the noble levies of Greater Poland into surrender on 25 July 1655. By the early autumn it had overrun much of Lesser Poland as well. Meanwhile a smaller Swedish force secured the Daugava estuary. In its sights were Polish–Lithuanian Livonia, Courland, Samogitia, and the western parts of Lithuania propria, lands vital for maintaining communications between Swedish Livonia and the forces in the Polish Crown. Sweden had less interest in the Belarusian and Ukrainian territories.

Radziwiłł's decision to recognise Charles X as Grand Duke of Lithuania required support beyond his relatives, clients, and co-religionists. The Declaration of Kėdainiai, signed by 550 nobles on 17 August 1655, set conditions to any new union with Sweden. Nevertheless, the bishop of Vilnius, Jerzy Tyszkiewicz, regarded the terms as unacceptable: 'By this surrender we are dissolving the sacred union with Poland, whose inviolability was sworn by our ancestors; those of us who sign will be branded for eternity with the mark of destruction for betraying our loyalty to our king and our fatherland.'[14] Yet as the bishop manoeuvred this way and that, and as the Swedes took over the western parts of Lithuania, he tacitly authorised his suffragan bishop to sign the less favourable final agreement endorsed by more than 1,000 nobles at Kėdainiai on 20 October 1655.

The Kėdainiai Union remains one of the most controversial events in the shared history of Lithuania and Poland. The Nobel Prize-winning novelist Henryk Sienkiewicz largely shaped Polish memories by depicting the event in *The Deluge* (1886) as the treason of two dastardly Calvinist Radziwiłłs—Janusz II and his cousin Bogusław—against their Catholic and Polish fatherland. Jerzy Hoffman's cinematic masterpiece of 1974 breathed fresh life into that verdict. At neither time was it possible to do more than hint that the Commonwealth was fighting for its life against Muscovy as well as against Sweden. On 13 September 1655 in the smouldering wreckage of Vilnius, Tsar Aleksei proclaimed himself Grand Duke of Lithuania, and soon afterwards John Casimir went into exile in Silesia. Radziwiłł's case was that Poland had defaulted on the basic premise of the union—common defence against Muscovy—whereas he obtained the Swedish king's promise to restore the Grand Duchy's lost lands. Lithuanian collective memory honours Jonušas II Radvila as a patriot. In 2006 a striking monument was erected on the marketplace of Kėdainiai.

Yet Janusz II Radziwiłł lost. Many of the Grand Duchy's magnates and most of the remnants of the Lithuanian army joined a confederation in support of John Casimir. Their example was followed in the Polish Crown. Partisan warfare wore down the Swedes, whose pillaging and profanation lost them support. Denied reinforcements, Radziwiłł died in his castle at Tykocin in Podlachia on the last day of 1655. John Casimir returned to Poland the next day, and by the end of 1656 the Swedes were reduced to a few garrisons. Meanwhile, a Swedish–Muscovite war broke out in Livonia, which enabled a truce between the Commonwealth and Muscovy in November 1656. For the price of an unenforceable promise to elect Aleksei as successor to John Casimir, the Commonwealth bought itself time while it dealt with a fresh threat to its existence. In December 1656, Charles X agreed to partition Poland–Lithuania with the prince of Transylvania, George II Rákóczi the Elector of Brandenburg, Frederick William; Bohdan Khmel'nyts'kyi; and Bogusław Radziwiłł, who would get the palatinate of Navahrudak (much of which he owned anyway). But as often happens, the parties to a carve-up fell out between themselves. In 1657, Rákóczi's invasion of Lesser Poland failed, while Frederick William changed sides in exchange for sovereignty over Ducal Prussia. He protected his cousin Bogusław Radziwiłł. Khmel'nyts'kyi's death in August 1657 removed a major obstacle to an alliance between the Commonwealth and the Zaporizhian Cossacks.

The agreement reached with the new Cossack hetman, Ivan Vyhovs'kyi, at Hadiach on 16 September 1658 would have established a commonwealth of three nations, although the term was never used officially. The three south-eastern palatinates of the Polish Crown were to become the Duchy of Ruthenia, with its own senators, dignitaries, treasury, and offices broadly analogous to those of the Grand Duchy of Lithuania. The Union of Brest was sacrificed. Orthodoxy would be the dominant religion within the new Duchy, and Orthodox bishops would enter the senate. The crux was the ennoblement of 1,000 Cossacks, with the hetman empowered to ennoble a hundred more each year. This, combined with the provision for existing nobles to return to their estates, and the endowment with vast properties of Vyhovs'kyi and his family, sparked a revolt among less favoured Cossack soldiers and peasants who feared being forced back into serfdom. The ratification of the treaty by the King and sejm (albeit with reservations) did not ensure its successful implementation. Muscovy renewed the war, only to suffer a spectacular defeat by Vyhovs'kyi and his Tatar allies at Konotop on 8 July 1659—a battle now celebrated by independent Ukraine. Nonetheless, later that year Vyhovs'kyi was deposed by his fellow Cossacks, who rejoined the Muscovite side. Historians debate whether the Union of Hadiach ever stood a chance. It would return as an ideal two centuries later.

By this stage the Muscovite occupation of most of the Grand Duchy of Lithuania had lasted five years, and the toll of war—with famine and plague following in its wake—often seemed apocalyptic. Yet survivors tried to adapt. Especially after the 1656 truce, the Muscovite authorities sought to reanimate the desolate city of Vilnius.[15] Among the exiles, just as among those who stayed or returned to rebuild, were people of all faiths. Muscovite treatment of Jews was less harsh in Lithuania propria than further east, but the invasion undoubtedly inflicted a severe blow on Lithuanian Jewry. Both town and country during the occupation remained confessionally diverse, and the division between local Ruthenians and Muscovite newcomers remained palpable. Nevertheless, tensions and suspicions were inevitable as Orthodox burghers and nobles moved up the pecking order, and the Ruthenian language became more prominent in the public sphere. Property disputes overlapped with accusations of disloyalty. There would be recriminations after the Muscovites were expelled in 1660. The principle of parity in the city council between 'Latins' and 'Greeks' would later become parity between Catholics of the Latin rite and Uniates.

Peace with Sweden, concluded in May 1660, allowed the Commonwealth to concentrate its depleted forces against Muscovy. On 28 June 1660, the main Lithuanian army, commanded by Hetman Paweł Sapieha and supported by a Crown division, destroyed a Muscovite army at the Battle of Polonka. The rapid exploitation of the victory enabled the liberation of most of the Grand Duchy west of the River Dniapro. Meanwhile Crown forces defeated the Muscovites and Cossacks in Ukraine. The successes continued into the following year, bringing a bloody reckoning with the invaders. On 11 February 1661, the overwhelmingly Orthodox townspeople of Mahileŭ rose up and killed the Muscovite garrison, and their example was followed elsewhere. Although the city of Vilnius had been freed on 11 July 1660, the fanatical Muscovite commander, Daniil Myshetskii, prolonged the siege of the two castles for seventeen months. His surviving seventy-eight soldiers handed him over to the Lithuanian army on 3 December 1661. A week later he was executed for war crimes in front of the city hall.

A COMMONWEALTH OF TWO NATIONS?

A bright future seemed imminent, as the standards of the routed Muscovites were laid before the monarch during the sejm that opened in Warsaw in May 1661. Yet John Casimir chose this moment to prophesy the country's partition by the countries' neighbours, unless his proposals to strengthen the monarchy were accepted. At the time, his warnings seemed hyperbolic. The Commonwealth wasted its best opportunity to win the war against Muscovy, initially because its victorious soldiers formed confederations to demand their arrears of pay. Mutinous soldiers even murdered the field hetman of Lithuania, Wincenty Gosiewski, in 1662. Following the restoration of a semblance of order, during the winter of 1663–64, John Casimir led the Crown and Lithuanian armies into Muscovite territory but could not win a decisive victory. Negotiations dragged on for two and a half years as the war—dubbed the 'forgotten war' by the Belarusian historian Henadz Sahanovich—petered out.[16] The truce, concluded early in 1667, brought the return of the palatinates of Vitsebsk and Polatsk, as well as the part of Livonia not ceded to the Swedes, but not other lands seized by the Muscovites. In 1686, the truce congealed into a treaty of 'eternal peace'. The Commonwealth acknowledged its loss of Smolensk, Kyiv, and Ukraine beyond the Dnipro.

Exhaustion, whose consequence was mutinous unpaid soldiers, was not the only reason why victory eluded the Commonwealth. Political strife escalated into another civil war. The main protagonists were the King and Queen on the one side, and the Crown Grand Marshal Jerzy Lubomirski on the other. They had clashed during the Swedish Deluge, when the royal couple made the designation of a successor to the throne during the King's lifetime the centrepiece of its plans for reform. The perilous prospect of a wartime interregnum softened republican opposition to the idea itself, but the question of the candidate divided the elites. Lubomirski led the opposition to the French candidature favoured

LITHUANIA

by the King and Gueen, who were accused of trying to introduce French-style absolute rule. The monarch responded in 1664 by instigating the sejm court to sentence Lubomirski to infamy and banishment. For almost two years, Lubomirski's supporters paralysed the body politic, while he himself led the King's army a dance before finally defeating it in battle in 1666. The victorious rebels slaughtered thousands of royalist prisoners. Restored to his good name but not his offices, Lubomirski died in exile, while the royal court abandoned its reforms. Grief-stricken after the death of the Queen, the King abdicated in 1668. He saw out his days in Paris as abbot of Saint-Germain-des-Près.

During this second civil war, John Casimir seemed to have the measure of the Grand Duchy of Lithuania. Despite the shortage of troops to fight the Muscovites, Lithuanian units marched to the Polish Crown to fight the rebels. But the price the King paid was reliance on the Pac family. The clan's fortunes climaxed under the leadership of the gifted chancellor, Krzysztof, and his less cerebral cousin, Hetman Michał Kazimierz. Their episcopal brothers preferred confronting 'heretics' to providing pastoral or political leadership. The chancellor's brother Mikołaj Stefan Pac exchanged the castellany for the bishopric of Vilnius, having consigned his wife to a nunnery. After the most violent religious tumult yet in Vilnius in 1682, he 'backed the Jesuit Academy against the Calvinist community, protected the accused, blamed the victims, and effectively sabotaged the administration of royal justice.'[17]

As the Counter-Reformation reached its zenith, the Pac family left magnificent architectural legacies. Chancellor Krzysztof founded the largest monastic complex in Lithuania at Pažaislis on the banks of the River Nemunas outside Kaunas. He named the site Mons Pacis (literally the Mountain of Peace, but also a pun on the family name). The austere rule of the Camaldolese order contrasted with the baroque opulence of the buildings. At its heart is a marbled hexagonal church with a concave facade, under whose portal rests the chancellor. The dome and towers were not completed until the mid-eighteenth century. After many reversals of fortune, including functioning as a psychiatric hospital during the Soviet period, the church and monastery were returned by independent Lithuania to the Sisters of St Casimir in the 1990s, and then carefully restored.

Michał Kazimierz Pac re-founded the monastery and church of the Lateran canons just outside Vilnius at Antakalnis. He was reputedly inspired to do so by his narrow escape while hiding from mutinous troops in the ruined buildings in 1662. Nothing can prepare the visitor or worshipper for the interior of the church of Saints Peter and Paul. 2,000 human figures, fantastical and living creatures, and other objects and symbols sculpted in white stucco seem to cavort in riotous abandon, yet they are carefully arranged to convey the teachings of the Catholic Church. The hetman had himself interred so that those entering the church would step on his tombstone, which bears the undeniable epitaph *Hic iacet peccator* (Here lies a sinner). This stone, fractured by a falling sculpture, was later moved to the wall. In another pun, the façade bears the appeal *Regina pacis funda nos in pace* (Queen of Peace, protect us in peace).

The Pac family drifted into opposition towards the end of John Casimir's reign, before supporting the election to the throne of Michał Korybut Wiśniowiecki in 1669. The monarch claimed descent from Gediminas via his son Kaributas, but there his merits ended. The task of rehabilitating this multilingual non-entity has so far defeated every historian who has attempted it—although the blame for the calamitous turn of events has been spread wide. During King Michael's four-year reign, the Pac family extended its clientele and consolidated its domination of the army and principal institutions of the Grand Duchy of Lithuania.

LITHUANIA

Hetman Pac's relations with his Crown counterpart, Jan Sobieski, were toxic. Their mutual loathing contributed to the Commonwealth's humiliation by the Ottoman Empire in 1672, temporarily reducing it to a tributary state. Pac's insubordination was one reason why Sobieski could not fully exploit his victory over the Ottomans at Khotyn a year later. Sobieski, elected to the throne as John III in 1674, had little grasp of Lithuanian affairs, despite having married his sister to Michał Kazimierz Radziwiłł, the head of the Catholic branch of the family. The Pac clan remained uncontrollable for several years, before royal patronage gradually helped the Sapiehas to ascend once more. After the hetman died in 1682, followed to the grave two years later by the chancellor, the Pac faction fell apart.

The hapless monarch jumped from the frying pan into the fire, because the Sapiehas, led by the gifted treasurer, Benedykt and his less cerebral brother, the palatine of Vilnius and grand hetman, Kazimierz, built a social, economic, political, and military hegemony in Lithuania that lasted until the end of the century. The combination of the offices of hetman and treasurer in one family proved crucial. The Grand Duchy's fiscal-military system was no longer fit for purpose, but control of it enabled the Sapiehas to reward their supporters and intimidate their opponents. They could enforce favourable court verdicts and ignore those that went against them. The treasurer's misuse of public funds went unchecked, while the hetman quartered soldiers where he pleased, including the estates of his fiercest critic, the bishop of Vilnius. When Bishop Konstanty Brzostowski excommunicated the hetman in 1694, the latter intensified the ruinous military exploitation of episcopal property. The stakes rose yet higher after the death of the heiress of the Calvinist line of the Radziwiłłs, Ludwika Karolina. The Sapiehas sought to prevent the surviving Catholic branch of the Radziwiłłs from inheriting her latifundia.

A COMMONWEALTH OF TWO NATIONS?

King John III had cause to regret assisting the Sapiehas as early as 1683. Hetman Kazimierz led the Lithuanian army on a plundering spree in northern Hungary (now in Slovakia) rather than join the monarch in defeating the Ottoman host outside Vienna. Nonetheless, the Sapiehas repeatedly prevented the King from realigning the Commonwealth with France and helped to keep the Commonwealth in the Holy League against the Turks. This geopolitical clash was one of the reasons why the parliamentary system broke down during the second half of Sobieski's reign. Foreign diplomats worked with magnate factions to prevent the sejm from agreeing measures contrary to their courts' interests.

The means of this destruction was the notorious *liberum veto*. The sejm had long reached its decisions by consensus, hammering out compromises to preserve the unity of the Commonwealth. However, before legislative and fiscal measures could be written into the law books, they needed a threefold, uncontested acclamation during the concluding sessions of the sejm, when the King, senators, and envoys deliberated together. Otherwise, even measures provisionally agreed earlier were lost. Since 1569, the common Polish–Lithuanian sejm had more business to transact, but no more time was available unless it agreed—by consensus—to prolong its deliberations. When agreement was not forthcoming, the sejm dispersed without concluding successfully. In 1652, however, Władysław Siciński, envoy for Upytė (Upita) in the Grand Duchy of Lithuania and usually considered a client of Janusz II Radziwiłł, protested against the prolongation of the sejm and left Warsaw. Because he could not be persuaded to return and retract his protest, the marshal of the sejm deemed it legally binding. The resultant consternation inspired calls to reform parliamentary procedure to prevent the problem recurring. However, the breakdown of political trust during the 1660s vitiated these attempts and further sejms failed. Respectable parliamentarians justified the *liberum veto* as the last resort of the virtuous few against royal attempts to subvert freedom by corrupting the majority. 1669 brought another milestone: an envoy objected to the continued deliberations of the sejm before its six-week term had elapsed, the objection was upheld, and the sejm duly broke up.

Four of the six sejms of Michael's reign failed in this way, before the next decade brought respite. Only one of the six sejms held until 1685 was broken up. The parliamentary history of John III's reign is also notable for three sejms being held in Hrodna (in 1678–79, 1688, and 1693), realising the long-standing Lithuanian demand for every third sejm to be held in the Grand Duchy. But of these three, only the first concluded successfully. All but one of the six sejms held between 1688 and 1695 were lost to the *liberum veto*. In 1688, the sejm was 'ruptured' even before the marshal or speaker was chosen—that is, before it was legally constituted. On this occasion, and on several others, the monarch—via his supporters—was responsible for the use of the *liberum veto*. The *liberum veto* was also used to wreck sejmiks (local assemblies). Those that did conclude successfully constrained their envoys' freedom of action with ever longer—and ever less realistic—instructions. Envoys were sometimes instructed to break up the sejm if their sejmik's demands were not met. Crown sejmiks were more likely to indulge this prescriptive tendency. In Lithuania, magnates exercised greater control over the drafting of instructions. The ailing Sobieski shrank from the extreme remedy of calling on ordinary nobles to saddle their horses for a multitudinous 'equestrian sejm'. Like several other monarchs, he used meetings of the senate council to deal with matters, such as diplomatic missions, that did not require legislation.

John III's death on 17 June 1696 inaugurated a long and turbulent interregnum. The horns of the Commonwealth's usual dilemma between Vienna and Versailles were sharpened both by

A COMMONWEALTH OF TWO NATIONS?

the ongoing war with the Ottoman Empire, which still occupied parts of Podolia, and by the impending contest between Austria and France for the Spanish Habsburg inheritance. The Grand Duchy of Lithuania was riven between the Sapiehas and their rivals, who began to be called 'republicans'.

A coalition of magnates and middling nobles rallied around the cause of *coequatio iurium*—that is, the equalisation of the rights and laws of the Grand Duchy of Lithuania with those of the Polish Crown. This meant reforming, rather than abandoning the Third Lithuanian Statute. Although the provision that court verdicts would henceforth be written in Polish rather than Ruthenian breached the Grand Duchy's traditions, ordinary nobles found reading, let alone writing, Cyrillic script increasingly difficult. During the eighteenth century, Lithuanian sejmiks sporadically endeavoured to have barely legible old acts, vulnerable to damp and fire, translated into Polish and securely archived—testimony to the civic importance of clear property rights. In the Polish Crown, by contrast, Latin long remained the language of most legal documents. The main purpose of equalisation was to prune the powers of the Lithuanian ministers (hetmans, marshals, chancellors, and treasurers) which exceeded those of their Crown colleagues. It would also be easier to bring ministers before the courts for their abuses of power. The Sapiehas could not prevent these reforms being agreed in 1697, but they obstructed their implementation.

As the royal election approached, several German princes and John III's eldest son, Jakub Sobieski, appealed to anti-French opinion in the Commonwealth and vied for Austrian support. But having pipped them all at the post, the Elector and Duke of Saxony, Friedrich August Wettin, squared up to the French candidate François-Louis de Bourbon-Conti, a distant cousin of Louis XIV. The twenty-seven-year-old Saxon cultivated his reputation as a new Hercules, manifested by feats such as breaking horseshoes with his bare hands. He also proclaimed his virility, although his one legitimate son and fewer than ten known bastards were a small fraction of the 354 offspring with which he was later credited. He was also considered a capable soldier. Above all, his fresh conversion/apostasy from Lutheranism to Roman Catholicism caused a sensation: the Electors of Saxony traditionally led the Protestant cause in the Holy Roman Empire.

Two rival monarchs were proclaimed on the election field on 27 June 1697, but it was the supporters of King Augustus II who acted decisively and arranged his coronation in Kraków for 15 September. The Saxon marched into Poland at the head of his troops while the French court waited on events. By the time Conti arrived in Gdańsk with a small contingent of soldiers, it was too late. The Sapiehas negotiated with him, before he sailed away again, and they acknowledged Augustus. The 'republicans' had not hesitated to do so. Despite support for the Saxon monarch across the Lithuanian political scene, tensions mounted until the two armies confronted each other at Valkininkai (Olkieniki) on 18 November 1700. In a ferocious battle, the 'republican' confederation overwhelmed the Sapiehas' better trained, but smaller force. The thousands of corpses included the hetman's son Michał. His uncle and father had fled the field. The victors condemned the brothers Sapieha to exile, expropriation, and infamy.

The outcome prompts further reflection on the problem of 'magnate oligarchy' in the Grand Duchy of Lithuania. Oligarchy, as classical authors informed better educated nobles, resulted from the corruption of aristocracy—rule by the best for the public good—by an unchecked accumulation of wealth and power in the hands of a self-serving elite. The first point is that wealth and office were concentrated more narrowly in the Grand Duchy of Lithuania than in the Polish Crown. Vast wealth and high office translated into tangible influence over poorer nobles—at sejmiks, in the law courts, in the marriage market, and in employment. However, it did not guarantee their obedience. The second point is that bonds between patrons and clients were relatively stable at district level. At the level of the Grand Duchy of Lithuania, during periods of uncertainty, they could shift like a kaleidoscope. Patterns lasting for a generation were exceptional. Noble families could still rise from obscurity and sink back again. Third, the fragility of family-based hegemonies was compounded by the ease with which determined opponents could frustrate their positive initiatives. For example, when the Pac clan and the royal court tried to muster the Grand Duchy's resources for war against the Turks, their opponents used the *liberum veto* to break up the Lithuanian convocation held in Vilnius in 1671. Finally, the general crisis of the later seventeenth century dampened, but did not extinguish public spirit among ordinary Lithuanian nobles. Part of the remedy for the Sapiehas' misrule were 'republican' reforms involving the equalisation of the rights and laws of the Grand Duchy with those of the Crown. These testified to civic maturity within the shared Commonwealth.

Crown nobles saw things differently. The vengeful treatment meted out to the Sapiehas raised the spectre of a fearsome alliance between Augustus II and his Lithuanian henchmen. The moment was seized by their opponents who, in an example of 'fake news', circulated an act purportedly agreed by the 'republicans' in Vilnius on 24 November 1700 (when its alleged authors were in fact elsewhere). This document rejected 'despicable Polish freedoms', and proclaimed Augustus the absolute, hereditary ruler of the Grand Duchy of Lithuania. The public executioner in Warsaw burnt a copy during the sejm of 1701. Authentic documents drawn up in the name of the 'republicans' feature the term 'the Commonwealth of the Grand Duchy of Lithuania', although they also refer to the 'entire nation' or the 'Estates' of the Grand Duchy of Lithuania within the

LITHUANIA

Commonwealth as a whole. These, and more casual usages of 'the Lithuanian Commonwealth' (*Rzeczpospolita litewska*), provoked exaggerated fears in the Polish Crown for the union. Fears of the monarch's intentions were better founded. Augustus II routinely bypassed the Commonwealth's procedures, making use of Saxon officials, diplomats, and soldiers.

Things went from bad to worse during the first two decades of the eighteenth century. From an afflicted but still sovereign polity, the Commonwealth became a storehouse and highway for foreign armies. Ravaged time and again by pillage, epidemics, and famine, Poland–Lithuania ended the Great Northern War (1700–21) in the Russian sphere of influence. Much of the responsibility lies with Augustus II. In 1697, the young Tsar Peter I was still feeling his way. Once crowned, Augustus sought Peter's support and bartered the Commonwealth's interests for his own.

In the summer of 1698, the tsar returned to Moscow from his 'great embassy to the West'. He met Augustus for an epic drinking bout at Rava Rus′ka (now the site of a Ukrainian–Polish border crossing). Exactly what they said (or slurred) to each other remains speculation, but—probably at Peter's instigation—they agreed to ally with Denmark against the new King of Sweden, Charles XII. Their cunning plan failed to reckon either with the teenager's martial genius or with his father's fiscal-military reforms. Trusting too readily in promises of a revolt among Livonian nobles against Swedish rule, Augustus sent a force to take Riga in the spring of 1700. It failed, not least because the cannon balls were the wrong size for the cannons. Meanwhile the Swedes first knocked the Danes out of the war. Next, during a snowstorm on 30 November 1700, they annihilated Peter's larger army at Narva. The Swedish son of Mars then fixated on the Saxon Hercules. Charles invaded Courland in July 1701. During 1702, the Swedes moved through the Grand Duchy of

A COMMONWEALTH OF TWO NATIONS?

Lithuania, routed a larger Saxon and Polish army in Lesser Poland, and took the Commonwealth's principal cities (although the 'republicans' regained Vilnius). It takes hindsight to pronounce this string of victories a fateful strategic error. But Peter I used the respite to reform his military and fiscal base, pick off Swedish garrisons in Livonia, and found St Petersburg. By the time Charles marched deep into Ukraine in 1708, the exhausted and outnumbered Swedes were facing a formidable enemy.

The war between Charles and Augustus played out differently, partly because of the Commonwealth's politics and values. In May 1700 the senate council refused to declare war on Sweden, although some Lithuanian foes of the Sapiehas joined in Augustus's abortive assault on Swedish Livonia. When the battered Sapiehas turned to Charles for protection, the 'republicans' supplicated Peter's support. Unaware of contingency plans in Moscow to annex most of the Grand Duchy of Lithuania, they gradually became more dependent on the tsar and negotiated with his representatives directly. Lithuanian resistance to the Swedes helped to prevent the relief of isolated garrisons in Livonia.

Charles took no account of the Commonwealth's formal neutrality as his forces criss-crossed its territory, spreading havoc. In 1703, the sejm rejected his demands to depose Augustus. Moreover, it agreed to a joint army of 48,000 regular soldiers, supplemented by Saxons, mercenaries, and the general levy, although the actual numbers raised fell short. In 1704, Charles commanded his supporters to elect as King a compliant magnate from Greater Poland, Stanisław Leszczyński. This pseudo-election (followed by a makeshift coronation in Warsaw) flouted the Commonwealth's laws and customs. The so-called alliance with Sweden was a pact of subjection and exploitation. In 1706, Charles marched into Saxony and forced Augustus to abdicate as King of Poland and Grand Duke of Lithuania. However, many nobles denied the legality of the abdication. The tsar played his cards closer to his chest, and did not wholly alienate Augustus's supporters. They prevented Leszczyński's adherents from aiding Charles as he marched into Ukraine.

The Swedish king's other hope also failed. Cossack Hetman Ivan Mazepa switched sides in a bid for independence, but in July 1709, he fled from the battlefield of Poltava along with Charles XII and died later that year in exile. The following April at Bender (now Tighina in Moldova), Mazepa's successor Pylyp Orlyk issued the *Pacts and Constitutions of the Laws and Liberties of the Zaporizhian Army*. This remarkable document, preserved in Latin and Ukrainian versions, was partly a manifesto for action, and partly a historical narrative. Its provisions for governance testify to the internalisation by the Cossacks of the Commonwealth's principles of liberty, consensus, the division of power, and the rule of law. Claimed by Ukrainians as the world's first written constitution, it could not take effect. The gradual elimination of the Cossacks' autonomy had already begun.

Despite Peter's victory at Poltava, the Great Northern War lasted another twelve years. As Charles fled the field, he owed his life to his companion in arms, Stanisław Poniatowski. This modestly born nobleman from the Polish Crown had previously served the Sapiehas. Poniatowski's command of the Turkish language helped Charles to bring the Ottoman Empire into the war. Peter came within a whisker of destruction when surrounded on the River Prut in 1711. Charles eventually made his way back to Sweden, which he defended bravely until he was killed during a siege in 1718.

The result at Poltava did end Leszczyński's miserable reign. A general council assembled in Warsaw in the spring of 1710 and acknowledged Augustus II. Sejmiks in the Grand Duchy of Lithuania approved and did their best to implement the taxes and troop recruitment agreed in Warsaw, testifying to resilience

A COMMONWEALTH OF TWO NATIONS?

in adversity, as Mindaugas Šapoka has argued.[18] Plague, the coldest winter ever recorded, and famine ravaged the region. Augustus had returned to Poland as Peter I's client, but with the tsar preoccupied with the Ottomans and Swedes, the years after 1710 offered the King his best chance to reconcile with the political nations of the Polish Crown and Lithuania, and possibly even to escape from the Muscovite cage. It was not to be. Augustus, still hoping to institute a hereditary monarchy, had not yet learned to respect the constitutional rules. His reliance on the Saxon army aroused fears for nobles' liberty and property. Led by Hetman Ludwik Pociej, Lithuanian nobles formed a confederation against the King in Vilnius in August 1715. Three months later, nobles in the Polish Crown followed suit, and an armed confrontation ensued. The tsar's ambassador posed as the nobles' champion and mediated a compromise fiscal and military settlement between the confederates and the King in November 1716. The sejm silently ratified it on 1 February 1717.

Even at this late stage, the Commonwealth was not yet a protectorate of the tsar. A swell of anger obliged Peter to withdraw his rapacious troops from the country. In retrospect, the point of no return probably came at the sejm of 1719–20, when the tsar's diplomats incited the Crown and Lithuanian hetmans, who faced further restrictions on their powers, to block the Commonwealth's entry into an alliance with the courts of Vienna, London, Hanover, and Dresden. Not for the last time, the court of St Petersburg manipulated the dysfunctional political system to prevent military reform and geopolitical emancipation. The collapse of the Commonwealth's status was reflected in its exclusion from the peace treaties that concluded the Great Northern War. On 2 November 1721, Peter I celebrated his victory by taking the title of Emperor and Autocrat of All the Russias (*Imperator i Samoderzhets Vserossiiskii*).

LITHUANIA

iv. *Christians and Jews in Town and Country*

The cumulative effects of seven decades of warfare on the Commonwealth's own territory were devasting. Marching armies ravaged towns and villages, and in their wake pestilence and famine cut down humans and livestock alike. The shortage of manure made the land less fertile. The effects were worsened by the nadir of the 'Little Ice Age' which shortened the growing season. The average ratio between the number of grains sown and harvested fell from about 1:5 in the sixteenth century to below 1:3 by the end of the seventeenth. Forests, populated by wolves, grew back as fields and pastures were abandoned. The Grand Duchy of Lithuania—situated north and east of the Polish Crown—suffered disproportionately. The calamities of the 1700s snuffed out the modest demographic and economic recovery that had begun after the main theatre of war shifted south in the late 1660s. It has been estimated that the Grand Duchy's population of about 4.5 million around 1650 shrank to less than 2 million (on a smaller territorial base) around 1720. Most towns were repeatedly decimated.[19]

Magnates with dispersed latifundia and private militias were best placed to weather these merging storms. If one of their towns was destroyed, they could resettle survivors in another. For an unlucky middling noble family whose estate had been in the path of one or more armies, the price of rescue might be deeper dependency on an aristocratic patron—a slide from respectable clientage into leaseholding or employment. Hard-pressed nobles sought to limit their losses by demanding heavier labour services from the surviving peasants. But by the eighteenth century, up to two thirds of Samogitian nobles had no serfs at all. Such families had to work their farms themselves, or else even hire out their labour occasionally to wealthier peasants. Others moved to towns. If nobles could not live respectably by serving richer nobles, or by working in the law courts, they might take up urban occupations at the temporary cost of their hereditary privileges. Their families might recover their ancestral status if they could abandon degrading plebeian employments.

Peasants' situations varied greatly. Dues in cash and kind, rather than labour, were normal in the well-connected belt stretching from Livonia across the north of the Grand Duchy of Lithuania. In some other regions, the days of obligatory labouring for the lord might even exceed the number of days in the week. However, such requirements were for a full plot (typically around thirty hectares), and the minority of peasants who cultivated this much land could afford to have the work carried out by junior family members and hired hands. For the peasantry in general, the trend was unmistakeably towards impoverishment and servitude. One of the most physically and morally debilitating aspects of the interlocking dependencies known as serfdom was the lord's monopoly of the production and sale of alcohol. This was often leased to Jews. This might even mean that serfs were obliged to purchase set quantities of beer and vodka from their lord's tavern, whether or not they drank it. Most probably did, contributing to premature mortality and domestic violence. Some peasants resorted to sabotage or to flight, more rarely to violent rebellion, but most village communities ran their own internal affairs and assured the villagers' obligations. The instinct for self-preservation tempered hostility on both sides of the social divide.

Although the dead weight of the manorial economy disincentivised innovation, by the 1730s demographic recovery was irrefutable. As the climate gradually warmed up after the 'Little Ice Age', epidemics and famines became rarer and more localised. The general upswing was not reversed either by the Russian military intervention that secured the throne for the late king's son as Augustus III in 1733, or by the civil conflict that followed, or by the marches across Poland–Lithuania by Russian and Prussian armies during the general European wars of 1740–48 and 1756–63. The overall population of the Commonwealth probably rose from about 6–7 million in the aftermath of the Great Northern War to about 12.5 million on the eve of the first partition in 1772 (with an outlying estimate of 14 million). During this time, the population of the Grand Duchy of Lithuania bounced back to about 3.75 million.[20]

The Catholic Church of both rites—Latin and Ruthenian—benefited greatly from economic and demographic growth. Buoyant revenues and legacies, particularly to the religious orders of both sexes, paid for splendid ecclesiastical architecture. Peace, and the Church's apparent triumph over its 'heretical' and 'schismatic' foes, encouraged celebratory expenditure. A characteristic late baroque and rococo style spread from Vilnius to the farthest reaches of the Grand Duchy of Lithuania and Livonia in the middle decades of the eighteenth century. Tapering towers topped rippling facades. Among the finest churches of this kind were those of the Priests of the Mission in Vilnius, in an elevated position east of the city walls, and of the Uniate Basilian Fathers at Beraz'vechcha. The Belarusian Soviet authorities had this jewel blown up around 1970. The surviving monastic buildings are still a prison at the time of writing. This elegant style crossed confessional boundaries, particularly in the work of the mason turned architect Johann Christian Glaubitz. Besides rebuilding the church of his own Lutheran community in Vilnius, he also designed a new facade for the university church of Saints John and John; reconstructed the Uniate monastery of the Holy Trinity; designed the interior, including a huge iconostasis, of the Orthodox church of the Holy Spirit; and even reconstructed the cavernous interior of the Great Synagogue, which accommodated several thousand worshippers.

The growth of the Jewish population was especially rapid, especially on latifundia in the east of the Commonwealth. Here magnates saw Jews as the best agents of commerce, while being less truculent than Christian burghers. The census of Jews conducted in 1764–65 indicates an overall population in the Commonwealth of about 750,000, of whom just over a quarter resided in the Grand Duchy of Lithuania. This amounted to a tripling of the Jewish population since the beginning of the eighteenth century. Among the reasons for faster demographic growth among Jews than among Christians were the networks of familial and communal support that enabled both lower ages of marriage and better midwifery. The former increased the birth rate, while the latter reduced the death rate among infants and child-bearing women. Ritual ablutions and lower rates of alcoholism doubtless helped as well. However, this growth had its price: most Jews struggled to make ends meet as artisans and petty tradesmen.

There were no ghettoes as such in the Grand Duchy of Lithuania. Moreover, Christian burghers' efforts to obtain the coveted privilege of *de non tolerandis Iudaeis*, and thus to expel Jews from towns, met with no lasting success. The privileges granted to Jewish communities in Lithuania sometimes permitted or forbade residence in specified quarters or streets—or even on sides of streets. But many Jews could reside and trade in parts of towns theoretically closed to them, when they did so in a *jurydyka*—a property belonging to a noble, or even to an ecclesiastical institution, which was not subject to the jurisdiction of the town council. These properties grew rapidly in number, not least because many nobles took up residence in the larger towns. After the Muscovite occupation, nobles constituted up to a quarter of the population of Vilnius.[21] More Jews also settled in suburbs beyond town walls as the eighteenth century progressed. Lobbying to loosen these limitations sometimes succeeded—as in Vilnius in 1742, after which only two main throughfares remained closed to new purchases by Jews. Nevertheless, rabbis and priests alike discouraged Jews and Gentiles from social and cultural intercourse, and they usually lived 'together, but apart'.

Jews and Christians mostly encountered each other as buyers and sellers, as lessees and owners, and as employers and employees. Jewish law, the canon law of the Catholic Church, and the respective privileges issued to Jews and Christian burghers by monarchs and aristocratic founders all regulated the livelihoods open to Jews. Moneylending, for example, had to comply with all three frameworks. There could be restrictions on conducting business on both Jewish and Christian holy days, on trading in non-kosher meat, or in other commodities, and on Jews employing Christian servants (albeit sometimes only on the Sabbath). Christian traders and artisans often accused Jews of forming cartels and other unfair business practices to undercut and squeeze out competitors, but they usually refused to admit them to the guilds. Jewish craftsmen formed fraternities of their own, but as the decades passed, Christian guilds sometimes admitted Jewish 'half-brothers', when instructed to do so by owners of private towns. Jews predominated among tailors, dressmakers, haberdashers, furriers, butchers, glaziers, gold- and silversmiths, and brewers and distillers. Some traders engaged in door-to-door selling. Significant numbers of Jews also transacted with noble landowners. They leased inns, taverns, mills, and even the administration of entire landed estates, in a system known as the *arenda*. Nobles' expectation of a promptly and regularly paid fixed income, and Jewish leaseholders' incentive to maximise profits from a monopoly inevitably caused tensions with the involuntary consumers and producers—Christian peasants.

The foundation of Jewish autonomy in the Polish-Lithuanian Commonwealth was the communal organisation or kahal. These varied in age and importance, but they all had fiscal, judicial, welfare, sanitary, educational, and religious responsibilities. It was the kahal, for example, that chose and employed the rabbi.

A COMMONWEALTH OF TWO NATIONS?

Although its two dozen or so members were elected from among the senior male members of the community, the kahal itself could often choose its electors. Broadly democratic organs thus slid into self-reproducing local oligarchies, and grievances mounted at unfair allocations of burdens and benefits. In private towns, kahals' principal external relationship was with the noble proprietors, whereas in royal towns they had to manoeuvre between several centres of power—royal *starosta*s with judicial responsibilities, town councils, and the Catholic hierarchy.

As the centuries passed, the Jewish population grew, and the fiscal burdens on Jews increased, so Jews' endeavours at collective representation took on specific institutional forms. From the Commonwealth's perspective, the Vaad Arba Aratsot or Council of the Four Lands (Lesser and Greater Poland, Lithuania, and Ruthenia) established in 1587 was a convenient way to handle the taxation of the Jewish population. For the representatives of Jewish communities, the Vaad's meetings also served to compare rulings on points of Jewish law, and to co-ordinate lobbying at the royal court, the sejm, or sejmiks. Its rulings bound all Polish–Lithuanian Jews. In 1623, the Council of Lithuania (Vaad medinat Lita) became a separate body, mainly because new taxes on Jews were levied in different ways in the Polish Crown and the Grand Duchy. The different legal environment under the Third Lithuanian Statute probably also contributed to the split. When necessary, representatives of the two Councils would meet on the border between their jurisdictions, at Tykocin in Podlachia. This market town—Tiktin in Yiddish—became a major centre of Jewish learning, and its synagogue is now one of the best preserved in Poland.

Three major communities were instrumental in forming the Lithuanian Vaad: Brest, Hrodna, and Pinsk. In 1652 they were joined by Vilnius, and in 1691 by Slutsk as the major communities that sent provincial elders and rabbis directly to the Council.

LITHUANIA

These five communities each maintained their own authorised copy of the book of the Council's decisions—the *Pinkas*. Lesser kahals, grouped in districts, sent their delegates to present tax registers and expenses. The Council maintained its own treasury, officials, and archives. It also constituted the court of appeal for disputes between Jews. Its assemblies rotated between the major communities, meeting for four to six weeks every three years or so in the seventeenth century, but less frequently in the eighteenth. Among the Vaad's concerns were inter-confessional relations. It sought to guard against Christian proselytising and avoid conflicts by maintaining cultural and social barriers. The Council of Lithuania also defended the economic interests of established Jewish residents against newcomers, which perhaps helps to explain why the Jewish population did not grow quite as fast in the Grand Duchy of Lithuania as it did in the south-east of the Polish Crown.

By the middle of the eighteenth century, Jewish communal institutions were deep in debt, often to Catholic religious orders. Both councils were encumbered by loans taken out to cover the fiscal shortfalls of individual kahals. The Lithuanian Vaad met for what turned out to be the last time in Slutsk in 1761. The convocation sejm of 1764 ordained a census to determine the size and assets of Jewish communities, while the Crown and Lithuanian treasuries sought to discover the extent of communities' debts and to supervise repayments to creditors. The census cost the Jews of Lithuania 45,000 złotys. The problem was not resolved before the third partition, by which time the debts of the Vilnius kahal amounted to at least twenty-one times its annual income. The de facto abolition of the two councils might in hindsight be viewed as an enlightened, centralising development that ended 'a state within a state', but more pragmatically, neither Vaad could serve its fiscal purpose. The Commonwealth took Jewish taxation in hand by dealing directly with the kahals, which continued

A COMMONWEALTH OF TWO NATIONS?

to operate. The long experience of self-rule did however bequeath an intangible parliamentary legacy to the Jews of the region; not for nothing have the two Vaads often been called Jewish sejms.

The most distinguished Jewish figure of eighteenth-century Vilnius was Eliyahu ben Shelomoh Zalman, known as the Gaon (genius). Although he did not hold formal office, stories of the extraordinary erudition and powers of memory of this retiring scholar spread his fame and authority throughout the Jewish world. He contributed mightily to his city's sobriquet as 'the Jerusalem of Lithuania'. His priority was to study, annotate, and elucidate the vast body of Talmudic writings that expanded on the Tanakh or Hebrew Bible, but he also had a formidable knowledge of mystical, kabbalist texts. The Gaon envisaged an auxiliary role for secular learning, including philology, as a tool for the better understanding of Scripture, but he kept his distance from the Jewish Enlightenment, or Haskalah. Its supporters—the maskilim—postulated greater integration into the non-Jewish world.

A stickler for the strict observance of Jewish law with all its implications on how to live (*halakha*), the Gaon deployed his personal authority against a less scholarly, more emotional movement: Hasidism. This offered every Jew a personal and prayerful relationship with God. Hasidism began to spread north and west from Podolia during the second half of the eighteenth century, to the consternation of its orthodox critics. The Gaon participated in solemn exclusions of Hasidists from the Vilnan community in 1772 and 1781. However, as the repetition of the act suggests, Hasidism proved too attractive, especially to poorer Jews who felt marginalised or exploited by their communities, to be eradicated. Not only did it grow back, but throughout the nineteenth century, its followers—the Hasidim—would contest the leadership of Lithuanian Jewry with the rabbinical establishment, or Misnagdim.

LITHUANIA

These internal controversies contrast with the fundamental challenge to Judaism presented by the Podolian Jew, Jacob Frank. He claimed to be the reincarnation of the reputed Messiah, Sabbatai Zevi, who became a Muslim in Istanbul in 1666. Frank began to preach his 'revelations' in the south-east of the Commonwealth in the mid-1750s. Orthodox rabbis excommunicated him and his followers, pushing them into the arms of the Catholic Church. In two public disputes held before the Catholic hierarchy, the Frankists rejected the Talmud, 10,000 copies of which were duly burned. Frank and thousands of his supporters were baptised but the Church charged him with heresy in 1760 and confined him in the monastery at Częstochowa. Released by the Russians in 1773, he spent his final years in Offenbach in Hesse, generously maintained by his devotees.

The chief significance of Frankism for the Grand Duchy of Lithuania lay in the Third Lithuanian Statute's provision for the ennoblement of Jewish converts to Christianity. The Mariavite Sisters, established in 1737 by the Lithuanian episcopate to look after female converts from Judaism, expanded their network. However, the mass influx into the nobility of unconventional neophytes diminished the attractions of proselytisation for *szlachta* and clergy alike. Some Frankists endangered their former co-religionists by alleging that Jews made use of Christian blood in their ceremonies. The Blood Libel gained credence, soon after the trials, tortures, and executions at Zhytomyr in Ukraine in 1753. It would take more than thirty years for trials for 'ritual murder' to cease, as a result of persuasion by learned Jews and Christians, including the Commonwealth's last monarch.

v. *Sarmatians and Revolutionaries*

Stanisław Poniatowski, the namesake and fourth son of Charles XII's former companion, was born at Voŭchin, near Brest, in

A COMMONWEALTH OF TWO NATIONS?

1732. He later became the first Grand Duke of Lithuania born in the Grand Duchy for more than three centuries. Although panegyrics composed in his honour sometimes emphasised his Lithuanian nativity, King Stanisław August was a determined proponent of an integrated Polish state and nation, before events took a different course. Astrological portents supposedly attended his birth, but his prospects of a major inheritance were slim. His parvenu father Stanisław had married the formidable Konstancja, née Czartoryska. She was born into an old princely family that traced its lineage back to Gediminas. However, the clan only catapulted itself into the first rank of the Commonwealth's magnates when Konstancja's younger brother, August Czartoryski, married the richest heiress in the Commonwealth, Zofia née Sieniawska. Her dowry included the latifundium of Shkloŭ, but most of her estates and clients were in the Polish Crown. August's elder brother Michał Czartoryski inherited most of the parental estates in the Grand Duchy of Lithuania. Serving as vice-chancellor and then as chancellor, he was the leading player in Lithuanian politics between the 1720s and the 1760s, heading a network of allies, clients, and fixers. The Czartoryskis and Poniatowskis constituted the *Familia*, which operated as a cohesive political grouping across the Commonwealth. They gained a reputation as intelligent supporters of much-needed fiscal, military, and judicial reforms.

They were unable, however, to implement any of their proposals during the politically stagnant reign of Augustus III (1733–63). The Commonwealth's second Saxon monarch owed his throne to Russian military intervention against the supporters of Stanisław Leszczyński. Although this exiled ex-king was chosen by most electors at his second attempt in 1733, as the father-in-law of Louis XV of France he was unacceptable to the courts of St Petersburg and Vienna. Augustus III paid his bill in 1738 by investing Tsaritsa Anna's favourite, Ernst Biron, as hereditary

LITHUANIA

Duke of Courland. The duchy would otherwise have reverted to the Commonwealth. Russian diplomats worked with their Austrian and Prussian colleagues to ensure that all attempts at fiscal and military reforms failed. Factional rivalry eased their task. A pacification sejm succeeded in 1736, but the next ten sejms held between 1738 and 1762 either ran out of time or were broken up by the *liberum veto*. Many sejmiks were also ruined in this way, although the Kaunas sejmik, where local families kept the magnates at arm's length, had an enviable record of never once succumbing to the *veto*. The tribunals became the main arena for factional contests. Coalition-building among the dozen or so magnate clans of the Grand Duchy of Lithuania was an art whose difficulty was compounded by different relationships in the Polish Crown, and at the monarch's court in Dresden.

The *Familia*'s principal Lithuanian rivals were usually the Radziwiłłs of the surviving Niasvizh branch. The men were noted more for their vast wealth, eccentric tastes, and extravagant hospitality than for any cerebral qualities. The women were more impressive: Anna née Sanguszko energetically ran vast estates on which she established manufactories and foundries. But her autocratic character stimulated the mixture of theatrical and sadistic inclinations that marked her younger son Hieronim Florian. The elder son Michał, known as the 'little fish' (*Rybeńko*), achieved nothing of note as a senator and hetman, but he married a poet and playwright, Urszula née Wiśniowiecka. She staged her Polish-language dramas, including adaptations of Molière, in the court theatre at Niasvizh. Their eldest surviving son, Karol Stanisław Radziwiłł, did not inherit her intellect. He was known, after his characteristic mode of address, as 'My dear Sir' (*Panie Kochanku*). Reputed to be near-illiterate, his polar opposite was the younger Stanisław Poniatowski, whose mother Konstancja instilled in him an aversion to ignorance and boorishness. The future king's own abstemiousness towards alcohol

A COMMONWEALTH OF TWO NATIONS?

also helps to explain why so many ordinary nobles adored the legendary drunkard Karol Radziwiłł who magnified their own vices and virtues.

The culture clash within the eighteenth-century *szlachta* can also be summed up sartorially. For decades, the western European apparel of frock coat, breeches, stockings, and buckled shoes, accompanied by a powdered periwig and clean-shaven face, advanced at the expense of the traditional long overcoat (*kontusz*) girthed with a silk sash, many of which were woven at the Radziwiłł manufactory in Slutsk. A doublet (*żupan*) and soft leather boots completed the attire. Full beards were less common than in the mid-seventeenth century, but whiskers were expected, and the head was partly shaved. Foreigners associated this costume with the Ottoman, Tatar, or Persian 'Orient', whence many elements of it came, but to most of the Commonwealth's nobles it was unequivocally their own. Those who cultivated French fashions might mock their traditionally attired and shorn 'brethren' as 'moustaches' or 'Sarmatians'.

The latter term reflected the long-standing, if inchoate belief among Polish nobles of their descent from the valiant Sarmatian warriors (and female 'Amazons') who had battled the ancient Roman legions. Medieval geography preserved the names of *Sarmatia europaea* and *Sarmatia asiatica* for the lands north of the Black Sea. 'Sarmatia' proved a useful name for Renaissance-era historians. During the sixteenth and seventeenth centuries, this cartographic survival morphed into a way of life. The Sarmatian myth and aesthetic spread to Ukrainian Cossacks, Prussian burghers, and nobles of the Grand Duchy of Lithuania. The grandest Lithuanian families claimed Roman ancestry via the legendary Palemon and his companions, but the two concepts co-existed easily enough. However, in the mid-1760s, a pejorative 'ism' was coined—*sarmatyzm*—as a satirical shorthand for ignorance, prejudice, and superstition, the opposite of 'enlightenment' (*oświecenie*), which had hitherto been a religious metaphor. The insult was felt deeply. Within two decades, the tide turned towards neo-Sarmatian patriotism, manifested by 'uniforms' that distinguished each palatinate of the Commonwealth by the different colours, collars, and caps of essentially the same national costume. Poets ridiculed frock-coated fops. In his greatest poem, *Pan Tadeusz*, completed in 1834, but set in 1811–12, Adam Mickiewicz captured his elders' memories of the consternation caused by foreign fashions in the Navahrudak district in the 1770s and 1780s.

The younger Stanisław Poniatowski was destined by his parents for a career in diplomacy and politics, hence the emphasis in his education on languages, including English, and a grand tour that took in the Netherlands, France, and England. (The youngest son, Michał, destined for the Church, went to Italy instead.) The avuncular British diplomat and libertine poet, Sir Charles Hanbury Williams, took Stanisław under his wing. As ambassador to Russia from 1755, he taught Poniatowski—his secretary—the diplomat's craft. Stanisław's journey north took him through Vilnius. He noted the traces of its former grandeur, and rebuilding after fires. In St Petersburg, Williams presented Poniatowski to the Grand Duchess Catherine, the neglected wife of the heir to the Russian throne. And after their love affair ignited, Williams suggested to Catherine that she make Stanisław King of Poland.

Having disposed of her hapless husband, Peter III, in the summer of 1762, Empress Catherine II decided that Stanisław should succeed Augustus III, who died on 5 October 1763. She mistakenly assumed that her former lover would be a pliant instrument of her will. He naively believed that because she intended to reform the Russian Empire in an enlightened spirit, she would support his efforts to do likewise in the Commonwealth. Poniatowski's uncles, who should have known better, hoped that she would install them in power and enable them to strengthen their country's institutions on their own terms.

A COMMONWEALTH OF TWO NATIONS?

The German-born and Lutheran-raised tsaritsa needed an early foreign-policy success. She would show foreign courts, Russian nobles, and Orthodox clergymen that she decided the the Commonwealth's royal election. The Czartoryskis obligingly invited her armed intervention. Their 'republican' opponents were led by Karol Radziwiłł and Crown Grand Hetman Jan Klemens Branicki, who campaigned for the throne against his much younger brother-in-law Poniatowski. Catherine's ambassador cut a deal that permitted the *Familia* to implement some long-planned reforms during the convocation sejm that met in the spring of 1764 to prepare the election. These included allowing the sejm to transact business from the newly established Crown and Lithuanian treasury commissions by an obscure formula that permitted majority voting. Lithuanian envoys aired an old aspiration—raising the bishopric of Vilnius to an archbishopric—but the Czartoryskis refused to support the motion. Radziwiłł and Branicki went abroad after their forces lost skirmishes with Russian troops, clearing the way for 5,584 nobles to elect Poniatowski King outside Warsaw on 7 September. In a breach with tradition, he was crowned in Warsaw on 25 November 1764.

The new monarch was an eloquent orator. The further and faster reforms he desired would include closer integration of the Grand Duchy of Lithuania and the Polish Crown. He told the 1766 sejm that 'we have a kind of new, or rather second creation of the Polish world before us. It is the critical moment, when almost everything must be moved at once'.[22] The King admired Father Stanisław Konarski who had renovated the schools of the Piarist Order in the spirit of enlightened Catholicism, aiming to educate elite noble youth as good Catholics and good citizens. The Jesuits followed suit. Above all, Konarski had 'dared to be wise' (as the royal medal struck in his honour proclaimed) by demolishing the arguments for the *liberum veto*. He advocated reforms to facilitate government while safeguarding republican liberty. Institutions should be designed for sinful men, rather than mythologised ancestral virtue.

Stanisław August's early 'reform fever' included an 'enlightened' essay periodical (*Monitor*), a national theatre, a currency revaluation, a cannon foundry, and a military academy. Several monarchs had been obliged by their *pacta conventa* to establish a cadet corps to train young nobles as officers, but only Poniatowski kept his promise. The King's elegant and erudite cousin, Prince Adam Kazimierz Czartoryski, took his responsibilities as commandant of the Knights' School seriously. The curriculum would enlighten and form citizens, as well as train soldiers.

Among the first students of the Knights' School in Warsaw was an obscure youth from the palatinate of Brest, born in 1746, who had been schooled by the Piarists at Liubeshiv. Not only was his conduct exemplary, his draughtsmanship persuaded the King to send him to Paris on a scholarship. During a five-year stay there, the young man mastered modern fortifications and military architecture. He came from a modestly situated noble family of Ruthenian origin, which over the centuries had moved from Orthodoxy through Calvinism to Latin-rite Catholicism. The family manor house at Merachoŭshchyna was reconstructed as a museum in the twenty-first century, and Belarusians have claimed him as their own. Within the Commonwealth, he called himself a Lithuanian (*Litwin*), but abroad, he was a Pole. He was Tadeusz Kościuszko.

By the time Kościuszko left for France in 1769, the Commonwealth was in chaos. Not only had the reforming king provoked opposition among the nobility, but the neighbouring monarchs had reined in his ambition. Frederick the Great of Prussia forced the abandonment of the new general customs system which had both increased state revenue and stimulated internal trade. Catherine II, alerted to the danger of the *liberum veto* being fur-

A COMMONWEALTH OF TWO NATIONS?

ther restricted at the 1766 sejm, had it reinforced instead. She outraged the Catholic *szlachta* by insisting on equal political rights for the Protestant and Orthodox nobles whom she wished to manipulate. Stanisław August tried in vain to persuade her that while greater religious liberty was achievable, equal political rights were not. Rebuffed by the sejms of 1764 and 1766, she had her ambassador, Nikolai Repnin, organise confederations in the Grand Duchy of Lithuania and the Crown, directed against the King. Repnin then had two bishops and a hetman seized and sent to Russia, where they spent five years in captivity. Cowed into submission, the confederated sejm of 1767–68 passed all the desired legislation.

Before this compliant sejm ended in the spring of 1768, a rival confederation was formed for 'faith and freedom' at Bar in Podolia. It opposed 'heretics' and 'schismatics', Poniatowski's reforms, and Russian violations of the Commonwealth's laws. The Ottoman Empire declared war on Russia, and guerilla fighting engulfed the Commonwealth. A formally separate Lithuanian confederation gathered much of the nobility, from magnates to landless nobles. One of the most spectacular actions was the daring cavalry raid across much of the Grand Duchy and into the Russian Empire led by Szymon Kossakowski. We shall encounter him again. However, individual heroics could not substitute for organisation, numbers, weapons, and training, and by the spring of 1772 the insurgency was over.

The courts of St Petersburg and Berlin had already agreed a partition of the Commonwealth. Catherine II, having encountered obstruction from the King and his uncles, and resistance from the confederates, was now willing to satisfy her own courtiers' appetites by annexing strategically vital lands in the northeast of the Grand Duchy of Lithuania. Frederick II was permitted to take Royal Prussia, thereby joining East Prussia with the main body of his territories, but without the cities of Gdańsk and

Toruń. The rulers of the Austrian monarchy, Maria Theresa and her son Joseph II, annexed populous lands in the south, which they renamed Galicia and Lodomeria after an old Hungarian claim, rather than fight both Russia and Prussia. The three powers thus took about a third of the Commonwealth's lands and inhabitants, leaving it with territories more unlike those of the current Republic of Poland than at any time previously. Three quarters of those lands now lie in Ukraine, Belarus, Lithuania, and Latvia.

Stanisław August's publicity campaign demonstrated the flagrant illegality of the partition to European opinion-formers, but the threat of further annexations made him desist. The sejm summoned in 1773 ratified the partition treaties, despite a dramatic protest by three Lithuanian envoys, led by Tadeusz Reytan of Navahrudak, which delayed the proceedings by three days. Had they succeeded, the sejm would not have been confederated, but rather would have been susceptible to the *liberum veto*. The fact that they were overridden proved Konarski right. The *veto* allowed corrupt minorities to frustrate the will of virtuous majorities, but it did not enable virtuous minorities to save the Commonwealth from corrupt majorities. This sejm also established a form of government designed to keep the amputated Commonwealth in tranquil obedience to Russia. Between sejms, a thirty-six-member Permanent Council would supervise government. It took over some of the royal prerogatives, although the King chaired it and had the casting vote. Each councillor, elected by the sejm from among the senators and envoys, also sat in one of the treasury, military, police, justice, and foreign affairs departments.

Stanisław August convinced the Russian ambassador, Otto von Stackelberg, to persuade the empress to permit the strengthening of the Permanent Council in 1776. This was achieved by marginalising the supporters of the aristocratic opposition at yet another confederated sejm. Afterwards, Catherine II rejected requests for parliamentary confederations, so the five 'free' sejms held between 1778 and 1786 yielded little legislation. The Russian ambassador held the ring between the king and his opponents. Nevertheless, the monarch used institutions to advance incremental reform on a wide front.

The Permanent Council's military department took over from the separate Crown and Lithuanian military commissions, reducing further the hetmans' authority. Over the next decade, a modest budget surplus allowed the small Crown and Lithuanian armies to grow from about 16,000 to 18,000 men. More significantly, these forces, especially the artillery, benefited from improved training and weaponry. The successors to the hussar and armoured formations of old were reorganised into the National Cavalry—the ancestor of the lancers made famous by the Napoleonic wars. There was, however, no commission for Tadeusz Kościuszko after his return from France in 1774. Having been refused the hand of his beloved Ludwika by her father, Lithuanian Field Hetman Józef Sosnowski, he returned to Paris. There, Benjamin Franklin, impressed by his mathematical skills, recommended him to George Washington. Kościuszko crossed the Atlantic.

Meanwhile, the justice department of the Permanent Council tried to improve the workings of the court system across the Commonwealth. The police department devoted itself to urban reform, sometimes encountering obstruction from town councillors and *starosta*s with judicial responsibilities in royal towns. However, the sejm of 1776 dealt a severe blow to the pride and prosperity of urban citizens in the Grand Duchy of Lithuania by removing municipal rights from all but eleven royal towns, claiming that they were more like villages. But this measure did not affect the more numerous private towns, and after the partition steady economic and demographic growth resumed. The 1790 tax returns indicate that up to half a million people lived

LITHUANIA

in seventy larger and 457 smaller urban settlements in the Grand Duchy.

Towns grew at varying rates. None approached Warsaw whose population quadrupled between the mid-1750s and early 1790s, reaching 115,000–120,000. Part of Warsaw's growth came from migration from the western reaches of Lithuania. Lithuanian towns also attracted migrants. Kaunas, where the number of households recorded for tax purposes more than doubled in fifteen years, attracted so many Lutherans from East Prussia that the elderly Catholic parish priest worried his flock would succumb to 'heresy'. At the other end of the Grand Duchy, Mazyr saw still faster growth, although the Radziwiłłs' town of Slutsk grew only slowly.

Most immigrants to Vilnius came from the nearer parts of Lithuania, but some arrived from the Polish Crown and even further afield. Few applied for urban citizenship, for which a master craftsman or trader's recommendation was needed.[23] Most of the expansion took place beyond the crumbling city walls in the suburbs, where two thirds of the 1,552 recorded possessions were located in 1790. However, fewer than half of the possessions remained under the jurisdiction of the city council. The rest were exempt *jurydyki* owned by nobles or the Catholic Church.[24] Magnate families maintained palatial residences on the principal streets, while moderately wealthy nobles built outlying manor houses with gardens and orchards. Closer to the walls were tanners' workshops. Nevertheless, the rise in the Jewish population within the walls was such as to prompt a court verdict in 1783, further relaxing restrictions on their residence. Historians have variously estimated the population, including the suburbs, at between 11,000 and 24,000.[25]

Upstream at Verkiai was the delightful palace of the bishop of Vilnius, Ignacy Massalski, designed by Wawrzyniec Gucewicz. This remarkable man was born to peasant parents near Panevėžys

A COMMONWEALTH OF TWO NATIONS?

as Laurynas Masiulis. He was educated by the local Piarists, before entering the seminary of the Priests of the Mission, where he was talented-spotted by the bishop, released from his clerical vocation, and sent abroad to study architecture. After his return he designed the austerely classical city hall and cathedral in Vilnius. The latter had collapsed in 1769 and the rebuilding was not completed until the end of the century. The bishop, addicted to cards, was perennially short of money. Ennobled in 1790, Gucewicz became a professor at the university in 1793. He died after falling from the scaffolding around the cathedral.

In contrast to the military department, the treasury department of the Permanent Council supervised the activities of the two existing treasury commissions that employed most of the Commonwealth's salaried officials. Thanks to the research of Ramunė Šmigelskytė-Stukienė and other scholars on felicitously preserved sources, more is known about the public servants of the Grand Duchy of Lithuania than about their counterparts in the Polish Crown. For example, the young aristocrat Michał Kleofas Ogiński proved a conscientious and effective treasury commissioner after 1786. He postulated changes to customs posts to minimise losses caused by Prussian manipulations of the treaties, and advocated a seaport near Palanga. This would be linked by a canal to the Nemunas, opening up much of the Grand Duchy to overseas trade.[26] Two major canals were begun to connect the Baltic and Black Seas. Stanisław August visited them in 1784. At the sejm held that year in Hrodna, he spoke about the dredged channels and elevated roads that enabled communication across the marshlands.

The limits of the possible are shown by the career of Antoni Tyzenhauz. This is known thanks to a thorough monograph researched and written in interwar Vilnius by Professor Stanisław Kościałkowski. The historian recreated his work in postwar exile in London, where it was posthumously published by subscription.[27] Hailing from a family of Livonian origin, Tyzenhauz became court treasurer of Lithuania in 1765, and soon multiplied the revenues from the royal domain estates. The dozens of manufactories he founded in and around Hrodna produced goods from textiles to carriages. He renovated small towns and founded new settlements, even in the depths of the Białowieża Forest. However, his over-reliance on serf labour, with greatly increased norms, led to low quality, poor productivity, and in the end to mass flight. Tyzenhauz also kept a tight grip on the lease-holding *szlachta* of the region. He managed royal patronage in the Grand Duchy so effectively that the King's party became Tyzenhauz's party. He could block further integration of Lithuania with the Polish Crown. However, resentment of Tyzenhauz's high-handed methods mounted. When he defaulted on the payments due to the King at the end of the 1770s, his position collapsed, and few of his hastily erected enterprises survived him.

From a long-term perspective, the most significant advances came in education. Pope Clement XIV's suppression of the Jesuits in 1773 threatened disaster, as the Society of Jesus ran more schools and colleges in the Commonwealth than all the other orders put together. Moreover, it had raised its pedagogical game, and Vilnius University again sparkled with intellectual activity. The brightest star in its firmament was Marcin Poczobut. Named astronomer royal in 1766, he later became a Fellow of the Royal Society in London. Ambassador Stackelberg allowed Stanisław August a consolation prize in the form of the Commission of National Education, established by the sejm in 1773 to take over Jesuit property and schools. Much of the property was looted by the same clique paid by the ambassador to procure the ratification of the partition treaties, but enough remained to sustain a network of schools. The commissioners and their helpers, many of them ex-Jesuits and Piarists, developed an enlightened curriculum and textbooks for all schools supervised by the commission.

A COMMONWEALTH OF TWO NATIONS?

Bishop Massalski, the first chairman, encouraged the gifted preachers in his circle, notably Michał Franciszek Karpowicz, to attack the abuses of serfdom. The bishop was an enthusiastic founder of parish schools that also taught girls, but he was hopeless with money and was soon replaced. The King's youngest brother, Michał Poniatowski, took charge of the commission and put the finances in order. As bishop of Płock from 1773 and archbishop of Gniezno from 1785, he established the model of an industrious episcopal administrator, enforcing higher standards of conduct, learning, and even hygiene via reams of regulations, in the spirit of the Catholic Enlightenment.

The post-Jesuit university in Vilnius was reorganised in 1780 into the Principal School of the Grand Duchy of Lithuania, analogously to Kraków University in the Polish Crown. These two academies were responsible for training teachers and inspecting schools. Thanks to the tact and moral authority of Rector Poczobut, the reform was implemented more smoothly in Lithuania than in the Polish Crown, where the abrasive Reverend Hugo Kołłątaj shook up Kraków University as visitor and rector. However, Poczobut had to leave his telescopes to deal with complaints from burghers, Jews, and officials assaulted by riotous students, from demoralised former Jesuit teachers, and from parents demanding the return of rote learning in Latin. Undeterred, the commission's schools and universities helped to form a generation of enlightened and patriotic citizens, ready to meet the challenges of the nineteenth century. It was, however, the alumni of the reformed Piarist and Jesuit schools of the 1750s and 1760s who set the tone of the transformative Great Sejm of 1788–92.

For those few glorious years, the limits of the possible seemed to vanish. The Russian Empire was fortuitously distracted. A few years after Catherine II's victorious peace with the Ottoman Empire in 1774, the strategic turn towards the south advocated by her partner in love and power, Grigorii Potemkin, brought about a diplomatic realignment. Catherine jilted Frederick II for the Austrian ruler, Emperor Joseph II. With Joseph's connivance she annexed the Crimea in 1783. As another Russo–Ottoman war loomed, Frederick II's nephew, King Frederick William II, violently pulled the anaemic Dutch Republic into a Triple Alliance with Great Britain. France, on the verge of bankruptcy after backing the American cause in the War of Independence, railed impotently.

Stanisław August seized an opportunity to greet Catherine II in May 1787 as she sailed down the Dnipro on her way to tour the Crimea. He proposed an unequal alliance, in which Polish–Lithuanian forces would fight alongside Russian armies in the forthcoming war. This would require fiscal and military expansion, deliverable only by a confederated sejm that could decide by majority vote. He hoped to assuage dented national pride. For years, Russian, Prussian, and Austrian troops had violated the truncated Commonwealth's borders at will, and carried away its natural and human resources. However, the empress kept him waiting for over a year before accepting a scaled-down plan. Meanwhile, a 'ferment of minds' left the political nation ripe for revolution.[28]

Within weeks of the sejm opening and forming itself into a parliamentary confederation on 7 October 1788, the King, the Russian ambassador, and even the aristocratic leaders of the opposition lost control of the situation. Elected envoys considered themselves the embodiment of the sovereign Commonwealth. The sejm exultantly acclaimed an army of 100,000 men (later scaled down to 65,000). It then imposed taxes on *starosta*s, the clergy, and the landed nobility (at 10 per cent of their permanent and secure income). To deny the King control of the enlarged army, the sejm replaced the military department of the Permanent Council with a joint military commission for the entire Commonwealth, having gained the assent of the Lithuanian envoys and senators. The sejm took direct control of foreign relations.

A COMMONWEALTH OF TWO NATIONS?

Encouraged by the skilful envoy of the King of Prussia, it jettisoned the Russian 'guarantee' of the Commonwealth's form of government (imposed in 1768 and adjusted in 1775 and 1776) by abolishing the Permanent Council in January 1789. This 'ruling sejm' prolonged itself indefinitely.

The reclaiming of sovereignty was linked to a revolution in political culture. Words and decisions now had consequences. The sejm's foremost orator was Kazimierz Nestor Sapieha. His mother Elżbieta had persuaded the king to appoint her teenage son to the lucrative post of general of the Lithuanian artillery. She was sister to Crown Grand Hetman Ksawery Branicki, who later married Potemkin's favourite niece and so joined the extended imperial family. Some feared that the mercurial and hedonistic Sapieha might be part of his uncle's double game between Russia and the Commonwealth. Confederations manifested the double composition of the Commonwealth, and so the parliamentary confederation established in October 1788 needed a marshal from the Grand Duchy, alongside a marshal from the Crown. The latter was the moderate, honest broker, Stanisław Małachowski, who actually presided over the sejm. Sapieha, chosen by 'the Lithuanian province' as its marshal, often held the assembly and its spectators spellbound with his improvised oratory. He rode the neo-Sarmatian wave, when in December 1788 he had his flowing locks ceremoniously trimmed by the Commonwealth's grandest dame. Izabela Czartoryska, the granddaughter of Michał Czartoryski and the wife of Adam Kazimierz, was a consummate orchestrator of political theatre. Later that day, Sapieha walked into the chamber clad in *kontusz* and sash.

Citizens (including burghers) could now freely debate what needed to be done. Floods of speeches, sermons, pamphlets, poems, and riddles surged out of Warsaw into provincial towns. Unlike in the past, most of these writings were printed. Clashing opinions were discussed, for example, during the signing of quar-

LITHUANIA

terly contracts, or at sejmiks that met to elect judges and local officials. One of the sejm's most successful reforms established elected local government bodies. The Civil-Military Commissions of Good Order linked provincial communities with the sejm and central government commissions in Warsaw. Lithuanian towns participated in the wider movement for urban reform, being motivated to restore the municipal rights removed from most royal towns in 1776. Vilnius, with its tribunal and university, had a lively political, social, cultural, and intellectual scene.

Stanisław August gradually regained trust among parliamentarians and public opinion, partly by accepting decisions he had warned against, such as the alliance with Prussia concluded in March 1790. That summer it became evident that his opponents would be unable to carry their preferred form of government through a divided sejm. Royalist orators, including the Lithuanian envoy Tadeusz Kościałkowski, stirred up middling nobles' grievances against the magnates. Stanisław August's candidates did well at the sejmiks that in November 1790 elected a second set of envoys to deliberate alongside those elected in 1788. These sejmiks also produced instructions that are perhaps the most complete expression of the values, opinions, and prejudices of the middling *szlachta*. Opposition to hereditary succession to the throne, grumbling about taxes and timewasting, calls for the return of the Jesuits, and hostility to pedagogical novelties and far-reaching social reforms echoed across the Commonwealth. A few sejmiks demanded the return of archives to the Grand Duchy of Lithuania. In December 1790, the leader of the aristocratic opposition, Ignacy Potocki, the court marshal of Lithuania, swallowed his pride and asked the King to draft the new constitution. Drafts went back and forth between them during the winter and spring, before they brought in the radical priest and pamphleteer Hugo Kołłątaj to add the finishing touches.

The first step to the new constitution was the passing of the law 'Our Free Royal Towns in the Territories of the Commonwealth' on 18 April 1791. This reform formally maintained the noble monopoly of lawmaking by limiting the burghers to elected plenipotentiaries who would advise the sejm in economic and urban matters. But the law granted townsmen extensive self-government and individual rights, including the old noble privilege of immunity from incarceration without trial. Provisions for hundreds of burghers to be ennobled were intended to break down barriers between them and the *szlachta*—to whom urban occupations were opened. And many nobles did take urban citizenship. After it was pointed out in debates by envoys from Greater Poland and the Grand Duchy of Lithuania that preference for Catholics in municipal office would ignore confessional realities and undermine the goal of encouraging immigration, at Sapieha's suggestion the law made no mention of religion. This was a notable victory for advocates of wider religious toleration.

Three weeks later, on 3 May 1791, the 'Law on Government' was sprung on the sejm. The previous evening, about eighty reliable senators and envoys had approved a final draft. After an emotional debate, all but a handful of parliamentarians swore fidelity to the new constitution. Two days later, this unorthodox procedure was rectified by the sejm's unanimous endorsement of the 'Law on Government' and its formal inscription into the law books. This was a constitution in the older sense of the word—a statute agreed by the sejm—but also in the newer sense. Like the constitution of the United States of America, ratified in 1788, it was a framework for the form of government, the relationship between citizens and government, and the shared values of the polity. After the preamble, which explains the need to seize the moment, the constitution deals with religion and the social order, introducing an inclusive concept of the nation. It then sets out the relationship between the nation and its form of government. It concludes with a declaration about propagation and enforcement.

Articles five through eight, devoted to the form of government, balanced the sovereignty of the nation with an asymmetrical division of the legislative, executive, and judicial powers. Article six abolished the *liberum veto* and future confederations, weakened the senate, declared elected envoys 'representatives of the entire nation' and therefore unbound by instructions, applying the principle enunciated by Edmund Burke in Great Britain. Article seven constrained the monarch, especially after the succession of Frederick Augustus, the Elector of Saxony (the grandson of Augustus III) whose sole daughter and her future husband were to found a new dynasty. At the same time, the King headed the executive power under the supervision of the legislature. Article eight provided for the election of judges at sejmiks.

The often archaic-sounding language is in fact open-ended and didactic. This is particularly apparent in the preamble and first four articles, devoted respectively to religion, the nobility, the towns, and the peasants. Although the Roman Catholic faith was reassuringly declared the national and dominant religion, with conversion to other religions prohibited, no penalty was (yet) specified for 'apostasy'. Moreover, religious freedom and security were assured to *all* people of *all* faiths, not just members of tolerated confessions. On the face of it, the second article of the constitution flattered nobles and confirmed their ancestral privileges. Yet its concept of liberty emphasised individuals' security and property, subtly preparing the ground for Kołłątaj's vision of a nineteenth-century nation, in which active citizenship would be based on property and education, rather than birth. The third article incorporated the law on towns as a whole, and presented the burghers to the *szlachta* as allies in the cause of liberty. The fourth article declared 'Peasants and villagers' the most numerous and useful part of the nation under the protection of law and government. This article has often been criticised for offering the peasants only warm words, but its provision for any immigrant into the 'territories of the Commonwealth', including people who had previously left, to enjoy the freedom

A COMMONWEALTH OF TWO NATIONS?

to settle in town or country and to contract for their labour, would surely have finished off serfdom within a generation. However, this would not happen immediately, as units of the Lithuanian army forcibly reminded peasants who refused to perform labour services that summer.

The predominant references to the community were 'the nation', 'Poland', 'the Fatherland', and 'the country'. Stanisław August and Kołłątaj doubtless intended these terms to help the Polish nation evolve from a community of noble citizens to a community of all the inhabitants of the country. The constitution's reticence in referring to the Commonwealth (*Rzeczpospolita*, mentioned just twice) and the Grand Duchy of Lithuania (restricted to the royal titulature, privileges issued by Grand Duke Vytautas, and one reference in the conclusory declaration) did not go unnoticed. A few critics alleged that a free republic had been transformed into a monarchy. Later legislation, which detailed the workings of the legislative, executive, and judicial organs, extended the restrictions on the royal prerogative and introduced qualified, rather than simple majority voting for the most important laws and new taxes. These later laws were also worded more traditionally, referring to, for example, 'the Most Serene Estates of the Commonwealth'.

Contrary to what was long asserted in Lithuanian and Polish textbooks, the Constitution of 3 May did not end the separate statehood of the Grand Duchy of Lithuania by merging it into Poland. But it did leave the question open. As the doyen of twentieth-century Lithuanian historians, Adolfas Šapoka, noticed just before the Second World War,[29] the doubts were resolved during the debates over a new joint treasury commission in October 1791. Konstanty Plater, castellan of Trakai, distilled the essence of the Lithuanian case: 'in the circumstances of the union, Lithuania cannot be considered as a province with regard to a single body, but as one nation with regard to another'.[30] On

20 October, the sejm unanimously agreed a solemn law, to be considered part of the act of union. This 'Mutual Pledge of the Two Nations' guaranteed parity in current and future executive organs, and in the respective hierarchies of ministers and officials. As its title suggests, it enshrined the principle that 'two nations' (or at least a 'double nation'), rather than three equal provinces, comprised the Commonwealth. That said, the text also refers to 'our shared fatherland, the Polish Commonwealth'. The concepts of Poland and Lithuania were not mutually exclusive, and the name of the state was not formally fixed.[31] The law establishing the joint commission was entitled 'The Treasury Commission of the Commonwealth of the Two Nations' (*Komissya skarbowa Rzeczypospolitey Oboyga Narodów*). This is an extraordinarily rare usage in an official document of the term now generally used in Lithuanian to refer to the Commonwealth: *Abiejų Tautų Respublika*.

This reassuring turn in legislation was combined with a campaign to persuade the *szlachta* of the merits of the new constitution. Particularly eloquent were the sermons preached by Karpowicz in Hrodna, Vilnius, and to his own sejmik at Prienai in February 1792. The assembled nobles swore a strongly worded oath to defend the constitution. In effect, they participated in a referendum. Across the Commonwealth, not a single sejmik criticised the constitution, although eight passed over it in silence. Seventy sejmiks (90 per cent) either voted thanks, made a solemn pledge, or swore an oath. The *szlachta*'s endorsement was warmer in Lithuania than in the Polish Crown. No fewer than twenty-seven of the thirty-two Lithuanian sejmiks swore an oath—the highest form of support—and not one remained silent. Suggested explanations include a stronger reflex of deference to the monarch among Lithuanian nobles. Without doubt, the constitution entered the national *sacrum*.

The better the Commonwealth's future prospects, the more intolerable they became for the tsaritsa. On hearing the news of

A COMMONWEALTH OF TWO NATIONS?

the constitution, Catherine II began to plan either to return the Commonwealth to its former subservience, or to destroy it altogether. Peace with the Ottoman Empire freed her hands. By the start of 1792, she had gathered about two dozen malcontents who obediently supplicated her armed intervention to restore their liberty. The leaders in the Polish Crown were the Commonwealth's richest magnate, Szczęsny Potocki, and the two Crown hetmans: Ksawery Branicki and Seweryn Rzewuski. They formed a confederation in St Petersburg at the end of April 1792, but postdated the act to 14 May, supposedly in Potocki's Ukrainian border town of Torhovytsia, better known by its Polish name—Targowica. '*Targowica!*' is now a Polish synonym for treason, and so it functions in Mickiewicz's *Pan Tadeusz*. However, the Grand Duchy of Lithuania was to be confederated separately, first locally and then centrally. In practice, only a few district confederations preceded the General Confederation of the Grand Duchy of Lithuania formed in Vilnius on 25 June 1792, as Šmigelskytė-Stukienė has shown.[32] The real leaders of the Lithuanian confederation were Szymon Kossakowski, now a lieutenant-general in Russian service, and his brother Józef, the bishop of Livonia. Their incomes had never matched their ambitions.

Two Russian armies, totalling 98,000 men, invaded the Commonwealth on 18 May 1792. Against them were mustered about 45,000 soldiers able to fight. The commander of the Lithuanian army was Ludwig of Württemberg, son-in-law to Izabela and Adam Kazimierz Czartoryski. Loyal to his uncle, the King of Prussia, who refused to honour his alliance with the Commonwealth, the prince feigned illness, paralysing the army for the first few days of the campaign in the Grand Duchy. Even after his dismissal, things did not improve, as the main Lithuanian corps broke under cannon-fire at Mir and retreated in disorder. However, the fighting spirit stiffened in July, with hard fighting along the Neman and Bug. The campaign in the Polish Crown, where larger forces were engaged on both sides, went better, but the result was similar: a retreat to the line of the Bug.

Kościuszko commanded the rearguard of the Crown army. After the War of American Independence, he came home in 1784 with an excellent reputation as a military engineer, but little money or prospects. For several years he struggled to run the modest family estate at Siakhnovichy. Convinced that all humans were fundamentally equal, he halved the serfs' labour services and abolished floggings. He had also befriended native Americans and African Americans, and in his testament left his American backpay for the emancipation and education of Thomas Jefferson's slaves. Alas, Jefferson failed to execute his friend's will. Meanwhile, in 1789, the expansion of the Commonwealth's armies finally brought Kościuszko a major-general's commission. Although he would have preferred to serve in the Lithuanian army, he was posted first to the Greater Poland division, and then to the principal Crown corps in Ukraine. At Dubienka on the River Bug on 18 July, his division held its fortified positions against a larger Russian force, inflicting severe casualties, until the danger of being outflanked prompted a controlled retreat towards Warsaw.

The result of this undeclared war of aggression was still in doubt when Stanisław August, supported by most ministers present in Warsaw, bowed to the empress's ultimatum on 23 July. He ordered the Crown and Lithuanian armies to cease fire and dislocate to peacetime quarters further west. Kościuszko and other senior officers resigned in protest and went into exile in Saxony. The King's plan was to take over the counter-revolutionary confederations, and thereby save some of the reforms of the Great Sejm. Many nobles followed his example and joined the local confederations 'around the king'. But his gambit failed: the confederates and their Russian backers pitilessly exposed the weakness of his position.

A COMMONWEALTH OF TWO NATIONS?

Confederate corruption and coercion assumed pathological dimensions in Lithuania. The brothers Kossakowski tried to build a satrapy of their own, possibly in a separate union with Russia. With Austria and Prussia tied up in a war with revolutionary France, Catherine II picked her moment. Having learned her logistical lessons, she annexed vast swathes of strategically and economically vital territory in what is now central Ukraine and Belarus. A commemorative medal showed the lands annexed in the first and second partitions and proclaimed that she had recovered what had once been lost. Prussia was allowed to take the remaining parts of Greater Poland and the cities of Gdańsk and Toruń. Austria got nothing. The Commonwealth was left as an oddly shaped rump, but the old Lithuanian heartlands remained.

Once again, the Commonwealth had to ratify the partition treaties. Russian troops ensured these were rammed through the last sejm of all, held in Hrodna in the summer and autumn of 1793. The new form of government laid bare the state's subjection to Russia. The Commonwealth could survive only as long as it suited the empress. However, it seems unlikely she wanted General Otto Igelström, her plenipotentiary in Warsaw, to provoke an uprising that might provide a pretext to dismember Poland–Lithuania entirely. Her best units were on the Ottoman frontier when Kościuszko proclaimed the insurrection in Kraków in March 1794, and it was not until July that they could march against the insurgents.

Before the Russian army crushed the uprising, the Commonwealth once more demonstrated its vigour and potential. The contribution of peasant scythe-men to Kościuszko's early victory over the Russians at the battle of Racławice, the proclamation he issued from the camp at Połaniec on 7 May 1794, reducing the burdens of serfdom, and Warsaw's withstanding of a two-month Prussian siege, are all well known to Poles. Yet the insurrection in the Grand Duchy of Lithuania was more radical than that in the Polish Crown. Although the insurrection was first proclaimed at Šiauliai on 16 April in relatively traditional terms, radical conspirators such as Major-General Jakub Jasiński soon set the tone. Vilnans rose up and expelled a large Russian garrison on 23–24 April. On 25 April, Szymon Kossakowski, discovered hiding behind a chimney during the fighting, was tried for treason and hanged in front of the city hall.

The Supreme Governing Council of Lithuania took charge, attending to the challenges of recruiting, provisioning, arming, and motivating the insurgent forces. It issued some of its proclamations in Lithuanian, Ruthenian, and Latvian, while the Constitution of 3 May and some of Karpowicz's sermons were also translated into Lithuanian. These were probably the earliest political, as opposed to strictly religious texts to be written in the language. Somewhat ironically, while Jasiński, a Crown Pole, led the 'Lithuanian nation' in arms, Kościuszko, a native of the Grand Duchy, reined in its autonomy and centralised decision-making in Warsaw.

The Lithuanian insurrection's successes included its spread to Courland at the end of June 1794. Latvian-speaking serfs turned on their German-speaking lords with sanguinary relish. On 29 July, the modest force commanded by Major-General Romuald Giedroyć, composed mostly of peasant scythe-men, put a larger Russian army to flight at Saločiai, close to the border with Courland. A little earlier, on 23–24 July, the garrison and people of Vilnius repelled Russian attempts to storm the city. However, when the Russians returned on 11–12 August, Lieutenant-General Antoni Chlewiński capitulated, amidst accusations of treason. The remaining Lithuanian forces retreated towards Warsaw, where most of them, including Jasiński, were cut down defending the suburb of Praga on the foggy morning of 4 November. General Aleksandr Suvorov's army then butchered the mostly Jewish civilian population. Among those who sur-

A COMMONWEALTH OF TWO NATIONS?

vived to fight again was Colonel Berek Joselewicz, a horse trader from Samogitia, who formed and led a religiously observant Jewish militia unit. Terrified Warsaw surrendered the following day. Kościuszko himself had already been defeated, wounded, and captured at Maciejowice on 10 October. When released from captivity in St Petersburg, his travels took in Sweden, England, America, France, Austria, and Switzerland, but he didn't return home alive.

The Russian army re-occupied the Grand Duchy of Lithuania and enforced oaths of loyalty from the *szlachta*, anticipating the Commonwealth's demise. Catherine II adjudicated the rival Prussian and Austrian claims and dictated the terms of the partition treaty signed in St Petersburg on 24 October 1795. The Russian Empire annexed Courland, western Volhynia, and most of the remaining territories of the Grand Duchy of Lithuania. The exception were the lands south and west of the River Nemunas that went to Prussia.

Stanisław August's last act as Grand Duke of Lithuania was to abdicate, on the empress's terms rather than his own, on 25 November 1795. Until this point, he could reasonably argue that he had always chosen what he had judged to be the lesser evil for his country. No longer. The ex-king died in comfortable captivity in St Petersburg in 1798, and was buried there. However, the Soviet authorities returned his coffin to the interwar Polish state in 1938. He was interred in the church at his birthplace, Voŭchin, but the postwar frontier shift marooned the royal remains on the Soviet side. By the time the Polish regime decided to reclaim them in 1988, only fragments of the Commonwealth's last monarch's robes and insignia were left. These were reburied in Warsaw's cathedral in 1995.

The unflagging controversies over the intentions and actions of the last Grand Duke of Lithuania should not obscure the essential point about his reign. In the most unpromising circumstances, the Polish–Lithuanian Commonwealth demonstrated its underlying civic strength, and its ability to renew itself—economically, socially, culturally, intellectually, and in the end, politically. It was 'not a failed state [...], put out of its anarchic misery by its better governed neighbours',[33] but a going concern. It was for this very reason that the neighbouring monarchs eliminated this demographic, geopolitical, and ideological threat to their expansionist and absolutist states. We cannot be certain how the Commonwealth would have evolved, had it by some miracle survived the revolutionary and Napoleonic turmoil and dropped a safe anchor in Europe's legitimist harbour after 1815. It would not have been immune to the forces of nationalism. What we can say is that by 1792, the Commonwealth was swiftly travelling towards the inclusion of all its inhabitants in a flourishing civic community. Moreover, in the last few years before the third partition, the long drift towards a Polish Commonwealth with three provinces was reversed. The Commonwealth of the Two Nations went down fighting.

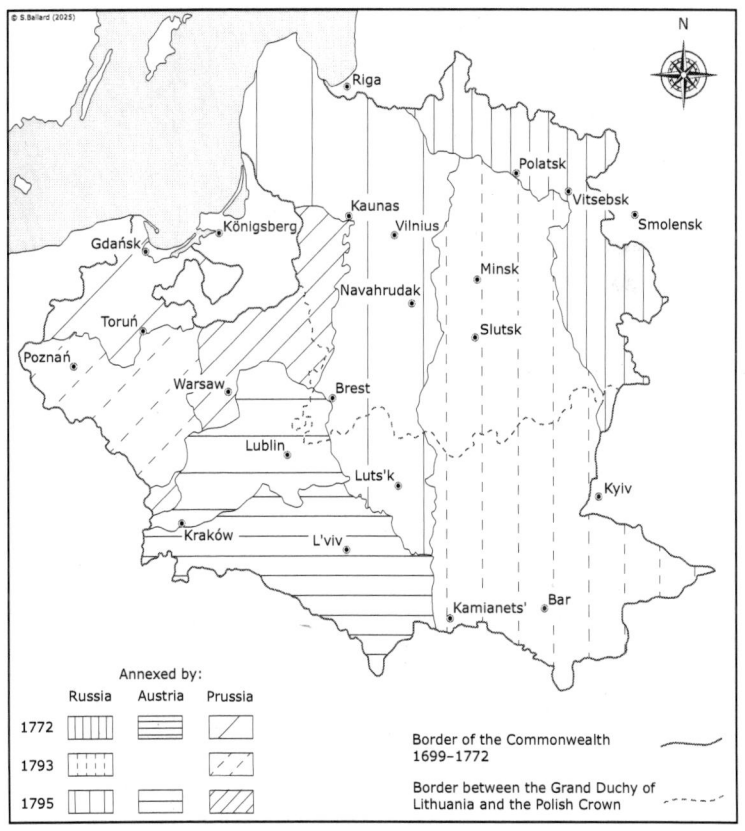

Map 5: The partitions of the Commonwealth, 1772–95

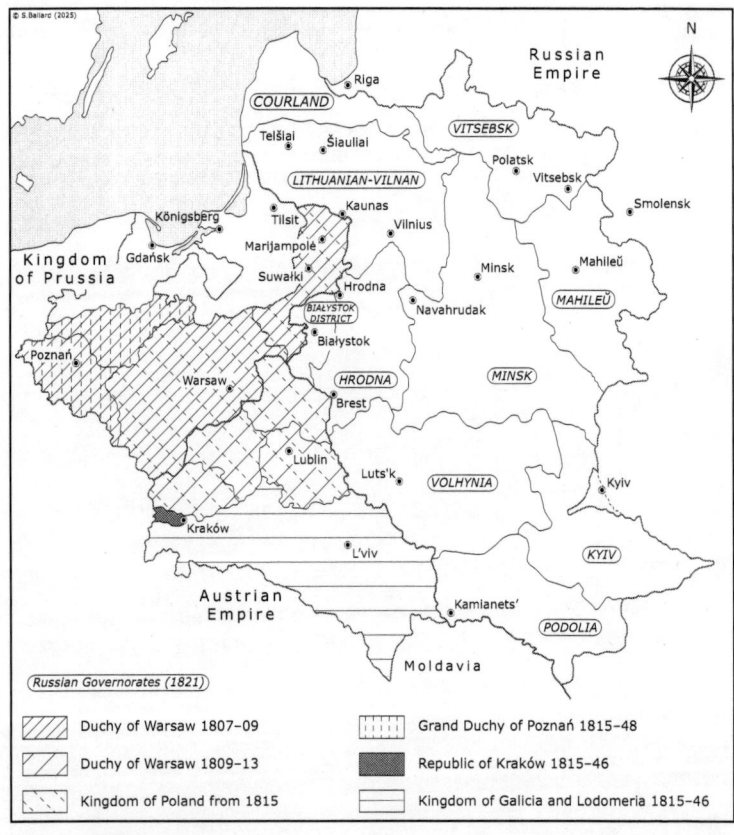

Map 6: The lands of the former Polish–Lithuanian Commonwealth, 1795–1846

4

UNDER IMPERIAL RULE

(1795–1914)

The Grand Duchy of Lithuania lived on as memory and myth. A handful of its self-proclaimed 'last citizens' even lived into the twenty-first century. Nevertheless, as the decades passed, implacable political, economic, and demographic processes wrought profound changes on the lands and peoples of the former Polish–Lithuanian Commonwealth. In the territories annexed by the Russian Empire, policies including military conscription, taxation, policing, surveillance, schooling, and infrastructure slowly and unevenly altered communities, often with unintended consequences. 'Modernisation' proceeded faster and further in the Kingdom of Prussia, which in 1871 became the dominant part of the new German Empire. Here, consequences were more predictable: almost all of the remaining Lithuanian-speaking population of Lithuania minor in East Prussia assimilated into the German-speaking population. The Grand Duchy of Lithuania's territories on the left bank of the River Nemunas became part of 'New East Prussia', and then of the Duchy of Warsaw created by Napoleon in 1807, before becoming the north-eastern 'panhandle' of the

LITHUANIA

Kingdom of Poland established by the Congress of Vienna in 1815. This 'Congress Kingdom' was subjected to the Russian emperors, but throughout the following century it was governed differently from the lands directly incorporated into their empire. Most of the territories of the Grand Duchy of Lithuania became Russian imperial governorates (*guberniie*). District boundaries were largely unaffected. For several decades, the core lands of the former Grand Duchy formed the Lithuanian–Vilnan and Hrodna (Grodno) governorates. Further east were the Belarusian governorates of Minsk, Mahileŭ (Mogilev), and Vitsebsk (Vitebsk). Informally, the name of Lithuania lasted much longer, even in Russian usage.

Both the frontier with Prussia and the differing experiences of tsarist autocracy on the two banks of the River Nemunas affected the formation of the modern, ethno-linguistic Lithuanian nation. So did other national movements. By the beginning of the twentieth century, four increasingly competitive, but socially inclusive and self-consciously 'modern' national movements had emerged in the former Grand Duchy of Lithuania: Poles, Lithuanians, Belarusians, and Jews. Rival national activists endeavoured to 'awaken' national consciousness among the rural and urban populations. Sometimes these 'handsome princes' raced to plant the first kiss on the same 'sleeping beauties', and then jealously to guard them. In broad outline, the Lithuanian case fits the Czech scholar Miroslav Hroch's three-stage model for 'smaller European nations' during the nineteenth and early twentieth centuries: enthusiasts' study of folklore and language (A) laid the foundations for a historicised and politicised national cause (B), which grew into a mass political and social movement (C).[1] However, it needs qualifying: the promotion of national culture has never ceased to be central to Lithuanian nationalism. Most nobles and post-noble urban professionals long considered themselves both Polish and Lithuanian, and saw no reason to choose between their overlapping identities. And the staunchest modern Lithuanian nationalists spoke and wrote Polish fluently.

These rival nation-building programmes clashed with the Russian imperial state that sought to divide and rule its subject peoples. It also tried to impose on them varying policies of 'Russification', with varying degrees of success. The Russian Empire could not match the state-driven nation-building projects of later nineteenth-century France, Great Britain, or Italy. Lithuanian national activists feared for the fate of the Lithuanian language, but it never approached the near-extinction experienced by most of the Celtic and Gaelic languages. Different again were the symbiotic relationships between multiple national movements and the overtly multinational state in the Habsburg monarchy (albeit after 1867 only in its 'Austrian' half). There would, however, be some similarities to the situations of Slovaks, Romanians, and Serbs whom the Kingdom of Hungary tried to 'Magyarise', but with inadequate resources.

The gradual parting of the ways between the anti-Russian national causes began after the failure of the 1863–64 uprising. This insurgency was the last serious attempt to restore the Polish–Lithuanian Commonwealth (or rather, a vision of what it could have become). Henceforth the Grand Duchy of Lithuania became either a fading object of nostalgia, or a multinational, multilingual, and multicultural ideal—a 'Switzerland'—espoused by an eloquent minority of intellectuals, most of them well born and well to do. While these Polonophone 'homelanders' (*krajowcy*) have in recent decades been presented as 'a refreshing alternative to the chauvinistic and murderous "solutions" of the twentieth century', they nuance rather than transform the broader picture.[2] The tsarist regime's repressive policies varied in intensity across time and space, but they could never be ignored. The concessions it made during and after the 1905 revolutions across the Russian Empire enabled the Lithuanian, Polish, and—

LITHUANIA

to a lesser extent—Belarusian and Jewish national movements to compete vigorously in public life, accelerating their development and mutual estrangement. Nonetheless, full articulation of their incompatible goals remained beyond the horizon until the First World War.

i. *Romantic Lithuania*

The partitioning powers tried to stem the rising tide of social mobility that marked the last years of the Commonwealth. The Prussian kingdom sought to anchor in the rule of law a rigid society, ordered by estate. A decade of peace and high grain prices after 1795 brought prosperity to wealthy landowners, but pettifogging officialdom irked nobles and burghers alike. They were no longer self-governing citizens, but highly regulated, highly taxed subjects. Under Prussian rule, peasants might more easily appeal against their lords to the state courts, but they were also liable to military conscription. No similar trade-off applied to peasants in the Russian Empire, except for the Baltic provinces of Livonia and Estonia. Here, reforms in 1804–05 and 1816–19 limited and then abolished personal serfdom, laying early social foundations for the Latvian and Estonian national movements. However, these reforms did not apply to the mostly Latgalian-speaking and Catholic peasants of former Polish–Lithuanian Livonia, which was part of the governorate of Vitsebsk. With the partial exception of Courland, in the lands annexed by Russia from the Commonwealth, labour services rose, the burden of taxation and the risk of impressment into the army multiplied, and serfs became more dependent on their masters and mistresses. Complainants to the state authorities were punished with hard labour. The situations and status of the peasants of the empire's Lithuanian lands varied, but the trends were unfavourable. Most plots shrank, and the proportion of personally free

UNDER IMPERIAL RULE

peasants fell from 28 per cent in 1795 to fewer than 6 per cent in 1858.[3] The tsarist regime stationed troops along the Prussian border to deter runaways and deserters. It also guarded the frontier with the Duchy of Warsaw, where the Napoleonic reforms brought peasants personal freedom, although not possession of the land they farmed.

The tighter manorial system satisfied most noble landowners in the territories annexed by the Russian Empire. Momentum for social reform was lost with the sovereign Commonwealth. Few nobles tried to abolish personal serfdom and commute labour services to cash rents in their own estates. Hereditary privileges, including exemption from the poll tax, consoled most nobles. They could pursue careers in the civil administration, army, and navy. When Catherine II's son Paul I (reigned 1796–1801) ended the military occupation of the Lithuanian and Belarusian lands, he restored the familiar district courts and sejmiks, with their elected judges and officials. Most of the Third Lithuanian Statute continued in force as the law of the land. Paul's idealistic son Alexander I (reigned 1801–25) extended his father's amnesty for the insurgents of 1794 to those who had emigrated. Alexander not only listened to the liberal ideas of Prince Adam Jerzy Czartoryski, who had been sent to St Petersburg to recover his family's confiscated estates, but even made his friend de facto foreign minister between 1804 and 1806. Czartoryski's hostility to Napoleon was part of his vision of a just and peaceful European order, which included a restored Polish–Lithuanian state under Alexander I.

These two tsars' warm support of religion encompassed the Catholic Church, albeit subjected to their own authority at the expense of the pope's. They had a loyal and energetic partner in Archbishop Stanisław Siestrzeńcewicz. Born into the Calvinist *szlachta* of the Vaŭkavysk district, he was educated in Berlin and Königsberg and became a pastor before converting to Catholicism and attaching himself to Bishop Ignacy Massalski. Catherine II had on her own authority made him head of all Catholics of all rites in her empire. Rome acquiesced in 1783. In other respects, the Catholic clergy, especially plump prelates amply cushioned by multiple benefices, had little cause for complaint. The empress refused to acknowledge the papal suppression of the Society of Jesus, and the grateful Jesuits served her empire as educators. For a generation the Jesuit college at Polatsk flourished. Even the pressure on Uniates to 'return' to Russian Orthodoxy eased for a generation.

As long as taxes were paid, recruits provided, violent disorder avoided (or at least covered up), and bribes paid to higher-level Russian officials, the imperial state generally left local affairs to the *szlachta*. Although the tsarist regime challenged the status of those numerous nobles who owned little or no land, it lacked the bureaucratic resources to deal with them. For several decades, those who fell between the legal categories of landowning nobles and personally free peasants were largely left alone. Villages populated entirely by serf-less noble families were still common in Samogitia and the hinterland of Hrodna. The inhabitants of small towns continued to live, trade, gossip, and worship according to familiar rhythms. For these decades were the heyday of the *shtetl*—the word for small town in Yiddish.

The first partition of the Commonwealth brought the Russian Empire a large Jewish population. Like other non-noble populations, Jews faced restrictions on their mobility, but only in the 1790s were they formally forbidden to move deeper into the empire, thereby creating the so-called Pale of Permanent Jewish Settlement. Its exact boundaries took shape gradually, but in effect they enclosed the lands annexed from the Polish–Lithuanian Commonwealth, the Cossack Hetmanate, and the Crimean Tatars. Catherine II probably intended to shield Russian merchants from competition. Among officials, phobias that had largely barred Jews from Muscovy for centuries merged with Enlightenment-era convictions that these 'parasitical' and 'superstitious' people required reform in order to turn them into 'useful subjects'. Several decisions, whether to expel Jews from the countryside or to transform many of them into farmers and workers, proved impracticable and were reversed, in part through lobbying at the imperial court. As long as the poll tax (doubled in return for dispensation from military service) and other levies were paid, Jewish communities experienced benign neglect. Taverns leased to Jews remained a familiar feature of the landscape. What did change was the number of Jews in the empire. The Jewish population more than doubled after 1795, reaching about 1.2 million in 1820.[4] These figures are estimates, because as late as 1840 the state authorities believed that at least a quarter of Jews remained unregistered.

Such was the slow-moving world of the young Adam Mickiewicz. Poland's greatest bard was born in 1798 in Navahrudak, into a minor noble family of mixed Ruthenian, Lithuanian, and possibly Jewish (Frankist) descent. He grew up amidst relatives and neighbours who cultivated ancestral virtues. Then in the summer of 1812, the irruption into these backwaters of Napoleon's *Grande Armée* looked set to change almost everything. Over two decades later, Mickiewicz created his masterpiece, the epic poem *Pan Tadeusz* (1834). With affectionate humour he evoked the customs and climate, the flora and fauna, and the characters and quarrels of his homeland—not least the tavern leased by Jankiel. This 'honest Jew' both spied for the Polish cause and evoked it on the dulcimer. The exiled poet recalled the joy and hopes aroused by the arrival of Polish soldiers and the restoration of the Polish–Lithuanian union. He even imagined the emancipation, enfranchisement, and endowment with land of the local serfs by the eponymous hero (named after Kościuszko) and his high-born fiancée Zosia. But the realities of 1812 were harsher than the myth.

LITHUANIA

The campaign began glamorously. Napoleon's main army crossed the River Nemunas near Kaunas on 24 and 25 June 1812 ('Napoleon's Hill' offers a splendid view). He entered Vilnius on 28 June, just two days after Alexander I had hosted a glittering ball there (some ladies danced with two emperors within a week). Napoleon stayed a fortnight while he pondered his options. His goal—to force Alexander back into the Continental System designed to bankrupt Great Britain—was incompatible with his vague promises to restore Poland. From a military perspective, most of the Commonwealth could have been re-established in 1812, especially if the *Grande Armée* had not marched on past Smolensk, but the Russian Empire would not have accepted peace on such terms. To maintain a restored Poland–Lithuania, the French Empire would have been drawn into a war in the east as intractable as the 'Spanish ulcer' in the west. Resources would have flowed in the wrong direction. Napoleon promised and hinted just enough in Warsaw and Vilnius to rally many Lithuanian nobles and burghers to his cause. The Lithuanian Government Commissioners, mostly wealthy landowners who had held office in the last years of the Commonwealth, did their best to organise supplies and recruits. Questions about the future relationship of the Polish Crown and the Grand Duchy of Lithuania remained unanswered. Napoleon's studied ambiguity also extended to social questions. He would not risk chaos by proclaiming an end to serfdom.

At over 600,000 men, the *Grande Armée* was the largest force yet mustered in Europe. Two thirds came from the engorged French Empire, which stretched through the Low Countries to the northern fringes of Germany, as well as half-way down Italy, and even into Illyria. The next largest contingent, almost 100,000 soldiers, was Polish. However, such a host lacked the manoeuvrability that was a hallmark of Bonaparte's early triumphs. The roads were inadequate for maintaining communication or deliv-

UNDER IMPERIAL RULE

ering supplies. Most rivers had to be forded. The territory between the Rivers Nemunas and Dniapro, much of it forest or marsh, could not provision such a host. Foraging degenerated into pillage, as hungry soldiers ransacked manors, villages, and small towns, and some stooped to rapine and murder. Peasants vanished into the woods at the approach of either army. Troops usually treated Jewish traders—often the only people who could obtain food and drink for them—with contempt. The army, alternately drenched by thunderstorms and scorched by the sun, caked in mud and choked by dust, and tormented by mosquitoes, horseflies, ticks, and wasps, lost many more men and beasts to disease and exhaustion than in fighting the retreating Russians. But the fittest of the *Grande Armée* survived the marches and the bloody battlefield of Borodino, and entered Moscow on 14 September 1812.

Five weeks later, about 95,000 soldiers, accompanied by about half as many civilians, left Moscow. But winter came early. The retreating army narrowly escaped destruction while crossing the icy River Biarezina. As temperatures plummeted, the survivors staggered back into Vilnius between 7 and 9 December. Tens of thousands of frostbitten men at the limits of endurance could go no further when ordered to resume the retreat. Napoleon himself had gone on ahead. As the last units of the *Grande Armée* recrossed the Nemunas, most of those left behind were dying in captivity, or in the makeshift monastic hospitals of Vilnius. One pit excavated in 2002 yielded the remains of about 3,000 soldiers and a few dozen women. Analyses revealed the ravages of typhus, carried by lice. The reburial of many soldiers with full military honours at the Antakalnis Cemetery manifested Franco–Lithuanian solidarity, obscuring the probability that about half of the dead were not French at all.

Bountiful harvests in 1813 and 1814 helped the Lithuanian and Belarusian lands to recover from the wartime devastation. The tsar forgave nobles who had backed Napoleon and life

LITHUANIA

returned to normal. The Vienna treaties not only approved Alexander's new title of King of Poland, but also allowed him the possibility of uniting the lands Russia had taken from the Commonwealth in 1772, 1793, and 1795 with his diminutive Polish kingdom. Hopes rose that Lithuania might share the constitutional form of government on the other bank of the River Nemunas. The Vilnan social and cultural scene flourished. Mickiewicz debuted in the *Vilnan Weekly* (*Tygodnik Wileński*) founded by the charismatic historian and democrat, Joachim Lelewel. The most prominent publisher was Józef Zawadzki. Alongside Polish-language books and periodicals, his firm also published some works in Lithuanian.

Nowhere did the future seem more luminous than at the Imperial University of Vilnius. Since its reform in 1803, the university had been the hub of a vast educational district encompassing the lands of the former Commonwealth under direct Russian rule. The district's curator, Adam Jerzy Czartoryski, presided over an expanding system of Polish-language schools. The mostly noble pupils followed an enlightened curriculum that drew on that of the Commission of National Education. In the Lithuanian-speaking areas, especially in Samogitia, some of the teaching in the first few classes was in Lithuanian. Here as many as a third of the pupils of some schools came from peasant families. Many poorer nobles remained bilingual in Polish and in Samogitian dialect. Within the Lithuanian governorates, seventy secondary schools with almost 350 teachers and over 10,000 pupils in 1803 grew to 430 schools, almost 1,000 teachers, and over 21,000 pupils in 1820.[5] By the end of Alexander I's reign, more of his subjects could read and write in Polish than could read and write in Russian.

Jan Śniadecki was rector of Vilnius University between 1807 and 1815. Like his predecessor and fellow astronomer Marcin Poczobut, he recruited talented professors and students. It would help the university's cause that the rector praised Alexander's munificence even when welcoming Napoleon in 1812. In 1816, Polish replaced Latin as the principal language of instruction. A proposal for a chair in the Lithuanian language was discussed but rejected in 1822. The venerable Śniadecki stood on one side of a generational divide between the 'classics' and the 'romantics'. Mickiewicz satirised him just as William Blake caricatured Isaac Newton: obsessed with what he could discern through the cold glass of his lens, but insensible of his beating heart. The youthful poet belonged to two secret student societies: the Philomaths (lovers of knowledge) and the Philarets (lovers of virtue). Their causes included projects for the emancipation and education of the enserfed peasantry.

The 'liberal' Alexander is often contrasted with his martinet younger brother Nicholas I, who succeeded him in 1825. Around 1820, however, Alexander became more autocratic. Not only did he reject proposals for emancipating the serfs, but he also closed down the Jesuits and the Freemasons. In 1823, Czartoryski had to resign and some of the university's professors were dismissed, including Lelewel. Rumours of conspiracies led to arrests, interrogations, and trials of students. Mickiewicz was among twenty young men exiled into the depths of the Russian Empire. By later standards he got off lightly. His five years in Moscow and St Petersburg, where he befriended Aleksandr Pushkin, stimulated his art. In 1828, Mickiewicz published the subversive poem *Konrad Wallenrod*, which escaped censorship. It told of how a pagan Lithuanian boy captured by the Teutonic Knights rose to lead them (the historical Konrad von Wallenrode was grand master in 1391–93). After a minstrel had awakened him to his true heritage, Wallenrod deliberately led the Order to defeat. The questionable ethics of 'Wallenrodism' have since provoked controversy in both Lithuania and Poland. The poem even inspired Amilcare Ponchielli's opera *I Lituani* (*The Lithuanians*), staged in Kaunas in 2020.

LITHUANIA

Mickiewicz had earlier won renown with *Grażyna*, written while a schoolmaster in Kaunas in 1822–23. This classically structured epic poem recast themes from Homer's *Iliad* as a 'Lithuanian tale' set in the times of Grand Duke Vytautas. It was supposedly recreated from a surviving manuscript and the memories of the people of his own Navahrudak district. The poet invented the name of its heroine: *graži* in Lithuanian is the feminine form of 'beautiful', and Gražina remains a moderately popular Lithuanian name to this day. The beautiful, tall, virtuous, and courageous heroine takes her wavering husband's place and dies in battle against the Teutonic Knights. Did she inspire a young lady from an aristocratic Livonian family, who died after leading a unit against the Russians throughout the uprising of 1831? Mickiewicz reveals—or perhaps assigns—her identities at the end of his poem *Death of the Colonel*: 'It is a Lithuanian, a virginal heroine / The insurgents' leader—Emilia Plater'.[6]

What did Mickiewicz and his contemporaries mean by 'Lithuania' and 'Lithuanian'? It may seem a riddle that a native of present-day Belarus began the most famous poem in the Polish language with the words 'Lithuania, my fatherland!'* By my reckoning, the 9,847-line text of *Pan Tadeusz* mentions 'Lithuania', 'Lithuanian', 'Lithuanians', and their variants ninety times, while it refers to variants of 'Poland', 'Polish', and 'Poles' eighty-seven times. The meanings of these terms depend on their contexts. Many references evoke Lithuanian customs, countryside, and climate, but other usages are political. Occasionally Lithuania appears as a partner of Poland, but more often it partners 'the Crown' as a constituent part of Poland. The Lithuanians

---

* '*Litwo, Ojczyzno moja!* Sometimes this is rendered as 'motherland', 'homeland', or 'country', but the Polish word *ojczyzna*, although feminine in gender, is derived from the word for 'father'. So are the equally feminine Belarusian *aichyna* (айчына), the Lithuanian *tėvynė*, and the Latin *patria*.

of the poem are thus also Poles, but their layered national identities do not exactly correspond to those of the inhabitants of the former province of Greater Poland within the former Crown. Mickiewicz's Lithuanian nobles remember, mourn, celebrate, and aspire to 'Poland' more often than they recall 'the Commonwealth'—*Rzeczpospolita*—which features just four times. 'Our Crown' and 'our Lithuania' are compared to the twin stars Castor and Pollux, to two sisters desirous of being reunited, and finally to storm-crossed spouses. It takes hindsight to know that they would never again be conjoined.

Mickiewicz's Navahrudak district was one of the historical heartlands of the Grand Duchy of Lithuania, but most of its population spoke dialects of Belarusian, not Lithuanian or Polish. The challenge of bringing *Pan Tadeusz* to the Belarusian-speaking peasantry, who identified with their religion and their localities, rather than with any nation, and referred to their language as 'simple speech' (*prosta mova*), was taken on by a son of a minor noble leaseholder, Wincenty Dunin-Marcinkiewicz (Vintsent Dunin-Martsinkevich). Having studied medicine in St Petersburg, he settled in the countryside near Minsk and devoted himself to educational, theatrical, and literary work. This included the libretto of the opera *Idyll* (*Sielanka*), first performed in Minsk in 1852, which was partly written in Belarusian, and partly in Polish. The music was written by Stanisław Moniuszko, who came from a noble background near Minsk, spent eighteen years as an organist in Vilnius, and won fame as the father of Polish national opera. For *Pan Tadeusz*, however, the literary and philological challenges were daunting: the Ruthenian language of the Lithuanian Statutes was long in disuse for high culture, while the dialects spoken by peasants were far from codification. The political obstacles proved decisive. Objecting to the use of the Latin alphabet, the tsarist censors confiscated the manuscript after the translation of the first two of the poem's twelve books was submitted for publication in Vilnius in 1859.

LITHUANIA

Mickiewicz shared his interest in Lithuanian folklore, legends, antiquities, and history with a growing circle of scholars. Some, like the Vilnan antiquarian, historian, and statistician Michał Baliński, wrote in Polish of their compatriots' Lithuanian, yet simultaneously Polish heritage. A crucial impulse came from a prelate of Vilnius Cathedral, Ksawery Bohusz (Ksaveras Bohušas), who was arrested by the Russians in 1794 and released the following year. His treatise *On the Beginnings of the Lithuanian Nation and Language*, read to the Society of the Friends of Science in Warsaw in 1806 and published in 1808, demonstrated the antiquity of the Lithuanian language and its similarity to Sanskrit. Lithuanian, argued Bohusz, might serve as a language of high culture. Among the responses to his challenge was a versed epistle addressed to him in Samogitian dialect, published in 1812. Its author was a lawyer, Dionizy Paszkiewicz (Dionizas Poška), born into a modest noble family and educated at the Commission of National Education's school at Kražiai. He published little else in his lifetime, but he did leave the manuscript of an epic poem 'The Peasant of Samogitia and Lithuania' (*Mužikas Žiamajčziu ir Lietuwos*). Fascinated by traces of the distant Lithuanian past, he opened a small museum of antiquities in 1812.

In the next generation, Szymon Staniewicz (Simonas Stanevičius), another minor noble who attended the Kražiai school and Vilnius University, made his living as a tutor. In 1829 he published in Vilnius a grammar, a collection of thirty *Songs of the Samogitians* (*Daynas Žemaycziu*), and his own *Six Fables* (*Szeszes pasakas*), which wove folklore into themes from Aesop. Later he engaged in critical research on folklore and history, although he never finished his work on Lithuanian mythology, which he wrote in Polish. Staniewicz's pupil and patron was Count Jerzy Plater (Jurgis Pliateris). During his short life, he wrote numerous unpublished studies on Lithuanian language and literature, mostly in Polish, but some in Lithuanian. He also collected about 3,000 manuscripts and books, some of them in Lithuanian, Latvian, and old-Prussian.

Plater was related to Józef Arnulf Giedroyć (Juozapas Arnulfas Giedraitis), who succeeded his less reputable uncle as bishop of Samogitia in 1802. While treading a fine political line, Bishop Giedroyć encouraged his clergy to learn to preach in the language of their parishioners. He promoted the teaching of Lithuanian in primary and secondary schools. A patron of scholars and writers, he translated the New Testament into Lithuanian, dedicated his work to Alexander I, and had it published by the Priests of the Mission in Vilnius.[7]

Rich or poor, these figures of the 'Samogitian revival' were of noble birth and spoke and wrote literary Polish. They also studied and promoted the Lithuanian or Samogitian language because of their interest in the culture of their homeland and its rural population. Some of them were directly influenced by Johann Gottfried Herder's concept of the unique spirit of each people—the *Volksgeist*—best preserved in folklore and folksong. However, even before the eighteenth century had ended, a few upwardly mobile people of humbler origins had begun to write about ordinary folk in their native tongue.

Staniewicz and Plater spent the period of the 1830–31 uprising in East Prussia, where they compared notes with the Lutheran pastor and professor Martin Rhesa (Martynas Rėza). He was the son of an innkeeper at Karvaičiai (Karwaiten), a village on the Curonian Spit buried by the encroaching sand dunes in 1797 (the consequence of deforestation, accelerated by the Russian army during the Seven Years' War). Rhesa studied theology in Königsberg, and was ordained, but he later resigned his parish to concentrate on his study of languages and his publishing work. As convenor of the Lithuanian language seminar at Königsberg University, Rhesa was the last great champion of Lithuanian heritage in the Prussian kingdom—albeit less as a creator than as a scholar. In 1818 he published surviving parts of *The Seasons* (*Metai*), the first major poem to have been written in Lithuanian. The structure of this work corresponded to the peasants' annual cycle of work on the land. Traditional virtues of honesty, piety, duty, and perseverance are personified by the native Lithuanians (*Lietuvninkai*), while privileged colonists from afar import moral corruption. Rhesa also published an abridged German translation. The poem's author was Kristijonas Donelaitis (1720–78), a son of free peasants, who diligently studied literature and science, and became a pastor who stayed close to his flock. His parish of Tollmingkehmen is now in the Kaliningrad exclave of the Russian Federation. The former church became a memorial and museum in 1964.

More rebellious was the Catholic priest Antanas Strazdas, born into a peasant family in the north-east of today's Lithuania in 1760. He too was close to his rural parishioners, but in 1828, he was accused of conduct unbecoming his priesthood and was confined in the Pažaislis monastery near Kaunas. Few of his poems were published in his lifetime; like his behaviour, they broke the rules of classical decorum. In *The Thrush* (*Strazdas*), part of a slim collection of sacred and secular songs published in 1814, the poet sings through the eponymous bird about the peasants' burdens and consolations.

From the longer-term perspective of nation-building, the author of the first histories written in Lithuanian made the crucial intellectual contribution. In order to graduate in law from Vilnius University, Simonas Daukantas claimed to be of minor Samogitian noble stock, signing himself 'Szymon Dowkont', but he may well have been born into a free peasant family. The uncertainty testifies to blurred social, legal, and cultural boundaries between the wealthier peasants and poorer nobles at the end of the eighteenth century. His uncle (a priest) paid for his education in Kretinga,

Kalvarija, and Vilnius. Later he worked as an official in Riga and St Petersburg until he retired in 1851. In 1822 Daukantas completed a historical work entitled *Deeds of the Ancient Lithuanians and Samogitians* (*Darbay senuju Lituwiu yr Žemaycziu*), up to Jogaila's death in 1434. He dedicated it to Lithuanian mothers as teachers of their children. The following decade he finished a history of Samogitia up to 1572. These substantial works remained in manuscript, for circulation among kindred spirits, but in 1845/46 he published in St Petersburg a work of ethnography entitled *The Character of the Ancient Lithuanians, Highlanders, and Samogitians* (*Budą Senowęs Lëtowiū, kalnienū ir Žamajtiū*). He also wrote and published Lithuanian-language booklets of advice for farmers, an elementary school primer with religious and secular texts, and a Latin–Lithuanian dictionary. He never finished his Polish–Lithuanian dictionary. Although he created many neologisms, sometimes drawing on Latvian, he pursued a purer Lithuanian language, and in his own work he moved away from the rural Samogitian idiom of his youth.

Daukantas's significance lay not in any critical rigour, for he repeated tall stories as if they were historical facts, having read them in older histories and chronicles, or listened to them in folksongs. Even an unpublished text by Mickiewicz took him in. What mattered was that he conceived the Lithuanian nation as an ancient community that remained vigorous among the peasantry and could yet regain its former greatness. As his works gradually entered circulation during the decades that followed, the 'fathers' and 'mothers' of the modern Lithuanian nation adopted his vision of the national past, present, and future. This turning away from the Polonophone nobility (to which Daukantas claimed to belong) went hand in hand with a negative evaluation of Lithuania's union with Poland. After Vytautas, it had been downhill all the way. Daukantas shared this part of his stance with a still less sceptical historian with whom he corresponded. Teodor Narbutt published his pioneering Polish-language *History of the Lithuanian Nation* in Vilnius between 1835 and 1841. He concluded his ninth and final volume by 'breaking his pen' at the death of Sigismund Augustus in 1572, thereby writing off the history and heritage of the Polish–Lithuanian Commonwealth as a lost cause.

Narbutt's and Daukantas's contrast between medieval greatness and early modern decline was akin to the message of František Palacký's *History of the Czech Nation in Bohemia and Moravia* (first published in German in 1836 before being translated into Czech). After lauding the Hussite revolution of the fifteenth century as his nation's zenith, Palacký ended his narrative with the ascent of the Habsburgs to the Bohemian throne in 1526. However, the Protestant Czech historian would later be active in the public life of the Habsburg monarchy, something unimaginable for his Lithuanian counterparts in the Russian Empire.

For all the long-term intellectual and cultural significance of what was achieved at this time, the numbers of those involved in studying and promoting Lithuanian and Samogitian language and folklore remained extremely low throughout the first half of the nineteenth century. Rather more numerous were those who valued such work as an antiquarian hobby. Although the polemical thrust of Narbutt's history created a stir among the mid-century reading public, as yet the publication of a few volumes of poems and songs in Lithuanian, along with larger numbers of prayer books and almanacs, in no way threatened the prestige of Polish. In the conditions created by Alexander I's forbearance, Polish high culture flourished until 1831 and survived everything the Russian Empire threw at it thereafter.

ii. *Risings and Reprisals*

The tsarist regime responded to the insurrection that liberated Warsaw on 29–30 November 1830 by imposing martial law on the Lithuanian and Belarusian lands. A full-scale Polish-Russian war began in earnest in February 1831. On 25 March, radical nobles and students proclaimed the Lithuanian uprising at Šiauliai (where the 1794 insurrection had also been launched). The rising spread eastwards and southwards, although the insurgents could take neither Kaunas nor Vilnius. Proclamations in Lithuanian encouraged peasants to join in, avowing that serfs would become 'true free Poles'. Many peasants did fight, especially in the Telšiai district, where an announcement of military conscription had already led villagers to revolt. Some even sang 'Poland is not yet lost, while Samogitians live' (*Darbai lenkai naprapule / Kol žemaitiai gyvi*),[8] adapting the 1797 song of the Polish legions in Italy, which became Poland's national anthem in the twentieth century.

In May 1831, the Russian Army concentrated sufficient forces to turn the tide—disheartening most peasants—before relief forces arrived from Poland. Since 1815, the kingdom maintained its own, well-trained regular army, but in June the Russians defeated the Polish corps outside Vilnius. The beaten Polish general was Antoni Giełgud, a scion of an old Lithuanian noble family (from which the actor John Gielgud also descended). After further setbacks, most of the Polish forces crossed the Prussian border in mid-July and were disarmed and interred. As the ineffectual Giełgud handed over his weapon, one of his own officers shot him dead. Effectively the uprising in Lithuania was over, although some partisans held out in the woods until November.

The real Emilia Plater had scornfully refused to seek safety in Prussia, but in the end hunger, fever, and exhaustion stopped her from reaching Warsaw. She found refuge with a noble family who passed her off as a governess. Broken in health, she died, aged twenty-five, on 23 December 1831 and was buried nearby at Kapčiamiestis, now close to Lithuania's open border with Poland and fortified frontier with Belarus. Inscribed on the pedestal of her statue, erected in 1999, is a Lithuanian translation of Mickiewicz's *Death of the Colonel*.

Reprisals commenced on both banks of the Nemunas. In the Lithuanian and Belarusian governorates, several thousand insurgents were deported to Siberia, and hundreds of estates were confiscated. Peasants were liable to be brutally flogged and then conscripted into penal battalions. Nicholas I's regime blamed the Catholic Church for supporting the 'rebellion'. From 1832 it dissolved many monasteries, convents, and seminaries. Confiscation of most remaining ecclesiastical lands was intended to reduce the clergy's influence on the peasantry, but it removed a major source of social antagonism. Bishops' powers to appoint priests to parishes were limited, and sermons censored. Catholic priests could no longer baptise the children of confessionally mixed marriages. Pope Gregory XVI, who in 1832 had condemned the uprising, protested against these policies in vain.

The papacy would not or could not defend the Uniate Church. The tsarist regime gradually undermined its identity and structures before suppressing it altogether in 1839. The synod of Uniate clergy summoned to Polatsk to annul the Union of Brest did so in the cathedral rebuilt a century earlier by Glaubitz for the Basilian Order—as a pearl of the Vilnan Baroque. The Uniates were thus deemed to have returned to Russian Orthodoxy, except for those in the diocese of Chełm in the Kingdom of Poland, which survived until 1875, and those in Austrian-ruled Galicia, where the Greek Catholic Church played a major part in building the modern Ukrainian nation.

In 1833, the empire's deputy education minister, Sergei Uvarov, summed up the regime's doctrine of Official Nationality as 'Orthodoxy, autocracy, nationality'. To him and other officials, Catholicism and Polishness were intrinsically linked and irremediably hostile. The discovery, trials, and executions of further conspirators in the 1830s and 1840s confirmed their suspicions.

Such functionaries elaborated the slogans used by Catherine II to justify the partitions of the Commonwealth: only malign Polish influence had diverted the Lithuanian and Belarusian lands from their once and future Russian destiny. They conceived 'nationality' in terms of an overarching Russian nation, in which the elder 'Great Russian' (*velikorossiiskie*) brothers led junior 'Little Russian' (*malorossiiskie*) and 'White Russian' (*belorossiiskie*) or 'West Russian' (*zapadnorossiiskie*) siblings. The name of Lithuania was not banned, but from 1840 the reorganised Lithuanian and Belarusian governorates were renamed the North-Western Province. Within it, the Kaunas, Vilnius, and Hrodna governorates would until 1912 constitute a general-governorate of Vilnius. Senior administrative posts would be held by imported officials, while Russian replaced Polish at all levels of public administration. Recently codified Russian laws were imposed on the annexed territories in place of the Third Lithuanian Statute.

Education regressed. Many elementary and secondary schools were closed, while in those that remained, the curriculum was shorn of such dangerous subjects as logic, ethics, natural law, political economy, natural science, and of course Lithuanian and Polish history. However, the shortage of trained teachers frustrated the regime's aim for all classes to be taught in Russian. Vilnius University was closed in 1832. Because of the shortage of trained physicians and surgeons, the medical faculty survived as a separate academy for a further decade. With Warsaw University also shut, the former Grand Duchy's elites had to choose between going abroad for higher education, and attending university in St Petersburg, Moscow, or Kyiv.

Nicholas I also ended what would be remembered by Jews as 'a golden age' when they 'were largely left alone and allowed to manage their own affairs'.[9] The tsar, deeply prejudiced religiously, culturally, and economically against Jews, believed that they should be strictly regulated, repressed, exploited, and whenever possible, converted. His policies wavered between coerced assimilation and discrimination, and they caused much suffering and division. From 1827 onwards, he had tens of thousands of Jews pressed into the army. These mostly underage, poor Jews were selected by their own kahals and seized by Jewish *khappers* ('grabbers'). Given little opportunity for religious observance, many of these boys converted to Russian Orthodox Christianity. The regime abolished the kahals in 1844, but Jews continued to be taxed and judged separately. The difference was that the Jews who were now assigned responsibility lacked their predecessors' legitimacy. Policies to force Jews into 'productive' classes of merchants, urban property owners, artisans, and farmers had some effect. Some Jews prospered in those roles, but as the population grew, the number of impoverished and persecuted Jews in both town and countryside remained far greater.

A minority among the 'enlightened' Jews (Maskilim) initially welcomed tighter censorship of books in Hebrew characters, state control of private Jewish schools, and the new state institutions that taught a mostly secular curriculum. Uvarov, who oversaw these policies, sought 'to destroy in the Jews the fanaticism of separation'.[10] This small minority of Jews also supported laws banning distinctive Jewish dress, which were brutally, if haphazardly enforced and bitterly resented by the traditional majority, itself divided between the followers of Hasidism and rabbinical orthodoxy. The latter generated the Musar movement that blended strict observance with a stronger focus on ethics. However, the regime's goal of conversion brought disenchantment. The point of the Haskalah or Jewish Enlightenment was to equip Jews for the modern world, not to eradicate Jewishness.

The mixture of rigidity and inconsistency that characterised Nicholas I's regime made it impossible to achieve the 'de-Polonisation' advocated by the 'Russifying' ideologues and officials who saw potential Russians not only in the Belarusian-speaking,

UNDER IMPERIAL RULE

but even in the Lithuanian-speaking peasantry. The tsar's aversion to radical reforms, together with the chronic shortage of trained cadres of ethnic Russians in administration and education, helped the Polish–Lithuanian *szlachta* maintain its grip on the countryside. Many landowners still made use of Jewish managers and innkeepers. Nicholas knew that the cussed passivity of serfs inured to their lot constrained economic growth, but his regime took only modest steps to curb the excesses of lordship and subjection. These measures had the effect of further reducing the number of personally free tenant farmers, whose status was often levelled down to that of privately owned serfs in official surveys. A hidebound bureaucratic culture, in which matters for decision were passed upwards until they piled up on the emperor's desk, could not liberate the economic, social, and demographic potential of the empire.

The Crimean War (1853–56) exposed the creaking structures of autocracy. France and Great Britain found it hard to supply their armies via a long sea route, yet they did so better than did the Russian Empire by land. After the fall of Sevastopol, Alexander II, who had succeeded his father Nicholas I in April 1855, had to stave off fiscal collapse with concessions that called into question Russia's status as a great power. The terms of the 1856 Treaty of Paris demilitarised the Black Sea and its shores, as well as the Åland Islands in the Baltic Sea.

The conduct and outcome of the Crimean War convinced the new tsar of the need for comprehensive reforms. Any kind of civil society, capable of embracing the necessary changes made from above, and showing some modest initiative from below, required some relaxation of the stifling apparatus of control and coercion, which generated servility and evasion. But any loosening of the reins encouraged the aspirations of national activists, especially Poles. Concessions in education, censorship, religious freedom, and public administration in the Kingdom of Poland created a febrile atmosphere north-east of the Nemunas. Alexander II discouraged similar 'daydreams' when asked to restore Vilnius University and the use of Polish in public life in 1860, pointedly replying: 'here is Lithuania, not Poland'.[11]

The emperor needed a well-trained and well-equipped army, capable of rapid expansion in an emergency, like that of other continental European powers. The reform of 1874 made virtually all men liable for conscription. After several years of active service, soldiers would move into the reserve. Previously, recruits provided by peasant communities served for twenty-five years: the few survivors did not return to their original villages whose communities they would have disrupted. The abolition of serfdom was thus a pre-requisite for the creation of a modern military and preceded it by thirteen years.

Alexander II was long remembered as the 'liberator tsar'. His emancipation manifesto of 19 February 1861 ended the personal servitude of privately owned peasants: they could now marry and trade without their master's or mistress's consent. State-owned peasants gained similar privileges in 1866. But in an autocratic regime and a legally stratified society, direct subjection to the civil law did not entail civil rights. Peasants paid a high price to acquire much of the land they worked. The impact on landowners was cushioned by the transfer to them of much common land, a two-year transition period, and by a system of purchase and compensation facilitated by the state. Peasants would redeem their debt for decades to come. Collective responsibility for implementing the reform, and the increased taxes which accompanied it, rested with the local peasant commune or *mir*. Most former serfs became materially poorer. The onerous terms disappointed peasants in the Lithuanian and Belarusian lands, where many refused to perform the labour services required of them during the transition period. A new uprising was in preparation. Liberally inclined landowners occasionally tried to fraternise with villagers, as when nobles offered cigars to peasants who promised to join the rising, with comic results.

Meanwhile, in the Kingdom of Poland (where the *Code Napoléon* had abolished personal serfdom) the terms on which peasants might obtain land were still being discussed, when a pre-emptive round-up of recruits precipitated the proclamation of the uprising there on 22 January 1863. The Polish Provisional Government's manifesto 'To Our Lithuanian Brothers' (*Do braci Litwinów*) declared that there was 'neither lord, nor noble, nor peasant, nor Jew, but we are all brothers and live equal and the same before the Lord God and our dear Fatherland!'[12] The insurgents were divided between moderate 'whites' and radical 'reds'. The latter dominated the Lithuanian Provincial Committee, which on 1 February promised the peasants the land they farmed without payment, as well as five morgs (about three and a half hectares) of land for each landless peasant household. It also forbade transitional labour services. The 'whites' grew bolder after the French Emperor Napoleon III demanded the restoration of the status of the Kingdom of Poland, and Britain and Austria expressed their diplomatic support. The three powers made a diplomatic demarche in June 1863, although it did not extend to the Lithuanian and Belarusian lands. Russia rejected the ultimatum, and France would not wage war against Russia by itself.

The insurgency spread swiftly during the spring of 1863. The disbandment of the regular Polish army after the last uprising necessitated guerrilla warfare. At least 2,500 skirmishes took place, over a quarter of them in the Lithuanian and western Belarusian lands. Here the most successful commanders were 'reds': the Volhynian nobleman Zygmunt Sierakowski, a revolutionary who had met Garibaldi and Mazzini, and the warrior-priest and minor Samogitian nobleman Antanas Mackevičius (Antoni Mackiewicz). The latter's fiery sermons, delivered in Lithuanian, motivated many peasants to fight the Russians. After

LITHUANIA

Sierakowski's defeat, capture, and execution, Mackevičius and his men fought on against worsening odds, until his own capture and execution in December 1863.

In the Hrodna governorate, the key figure was the Podlachian nobleman, journalist, and lawyer Konstanty Kalinowski (Kastus´ Kalinoŭski). The previous year he had written and printed several issues of the pioneering newspaper *Peasant Truth* (*Mużyckaja Prauda*). It used the Latin alphabet to express the local Belarusian language. Drawing inspiration from Kościuszko, Kalinowski denounced the oppression, manipulation, and division of the people by 'the Muscovites', demanded radical social and political reforms and the restoration of the Uniate Church, and called for the cultivation of the Belarusian language. As the tide turned against the partisans during the summer of 1863, he became the uprising's plenipotentiary commissar for Lithuania. Betrayed in Vilnius in February 1864, Kalinowski was publicly hanged, rather than shot (as befitted a nobleman), on 26 March on Lukiškės Square. Awaiting execution in his cell, he addressed his *Letters from Beneath the Gallows* (*Listy zpad szybienicy*) in Belarusian to his compatriots, avowing that it was worth dying for the truth. He urged them to resist the empire's endemic violence, corruption, and falsehood, 'for only then will you live happily when no Muscovite remains over you'.[13]

Most of the bodies of executed 'rebels' were secretly buried in mass graves. In 2017 the remains of twenty insurgents were discovered during work to stabilise the slopes of Gediminas Hill in Vilnius. Two were identified as Sierakowski and Kalinowski. Two years later, the presidents of Lithuania and Poland attended the solemn reburial of these twenty soldiers at the Rasos cemetery, following a Requiem Mass at the cathedral. So did the deputy prime minister of Belarus, who was greeted by a host of fluttering white-red-white flags bearing the Pahonia. By now Aleksandr Lukashenko's regime was fast cooling towards the 'class warrior'

UNDER IMPERIAL RULE

Kastus' Kalinoŭski. In 2022, Belarusian volunteers fighting for Ukraine against Russia chose him as their patron. The names of the executed insurgents were written on the coffins and tombstones in Lithuanian, Polish and Belarusian.

The show of unity at the funeral belies increasingly intense debates (both scholarly and otherwise) over whether the rising was a 'Polish', 'Lithuanian' or 'Belarusian' cause (at one time it suited almost everyone to call it Polish). Some historians stress the endorsement by the likes of Mackevičius and Kalinowski of the right of the peoples of the Grand Duchy of Lithuania to self-determination—with or without the Poles. Others assert these heroes belonged to an overarching Polish nation, including Lithuania and Belarus. Insurgent leaders differed on a great deal, but all detested Muscovite autocracy. It was not yet time for the Polish–Lithuanian–Ruthenian path to fork. Many standards and the official seals of the insurrectionary government combined Poland's white eagle, Lithuania's chasing knight, and the Archangel Michael—symbolising Rus'. It was as if the Commonwealth had at last been perfected—two centuries after the Union of Hadiach.

The artist Artur Grottger planned three cycles of drawings about the uprising, entitled *Polonia*, *Lithuania*, and *Roxolania*, although he did not live to complete the last one, dedicated to the Ukrainian, Volhynian, and his native Podolian lands. In the first drawing of the *Lithuania* cycle, spectral Death stalks a primeval forest. In the second, a forester is woken by his wife. In the third, he and other insurgents swear an oath, while the culmination of the battle against the Russians is shown in the fourth scene. The slain forester's ghost returns home in the fifth. In the sixth and last drawing, his widow, in chains in Siberia, turns to an apparition of the Virgin and Child for consolation.

The man tasked with suppressing the 'rebellion' in the Lithuanian and Belarusian lands was Mikhail Murav'ev. As a youth, he had fought and been wounded at Borodino in 1812. He

LITHUANIA

joined like-minded 'patriots' in clandestine organisations, but he was eventually cleared of involvement in the Decembrists' attempt to prevent Nicholas I's accession in 1825. His brother and brother-in-law, however, were sent to Siberia. The zeal of the convert marked Murav′ev's subsequent service. He manifested his loyalty through relentless enforcement of anti-Polish policies in the governorates of Vitsebsk, Mahileŭ, and Hrodna between 1827 and 1835. He continued his ascent as a reactionary voice in the inner circles of the imperial government. However, Alexander II's reform agenda was less to his taste. The uprising revived his career, and in May 1863 he returned to his former stomping grounds as governor-general of the North-Western Province.

Murav′ev's counter-insurgency strategy, to comb the countryside with mobile columns, proved effective against the outnumbered partisans. During his two years in charge of the province, he revelled in his sobriquet of 'the hangman'. He often participated personally in public executions of insurgents—at least 128 in 1863–64. The regime confiscated thousands of estates in the Lithuanian and Belarusian lands and deported about 9,000 people to Siberia. The governor-general ordered terror against civilians, including burning down villages suspected of helping the insurgents. Noble landowners made humble addresses, swore oaths of loyalty, and paid additional contributions from their estates on pain of confiscation. Even unproven suspicion of sympathy for the uprising could result in a forced sale to a Russian buyer. Murav′ev altered the implementation of the land reform to the relative advantage of the peasants, hoping to drive more noble landowners into bankruptcy. He also replaced all local officials with Orthodox Russians and banned any use of Polish in public life. The North-Western Province was excluded from the scope of the 1864 reform establishing landowners' assemblies (*zemstvo*s), for fear they would be dominated by Polish nobles.

UNDER IMPERIAL RULE

The local Catholic clergy generally complied (in the end) with orders to condemn the revolt. Yet within three years of Murav'ev's arrival in Vilnius, the regime suppressed dozens of parishes and chapels, and most of the remaining monasteries and convents. It prohibited the building of new churches, the repair of existing ones, and even the erection of wayside crosses. Processions were confined to churchyards. Over 100 new Orthodox churches were constructed in the Lithuanian governorates, paid for by local taxes. Some of them served very few Orthodox believers.

Pressure on the Catholic laity to convert to Orthodoxy and to send their children to Russian-language schools had most effect east and south of Vilnius. Murav'ev was confident that the Belarusian-speaking populace could become loyal, Orthodox 'West Russians' within a generation. The success of these efforts was limited both by the local-mindedness and inertia prevalent in some of the least-developed regions of the empire, and by the continuing prestige of Polish culture, reinforced by the Polish loyalties of the Catholic clergy. 'Russification' rarely involved any serious effort to turn Poles into ethnic or even cultural Russians. Rather, it involved the exclusion of Catholics/Poles from public life, and efforts to weaken their economic and social position. Publishing in Polish all but ceased in the North-Western province for forty years, but Poles could still read Polish newspapers from Warsaw or St Petersburg, as well as illegal imports. The Polish language was banned from public schools, so parents sent their children to clandestine private schools or taught them Polish language, literature, and history at home. By the late 1870s it was obvious that Polish culture could not be eradicated, although some Polish–Lithuanian–Ruthenian nobles converted to Orthodoxy and advanced in imperial service. However, in the ethnic Lithuanian heartlands the regime's policies backfired spectacularly.

LITHUANIA

iii. *Temperance and Literacy*

Well before this latest round of reprisals, some Roman Catholic priests had cultivated the Lithuanian language. The repeated blows struck by the tsarist regime against the Church's institutional autonomy and property pushed it into concentrating on religious ministry. The repression ultimately strengthened the Church's authority. From the mid-1840s, the key figure was Motiejus Valančius. Born into a prosperous peasant family in western Samogitia in 1801, he later claimed minor noble origins and signed himself in Polish as Maciej Wołonczewski. Ordained in Vilnius, he worked as a teacher and librarian at the Kražiai college and then lectured at the Vilnius seminary. He became rector of the Samogitian seminary at Varniai in 1845. As bishop of Samogitia from 1850, he visited parishes and founded parish schools.

The temperance movement had been spreading around the Catholic world for two decades before Valančius took up the cause in August 1858. The print-run of his pamphlet *On Brotherhoods of Sobriety* (*Apej brotsvą blaivybės*) was 40,000 copies. The impact was astounding. According to official figures compiled in 1860, no fewer than 692,000 of the 835,000 Catholics in the Kaunas governorate belonged to brotherhoods sworn to abstinence from liquor.[14] Owners of distilleries and taverns suffered severe losses. So did the imperial tax authorities: during the first seven months of 1858, excise revenues from alcohol in the Kaunas governorate were 36,000 rubles, but in the last five months—just 5,000.[15] This social and economic mobilisation hit the interests of manors and the imperial state hard. For several years the authorities affected approval on moral grounds— the bishop had asked and obtained the tsar's permission. In the end, Murav'ev banned the fraternities as anti-state organisations. Nonetheless, the role played in the movement by Valančius and his clergy was crucial. Doubtless, the earlier loss of ecclesiastical income from distilling and brewing encouraged their support of temperance, but reports of religious euphoria in the villages cannot be dismissed as wishful thinking. There was a darker side to enthusiasm: police reports claim that persons caught drinking were ritually and physically humiliated by their priests and fellow parishioners.

Valančius's most personal writings were in Polish, but in Lithuanian he wrote the first history of the bishopric and diocese of Samogitia (*Žemajtiu Wiskupiste*, published in Vilnius in 1848) as well as shorter devotional and pedagogical works. There was a long tradition of publishing Lithuanian-language prayer-books and almanacs for the 'simple folk', but a scholarly history in Lithuanian for the educated clergy and laity was a novelty. Despite the regime's reduction of episcopal income, the bishop sponsored several lay writers. However, his cordial relations with Daukantas soured. Valančius reputedly asked Daukantas if he had written his rambling and credulous history of Samogitia when drunk. First as rector, and then as bishop, Valančius created two generations of pastorally committed priests from both peasant and minor noble backgrounds. The Samogitian diocese had recently been expanded at the expense of the diocese of Vilnius, so that it now included most of the Lithuanian-speaking population. After 1863–64, Valančius had to convince the regime of his loyalty, but he engaged in clandestine acts of civil disobedience whose long-term significance is hard to overstate.

From 1864 the Russian Empire permitted the publication of books in the Lithuanian language only in the Cyrillic alphabet. Murav′ev hoped that more elementary schools would gradually distance the tsar's Lithuanian-speaking subjects from the Poles and bring them closer to the Russians. Valančius would have none of it. By 1867 he had paid for the printing in the Latin alphabet of Lithuanian books in East Prussia and organised a network of people that smuggled these books across the frontier.

LITHUANIA

Within the first two years, no fewer than 19,000 copies had been distributed in this way. The bishop himself wrote, published, and distributed ten books against the regime's persecution of the Catholic Church. He denied the possibility of salvation outside the Catholic faith and urged parents to teach their children to read and pray at home, rather than send them to public schools.

Despite the regime's efforts to expand the network of Russian-language elementary schools, in the lands inhabited by Lithuanian-speakers there were fewer of them, relative to the population, than anywhere else in the European parts of the Russian Empire. Even counting the Asian regions, school attendance rates were among the very lowest. According to the 1897 census, in the Kaunas governorate 16.8 per cent of men and 4.7 per cent of women were able to read in Russian. Among those who declared the Lithuanian language as their own, these figures were just 12 per cent of men and a mere 1.3 per cent of women. In other Lithuanian-speaking regions they were lower still—lower than in any other part of the Russian Empire west of the Urals. However, the proportion of the Lithuanian speakers able to read (and usually write) in any language was over half, much higher than anywhere else in the empire, except the Baltic provinces where there were fewer obstacles to schooling in Latvian or Estonian. Moreover, more women than men were literate: 54.9 per cent, as opposed to 51.9 per cent in the Kaunas governorate.[16] These astonishing figures testify to a mighty mobilisation at parish-level: by the end of the nineteenth century, most ethnically Lithuanian children were being home-schooled. There were itinerant teachers of both sexes, but mostly, it was two generations of mothers who taught their own and their neighbours' children to read and write in their own language.

To this day, the book-smugglers (*knygnešiai*) remain among the most popular of Lithuanian national heroes and heroines. Their achievement was phenomenal: between 1865 and 1904, at an increasing tempo, over 1,830 Lithuanian-language publications in the Latin alphabet were distributed in the Russian Empire, almost all illegally. Most were printed in East Prussia. In addition, over 700 books and brochures were printed in North America, and some of these reached Lithuania (including two volumes of Daukantas's histories, published in the 1890s). The total number of illicit copies was about 6 million. By the turn of the century, Russian frontier guards were confiscating about 20,000 volumes a year. In contrast, so low was demand for Lithuanian-language publications in the Cyrillic alphabet that only sixty-six have been recorded in the same period.[17] About half the Lithuanian-language books distributed during these four decades were prayer-books, almanacs, and primers. But the proportion and variety of secular literature grew significantly from the 1880s. Works of medicine, economics, anthropology, grammar, bibliography, as well as literary prose and poetry all built on earlier foundations. The difference was that they were printed abroad. On 24 April 1904, in a belated effort to regain control of what Lithuanians read, Tsar Nicholas II rescinded the ban on using the Latin alphabet. He was persuaded to do so by the governor-general of Vilnius, Prince Petr Sviatopolk-Mirskii, whose ancestors had been Polish–Lithuanian patriots.

The explosion of publications contributed to the standardisation of the Lithuanian language. The fact that most books were printed in East Prussia contributed to the literary standard. Prussian Lithuanians' dialect was close to the 'West Highland dialect' (*Vakarų Aukštaičių tarmė*) spoken in the region between Kaunas and the north-eastern corner of the Kingdom of Poland, whence came so many prominent nationalists. They included the linguist Jonas Jablonskis, born near the Prussian border and schooled at Marijampolė. Having graduated in classics from Moscow University, he taught beyond the Lithuanian lands until 1903. Concealing his identity, he published his *Grammar of the*

LITHUANIA

Lithuanian Language (*Lietuviškos kalbos gramatika*) in Tilsit in 1901 and his *Syntax of the Lithuanian Language* (*Lietuvių kalbos sintaksė*) in Vilnius in 1911. From 1905 he contributed to several legally published journals under a pen-name, campaigning for purer expressions, even if not all fellow-journalists appreciated his rulings on correct usage.

To explain the phenomenon of Lithuanian-language literacy, we should also look to economic and social conditions. The lands inhabited by Lithuanian speakers were strategically vital to the Russian Empire, as reflected in the military garrisons and the routes taken by the railways (Vilnius and Hrodna were on the main line that connected St Petersburg to Warsaw by the 1860s), but they were peripheral to state-directed industrialisation. In turn, Vilnius was crucial to the modern Lithuanian national movement, but Lithuanian speakers were, by most standards, marginal to the city's life. The administrative, commercial, and cultural spheres were respectively dominated by Russians, Jews, and Poles.

Industrialisation, accelerating rapidly by the end of the nineteenth century, turned many Latvian-speaking peasants into the proletariat of Riga, whose fast-growing population was measured at 282,230 people (over a third of it Latvian) by the implausibly precise imperial census of 1897. Yet just 3,238 of the 154,532 inhabitants of Vilnius were then counted as habitual Lithuanian-speakers, contemptuously classified within 'Lithuanian-Latvian dialects' (*litovsko-latyshskie narechiia*). The same statistical exercise also recorded 61,847 speakers of *yevreiskii yazyk* (the Jewish language, that is, Yiddish); 47,795 speakers of *polskii* (Polish); and 30,967 speakers of *russkii* (Russian), which included 6,514 speakers of *belorusskii* (Belarusian) and 517 of *malorusskii* (Ukrainian), with the rest speaking *velikorusskii* (Great Russian). The garrison would have accounted for many of those. There were also 2,170 speakers of *nemetskii* (German). Curiously, 722 persons, nine tenths of them men, claimed their mother tongue was *tatarskii* (Tatar). No doubt religion played a role in suggesting answers, although respondents were asked about their native language.[18]

The figure for Lithuanian speakers may be an underestimate, because of the ubiquity of 'code-switching' (not least among domestic servants). But it hardly changes the essential point. Many more Lithuanian speakers lived and worked in Riga, St Petersburg, or Chicago than in Vilnius. In Kaunas, the 1897 census counted 4,092 native speakers of *litovskoe* (Lithuanian) and 606 of *zhmudskoe* (Samogitian), while over a third of the city's population of 70,920 spoke Yiddish, with most of the rest divided between Polish and the three recognised varieties of 'Russian'. Even in most smaller towns, Lithuanian speakers constituted a minority. In the towns of the Kaunas governorate, just 18,438 Lithuanian and Samogitian speakers were recorded, amounting to 11.4 per cent of a total urban population of 143,144. Among the urban middle classes, the few Lithuanian-speaking individuals used Russian or Polish in official, professional, and most social contexts.

The enterprising exception was the engineer Petras Vileišis. Born into a free peasant family in northern Lithuania, he graduated in mathematics from St Petersburg University and earned a fortune from designing and constructing railway bridges across the Russian Empire. Having long maintained contact with other Lithuanian nationalists and funded their clandestine publications, while contributing articles himself, he moved to Vilnius in 1899. His ironworks employed Lithuanian workers. With his savings Vileišis built a neo-baroque palace in the Antakalnis suburb, next to the stuccoed glories of the church of Saints Peter and Paul. At the end of 1904, the first legally printed newspaper in Lithuanian, the *Vilnius News* (*Vilniaus žinios*), rolled off the press in the palace basement. By 1908 he needed to earn his living again. His palace is now home to the Institute of Lithuanian Folklore and Literature.

LITHUANIA

Ninety-three per cent of those counted as Lithuanian speakers in 1897 lived in the countryside. Rural society was becoming increasingly stratified. The terms of emancipation, although designed to weaken the *szlachta*, placed a heavy burden on the peasants—too heavy for many. But while there was no Lithuanian middle class in the towns, something like it emerged in villages. A significant minority of peasants bought land, much of it from impecunious nobles. These industrious farmers expanded and consolidated their holdings, which became thriving businesses, linked by co-operatives. They employed labourers, in plentiful supply because of the growing population and the sub-division of smallholdings. When conflicts arose between wealthier and poorer villagers, the former often looked to parish priests for support, and generally received it.

For Lithuanian speakers, the most common path of upward social mobility was the Roman Catholic clergy, which enjoyed both prestige and a measure of material security. The proud prospect of a son in a black cassock motivated some peasant families to invest their modest surplus in schooling their more promising male offspring. The eldest (or failing that, the most reliable) son would inherit the farm, so the others had to get on in the world if they did not wish to end up labouring for their brothers. Daughters would—ideally—be married off to prosperous farmers. By no means all of these well-schooled young men chose the celibate lifestyle of the seminary. Many used their education as springboards to prosper in in the Russian- and/or Polish-speaking worlds, but some, whether as priests, schoolmasters, or doctors, provided role models for the increasingly literate rural population. The campaign to teach reading and writing in Lithuanian at home, backed by Catholic priests, implemented by women, helped to provide the cultural integration that rapid changes to the structure of rural society might otherwise have threatened. Petras Rimša's sculpture depicting a woman spinning while supervising a child studying a book of the Lithuanian language was acclaimed when it was exhibited in Vilnius in 1906. Its popularity has never flagged.

No educator was more meritorious than Julija Beniuševičiūtė-Žymantienė, better known by her pen-name 'Žemaitė'—the Samogitian woman. Her parents, from the minor nobility, served a wealthier family as steward and housekeeper at a manor near Plungė. Despite their best efforts to prevent her from mixing with the local peasants, in case it spoiled her Polish, she learned their language anyway. She embraced the causes of both social and national liberation during the 1863–64 uprising and later married a former insurgent and former serf, Laurynas Žymantas. Alas, he did not appreciate her literary talent. After three decades struggling to make ends meet and educate her own and her neighbours' children in Lithuanian, she got her break. The young writer Povilas Višinskis gave her some Lithuanian periodicals (about which more will be said shortly) and encouraged her to contribute to them. Debuting in 1895, 'Žemaitė' was soon writing stories, polemical articles, novellas, and plays. Her vigorous vernacular style conveyed a critical, realist take on the problems of peasant families, confronting alcohol-fuelled violence and sexual abuse from women's perspectives. At the same time, she evoked the sounds, smells, and sights of the countryside.

Mass emigration—whether within the Russian Empire or across the oceans—mitigated rural poverty but could not eliminate it. Hundreds of thousands braved the rolling ocean in 'steerage'. Eagerly awaited 'letters from America' encouraged families and neighbours to follow the example of those who made new lives for themselves. Statistics are imprecise, because before 1899, Lithuanian immigrants into the United States were registered as Russians, Germans, or Poles, while the recording of their names was haphazard. Perhaps a quarter of a million Lithuanian-speakers had arrived by this time, with a quarter of a million

LITHUANIA

officially recorded as Lithuanians between 1899 and 1914. Initially most of them sought farmland. A hub emerged at Shenandoah, Pennsylvania, the site of the first Lithuanian-speaking Catholic parish. The local priest, Father Andrius Strupinskas, came to the United States via Bolivia, having been exiled after the 1863–64 uprising. Soon, however, onerous but relatively well-paid work in factories and mines drew most immigrants to urban areas. Many people quietly assimilated into English-speaking North America, bequeathing slight ancestral traces to their descendants, but others felt the need to congregate, converse in their native tongue, and cultivate their traditions. Free of legal restrictions, Lithuanian associations and publications flourished. The Catholic *Lithuanian Gazette* (*Lietuwiszka Gazeta*) blazed the trail in 1879, but the Irish- and Italian-American domination of the Roman Catholic Church slowed the formation of Lithuanian-speaking parishes. Lithuanian speakers soon separated from Polish speakers. The conscious building of a national diaspora probably outpaced nation-building in the homeland.

The relationship between diaspora and homeland was satirised by the play *America in the Bathhouse* (*Amerika pirtyje*). Written by Antanas and Juozas Vilkutaitis, it was published in Tilsit in 1895 and performed in Mitau (now Jelgava), in America, and at Palanga on the Baltic coast in 1899. The plot is straightforward: a cunning tailor takes advantage of an old peasant, a Jew, to whom the peasant owes money, and an acquaintance who wishes to marry the peasant's daughter. The tailor, having been trusted to arrange the marriage and the dowry which will settle matters, instead seduces the daughter. She steals the money so they can depart for an easy life in America, but he locks her in the bathhouse and goes by himself. This evergreen comedy, the first to be performed in Lithuanian in Lithuania, still graces the repertoire.

A qualitative breakthrough for Lithuanian nationalism came in 1883 with the publication in Prussian Tilsit of a new periodical.

Many of the seventy or so contributors to *The Dawn* (*Auszra*, later written *Aušra*) hailed from the relatively prosperous peasantry of the governorate of Suwałki (created by the division of the Augustów governorate in 1867). In Lithuanian ethnography this is the Suvalkija region. Some of its Lithuanian-speaking farmers expanded their landholdings after 1864, taking advantage of the application of the land reform on terms more favourable to the peasantry and unfavourable to the nobility than elsewhere in the empire. Moreover, Russifying policies were less intensely applied here than in the North-Western Province, giving children better opportunities to learn both Lithuanian and Polish at school.

The first editor of *The Dawn*, Dr Jonas Basanavičius, is a case in point. Visitors to the reconstructed buildings of his birthplace (in 1851) at Ožkabaliai, about 20 kilometres north of the current Polish border, can see what 'the homestead of a wealthy Suvalkija region farmer would have looked like in the late 19th and early 20th centuries'. The wooden house, barns, and stables, arranged around a four-sided courtyard, convey solidity and self-confidence. This branch of the National Museum, opened in 1998, also memorialises the 'patriarch of the nation' through his writings and personal mementos including busts of Kościuszko and Mickiewicz. The surrounding oak wood, planted in 1989 as an initiative of civil society, has fourteen groves named after national figures.[19]

Basanavičius attended the secondary school at Marijampolė. His education enabled him to relate the songs and stories he had learned at home to historical and literary works in Polish and Latin. These extended his understanding of Lithuania's past glories and present subjection. Not feeling the priestly vocation that his parents had prayed and saved for, he withstood his mother's tears and his father's threats to cut him off without a penny. He studied medicine at Moscow University as the recipient of one of ten state scholarships for Lithuanians. After qualifying he practised as a doctor in Bulgaria until he could return home in 1905. In his spare time, he continued to immerse himself in Lithuanian history, folklore, and language. The conclusions he drew from his endless reading and note-taking were sometimes eccentric (for example in the field of racial phrenology—the 'scientific' study of skull shapes and sizes), but he hit more targets than he missed. He and other contributors to *The Dawn* rooted their linguistic, cultural, educational, social, and economic campaigns for a modern Lithuanian future in Daukantas's vision of the past: the true inheritors of Lithuania's medieval greatness were not its Polonised nobles, but its virtuous and industrious farmers. The importance of this history was proclaimed in the first issue by the motto *Homines historiarum ignari semper sunt pueri*—people who ignore history remain children forever.

The Dawn folded in 1886 after forty issues, but some of its contributors wrote for *The Bell* (*Varpas*), which was published monthly between 1889 and 1905. This periodical satirised the tsarist regime. It initially hosted views that ranged from Catholic to socialist, but its main thrust was secular, liberal, and democratic. After the withdrawal of socialist and Catholic writers from its columns, sixteen men from its liberal milieu founded the Lithuanian Democratic Party in 1902. Prior to 1915, its membership never exceeded seventy.[20] Like *The Dawn*, *The Bell* was printed in East Prussia and smuggled across the frontier. Its first editor and long-time contributor was Vincas Kudirka, who had also been born to a prosperous peasant family in the north-east of the mid-century Kingdom of Poland. In another typical progression, he entered the seminary in Sejny, but left when his lack of vocation became obvious, which angered his father. Like Basanavičius, he studied medicine, but in Warsaw. Kudirka's conversion to the cause was accomplished later—by reading *The Dawn*, as he wrote in the columns of *The Bell*: 'It seemed to me as if I heard the voice of Lithuania accusing me and at the same time forgiving: and you wanderer, where have you been until now?'[21] Earlier, at school in Marijampolė, he had sought to pass himself off as 'a Pole and thus as a gentleman'.[22] He first wrote poetry in Polish, which would later help him to translate Mickiewicz. Kudirka's passionate desire for Lithuanian culture to emulate Polish drove him on despite failing health. He propagated the replacement of Polish-style consonant-combinations such as 'sz' and 'cz' with reformed Czech diacritics, such as 'š' and 'č' respectively, which are used in modern Lithuanian spelling. For similar reasons, the title of *The Bell* began with a 'v', not a 'w'—*Varpas*.

The year before Kudirka died of tuberculosis he wrote and composed *Lithuania, our Fatherland* (*Lietuva, Tėvyne mūsų*, now officially translated as 'Lithuania, our Homeland'). *The Bell* published the words and melody, and it premiered for Lithuanians in St Petersburg in 1899. The hymn evokes a 'land of worthy heroes', 'past experience', 'the paths of virtue', 'truth and light', and 'our love for our native land' before culminating in a stirring call for unity. Despite the controversial absence of God from the text, in 1918 it became Lithuania's national anthem. The lyrics are carved into the monument to Kudirka on Gediminas Avenue in Vilnius, which was unveiled during Lithuania's millennium celebrations in 2009.

At up to 3,000 copies, the circulation of the practically oriented *The Farmer* (*Ūkininkas*), also edited by Kudirka, was greater than that of *The Bell*. Catholic periodicals kept pace with secular ones. The most successful of them, with a print-run of 2,000 copies between 1896 and 1904, was the *Guardian of the Fatherland* (*Tėvynės sargas*). It took a militant line against Russification, criticised an 'older' generation of 'Polonomaniacs', and challenged the Catholic Church's universalist rejection of nationalism. However, it did not embrace urban modernity, warning that Lithuanian villagers who moved to Vilnius or even Kaunas became demoralised and denationalised 'like snow in spring'.[23]

LITHUANIA

Religious loyalties, strongest in villages and small towns, could motivate protests. Feelings ran high after the events of 1893–94. Following Tsar Alexander III's order to demolish the Benedictine nunnery and church in Kražiai, local Catholic faithful, who had repeatedly requested that the fine baroque church serve the parish, maintained a vigil inside it. On 21 November 1893, a crowd forcefully resisted the attempt of the governor of Kaunas, at the head of seventy policemen, to remove those inside the church. The following morning, about three hundred Don Cossacks accomplished the task. Let loose on the town and surrounding villages, they arrested, and then whipped or raped dozens of Catholics accused of defying the tsar's will. Several died. The following September, seventy-one people (peasants, townspeople, and nobles) were put on trial in Vilnius, where Polish and Russian lawyers eloquently defended them. Thirty-six defendants were acquitted, while the judges petitioned the tsar to commute the sentences passed on the others. The case became an international cause célèbre, as exaggerated figures circulated of hundreds raped and killed. Lithuanian Americans protested at public rallies. The church was eventually handed over to the parish in 1908 and reopened in 1910. Although both Lithuanian and Polish speakers were involved, a common cause against tsarist autocracy splintered into contested memories. Lithuanians resented the presentation of Poles as the initiators and leaders of the defence, but Lithuanian denials of any Polish presence at the church offended Poles.

From the 1890s, some Lithuanian-speaking clergy and laity campaigned for Lithuanian to replace Polish in seminaries and in worship. While the Mass itself remained in Latin until 1970, in many parishes the language of prayers, hymns, sermons, and announcements was vocally (and occasionally violently) contested. Lithuanian activists, especially the Vilnan Society of the 'Twelve Apostles', one of whom was the tycoon Vileišis, scored several successes. Even in the city itself, additional services in Lithuanian were provided in some churches, and the small parish church of St Nicholas went wholly Lithuanian in 1902. Father Juozapas Ambraziejus was said to use the confessional to demand that penitents pray in Lithuanian. Confronting parishioners with a stark choice between the Polish and Lithuanian languages drove forward the process of national self-identification.

That said, most hierarchs tried to dampen down national disputes. They included Antanas Baranauskas, a gifted Lithuanian poet who served as suffragan bishop of Samogitia and then as bishop of Sejny. He took exception to articles in *The Dawn* questioning clerical leadership of the modern Lithuanian national cause. In a category of his own was a noble of Polonised Baltic German stock, Eduard von der Ropp. He earned his clerical spurs in Samogitia, Courland, and Tiraspol before becoming bishop of Vilnius in 1903. He aimed to create a broad Catholic political movement in the Russian Empire and was elected to the First Duma, but the regime exiled him to Georgia in 1907. He left the diocese in the hands of the suffragan bishop, Kazimierz Michalkiewicz, who supported Polish educational initiatives, but in 1911 ordained sermons, prayers, and catechism in both languages for all mixed parishes.

The most distinguished Catholic figure in the growing Lithuanian national movement was a mild-mannered professor at the Roman Catholic Theological Academy in St Petersburg, Father Jonas Mačiulis. Better known by his pen-name, Maironis, he headed the Lithuanian literary canon. Like Kudirka, he immersed himself in Polish literature before venturing into Lithuanian. Maironis's debut publication was a verse in *The Dawn* in 1885. Later he embarked on major poetic works that expressed his Romantic attachment to rural landscapes and heroic history. They include the lyrical *Voices of Spring* (*Pavasario balsai*) and above all, *Young Lithuania* (*Jaunoji Lietuva*), which called for a national awakening from a 500-year-long night. In 1904, he wrote an epic poem in Polish, *From the Hill of Biruta* (*Znad Biruty*), in which he appealed to Polonised Lithuanian nobles to learn their ancestors' language and customs, and so unite themselves with their peasant brethren. But he published it in America under a female pen-name, and his authorship was only revealed almost two decades later because he preferred his faith and art to politics. He might otherwise have experienced the unpleasantness generated by a similar, but more polemical appeal published in Polish in 1902 by 'Adomas Jakštas' (the pen-name of Father Aleksandras Dambrauskas). The principal riposte was titled *Never Ever!* (*Przenigdy!*).

As the twentieth century opened, Polish continued to spread not only in the countryside around Vilnius, where Lithuanian dialects had long since yielded to Belarusian ones, but also further west, around Kaunas, where many modestly situated noble families lived. Despite all the efforts of the Russian Empire, Polish was still associated with the Church, the manor, and the city, that is with high culture and social mobility. Moreover, most Polonophone priests, nobles, and professionals could not or would not take the Lithuanian language seriously. They became increasingly irritated by 'litvomaniacs'. At the same time, many Lithuanian-speaking parents linked their children's prospects to their learning Polish.

Even among Lithuanian national activists, uncomfortably aware that most of them found it easier to write in Polish than Lithuanian, there were anxieties about Polish or Polish-speaking wives. Writing in *The Bell* as 'Kėkštas' (the Jay), Jonas Macys claimed that 'only the half-Poles can supply our educated youth with a required number of educated female spouses' but 'the half-Polish woman [...] would sever the ties between the educated Lithuanians and the nucleus of the nation', resulting in 'national hermaphrodites'. It required 'a sacrifice to live with the intellectually weak and insufficiently educated [Lithuanian] woman', but those who married non-Lithuanians were 'renegades'. Kudirka countered that 'to marry a simple country girl is too difficult for an educated man', and suggested choosing suitable brides from Latvia or Prussia, as well as a strategy for educating peasant girls. Future President Kazys Grinius deemed the challenge of changing 'a half-Polish woman [...] into a true Lithuanian' preferable to a bored intellectual husband turning to 'cards and alcohol'. Bachelorhood was framed as a patriotic sacrifice akin to clerical celibacy, but some young activists honed their social graces and found their spouses at Polonophone salons and country estates.[24]

Among them was the future President Antanas Smetona. He entered the world in 1874 in a wooden, thatched-roofed cottage as the sixth child of former serfs. Educated first by his parents, and then in Palanga, Mitau (Jelgava), and St Petersburg, this lawyer developed a love of philosophy (especially Plato), and distaste for socialism and revolution. Encouraged by his inspirational teacher Jonas Jablonskis, he married Sofija Chodakauskaitė (Zofia Chodakowska), whom he had earlier tutored at her family's manor near Ukmergė. Her family was distantly related to the Piłsudskis, but it also cultivated Lithuanian language and tradition. Sofija's godmother was Gabrielė Petkevičaitė, of whom more below.

Many who espoused similar political ideologies also parted company along national lines. Clandestine discussions of socialist ideas began in Vilnius in the 1870s. Networks scotched by the tsarist police were soon re-established. Vilnan socialists established branches in Warsaw, Kyiv, Moscow, and St Petersburg. By the first years of the twentieth century, seven main, partly overlapping socialist parties operated covertly in the Lithuanian and Belarusian lands. These were the Social Democratic Party of Lithuania which had the largest membership and postulated a democratic foundation of Lithuania, Poland, and other countries; the Jewish Bund (Algemeyner Yidisher Arbeter-bund in Lite, Poyln un Rusland); the Russian Social Democratic Workers' Party; the Polish Socialist Party; the Social Democracy of the Kingdom of Poland and Lithuania; the Social Democratic Workers' Party of Russia; and finally, the diminutive Belarusian Socialist Assembly. The leadership and membership of the first of these parties became mainly Lithuanian-speaking.

We may skip the details of the socialists' splits and mergers, but the fundamental conflict was between internationalism and nationalism. Two sons of old, financially straitened Polish–Lithuanian noble families, both born in the Vilnius governorate, personified the opposing directions. One was Feliks Dzierżyński, who prioritised a general proletarian revolution, rejecting the cause of national independence. After years in and out of prison and labour camps, 'Iron Feliks' Dzerzhinskii would become the Bolsheviks' most murderous enforcer. The other was Józef Piłsudski. He too developed a hatred of tsarist autocracy during his miserable time at the same school in Vilnius, but he also imbibed his family's cult of the 1863 uprising and devoured Polish Romantic poetry. As a first-year student in Kharkiv, Piłsudski mingled with the 'terrorist fraction' of the revolutionary organisation called The People's Will (Narodnaia Wola). After serving a five-year sentence in Siberia, he returned to Vilnius and directed the activities of the Polish Socialist Party in Lithuania. A gifted journalist, he also specialised in spectacular actions such as robbing a post train to raise funds. His insistence on first achieving Polish independence by revolutionary deeds made him enemies in the international socialist movement. It complicated his relations with Jewish and Lithuanian socialists. Rival aspirations would be tested by the revolutions that racked the Russian Empire in 1905.

UNDER IMPERIAL RULE

iv. *Modern Lithuanian Nationalism and its Rivals*

The Japanese attack on the Russian Far East Fleet on 8 February 1904, followed three hours later by a declaration of war, sent shock waves through the Russian Empire. Japanese victories on land and at sea humiliated the tsarist autocracy and emboldened its domestic foes. In a further sign of changing times, the United States of America mediated the peace settlement in September 1905. The massacre of petitioners in front of the Winter Palace in St Petersburg on 'Bloody Sunday' (22 January 1905) escalated the strikes and protests. These often turned violent, especially in the cities of the Kingdom of Poland where Piłsudski (by now leader of the Polish Socialist Party) saw an opportunity to overthrow the regime and establish an independent Poland. The limited industrialisation of the Lithuanian and Belarusian lands meant that even the thousands of striking workers in Vilnius and Minsk (many of them Jewish) were not in the vanguard of the pan-imperial proletarian revolt. Peasant self-defence bands contested swathes of the countryside with paramilitary monarchist counter-insurgents and regular imperial troops. However, attacks on manors were far less frequent than in the vast communal agricultural zone of European Russia, or in Courland and Livonia. Violence against Jews remained rare, whereas murderous pogroms swept the lands further south and east.

The shaken Nicholas II promised a consultative assembly, and greater freedoms of speech, language, and religion. However, the tsar's promises failed to keep pace with rising expectations, leading to further strikes and protests in the autumn. Among the strikers were Vilnan railwaymen. The October Manifesto, reluctantly accepted by Nicholas II, admitted the bankruptcy of autocracy by granting a wide range of civil rights. Political parties would be able to contest elections to a legislative assembly (Duma).

On 11 November 1905, some Lithuanian activists published an appeal to their compatriots to elect representatives to a

Congress of Lithuanians in the *Vilnius News* (*Vilniaus žinios*). One of the initiators was Jonas Basanavičius, who with three colleagues sent a public memorandum to the imperial prime minister, Sergei Witte. This summarised the Lithuanian national narrative and demanded: Lithuanian autonomy; the use by the tsar of the title of Grand Duke of Lithuania; universal education in Lithuanian; the admission of Lithuanian to public administration; and political and religious freedom for all nationalities. The last of these demands should be set against the claim that Lithuanians were the original and legitimate inhabitants of a wide territorial area, and that other residents were either immigrants or 'slavicised Lithuanians'.

The Congress of Lithuanians, later hailed as the Great Seimas of Vilnius, met on 4–5 December 1905. Over 2,000 people squeezed into the ornate new, electrically lit City Hall. This was more than twice as many people as had been elected as delegates by their communes. Some came from East Prussia. Peasants formed the majority of participants, followed by professionals, workers, and priests. There were about a dozen sympathetic Jewish and Belarusian socialists, and a few Polonophones. Dr Basanavičius opened and chaired the sessions, but he had to accept a presidium that included social democrats and conservative Catholics, as well as a more political agenda than he had intended. The 'patriarch' addressed 'Lithuanian men and women' in his opening speech, but when some of the seven women participants tried to address the assembly, they were booed.

The most important of the four resolutions demanded:

> autonomy for Lithuania with a *seimas* in Vilnius, elected by universal, equal and secret ballot regardless of gender, ethnicity and religion. Such an autonomous Lithuania shall consist of present-day ethnographic Lithuania as a nucleus with those fringe areas which for various economic, cultural, ethnic or other reasons are attracted to the nucleus and whose population would be willing to belong to it.

UNDER IMPERIAL RULE

The claimed territory explicitly included Suvalkija.[25] The congress also called for schooling and local administration in Lithuanian, but it did not mention land reform, disappointing the peasant majority of delegates. But how might these heart's desires be fulfilled? Although Lithuanians needed 'to unite and together with the insurgent nations of Russia join battle' against 'the current tsarist government [...] our deadly enemy',[26] the delegates rejected violence and sanctioned only peaceful and passive resistance to the imperial state. Thanks to the prescient young leaders of the Lithuanian Peasant Union (Lietuvos valstiečių sąjunga, an offshoot of the Lithuanian Democratic Party), hundreds of rural delegates took home printed calls to refuse taxes and conscription, and to take over local administration and schools. Over half the communes of the Kaunas governorate did just that. On 3 December, the Russian governor of Suwałki reported 'a revolutionary firestorm which has taken on a mass character'.[27]

The tsarist regime restored its authority during 1906. Although the repression was less violent than in some other parts of the empire, martial law lasted in the Lithuanian governorates for a further three or four years. Constitutional liberties could be overridden by administrative *fiat*. Nevertheless, the regime failed to develop a coherent policy towards the nationalities of the region. Lithuanian social, cultural, and economic associations could operate openly, subject to surveillance and obstruction by suspicious officials. Basanavičius's moderately liberal Lithuanian National Democratic Party (another offshoot of the Lithuanian Democratic Party), encountered few problems from the police, whereas most social democrats were imprisoned or chose emigration. Catholic activists, shaken by the violence in the countryside, re-consolidated their position. Within a few years, the clergy exercised control of most Lithuanian-language periodicals. Supported by donations from Lithuanian Americans, the Catholic

LITHUANIA

association 'The Sun' (Saulė) established a seminary to train teachers in Kaunas. Most public schools in Lithuanian-speaking areas offered some teaching in the language, while the number of private schools with teaching in Lithuanian rose rapidly. By 1914 there were about fifty of these at a higher or lower secondary level, including one for girls in Marijampolė.[28]

The Lithuanian women's movement exemplifies tensions within Lithuanian nationalism. At its head was Gabrielė Petkevičaitė. She was born at her noble family's manor in northern Lithuania, where her parents, who sympathised with the common folk, imbued in her an ethic of service and encouraged her to learn Lithuanian. She began to write for *The Bell* in 1892. Žemaitė spurred her on. She would later add her pen-name 'Bitė', ('the Bee'), to her surname. Her choice reflected her accomplished beekeeping, as well as the insects' industriousness. Having been one of the seven female delegates to the Great Seimas of 1905, Petkevičaitė-Bitė presided over the first Congress of Lithuanian Women held in Kaunas in 1907. Recognising that 'peasant women [...] managed to preserve our nation from extinction', she called on women from the intelligentsia to educate future generations.[29] The event was marred by clashes between rural Catholic women and their priests on the one hand, and secular, educated, and well-dressed Vilnan women, supported by liberal and social democrat politicians, on the other. The former established a separate Lithuanian Catholic Women's Organisation the following year. Petkevičaitė-Bitė, Žemaitė, and others continued to defy conservative and clerical attempts to define women as home-makers, but family and caring responsibilities sapped the time and energy they could devote to their cause. Nor were secular male intellectuals always supportive. In 1910, the writer Sofija Kymantaitė-Čiurlionienė lambasted their complexes when faced 'with equally well-educated women'.[30]

Tsarist autocracy was beyond repair, but the constitutional and parliamentary monarchy formalised by the revision to the

UNDER IMPERIAL RULE

Fundamental Laws of the Russian Empire issued on 6 May 1906 rested on weak foundations. The tsar could still legislate without the Duma, as well as veto its decisions and dissolve it when he pleased. Moreover, its electoral procedures favoured wealthy landowners and businessmen over farmers and workers. Nevertheless, eight out of the fourteen deputies elected in 1906 to the First Duma from the Kaunas, Vilnius, and Suwałki governorates were ethnic Lithuanians, compared to four Poles, one Jew, and one Belarusian. Seven Lithuanians were elected to the Second Duma in 1907, including five social democrats from the Kaunas governorate. However, only four Lithuanians entered the less truculent and longer-lasting Third Duma later that year, three of them from the liberal Lithuanian Democratic Party. Four Lithuanians were also elected to the Fourth Duma in 1912. Russian parliamentarianism stimulated Russian nationalism. Lithuanian deputies heard that Catholic Poles, determined to prevent pagan Lithuanians from being absorbed into a higher Russian and Orthodox culture and civilisation, had artificially constructed their nation.

During this period, reforms introduced by Prime Minister Petr Stolypin allowed wealthier peasants to establish full ownership of the land they farmed. The policy owed much to his firsthand knowledge of Lithuania. The owner of an estate near Kėdainai, he had served as marshal of the nobles of the Kaunas governorate. The land reforms, which further stratified rural society, encountered resistance in the communal farming zone of the empire. Following Stolypin's assassination at the opera in Kyiv, the regime veered between concessions and crackdowns. The tercentenary of the Romanov dynasty in 1913 intensified the emotional turn away from Peter the Great's westward-looking empire towards an older, mystic bond imagined between the tsars and Muscovite 'Holy Rus''.

Mystic bonds of a different kind waft out of the music and paintings of Mikalojus Konstantinas Čiurlionis. The eldest of

LITHUANIA

nine children born to Polish-speaking parents, he grew up in the spa town of Druskininkai, where his father was the church organist. The boy's prodigious musical talent attracted notice. The aristocrat Mikołaj Michał Ogiński brought him to his orchestral school at Plungė in Samogitia, and then funded his musical studies in Warsaw and Leipzig. Čiurlionis composed sacral music, choral songs, and pieces for the piano, but his speciality became the symphonic or tone poem, a form that allowed his listeners to wander 'In the Forest' (*Miške*, 1901), or to contemplate 'The Sea' (*Jūra*, 1907). While teaching music to support himself, he studied as a painter in Warsaw. There, in 1906, he dedicated his work to Lithuania. The following year he moved to Vilnius and became a founding member of the Lithuanian Art Society (Lietuvių dailės draugija) and a participant in its annual exhibitions. His symbolic, increasingly abstract work, created using tempera and often structured as cycles or triptychs, evoked the seasons, the stars, and even 'the Creation of the World'. Pagan and Christian motifs fused, just as they did on the elaborately carved crosses in the rural cemeteries he depicted. In Vilnius, Čiurlionis met the well-travelled and educated writer of minor noble descent, Sofija Kymantaitė. She taught him Lithuanian, having learned it herself a decade earlier. They married in 1909, but two years later he died, exhausted by overwork. His finest paintings can now be enjoyed while listening to his music in the Čiurlionis National Museum in Kaunas.

As the above examples indicate, from 1905 onwards Lithuanian presses, schools, associations, and charities multiplied in Vilnius. In the last years before the First World War, two daily newspapers competed for advertising and readers: the liberal *Lithuanian News* (*Lietuvos žinios*), edited by Jonas Vileišis, the youngest brother of Petras, and the Catholic *Hope* (*Viltis*), edited by Antanas Smetona. Members of the Lithuanian Scientific Society (Lietuvių mokslo draugija), founded in 1907, vocally staked out their place in the city's public life. They protested—successfully—against a plan to build a water reservoir in Gediminas's Upper Castle. They planned a national museum in the city, combining natural sciences, art, and history. Without doubt, the Vilnan question had moved up the Lithuanian national agenda since the 1880s, when leading writers had lamented that Lithuanian was little spoken in Vilnius and that, as the cemeteries bore witness, 'others achieved greatness there'.[31] By the turn of the century, more Lithuanian activists had moved to the city, and visual images of its sacral and historical monuments spread. In 1905, the broad-based, well-organised Lithuanian national movement named Vilnius as the seat of the autonomous parliament.

In this vision, Vilnius would be the capital not of a multinational Lithuania in its historical borders, but of a Lithuanian Lithuania in its aspirational ethnographic boundaries, hosting other nationalities as minorities. Mainly for practical reasons, the Great Seimas chose the horizontal tricolour of yellow, green, and red (colours widely used in traditional motifs) as the national flag, instead of the banner of the chasing knight, the Vytis. Yet it also claimed continuity with the Grand Duchy of Lithuania. Vilnius, then best known to Lithuanian-speaking peasants through religious pilgrimages, symbolised that former greatness. Looking forward, as Smetona argued, 'the establishment of the Lithuanians in Vilnius' could bring the surrounding rural folk 'back to the Lithuanian nation'.[32] Vilnius was also the largest city in the region and a communications hub. The alternative of Kaunas, closer to the faithful Samogitian heartlands, enjoyed support among those Catholic activists who regarded Vilnius as a lost cause, and had low expectations of political autonomy. In and after 1905, the more ambitious view prevailed. The new incarnation of Lithuania would define itself both historically and ethnically. This goal would necessarily involve weakening and even breaking the role of Polish language and culture in public life. Once Poles began to take the Lithuanian project seriously, it would generate intense opposition, and the flashpoint would be Vilnius.

Even as Lithuanian civil society flourished, most early twentieth-century Vilnans considered themselves either Jewish or Polish (but rarely both, unlike in Warsaw or L'viv). Lithuanian-speakers remained in fifth place, after speakers of Russian and Belarusian. No subsequent official statistics significantly challenged the 1897 figures, which had indicated that 2.1 per cent of the city's population were native speakers of Lithuanian. Because the subjective linguistic test used in the census delivered such disappointing results, Lithuanian nationalists proposed ethnographic criteria—including customs, folk melodies, and building techniques—to determine people's nationality 'objectively'. In addition, Polonised forms of ancestral Lithuanian surnames could help to identify persons suitable for revindication. As we have seen, quite a few of the fathers and mothers of the modern Lithuanian nation came from old noble families, learned Lithuanian as a second language, and embraced the cause. But many more descendants of such families did not.

Many of these Polonophones considered themselves historical Lithuanians (*Litwini*) without rejecting their Polishness. They looked back to the Grand Duchy of Lithuania and accentuated their differences from the inhabitants of the former Polish Crown (*koroniarze*). For some conservative landowners, this attitude was largely expressed in paternalism. Others went further: the former Grand Duchy constituted a distinct country (*kraj*) which belonged equally to its overlapping nationalities—although not to the Russians. They sought a way for this country and its peoples to develop harmoniously in pursuit of the common good. They were referred to as *krajowcy*—a name variously translated, including 'regionalists'. That does not do justice to their patriotism, and I prefer 'homelanders'.

On the conservative side of the movement, the most prominent person was the aristocratic, French-educated Hipolit Korwin-

Milewski. He founded the *Vilnan Courier* (*Kurier wileński*) in 1905. The most democratic 'homelanders' supported land reform and universal suffrage. Among them, Michał Römer (Mykolas Römeris) was the most sympathetic to the Lithuanian cause. Descending from a Livonian noble family settled in northern Lithuania, Römer studied law in St Petersburg, history in Kraków, and economics in Paris, before returning to Lithuania in 1905. The following year he began to edit the liberal *Vilnan Gazette* (*Gazeta Wileńska*). Römer's book *Lithuania: A Study of the Rebirth of the Lithuanian Nation* (*Litwa. Studyum o odrodzeniu narodu litewskiego*), published in L'viv in 1908, remains the foundational analysis of the cultural, social, and political phenomenon, on which other scholars have since elaborated.

Another democratic 'homelander' was the Vilnan lawyer Tadeusz Wróblewski. Among those he defended in court were the sailors accused of mutiny on the battleship 'Potemkin'. He adopted the concept developed by Austrian socialists of personal cultural autonomy, rather than national-territorial divisions within the former Grand Duchy of Lithuania. Never a front-line politician, he collected books and manuscripts, including the archives of old Lithuanian noble families. In 1912 he opened a public library in Vilnius, named after his parents, although he was unable to provide a suitable building. After his death the Polish state bought the Tyszkiewicz Palace on the banks of the Neris to house the collections and opened the Wróblewski State Library in 1931. Ten years later, still in the same building, it became the Library of the Academy of Sciences of the Lithuanian SSR, a function it resumed after the Second World War. Among the additions to the collection is the archive of the Vilnius Cathedral Chapter, found in the foundations of the cathedral and deposited in the library in 1956. After Lithuania regained its independence, readers regained access to those holdings deemed unsuitable for Soviet citizens. The library was threatened with

LITHUANIA

the dispersal of its collections and sale of its palatial building, but protests by Lithuanian and international scholars not only saved its existence, but also restored the name of its patron. Since 2009 it has been the Wróblewski Library of the Lithuanian Academy of Sciences (Lietuvos mokslų akademijos Vrublevskių biblioteka). In this writer's experience, the spacious reading rooms, exceptional card indexes, and helpful staff make it the finest place for research into Lithuanian history.

'Homelanders' defended the local-mindedness (*tutejszość*) of Belarusian-speaking peasants as a form of local patriotism, rejecting the idea that they were 'unconscious' nationally and ripe for recruitment into this or that national project. But for the great majority of uneducated 'locals' (*tutejsi*) who might potentially have supported 'homeland' ideas, the step from a state of mind to a political ideology was too great a leap. Meanwhile the attractions of rival national causes, with their relatively straightforward slogans, grew rapidly. Political cooperation between the more democratic 'homelanders' and the more liberal Lithuanian nationalists did not survive the events of 1905, even if their social exchanges remained amicable. The 'homelanders' shared more aspirations with the leaders of the nascent Belarusian national movement, and some belonged to both camps.

Gradually drowning out the gentle melody of the 'homelanders' was the drumbeat of the harsher wing of modern Polish nationalism. Roman Dmowski cogently expressed the unsentimental imperative to keep up with the times in his *Thoughts of a Modern Pole* (*Myśli nowoczesnego Polaka*, 1903). Born to indigent post-noble parents near Warsaw, his exceptional intellectual discipline enabled him to become the chief ideologue of the clandestine National League (Liga Narodowa) founded in 1893, which in 1897 reformed as the National Democratic Party (Stronnictwo Narodowo-Demokratyczne). This formation operated in all parts of the former Polish–Lithuanian Commonwealth, although only from 1905 could it do so openly in the Russian Empire. Dmowski was a deputy to the first three Dumas, in which National Democrats and allied groups formed the Polish Circle. They achieved little there, for which they were attacked by their socialist rivals, who boycotted all four elections.

Dmowski regarded Piłsudski as an irresponsible adventurer. While both men belong to the spectrum of Polish nationalism (when understood neutrally), they held fundamentally different visions of Poland. For the man of action Piłsudski, a historical Lithuanian who often spoke contemptuously about Crown Poles, what counted was an independent Polish state, not its inhabitants' ethnicity, language, or religion. For Dmowski and his admirers, those things were vital. They blamed the anarchic *szlachta* for the downfall of the Commonwealth and for neglecting opportunities to turn most of its non-noble inhabitants into nationally conscious Poles. In their racialised, social-Darwinist mindset (shared with many educated people across Europe and the Americas), they conceived a Polish nation that needed discipline and leadership in the struggle for survival. Dmowski argued in *Germany, Russia, and the Polish Question* (*Niemcy, Rosja i kwestia polska*, 1907), that because the German national destiny depended on eastward expansion at Polish expense, Poles should seek accommodation with the Russian Empire, allied to France and Great Britain. Moreover, he viewed German culture as greatly superior to Russian (analogously, modern Lithuanian nationalists feared the strength of Polish culture more than they did Russian). National Democrats also believed that Lithuanian, Belarusian, and Ukrainian speakers could and should be assimilated into the modern Polish nation, thereby expanding its national territory and demographic mass, but they deemed Jews irremediably alien and hostile. In their agitation, older religious prejudices and economic grievances morphed into a modern, pseudo-scientific racial and antisemitic ideology (the word 'anti-

LITHUANIA

semitism' was coined in Germany in 1878 and soon spread far and wide).[33]

The National Democrats' bastion became Greater Poland, part of the German Empire, whereas in historical Lithuania they faced strong challenges from traditional conservatives, liberals, and socialists. They were also handicapped by their prioritisation of the Kingdom of Poland over concessions to Poles in the east. There were probably only a few dozen committed National Democrats in Vilnius on the eve of the First World War, but their ideas increasingly appealed to those who considered themselves simply as Poles (sometimes in response to the gauntlet thrown down by modern Lithuanian nationalism). For National Democrats, the idea of restoring the Grand Duchy of Lithuania in a federation with Poland was an anachronistic distraction from the national struggle. In claiming historical Lithuania for Poland, they appealed to the evidence of monuments and cemeteries for eastward spread of Polish culture, but they also put forward demographic and linguistic arguments. Because they believed the Jews should not count, Wilno (Vilnius) was a Polish city in a Polish hinterland. In most of the surrounding countryside, local dialects known as 'simple speech' functioned alongside cultured Polish and official Russian, serving different purposes, but since few villagers articulated any national consciousness, at least the Catholics among them could and should be made into committed Poles. This position won the National Democrats allies among the local Polish and Catholic clergy, despite the incompatibility of the doctrine of racial struggle with Catholic universalism.

The phenomenon of Belarusian-speaking, Catholic peasants becoming Poles galvanised Belarusian nationalists. In 1905 the Belarusian Socialist Assembly established a printing house in Minsk. However, the group's first newspaper, *Our Fate* (*Nasha Dolia*) experienced a false-start. After the confiscation of almost all the first few issues, the regime banned this subversive publication early in 1907. By then a more politically prudent weekly called *Our Field* (*Nasha Niva*, published simultaneously 'in Ruthenian and Polish letters') was spreading the message that it would 'serve *the entire oppressed Belarusian nation*, seeking to be a mirror to life, and from us, as from the mirror, light will disperse the darkness.' It also promised calm writing, based on 'cool reason'. Among its causes was elementary hygiene. Ceaselessly advocating social justice, the paper called for Belarusian peasants' solidarity with the impoverished majority of Jews who toiled in workshops and factories. For almost a decade the paper, edited from Vil'nia (Vilnius), involved as many as 3,000 regular or occasional contributors and had a four-figure print-run. It set linguistic standards and published poems and novellas. These included the debut work of Maksim Bahdanovich. Born in Minsk, his father was a bank clerk of peasant descent, while his mother was of Ruthenian noble stock. His poems, essays, and novels became part of the canon of Belarusian literature. The editors also published annual almanacs containing both practical information and literary news. Nevertheless, the scale of the task was implicit in the editors' pledge 'to endeavour that *all Belarusians*, who do not know that they exist, *would understand that they are Belarusians and human beings*, and that they should know their rights and help us in our work.'[34]

It has become a cliché that Belarusian nationalism was much younger and weaker than its rivals. Its main problem was not that the identified members of the Belarusian nation were overwhelmingly peasants, most of them downtrodden and illiterate. Nor was it decisive that few Polish–Lithuanian–Ruthenian nobles followed the examples of Wincenty Dunin-Marcinkiewicz and Konstanty Kalinowski. While these factors limited the pool of activists, they did make the message more coherent. The Belarusian national cause, like the Ukrainian one, fed on the social cleavages that beset Polish nationalism. Between the Rivers Neman, Prypiats', and Dniapro, millions of peasants (*muzhyki*) and their families knew they were not Polish lords (*pany*). Numbers were on the Belarusians' side. For what it is worth, the 1897 census counted 5,885,547 speakers of Belarusian and 1,658,532 of Lithuanian and Samogitian.

On the other hand, religious factors hindered the Belarusian cause. In the early nineteenth century, most Christians in the Belarusian lands were Uniates, but the Russian Empire abolished the Union in 1839. From 1905 it was possible to convert from Orthodoxy to Catholicism, but only into the Latin rite. Perhaps 20,000 descendants of Uniates chose this path, and naturally looked towards Vilnius as 'their spiritual capital'.[35] Due to the tsarist regime's long-standing identification of Roman Catholic churches as 'Polish', and Orthodox ones as 'Russian', the space in between all but vanished. The language of instruction in the Catholic religion was contested between the Catholic hierarchy, which wanted Polish, and imperial officials, who wanted Russian. Both sides feared that prayers in Belarusian would be a stepping stone to the loss of souls. In contrast, in Austrian Galicia the Greek Catholic Church flourished and became a Ukrainian national church. Lithuanian nationalists, for their part, contested the Roman Catholic Church with the Poles.

Linguistic factors also played their part. Belarusian dialects imperceptibly shaded into Polish and Russian on the Slavonic continuum between west and east. While Lithuanian speakers were not immune from the cultural prestige of Polish or the career advantages of Russian, Belarusian speakers with social ambitions were likely to find their national identity as Poles or Russians, before they could be convinced that they were 'in fact' Belarusians. As Timothy Snyder has observed, the fact that the claimed Belarusian national territory was not partitioned handicapped the cause, because there was no respite from tsarist oppression. Not only had Belarusians no equivalent to the freedoms enjoyed by Poles and Ukrainians in autonomous Galicia, but—even had much demand for Belarusian texts existed—the Lithuanian phenomenon of cross-border book smuggling was unattainable.[36] When the ban imposed in 1863 on publishing in Belarusian (even in Cyrillic script) was lifted in 1905, Belarusian nationalists found themselves far behind their rivals, especially in the race for mass literacy in the national language.

The regime's persistent assumption of a binary divide between loyal Orthodox Russians and disloyal Catholic Poles, and the rise of modern Lithuanian nationalism both contributed to the waning attraction to Belarusian nationalists of Litva (Lithuania) as the name of their country. Confronting the Muscovite appropriation of the heritage of Rus′, in 1910, Vatslaŭ Latoŭski, who had been born into the petty nobility and had previously (as Wacław Lastowski) been a member of the Polish Socialist Party, advanced the 'Krievan' theory. This held that Belarusians were of 'Aryan' stock, whereas the Great Russians were essentially descendants of the Mongols. The name came from a tribal formation mentioned in the oldest Rus′ian chronicles. Lastoŭski would later argue that while 'Belarus' was widely used, 'our ancient and true name is *Krivichi* and the country—*Kryviia*'.[37] Although such racialised theories had limited impact at the time, pejorative associations of 'Muscovites' with 'Mongols' have taken root, and are given academic plausibility by published philological and pseudo-genetic research.

The Jews of the Lithuanian and Belarusian lands, known as Litvaks, were still overwhelmingly defined by their religion in the 1860s, when Alexander II's reforms removed some of the barriers to their integration. For many Jews, little seemed to have changed by the 1900s, except that there were far more of them, despite the rising tide of emigration. Of the more than 5 million Jews counted by the 1897 census (slightly more by religion than by language), almost 1.5 million resided in the six Lithuanian and Belarusian governorates. Well over half of them lived in the countryside, but they formed at least half of the total urban population of the region. In Vilnius, Jews dominated the Old Town on both sides of German Street (*Daytshe gos* in Yiddish). Amidst innumerable shops, stalls, and workshops were many traditional elementary schools (*hedarim*, literally: rooms) and for advanced study—*yeshivot*. These institutions produced high levels of literacy in Hebrew letters, at least among men. At the same time, the growing minority of Maskilim studied at Russian or even German universities and moved into the professions, which enabled them to purchase or rent modern apartments or suburban villas. Their Russian was often better than their Yiddish. Many more Jews worked in factories, where socialist parties operated.

The early Zionist movement may be considered a Jewish form of nationalism which saw the only solution to European antisemitism in a Jewish nation-state. Not all Zionists as yet necessarily located their nation-state in Palestine, but the idea gained currency from the works of Abraham Mapu, a luminary of the Haskalah in Kaunas, who set his pioneering Hebrew-language novels in ancient Israel. Zionism also gained supporters in Vilnius, especially after 1902, when a world congress of religious Zionists begat the Mizrachi movement (whose religious nationalist successor-formations still play a controversial role in Israeli politics). However, the visit to the city of the movement's leader, Theodor Herzl, in 1903 did not delight all Litvaks. As an alternative to Zionism, the distinguished historian Simon Dubnow, a native of Mstsislaŭ but resident in Vilnius in 1905, promoted Jewish Autonomism, which emphasised linguistic and cultural distinctiveness as an antidote to assimilation. For their part, many religiously orthodox Jews believed it was sacrilegious to anticipate the coming of the Messiah by a premature 'return to Zion'. Rabbinical orthodoxy remained largely immune from

UNDER IMPERIAL RULE

Reform Judaism, even in the Moorish-style synagogue opened in 1903, where prosperous Jews worshipped. Others simply saw Lite (Lithuania) as their homeland.

The rulers and officials of the Russian Empire still regarded Vilnius as an 'awkward city'.[38] By the early twentieth century, the principal city of the North-Western Province, whose population was accelerating past 200,000, in some ways looked like dozens of other provincial capitals across the empire. The municipal authorities tried to address the chronic problems of sewerage, lighting, and transportation. However, they rejected trams as too noisy. Horse-drawn cabs and bicycles continued to provide the main alternative to walking for a generation to come (even today Vilnius has buses and trolley-buses, but not trams). Along St George's Avenue and in the 'New Town' rose apartment buildings for imperial officials and officers in a fussy, historicising style, while onion-domed Orthodox churches were placed to dominate the skyline. The regime inaugurated a monument to the 'hangman' Mikhail Murav'ev in front of the governor-general's palace in 1898. Six years later, next to the bell tower of the cathedral, a statue to Catherine the Great was ceremoniously unveiled, in the presence of prominent noble landowners who thought it prudent to attend. Its plinth rather desperately sought to legitimise the partitions with the inscription in Russian: 'that which was torn away, now returned'. Displays in the public library asserted the Russian character of the region. The imperial authorities feared Vilnius as an irreducible bastion of Polish culture. After 1905 that culture flourished openly, not only in print and on canvas, but also in new media such as cinema. Its flagship initiative was the Polish Theatre built on the initiative of Korwin-Milewski in 1912–14. It was known after its address as 'on Pohulanka' (now Basanavičius Street).

Less modern aspects of Vilnius on the eve of the First World War are evoked by the photographs of Jan Bułhak: arches binding narrow streets, pilgrims kneeling in the street before the Madonna of the Sharp Gate (*Ostra Brama*), domes, spires, towers, and belfries rising through mist and smoke. Influenced in his pictorial compositions by the painter Ferdynand Ruszczyc, who had earlier taught Čiurlionis, Bułhak created no less than 12,000 images of Vilnius between 1912 and 1915. *Belle-époque* Vilnius, in which it was still possible for friendships and marriages to bridge national and religious divides, and even for Poles and Lithuanians to join in each other's folk-dances at soirées, has cast its spell over twenty-first-century intellectuals. Mindaugas Kvietkauskas, currently dean of the Philology Faculty of Vilnius University and previously minister of culture, has explored the 'counterpoints' of the city's multilingual modernist literature.[39] The Vilnan poet Tomas Venclova imagines the early twentieth century as:

> a moment of balance, which could never afterwards be regained. All the nationalities enriched the identity of the city, even if they disagreed about its past and future. Nobody foresaw the approaching disasters. It seemed that history, in whichever way it would turn, was moving in the direction of tolerance, humanity, and openness.[40]

This enchanting metropolitan vision weaves together a better past and a better future. However, the great majority of the inhabitants of Lithuania (whether defined historically or ethnographically) lived in the countryside. 'The intelligentsia live their life, while the people live their own', warned a contributor to *Lithuanian News* in 1912.[41] Liberal, secular nationalists and democratic 'homelanders' have received most attention from historians and intellectuals, but by the early twentieth century, a Catholic and ethno-linguistic Lithuanian identity had rooted itself in the farming communities of Samogitia, Aukštaitija, and Suvalkija. The situation was more complex around Vilnius, and across the Belarusian governorates, but almost everywhere stances were hardening, not least between the clergy and anti-

UNDER IMPERIAL RULE

clericals. The politics of the Russian Empire were also poised between autocracy, nationalism, populism, and liberalism when millions of Europeans went to war in the summer of 1914.

Map 7: Actual and claimed Lithuanian territory, 1918–40

Fig. 1: The monument to Gediminas and the Palace of the Grand Dukes of Lithuania, Vilnius.

Fig. 2: Zygmunt Vogel, *The Church and Monastery of the Priests of the Mission*, Vilnius, c. 1800.

Fig. 3: Jan Matejko, *The Battle of Grunwald*, 1878.

Fig. 4: The interior of the Church of Saints Peter and Paul, Antakalnis, Vilnius.

Fig. 5: Franciszek Smuglewicz, *The Interior of the Great Synagogue*, Vilnius, 1785–86.

Fig. 6: Anonymous painter, *Nobles in the Uniforms of their Palatinates*, 1790s.

Fig. 7: Mikalojus Konstantinas Čiurlionis, *Samogitian Cemetery*, 1909.

Fig. 8: Artur Grottger, *Lithuania: The Forest.*

Fig. 9: Artur Grottger, *Lithuania: The Sign.*

Fig. 10: Artur Grottger, *Lithuania: The Oath.*

Fig. 11: Artur Grottger, *Lithuania: The Battle.*

Fig. 12: Artur Grottger, *Lithuania: The Ghost*.

Fig. 13: Artur Grottger, *Lithuania: The Apparition*.

Fig. 14: Petras Rimša, model for the *Lithuanian School*, 1906.

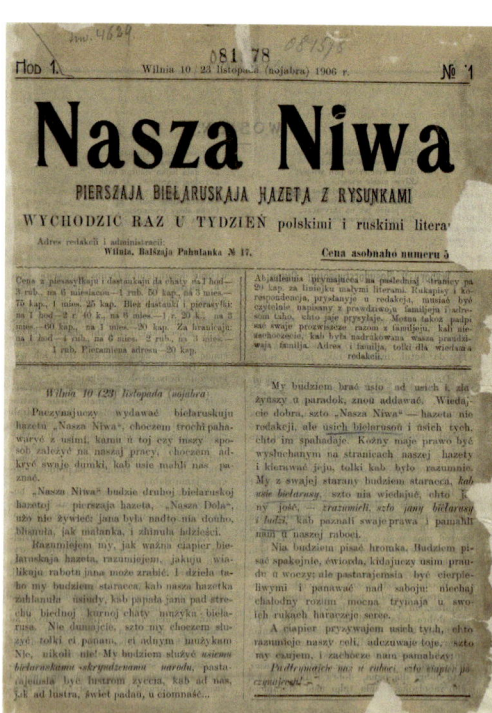

Fig. 15: The first issue of *Nasza Niwa*, 1906.

Fig. 16: Jan Bułhak, *Vilnius: the Bernardine Alley at Night*, 1912.

Fig. 17: Jan Bułhak, *Vilnius: General View*, 1912–16.

Fig. 18: The Council of Lithuania (*Lietuvos Taryba*) that later declared independent statehood. Photograph by Aleksandra Jurašaitytė (later Vailokaitienė). Standing from the left: Kazys Bizauskas, Jonas Vailokaitis, Donatas Malinauskas, Vladas Mironas, Mykolas Biržiška, Alfonsas Petrulis, Saliamonas Banaitis, Petras Klimas, Aleksandras Stulginskis, Jokūbas Šernas, Pranas Dovydaitis. Seated from the left: Jonas Vileišis, Jurgis Šaulys, Justinas Staugaitis, Stanisław Narutowicz, Jonas Basanavičius, Antanas Smetona, Kazimieras Šaulys, Steponas Kairys, Jonas Smigevičius.

Fig. 19: Deputies to the Constituent Seimas, 1920. From the left: Emilija Spudaitė-Gvildienė, Ona Muraškaitė-Račiukaitienė, Gabrielė Petkevičaitė-Bitė, Salomėja Stakauskaitė, Magdalena Draugelytė-Galdikienė.

Fig. 20: Kaunas modernism: The Pieno Centras building (1931–34) in 1938.

Fig. 21: Tragic heroes: Stasys Girėnas, Steponas Darius, and the *Lituanica*, 1933.

Fig. 22: 'The body is gone': clandestine photograph by George Kadish, 1943.

Fig. 23: The Jewish cemetery at Dieveniškės. Photograph by Wioletta Pawlikowska, 2024.

Fig. 24: Forest Brothers: Lithuanian partisans of the Vytautas military district, led by Kazimieras Kaladinskas (Erškėtis). Photograph by Juozas Karla, 1947.

Fig. 25: The Hill of the Crosses.

Fig. 26: Postcard of the Lazdynai estate, Vilnius, 1974.

Fig. 27: Trakai Castle, photograph by Augustas Didžgalvis, 2021.

Fig. 28: The Baltic Way in Šiauliai, 23 August 1989.

Fig. 29: Defending the Seimas, 13–14 January 1991. Photograph by Algimantas Žižiūnas.

Fig. 30: The cemetery at Norviliškės. Photograph by Wioletta Pawlikowska, 2024.

Fig. 31: A gravestone at Norviliškės. Photograph by Wioletta Pawlikowska, 2024.

5

BREAKING EMPIRES, MAKING NATIONS?

(1914–1940)

The First World War broke the empires of the Romanovs, Habsburgs, and Hohenzollerns, and from their wreckage emerged nation-states. The tide turned and the Nazi German and Soviet Russian empires broke the nation-states of Central and Eastern Europe.

The independent Republic of Lithuania fits this scheme quite well. It established itself at the high point of empire-breaking and nation-making in 1918–22. But after two largely successful decades, the Lithuanian nation-state was extinguished following the Nazi–Soviet carve-up of the region in 1939–40. However, the scheme lacks nuance. The First World War and its aftermath brought both the nationalisation of empires, and the imperialisation of nations. The German Empire (Reich) which occupied most of the historical Lithuanian lands was both nationalist and imperialist, Hitler's empire still more so. Stalin's Soviet Union imposed a different blend of imperialism and nationalism. Victorious Great Britain reached its imperial zenith, while losing most of Ireland to Irish nationalism. Even some of the successor-

LITHUANIA

states of Central and Eastern Europe resembled their imperial predecessors more than they cared to admit.

Despite the scale of death and destruction, until recently the First World War was relegated to the background of national narratives of independence—whether or not those stories had happy endings. Yet wartime conditions enabled overlapping nationalist, anti-imperial, and revolutionary causes to combust. The land question mattered more to rural majorities of populations than states' official languages, while violence produced more intense feelings of 'them' and 'us' than the most soaring patriotic rhetoric. Comradeship in exile and volunteering contributed to the spread of a shared national consciousness. All this applies to Lithuania.

If empires and nations could be broken, so could families. Most of the Römers opted for Poland, but when the 'homelander' Michał Römer's endeavours for compromise failed, he served Lithuania as Mykolas Römeris. Stanisław Narutowicz (also known as Stanislovas Narutavičius) signed the declaration of independent Lithuanian statehood in 1918. Yet his views were not so very different from those of his younger brother. A distinguished engineer who had electrified Switzerland, Professor Gabriel Narutowicz became the first president of the Republic of Poland in 1922, but he was assassinated four days after his inauguration by a fanatical Polish nationalist. The choices made by the Iwanowski family varied still more. Leonard Iwanowski was a Polish–Lithuanian nobleman who enjoyed a successful career as a chemical engineer and distiller in the Russian Empire, and a small estate near Lida. His eldest son Jerzy joined Józef Piłsudski's Polish Socialist Party and played a part in incorporating Vilnius into Poland, which he served as a minister and senator. The Vilnan lawyer Stanisław Iwanowski also chose Poland. Tadeusz (Tadas Ivanauskas) learned Lithuanian and became a professor of biology in Kaunas, where he established the Zoological Museum

BREAKING EMPIRES, MAKING NATIONS?

in 1919. The engineer Wacław (Vatslaŭ Ivanoŭski) became a leader of the Belarusian national cause before choosing Poland over the Bolsheviks. He lectured at Vilnius University before dying as a Belarusian collaborator with Nazi Germany. In contrast, his first wife Sabina, née Jaczynowska, hid Jewish women during the Nazi occupation. Their sons fell fighting for the Polish Home Army in 1944.

We should acknowledge the role of contingency, rather than imagine the fulfilment of national destinies—however strongly belief in national destiny motivated people to act. Unexpected opportunities arose. Some of them were seized—not least by Lithuanian leaders in 1918—and some were not. Foresight and luck played their parts as the limits of the possible changed rapidly and repeatedly, but all players in the game of nations and empires were constrained by choices made earlier. The odds were steep, yet as Tomas Balkelis puts it, 'by the late 1930s Lithuania hardly resembled the impoverished imperial Russian periphery of the early century'.[1] A similar verdict might be returned on the much larger Republic of Poland, despite the challenges of its own eastern peripheries. In contrast, the Belarusian state was stillborn, and the nation was only partly made before it was broken.

i. *From Occupation to Independence*

At the start of the First World War, most Lithuanian intellectuals stood by the Russian Empire. Gabrielė Petkevičaitė-Bitė wrote in her diary in September 1914:

> The German state is of much higher culture and in need of colonies: we would be exploited and denationalized, because the majority of our people have no self-awareness and they would not be able to stand against the power of such an iron culture. We don't have to fear these things from Russia.[2]

LITHUANIA

Jonas Basanavičius and two colleagues composed the 'Amber Declaration', read out in the Russian Duma on 4 September. It called on the Russian Empire to take Lithuania minor from Germany and unite the Lithuanian lands. The rhetoric was impassioned—'a common task of Lithuanian and Slav warriors is to combat [...] the all-devouring Germanism'—but it failed to persuade Russian ministers.[3] Soon afterwards the Prussian Landtag heard calls for Lithuania's unification within the German Empire. Either way, the possibility of the Polish lands being reunited under Russian aegis worried Lithuanian nationalists.

With the bulk of the German forces engaged in Belgium and France, two Russian armies marched into East Prussia. Famously, the German forces commanded by Paul von Hindenburg and coordinated by Erich Ludendorff outcommunicated, outmanoeuvred, and outgunned the Russians in the Battles of Tannenberg and the Masurian Lakes. The name given to the first victory avenged the Teutonic Knights after five centuries. The Russians attacked twice more, on each occasion inflicting pillage, rapine, and murder on civilians, before retreating. The Germans began their offensive in the spring of 1915 and took Kaunas on 18 August. The Russian authorities deported tens of thousands of Jews from their homes on suspicion of spying for the enemy. Russian landowners left of their own accord. In all, the order for 'scorched earth' displaced half a million people from the Lithuanian lands, mostly into the depths of the Russian Empire. As the Germans approached Vilnius, the Russians removed the fittings of 160 factories, as well as the statues of Murav'ev and Catherine II, before they left on 17 September.

The city council, dominated by local Poles, had already established a Civic Committee to represent Vilnans in relations with the Germans. The committee's twelve Poles from various political camps co-opted eleven Lithuanians, Belarusians, and Jews. The Lithuanian newspaper editor Jonas Vileišis became deputy chairman. The Belarusian leaders, Vatslaŭ Latoŭski and the brothers Ivan and Anton Lutskevich, were unable to find a suitable fourth candidate, so they asked the Polish socialist Aleksander Zasztowt to join the committee as a Belarusian. A scandal broke after the Polish relief committee in Switzerland, chaired by the novelist Henryk Sienkiewicz, sent funds to Vilnius not just for the Poles, but for all the city's communities. After most of the Poles on the committee objected, the German authorities distributed the money instead and soon afterwards restricted the committee's activities.

This fiasco did not bode well for intercommunal relations, already strained by the initial German proclamation in Vilnius issued on 18 September. In Polish, Russian, and German, Count Traugott von Pfeil greeted the city as the 'pearl in the glorious Kingdom of Poland'.[4] The following day Dr Basanavičius went to educate the German military command, but the posters had already been taken down. German plans for the nationalities of the occupied territories evolved. One variant under consideration in Berlin was to push the 'Polish Question' eastwards, facilitating the full Germanisation of the former Polish lands annexed by Prussia. On the other hand, General Ludendorff wanted to settle German veterans and refugees from Russia in the Baltic lands after the war. He considered the Poles both as the most serious contenders for statehood, and as the greatest potential obstacle to the emerging German war aims of economic, military, and political domination of *Mitteleuropa*. From this perspective, a restored Polish–Lithuanian Commonwealth, linked to other states between the Black and Baltic Seas, would be the worst conceivable outcome. The occupants therefore played off the Lithuanian Poles against their compatriots in the Kingdom of Poland, restricting communication between the two territories.

Ludendorff resisted any civilian oversight of Hindenburg as Supreme Commander of All German Forces in the East (Oberbefehlshaber der gesamten Deutschen Streitkräfte im

LITHUANIA

Osten, shortened to Ober Ost). This command was run by the Military Administration of Lithuania (Militärverwaltung Litauen). The territory was divided into six, later three, military districts. The shape of Ober Ost recalled the frontiers of the Grand Duchy of Lithuania between the second and third partitions. Its essential purpose was to identify and extract resources that Germany needed desperately because of the British naval blockade. To this end the occupants enforced draconian restrictions on movement. They also forced hundreds of thousands of underfed and physically maltreated people to build infrastructure for military purposes. Many folk hid in the forests, prompting reprisals for 'banditry'. The regime closed independently edited newspapers in the region's various languages, permitting only a few censored titles.

Onerous taxes, fees for permits, exorbitant requisitioning, and confiscation of property yielded a huge surplus over the costs of administration and investment. Between 1915 and 1918, the Germans extracted 90,000 horses, 140,000 cattle, and 767,000 pigs from Ober Ost. Almost 4 million cubic metres of wood were cut down.[5] Among the casualties were the bison of the Białowieża Forest, hitherto reserved for the tsar and his guests to hunt. The death rate also soared among humans weakened by malnutrition. Perhaps, however, alternative scenarios might have been even worse. The German advance ended mass conscription into the Russian army, which continued to take a heavy toll of Latvians and Estonians. Relatively little fighting took place in the Lithuanian heartlands.

Despite the practical and bureaucratic obstacles, national rivalries contributed to a bloom of cultural, scientific, and charitable activities in Ober Ost. As public demand for theatres, concerts, lectures, and bookshops grew, Lithuanians and Belarusians punched above their demographic weight in Vilnius. At first sight, the occupants' policies were relatively liberal regarding education. They permitted schools to be founded and run by all national groups, with teaching in any local language except Russian. By 1918, 1,350 public elementary schools were operating: 750 Lithuanian, 299 Polish, 164 Jewish, 89 Belarusian, 81 German, and 7 Latvian. The transformative effect was greatest in areas inhabited by hitherto unschooled Belarusian-speaking peasants. In teaching the German language, schools were expected to glorify Germany. 'Children's minds could be colonized from within through teaching "German from the inside"', explains the historian Vejas Liulevicius.[6] But too few local teachers could teach German at all, let alone in such a spirit. Traditions of clandestine schooling revived.

While the German occupants ruthlessly exploited resources, they also believed they brought *Ordnung* and *Kultur* to the filthy, slovenly, barbaric East. Contemplating a castle built by the Teutonic Knights from his headquarters in Kaunas, Ludendorff 'determined to resume that work of civilization [*Kultur*] at which the Germans had laboured in these lands for many centuries. The population, made up as it is of a mixture of races, has never produced a culture of its own and, left to itself, would succumb to Polish domination.'[7] He summed up the occupants' approach and assumptions:

> The Letts [Latvians] were opportunists, and awaited events. The Lithuanians believed the hour of deliverance was at hand, and when the good times they had anticipated did not materialize, owing to the cruel exigencies of war, they became suspicious once more, and turned against us. The Poles were hostile as they feared, quite justifiably, a pro-Lithuanian policy on our part. The White Ruthenians [Belarusians] were of no account, as the Poles had robbed them of their nationality and given them nothing in return. In the autumn of 1915 I thought I would like to obtain some idea of the distribution of this race. At first they were, literally, not to be found. Subsequently we discovered they were a widely-scattered people, apparently of Polish origin, but with such a low standard of civilization [*Kultur*] that it would be a long time before we could do any-

thing for them. The Jew [in the collective singular—R.B.] did not know what attitude to adopt, but he gave us no trouble, and we were at least able to converse with him, which was hardly ever possible with the Poles, Lithuanians and Letts. The language difficulties weighed heavily against us, and cannot be over-estimated. Owing to the dearth of German works of reference on the subject, we knew very little about the country or the people, and found ourselves in a strange world.[8]

German scholars soon set about documenting local folklore, as well as treasures of art and architecture, in which they found German traces.

The effects of the *Kulturmission* could be comic. A Vilnan diarist noted on 1 November 1915 that:

> for about a week an imposing number of German policemen in pickelhaubes and "Militär-Polizei" armbands has appeared on the streets of the city. [...] They issue instructions very energetically, particularly teaching the population how to walk along the street, that is, to keep on the right-hand side; they achieve this almost exclusively by pushes and shoves. They find this most difficult on narrow and busy streets.

Moreover, 'the greatest disorder was caused by German soldiers swaying along the streets from one beerhouse to another'.[9]

Order and culture required statistics. Ober Ost issued 1.8 million photographic identity cards, costing each identified person 1 mark. It conducted a census in Vilnius in the spring of 1916. If a person answered the question about their nationality by giving their religion, they were to be asked about their native language (in doubtful cases, the language spoken by their mothers). It yielded the following results: Poles: 50.15 per cent; Jews: 43.5 per cent; Lithuanians: 2.6 per cent; Russians: 1.46 per cent; Belarusians: 1.36 per cent; Germans: 0.72 per cent; others: 0.21 per cent. The outcome presented familiar challenges of interpretation to Lithuanian and Belarusian activists, who were in fact well represented among the representatives of the four Vilnan communities who carried out the survey under German instructions. The overall population was 141,000, about a third less since the start of the war.[10]

The German authorities applied the strategy of 'divide and rule'. Various national groups complained that they were singled out for harsher treatment than the others, although Hirsz Abramowicz later recalled: 'The German occupation during World War I oppressed everyone more or less equally'.[11] In April 1916, the German chancellor Theobald von Bethmann-Hollweg declared in the Reichstag that the nations—Poles, Lithuanians, Latvians, and Estonians—that lived between the Baltic Sea and the Volhynian marshes, liberated by the Germans and their allies, should not be returned to Russia. He did not mention the Belarusians or Jews, but his purposes were clear: to undermine pro-Russian calculations and stimulate rivalry for German support.

With the stakes raised, in September 1916 the 'homelander' Ludwik Abramowicz warned the Supreme National Committee of Poles in Austrian Galicia:

> The disdaining by the Polish nation of the rights of weaker peoples—the Lithuanians and Belarusians—to decide their own fates, the treating by it of the Lithuanian and Belarusian lands only as terrain for national expansion, the erasure of historical traditions for the doubtful gain that would be the acquisition of some sand and mud beyond the River Bug, would be unforgiveable mistakes, which would later constantly rebound on the further state development of Poland. The recognition of historical Lithuania as an indivisible whole should be the principle of Polish political thought.[12]

The warning would become a prophecy.

In Warsaw on 5 November 1916, the German and Austro–Hungarian authorities announced the restoration of the Kingdom of Poland. They specified neither its borders, nor its future relationship to Berlin and Vienna, but most Vilnan Poles rejoiced. Few of them supported the ideal of renewing the Polish–Lithuanian union on anything like equal terms; they desired the incorporation of historical Lithuania into Poland, if not as a whole, then in part. The memorandum sent to the German chancellor from Vilnius on 24 May 1917 by the Polish Committee (which had emerged from a Polish relief committee early in 1916), rejected the prospect of the Poles becoming a minority in a Lithuanian state, cut off from Poland. Alongside demographic arguments, it employed the rhetoric of a Polish civilising mission. Such an outcome was anathema to Ludendorff, 'as German rule in the territory under the Commander-in-Chief in the East must be based on the Lithuanians and the White Ruthenes.'[13] The Lithuanian riposte to the Polish memorandum not only condemned 'neo-Polish imperialism', but also clerical 'Polonisers', while Antanas Smetona persistently lobbied Berlin for a Lithuanian state with no connection to Poland and a capital in Vilnius.

The administrator of the diocese of Vilnius, Kazimierz Michalkiewicz, a signatory of the Polish memorandum, punished the five Lithuanian priests who had signed the response, but he was summoned to Rome and Pope Benedict XV sought a new bishop. Among the Lithuanian candidates was Aleksandras Dambrauskas ('Adomas Jakštas'), who in 1911 had compared nobles' Polishness to a 'grave and dangerous mental illness, similar to a mania'.[14] In November 1918, the pope announced his choice: Jurgis Matulaitis (Jerzy Matulewicz), the superior-general of the Marian Fathers. Born to a Lithuanian peasant family near Marijampolė, and now resident in Warsaw, Matulaitis personified conciliation, but he displeased many Vilnan Poles by greeting the faithful in both Polish and Lithuanian at his ingress.

The limits of the possible changed dramatically during 1917. In April, the United States of America entered the war on the side of the Anglo–French Entente, which promised an ultimate Allied victory and brought into play Lithuanian and Polish diasporas. The overthrow of the tsarist regime in Russia in early March changed the conditions for work among displaced persons. About half of the half-million refugees from the Lithuanian lands were ethnic Lithuanians. The Lithuanian War Relief Committee (Lietuvių draugija nukentėjusiems dėl karo šelpti) was founded in Vilnius on 21 November 1914. By 1915 it had 250 branches across the Russian Empire. These branches promoted moral and physical hygiene as they combated refugees' Russification or Polonisation. Particular attention was reserved for children. Among the teachers were the linguist Jonas Jablonskis and the writer Sofija Kymantaitė-Čiurlionienė. The belligerent powers largely relied on nationally organised groups to organise relief for refugees. When displaced persons came home, they might be mobilised for national causes. Between 27 May and 3 June 1917, a Lithuanian congress in Petrograd (as St Petersburg had been renamed) gathered 336 representatives of the refugees across a broad political spectrum. On the last day the congress voted by a narrow margin for 'a permanently neutral and independent Lithuanian state', but socialists saw opportunities for Lithuania in a federative Russia.[15]

Another Lithuanian conference met in Vilnius 18–22 September 1917, chaired by Basanavičius. The 214 participants comprised priests, peasants, and professionals in roughly equal measure, but no women. Essentially they discussed three linked questions: where would Lithuania be, how Lithuanian would it be, and what would be its relationship to Germany? Most ultimately agreed with Smetona's argument that, however hard to define, an ethnographic Lithuania was inevitable, given the stances of other nationalities. He believed that its prospects were better with orderly Germany than with revolutionary Russia. Stanisław Narutowicz rejected the clash of nationalisms, especially 'antisemitism and antipolonism', as he pleaded for an independent Lithuania that served all its peoples. The final resolution envisaged an independent Lithuanian state in its ethnographic borders, corrected in its economic interests, assuring cultural rights to minorities, and shaped by a constituent assembly in Vilnius. Lithuania might have special relations with Germany.[16]

The Lithuanian Congress chose a twenty-strong Council of Lithuania (Lietuvos Taryba). On 25 September, Aleksandra Jurašaitytė created the oft-reproduced photograph of its all-male members in her family's atelier off Cathedral Square. Four councillors were priests. A women's petition for representation attracted 20,000 signatures. Although Basanavičius took the place of honour, Smetona chaired the council, represented it in émigré conferences in Sweden and Switzerland, and did most of the negotiating with the Germans.

Following the Bolshevik coup in Russia, the German regime made its agreement to a Lithuanian state dependent on its subordination to Germany. Under pressure, on 11 December 1917 the Council announced the restitution of an independent Lithuanian state with its capital in Vilnius, breaking past links with other states (meaning Poland and Russia). The Council requested German assistance in rebuilding the state, which might be militarily and fiscally linked to Germany. Four left-leaning members—Mykolas Biržiška, Stanisław Narutowicz, Steponas Kairys, and Jonas Vileišis—suspended their participation in the council in protest.

Neither Germany nor Austria–Hungary invited Lithuanian representatives to the negotiations in Brest-Litovsk where they sought to reshape the region and further exploit its resources. After the peace treaty was signed on 3 March 1918, refugees could return home from Russia. About 350,000 refugees had done so by 1924, although 185,000 stayed. Many returned with a sense of national identity strengthened by shared privations and consolations.

BREAKING EMPIRES, MAKING NATIONS?

Meanwhile, in a speech to Congress on 8 January 1918, President Woodrow Wilson served notice that the United States wished to remake Europe and the world on anti-imperial principles. His Fourteen Points did not, however, articulate the principle of national self-determination. The implications of his demand that the Central Powers evacuate Russia, which should be assured 'the independent determination of her own political development and national policy', and of his postulate to restore independent Poland 'in the territories inhabited by indisputably Polish populations' spelled both threat and opportunity for the Lithuanians.[17]

In this situation, the Council of Lithuania decided to declare independence without conceding anything to Germany. After the text had been hammered out, the Council met in the cramped headquarters of the Lithuanian war relief committee over a café on Castle Street. Smetona, criticised as too pro-German, had agreed to give up the chair to Basanavičius, enabling the four dissenters to rejoin and sign. The concise resolution can be quoted in full:

> The Council of Lithuania in its session of February 16, 1918, decided unanimously to address the governments of Russia, Germany, and other states with the following declaration:
>
> The Council of Lithuania, as the sole representative of the Lithuanian nation, based on the recognized right to national self-determination, and on the Vilnius conference's resolution of 18–23 September 1917, proclaims the restoration of the independent state of Lithuania, founded on democratic principles, with Vilnius as its capital, and declares the termination of all state ties which formerly bound this state to other nations. The Council of Lithuania also declares that the foundation of the Lithuanian state and its relations with other countries will be finally determined by the Constituent Assembly, to be convoked as soon as possible, elected democratically by all its inhabitants.
>
> The Council of Lithuania by informing the government of Lithuania requests the recognition of the independent state of Lithuania.[18]

Independent statehood was thus 'restored', although it was not clear whether it had been interrupted in 1795 or in 1569.

Copies of the German version of the act reached Berlin. Although the German government refused to recognise the notification, several German newspapers published it on 18 February. In occupied Lithuania the declaration was printed on the front page of the *Echo of Lithuania* (*Lietuvos aidas*), the Council's official newspaper, founded by Smetona. The German authorities banned publication although the editor and Council member Petras Klimas hid several dozen copies and had them circulated by hand. The typed original and its duplicate are known to have been in the possession of Basanavičius and Smetona, but they are now only known from facsimiles. In 2017 Professor Liudas Mažylis found the handwritten notification in Lithuanian and German in the archive of the German ministry of foreign affairs. This document became the focal point of the centennial celebrations in 2018. Multitudes visited the small museum in the House of the Signatories to see the tangible bond between the nation's past, present, and future.

At the time, however, the declaration of 16 February had negligible practical effect. The Germans continued to govern Ober Ost. They also ignored the Estonian declaration of independence six days later. Wilhelm II announced his recognition of the Lithuanian state to a Lithuanian delegation in Berlin on 23 March 1918, but based on the declaration of 11 December 1917. The question of the head of state arose. Overriding protests that the question of a monarchy or a republic was for the Constituent Assembly to decide, on 13 July the majority of the Council forestalled a Hohenzollern candidature by inviting the Catholic Wilhelm von Urach, Count of Württemberg, to become King Mindaugas II. Without Berlin's approval this was a dead letter, and the Council annulled its invitation on 2 November 1918. This was his third unsuccessful bid for a throne. France had earlier denied him his inheritance as prince of Monaco, and he had come second in the contest to become the inaugural King of Albania in 1914. In 2009 his grandson Inigo visited Lithuania for the first time, and expressed his willingness to become King if asked by the Lithuanian people.

Meanwhile, left behind by the Lithuanians, the leaders of the Belarusian national cause took their own, rockier path towards statehood. Lastoŭski made an isolated call for an independent Belarus in 1916, but the revolution of March 1917 seemed to open perspectives for autonomy and radical land reform within a democratic Russia. An All-Belarusian Congress (Usebelaruski Zjezd) opened in Minsk on 17 December 1917. The 1,872 delegates included teachers, soldiers, officials, and a spectrum of left-leaning political parties. However, Bolshevik forces violently dispersed them on 31 December, and then suppressed other Belarusian organs. Some of the survivors fled to Vilnius, where in late January 1918 another Belarusian conference chose a council of fourteen.

Poles in Minsk rose up against the Bolsheviks on 19 February 1918. They formed a Polish–Belarusian city council, which on 21 February welcomed the German army. The same day, the executive committee of the All-Belarusian Congress proclaimed itself the supreme civilian authority of Belarus. Following the news of the Treaty of Brest-Litovsk, it proclaimed the Belarusian People's Republic (Belaruskaia Narodnaia Respublika) whose government was led by the socialist Yazep Varonka. On 25 March it declared independence and optimistically claimed territory from Białystok in the west to Smolensk in the east. Its leaders sought German aid, but Germany had undertaken at Brest-Litovsk not to create any new states within the remaining territory of Russia. The Bolsheviks advanced again in the autumn, and by the end of 1918 the Belarusian state had neither factual existence nor international recognition. Some of its leaders took

LITHUANIA

refuge in Lithuania, where Varonka briefly became minister for Belarusians in the Lithuanian government. The Council of the Belarusian People's Republic is now the world's oldest continuously existing government in exile. Its emblems draw on those of the Grand Duchy of Lithuania.

The Lithuanians fared much better, although they still faced daunting challenges. On 11 November, when the guns fell silent on the Western Front and Piłsudski took power in Warsaw, the Lithuanian Council named a government led by the diminutive, charismatic historian Augustinas Voldemaras. The Germans agreed to hand over power to the Lithuanians, but the Poles and the advancing Bolsheviks would contest the Vilnius region. Workers' soviets (councils) were established in the larger towns, competing for authority with German-approved town councils, and in Vilnius with a Polish Catholic workers' association.

As the Germans left Vilnius at the turn of the year, Polish militia units took over the city hall and surrounded the Vilnius Soviet. The socialist Mykolas Sleževičius, who had succeeded Voldemaras as Lithuanian prime minister on 26 December 1918, took a train to Kaunas on 2 January 1919. The Red Army took control of the city on 4 and 5 January. The northern prong of the Bolshevik offensive reached Telšiai on 25 January, opening the way for a pincer movement on Kaunas. Many volunteers answered the call to arms, buying time while the Lithuanian government cobbled together a regular army, despite the shortage of qualified officers. The new state authorities requisitioned provisions and horses from estates and larger farms, and levied cash contributions on towns. They also dissolved soviets and arrested their leaders. Meanwhile in Berlin, Smetona secured a 3-million-mark loan, which funded the purchase of weapons. German troops still stationed in the region and volunteers from Germany (the Freikorps) joined with Lithuanian forces to stop the Bolshevik advances in the second week of February 1919.

BREAKING EMPIRES, MAKING NATIONS?

The declaration of a Lithuanian Soviet Republic was published in Moscow on 18 December, but in Vilnius only six days later. At the head of its Lithuanian, Polish, Belarusian, and Jewish leaders stood the Lithuanian nationalist-turned-Bolshevik Vincas Mickevičius-Kapsukas. Although this regime employed terror less readily than its counterparts in Latvia and Estonia, on 14 January it decreed the nationalisation of estates and farms, except for the smallest plots. Peasants were unable to buy confiscated land. They had not expected collectivisation from the Bolsheviks' slogan of 'bread, land, and peace', and they resisted attempts to implement the policy. Worsening food shortages and unemployment were grist to the mill of the coalition government of nationalists and socialists in Kaunas, which promised Polish nobles' lands to the peasants.

Lenin ordered the merger of the weak Lithuanian and Belarusian Communist Parties, along with the two republics (thereby solving their rival claims to Vilnius). Mickevičius-Kapsukas headed the Socialist Soviet Republic of Lithuania and Belarus (shortened to LitBel) established on 27 February 1919. Neither Lithuanian nor Belarusian Communists showed enthusiasm for the merger. Nonetheless, the Bolsheviks continued their quest to reforge society. Some Lithuanian and Polish intellectuals agreed to work for the regime in various roles, mainly in culture. A decree issued on 22 March in five languages (Belarusian, Lithuanian, Polish, Russian, and Yiddish) proclaimed their equal and official status, but in practice Russian proved more convenient. Four days later, the regime announced that schooling would be compulsory, public, feeless, co-educational, and secular, with teaching in the pupils' native language. This policy also stirred resistance, especially on religious grounds.

Allied military and humanitarian missions arrived in the still unrecognised Baltic states in March 1919 (Latvia was the last to

LITHUANIA

declare its independence, on 18 November 1918). The Kaunas public fêted the Americans. The Germans decided to move on Riga, rather than help the Lithuanians take Vilnius. A Polish cavalry unit seized the moment and took Vilnius railway station on 19 April. It held it for two days, while more Polish troops arrived. A popular uprising helped to expel the Bolsheviks from the city. However, on 20 April violence erupted against Jews, perpetrated by many Polish soldiers and civilians. By the time order was restored on 22 April, several dozen Jews were dead, and up to 2,000 premises looted. Several hundred Jews, accused of collaboration with the Bolsheviks, were arrested and deported. Some had collaborated in various ways, but so had some Poles, Lithuanians, and Belarusians.

The pogrom in Vilnius was not an isolated incident. Two weeks earlier in Pinsk, a Polish unit summarily arrested 100 Jews and shot thirty-five of them, alleging that the town's Jews had supported the Bolsheviks. These events were part of a pattern of violence in the aftermath of the First World War, which reached far beyond Poland. Jewish communities were often saddled with collective responsibility for having adapted to the rule of whoever had previously been in charge. The scale and intensity of antisemitic violence was often exaggerated in Western press reports, but it cast a long shadow over the Jewish experience and memory of independent Poland.

Although Piłsudski has a (not undeserved) philosemitic reputation, he neither promptly nor unequivocally condemned the pogroms. He did, however, issue from Vilnius on 22 April 1919 a proclamation *To the Inhabitants of the former Grand Duchy of Lithuania* in Polish, Lithuanian, Yiddish, and Belarusian (the latter in the Latin alphabet). He declared: 'I want to give you all the ability to solve internal national and religious matters, as you will wish to, without any coercion or pressure from the Polish side'. The civil authority to be established would care for all

BREAKING EMPIRES, MAKING NATIONS?

without regard to religion or nationality and organise equal and direct elections with universal adult suffrage.[19] Piłsudski established the Civil Administration of the Eastern Lands (Zarząd Cywilny Ziem Wschodnich) in May 1919. It remained in charge of Polish-controlled territories for over a year, but it did not always meet his standards, because many of its personnel did not share his goals.

Nonetheless, the proclamation raised hopes among 'homelanders'. Might Piłsudski create a Polish-led federation from sea to sea, strong enough to hold back both Russia and Germany? He envisaged a restored Grand Duchy of Lithuania divided into three cantons. Kaunas and its hinterland would have ethnic Lithuanian leadership, Belarusian influence would be greatest in the eastern canton centred on Minsk, while Poles would lead the middle canton with a capital in Vilnius. But most Vilnan Poles' hero-worship of Piłsudski did not mean support for his plans. They wished to be part of Poland, even if that meant the relegation of Vilnius to a provincial town. From Pinsk, the lonely voice of Konstancja Skirmuntt argued that conceding Vilnius could maintain Polish culture in the life of independent Lithuania. The city council elections of September 1919 left the 'homelanders' crushed.

'Historical Lithuanians' were becoming an endangered species. Few Polonophones of the former Grand Duchy of Lithuania wished to follow the examples of Francophone Belgians or Swedish-speaking Finns. During the decades either side of 1900 they chose to be Poles. There is no reason to doubt either the authenticity of their choice or their right to make it, but the attendant vision of valiant Polish defenders of Latin civilisation in the Polish marchlands of Christian Europe had a price. It squeezed out the old ideal of a union of the free with the free, the equal with the equal. The shift made it harder for most Poles to understand what Mickiewicz had meant by 'Lithuania, my Fatherland!'

LITHUANIA

Ethnic Lithuanians were no more receptive to the idea of a federation. Mykolas Biržiška chaired the Provisional Committee of Vilnius Lithuanians (Laikinasis Vilniaus lietuvių komitetas), including Basanavičius and Kymantaitė-Čiurlionienė, which sustained the Lithuanian presence in the city. Despite Piłsudski's efforts to promote dialogue with the government in Kaunas via Römer and Stanisław Narutowicz (his cousin-in-law), even the most moderately expressed Polish and Lithuanian positions were irreconcilable. Not only did the Lithuanians reject second-rank membership of a Polish-led federation, but independent Lithuania would not grant the Polish language virtually equal status with Lithuanian. The Lithuanian government would neither abandon hope of Lithuanising the Polish-speaking population, nor risk the reverse process spreading. Nor could it accept an ethnographic Lithuania without Vilnius. One of the very few prominent Lithuanians who could contemplate any of these solutions was the poet Juozas Albinas Herbačiauskas (Józef Albin Herbaczewski). He taught Lithuanian at the Jagiellonian University in Kraków, taught Polish in Kaunas between 1924 and 1935, and finally returned to Poland. The slim chance of a reluctant compromise evaporated when a plot to establish a pro-Polish government in Kaunas was foiled at the end of August 1919. Narutowicz was involved in the planning. The rest of his life brought him disillusion with both Lithuania and Poland, financial hardship, and family tragedies. He shot himself dead on the last day of 1932.

The Poles advanced eastwards, while Lithuanians regained land from the Bolsheviks further north. There were some joint Polish–Lithuanian successes, such as the First Battle of Giedraičiai on 11 May 1919 (overshadowed by the second battle a year later, when the Lithuanians stopped the Poles). However, they fought over Suvalkija, and the town of Sejny changed hands many times. Balkelis writes of a cycle of 'intimate violence'

BREAKING EMPIRES, MAKING NATIONS?

between neighbours and paramilitary groups.[20] The Poles rejected the first demarcation line proposed by the victor of the Western Front, Marshal Ferdinand Foch, but his second proposal, of July 1919, became the basis of the future Polish–Lithuanian frontier in the area. The Allies made a further attempt to define Poland's eastern frontier in December 1919. The 'Curzon line' (named after the British Foreign Secretary) put Suwałki on the Polish side, but not Hrodna or Vilnius. This was a diplomatic blow for Poles and Lithuanians alike, but of little military significance.

Between July and December 1919, the Lithuanians also repelled an invasion of northern Lithuania by the 'West Russian Volunteer Army' led by Pavel Bermondt-Avalov. This anti-Bolshevik formation was allied to the German Freikorps in Latvia. The Entente equivocated; until the end of 1919, it backed the 'Whites' against the Reds in the Russian Civil War. The accumulated threats spurred social mobilisation, including the Lithuanian Riflemen's Union (Lietuvos šaulių sąjunga, shortened to šauliai— the riflemen), founded on 27 June 1919. It had women's and youth sections. Local self-defence groups, nationalist and revolutionary paramilitaries, and the regular army all contested the countryside. The strains told: Lithuanian army units stationed near Kaunas mutinied on 22–23 February 1920. Loyal units suppressed the rebellion, but grievances about rights, conditions, and non-Lithuanian-speaking officers were taken seriously.

Tensions also worsened between Lithuania and Latvia. The nascent Latvian state wanted the Baltic coast, while Lithuania desired the Ilūkste region on the left bank of the Daugava. In January 1920, Polish forces forestalled the Lithuanians and helped the Latvians to take Daugavpils and Latgale from the Bolsheviks. The consequences of this shared victory and common frontier would be felt in relations between Poland, Latvia, and Lithuania through the interwar period. However, a British diplomat achieved a mutually acceptable mediation of the Lithuanian–Latvian border in 1921. The exchanges of territory left Lithuania with the coastline around Palanga.

In the spring of 1920 Piłsudski concluded an alliance with the Ukrainian nationalist leader Symon Petliura. Poland would support the Ukrainian People's Republic established in 1917–18, but largely driven out by the Bolsheviks, in return for recognition of Polish sovereignty in eastern Galicia. The Polish and Ukrainian forces entered Kyiv on 7 May, but by mid-August the Soviet Russian counter-offensive reached the outskirts of Warsaw. On 10 July at Spa, in return for promises of Allied help, Poland's representatives offered to hand over Vilnius to the Lithuanians and pull Polish forces back to the Curzon line, but Moscow rejected the deal. Two days later, a Soviet–Lithuanian peace treaty was signed. Soviet Russia recognised Lithuania on the basis of self-determination, rather than any annulment of the partitions, but acknowledged territories including Vilnius, Hrodna, Lida, and Braslaŭ as Lithuanian. Among the consequences of the treaty was the liquidation of the ghostly LitBel, replaced by the Belarusian Soviet Socialist Republic.

The Red Army took Vilnius from the Poles on 14 July 1919. Lithuanian soldiers, delayed by a Polish unit which had not received orders to let them pass, arrived the next day and a joint parade was held. 'Kaunas is celebrating', proclaimed the Catholic newspaper *Freedom* (*Laisvė*), 'soon all our towns and villages will be celebrating too. Vilnius is ours!'[21] The joy was premature. Soviet Russia finally handed over the plundered city to Lithuania on 27 August. The Lithuanians also advanced in Suvalkija, but the Red Army reached Hrodna first. A revolutionary committee in Białystok, including Feliks Dzierżyński, prepared a Soviet future for Poland. A similar fate was envisaged for Lithuania, but between 14 and 16 August the Poles stopped the Red Army at the gates of Warsaw. The flanking counter-attacks ordered by

BREAKING EMPIRES, MAKING NATIONS?

Piłsudski threw the invaders into headlong retreat, and the Bolsheviks shelved their planned coup in Lithuania.

The 'Miracle on the Vistula' may have saved Lithuania (and much of Europe) from Communist revolution, but it did not improve Polish–Lithuanian relations. The Lithuanian government refused permission for Polish troops to march through territory claimed by Lithuania, but the Poles did so anyway. In the battle fought on both banks of the Nemunas at the turn of September and October, the Poles vanquished both Lithuanian and Soviet forces. The character of the fighting is suggested by the Lithuanian casualties: 34 killed, 103 wounded, more than 2,000 captured.[22] The Polish–Lithuanian truce of 7 October 1920 agreed a demarcation line as far as Bastuny, as the land beyond was still held by the Red Army. Because Bastuny lies almost due south of Vilnius, the city was very much up for grabs. Two days earlier, a preliminary Polish–Soviet peace was agreed in Riga.

To placate the Allies, who wanted the League of Nations to resolve the Vilnius question, Piłsudski disguised his move on the city as a 'mutiny' by soldiers of the 1st Lithuanian-Belarusian Division. He entrusted the task to Lucjan Żeligowski, a local lad who had gone to school in Vilnius (as he liked to remind people). When he marched into Vilnius from the south on 9 October, Lithuanian forces were too far away to stop them. As crowds cheered in his troops, Żeligowski dismissed the protests of the heads of the Allied military mission. Piłsudski had crossed his Rubicon.

On 12 October Żeligowski proclaimed himself the military head of 'Central Lithuania' (Litwa Środkowa). The Provisional Governing Commission spanned a spectrum of the local political scene. The name of the internationally unrecognised statelet suggested a 'cantonal' Lithuania in its historic territories, but there was no chance of that happening now. The loss of Vilnius and the ensuing threat to Kaunas both traumatised and mobilised the

LITHUANIA

Lithuanian nation-state. In the short-term, mobilisation encompassed volunteering, donations, requisitions, and surveillance. Landowners who served in the Polish army had their estates confiscated. The Lithuanians managed to halt the Polish advance and a truce, mediated by the League of Nations, was signed on 29 November 1920.

The League of Nations commissioned the former Belgian foreign minister Paul Hymans to find a solution. However, the Lithuanians wanted to confine the mooted plebiscite to disputed parts of Suvalkija, whereas the Poles wished to include the environs of Vilnius, Kaunas, Hrodna, Lida, and Ashmiany. Hymans predictably failed to persuade the Poles to cede Vilnius to the Lithuanians in return for political and cultural concessions. He just as predictably failed to persuade the Lithuanians to accept a federative arrangement with two cantons. The impasse left the incorporation of 'Central Lithuania' into Poland as the only likely outcome. Following elections, boycotted by most non-Polish inhabitants of the territory, the sejm of 'Central Lithuania' voted overwhelmingly for incorporation into Poland on 20 February 1922. After approval by the sejm in Warsaw, the requisite ceremonies took place in Vilnius on 18 April.

Mykolas Römeris, who had already made his choice and moved to Kaunas, wrote an open letter to Piłsudski, reproaching him for destroying any hope that Polish Lithuanians could participate fully in the life of independent Lithuania. The Riflemen's newspaper expressed the prevailing mood in 1923: 'Lithuanian, who is your greatest enemy? The Pole!'[23] Time did not heal the wound. Lithuania announced itself in a continuing state of war with Poland and refused to renew diplomatic relations. Mutual violence proliferated in the neutral zone brokered by the League of Nations until the zone's liquidation in February 1923, and vengeance was exacted after it was reduced to a demarcation or administrative line. Afterwards the Polish and Lithuanian regular armies patrolled the 'forbidden frontier', mainly against smugglers. Occasional fatal shots were still fired, railway, road, and telegraph communications were cut off, and birch trees grew in the approach roads. To cross legally, one had to set in motion a set of diplomatic and military wheels, as the British travel writer, novelist, lecturer, and informal spy Bernard Newman discovered in 1934.

If Polish language and culture had defined the 'other' for intellectual Lithuanian nationalists since the 1880s, then the Polish seizure of Vilnius ensured that Poland would become the defining 'other' for much of the Lithuanian population. Even in Samogitian villages, where Vilnius had been beyond the imaginary horizon, its loss stirred emotions. Every year, the Vilnius Liberation Union (Sąjunga Vilniui vaduoti), founded in 1925, marked 9 October as a day of national mourning. It organised meetings and ceremonies, and published illustrated books, articles, and maps of the capital. Membership peaked at 27,000 in 612 branches in 1937.[24]

Yet Lithuanian deaths fighting the Poles in 1919–20 amounted to only 232. Even when those who died fighting the Bolsheviks, the Freikorps, and the 'West Russian Volunteer Army' are added, the war dead total only a fraction of the Lithuanians killed serving in the Russian and German armies, or who died from malnutrition during the First World War.[25] The latter were not given memorials, but in Kaunas Juozas Zikaras designed the Monument to the Fallen Soldiers in the Wars of Independence, inaugurated in 1921. This pyramidal structure is constructed from stones brought from the battlefields, surmounted by a cross, a sword, and a shield, while a female figure lays flowers at a warrior's grave. Two years later an altar was built nearby with an eternal flame, and in 1934 an unknown soldier who had fallen in Ilūkste in 1919 was solemnly interred between the monument and the altar.

One more piece of the jigsaw remained: Lithuania minor. Although Lithuania had a shoreline around Palanga, it needed a deep-water port. However, Germans and German culture dominated not only the town of Klaipėda/Memel, but also much of the surrounding countryside. France administered and garrisoned the 'Memel-land' on behalf of the League of Nations. With no hope of regaining Vilnius, Lithuanian prime minister Ernestas Galvanauskas ordered a takeover of Klaipėda. Like Piłsudski, he needed deniability. Although the local Lutheran population of ethnic Lithuanian descent offered scant support, the German government tacitly connived at the operation, because it preferred to see the port in Lithuanian hands than in French. On 9 January 1923, 1,000 volunteers in civilian clothing took over Klaipėda. Sixteen Lithuanians and two Frenchmen were killed. France, Britain, and Germany protested, but Poland and the Soviet Union remained silent. On 24 January the seimas accepted the Klaipėdan request for incorporation. The arrangements for local autonomy were fixed in May 1924. The territory was in theory bilingual. The 1925 census purported to show just over half of the population among 141,000 were Lithuanian, although almost half of those deemed Lithuanians described themselves as Klaipėdans. The border with Germany was settled in 1928.

International recognition of Lithuania came slowly. Great Britain de facto recognised Lithuania on 26 September 1919, while France followed suit eight months later. Lithuania joined the League of Nations de facto on 22 September 1921, but the Entente powers withheld de jure recognition until 20 December 1922, almost two years after recognising Latvia and Estonia. On 17 February 1923 they accepted Lithuanian sovereignty over Klaipėda, which doubtless facilitated their recognition of Poland's claim to Vilnius on 15 March 1923. Independent Lithuania survived the 'titanic power struggle in Eastern Europe' partly because its leaders rode their luck, and partly because the state gained genuine support among the Lithuanian people.[26]

BREAKING EMPIRES, MAKING NATIONS?

ii. *Between Democracy and Autocracy*

On 14 and 15 April 1920, Lithuanian men and women elected the Constituent Seimas. Of the 112 deputies, five were women. On 15 May Gabrielė Petkevičaitė-Bitė inaugurated the proceedings in the Kaunas City Theatre. The only older parliamentarian, Simon Rosenbaum, yielded precedence as he did not speak Lithuanian (although Yiddish was permitted when necessary). The youngest deputy, Ona Muraškaitė-Račiukaitienė, aged twenty-four, acted as secretary. She was one of the victorious Christian Democrats who with their Christian Peasant and Christian Labour allies won fifty-nine seats. The left-leaning Popular Peasant bloc, to which Petkevičaitė-Bitė belonged, won twenty-eight seats, and the Social Democrats thirteen. The Jewish, Polish, and German committees had six, three, and one representative respectively. Smetona's equivocations on land reform cost the Nationalists (*Tautininkai*) dearly. They failed to win any seats, and he resigned the state presidency. The Christian Democrat Aleksandras Stulginskis, elected by the seimas as its presiding officer, became acting head of state, until under the terms of the constitution of 1 August 1922 he was chosen as President of the Republic of Lithuania.

Martial law was still in force, but the constitution envisaged a liberal, parliamentary form of government. All adult citizens would elect the unicameral seimas, whose eighty-five seats would be allocated by proportional representation, and whose terms would last three years. Lithuanian was the state's official language, but all citizens were promised equal individual rights before the law.

The census conducted in 1923 indicated a total population, not including the Vilnius and Klaipėda regions, of 2,028,971. More than half of the population was less than thirty years old, and only 15.8 per cent lived in towns with more than 2,000 inhabitants. Three quarters of the working population worked in the agricultural sector: a fifth of these were landless, while a quarter had less than 10 hectares. Using answers to the language question, the breakdown by nationality was announced as 83.9 per cent Lithuanians, 7.6 per cent Jews, 3.2 per cent Poles, 2.5 per cent Russians, 1.4 per cent Germans, and 1.4 per cent others. Of the hundreds of thousands of people of Lithuanian origin in the United States, several thousand returned, investing capital in land and firms. Many more stayed in America, but some of them sent significant sums to their families in Lithuania.

In the early 1920s, Jews constituted a third of the urban population and owned five-sixths of all businesses. Hoping for their support against Polish claims to Vilnius, Lithuania offered Jews far-reaching cultural and fiscal autonomy. There was a Jewish minister for Jewish affairs and a thirty-four-member elected council (vaad) decided on many Jewish matters. In contrast, Poland only reluctantly accepted its Treaty on Minorities in the summer of 1919, which obliged it only to support education in native languages. However, the Lithuanian state rolled back Jewish autonomy from 1924 onwards. Tensions concerned Jews' commercial dominance, their prominence in the professions, and their attitudes to Lithuanian language and culture. Most of the Jewish men called up to the army could not speak the Lithuanian language, so a much lower proportion of them were accepted into service than among ethnic Lithuanians. In Kaunas in February 1923, agitators smeared signs not written in Lithuanian in tar— Jews owned most of these businesses. Some of the roots of antisemitic violence during the Second World War can be traced to the aspirations of ethnic Lithuanians migrating into towns from villages. They expected to take first place not only in the public sphere, but in commerce as well. For their part, Zionist organisations encouraged Jews to emigrate to Palestine. Among the Jews who departed was Emmanuel Levinas who left for France in

1923. There he became one of the twentieth century's foremost philosophers of ethics.

The Constituent Seimas passed the land reform on 15 February 1922. Estates granted by the tsars, or belonging to those who had fought in the Polish army against Lithuania, were confiscated for the State Land Fund, as well as all lands in excess of eighty hectares (later amended to 150 hectares). Seventy-seven per cent of estate land was thereby confiscated, in exchange for nominal compensation (none was offered in Latvia), and then redistributed. More than a quarter of the 65,000 people who received land had served Lithuania as soldiers. The reform broke the socio-economic position of those Polish-speaking former nobles who opted to stay. Czesław Miłosz, of whom more below, captured their problems and outlook in his novel, *The Issa Valley* (1955). Overall, the proportion of the land held by peasants rose by 17 per cent, a less drastic change than in Latvia and Estonia, where the limit was fifty hectares. State-supported land banks helped increase investment in farms. Dairy cooperatives and refrigerators contributed to rising exports of milk and meat. The effects changed the pattern of settlement on former noble estates. Dispersed farmsteads replaced linear villages with three-field systems.

Hyper-inflation reduced the value of the post-German Ostmark. On 9 August 1922, a new currency was introduced, the litas. Backed by gold, the exchange rate was set at ten litai to one American dollar and remained stable. State investment in education increased. By 1937, 283,000 children were being taught by 5,110 teachers in 2,312 schools.[27] In 1922 the University of Lithuania was founded in Kaunas. Römeris became dean of the Law Faculty, and later served as rector. These achievements helped Lithuania to to rapidly become a fully-functioning, internationally recognised state with a growing economy and an educated workforce.

It was the political sphere that, perhaps predictably, brought disappointment. The First Seimas, elected in 1922, was deadlocked. The elections of 1923 produced a narrow majority for the Christian Democrats and their allies in the Second Seimas. Although four prime ministers came and went between 1922 and 1926, the Christian Democrats maintained their grip on government. As their refusal to end martial law, corruption scandals, and complacency sapped their popularity, Smetona bided his time.

Unwelcome changes to ecclesiastical boundaries made the first breach in the Christian Democrats' hegemony. Their own supporters were angered by the concordat of 1925 between the Holy See and Poland, which provided for the reorganisation of dioceses so that they fitted state borders. Several new bishoprics were erected, and those in Kraków and Vilnius raised to archbishoprics. The diocese of Sejny was already split de facto by the demarcation line into the Lithuanian part, governed from Vilkaviškis by the bishop, Antanas Karosas, and the Polish part, administered from Łomża by Romuald Jałbrzychowski. They continued in office with new titles. However, the new diocese of Vilkaviškis became part of the Lithuanian metropolitan province with an archbishopric in Kaunas, whereas the new diocese of Łomża belonged to the new metropolitan province of Vilnius. Despite his tact, Matulaitis was constantly criticised in Poland. In 1925 the pope accepted his resignation. Pius XI was the same Achille Ratti who had—unlike other diplomats—stayed in Warsaw as papal nuncio in August 1920 and formed an unlikely bond with Piłsudski. The pope raised Matulaitis to a titular archbishopric and entrusted him with negotiating a concordat with the Lithuanian government. John Paul II beatified him in 1987.

The first nominated archbishop of Vilnius, Jan Cieplak, had been the highest-ranking Catholic bishop in the Soviet Union. He survived arrest, a show-trial, a death sentence, and deportation, but he died in the United States before he could assume the role. Jałbrzychowski was then promoted. During his tenure of the archdiocese (de facto until 1940), he authorised the devotion of Divine Mercy, based on the visions experienced by Sister Faustina Kowalska (canonised in 2000) and the image painted at her direction in 1934. This picture, after being hidden in Soviet Lithuania and Belarus, and more recent controversies over its preservation in the church of the Holy Spirit in Vilnius, is now displayed and venerated in the Sanctuary of the Divine Mercy next door.

The Christian Democrats lost the elections of May 1926. The Third Seimas yielded a coalition government of the centre-left, headed by Mykolas Sleževičius. Smetona's Nationalists gained a parliamentary toehold. The seimas chose Kazys Grinius, formerly an author for *The Bell*, as president in place of Stulginskis. The minority votes cast for him might be compared to those that tipped the balance for Gabriel Narutowicz in Poland in 1922. Both the Christian Democrats and Nationalists professed outrage both at the government's dependence on the votes of Jewish, Polish, and German deputies and at its policies. These included the ending of martial law on 17 June (except in Klaipėda), the freeing of Communists from prison, and the abolition of the death penalty. Lithuania signed a non-aggression pact with the USSR on 28 September 1926, which implied Soviet recognition of Lithuania's claim to Vilnius, but also increased anxieties about Communist infiltration. Raucous and occasionally riotous demonstrations by left-wing activists, some of them speaking Russian and Yiddish, offended conservative, Catholic sensibilities. Concessions to national minorities included agreement to seventy Polish private schools, sparking protests against 'Polonisation'. The high number of Polish and Russian speakers in the municipal administration of Kaunas under the conciliatory mayor, Jonas Vileišis, grated on ethnic nationalists. Civil registration of births, deaths, and marriages hit the Catholic Church's finances, and the planned abolition of state salaries for ministers of religion compounded the blow. The Christian Democrat Father Mykolas Krupavičius exclaimed to thunderous applause in the seimas on 26 November: 'If you call national understanding patriotism, and national ideals fascism, in that sense I too am a fascist. And, as Lithuanian nationalists, we all are fascists!'[28] (Admittedly, Mussolini's regime had not yet bared all of its teeth.) Imprudent cuts to the army budget and the planned reduction of the officer corps created the conditions for a coup.

As dawn broke on 17 December 1926, troops commanded by junior officers overthrew the legitimate government of Lithuania. In parliament they arrested the prime minister, other ministers, and some of the deputies. The ringleaders asked Smetona and Voldemaras to take power. President Grinius had to dismiss Sleževičius, ask Voldemaras to form a government, and then resign himself. On 19 December, the seimas elected Smetona as president. The Social Democrats and Popular Peasants boycotted this session, but the Christian Democrats, in their fury at having lost power to the godless left, voted for their rival Smetona. The new regime re-imposed martial law and arrested more than 350 Communists in Kaunas alone. They were rapidly tried and sentenced on Christmas Eve for plotting against the Republic. Four leaders were executed by firing squad on 27 December. Parliamentary government did not last much longer. On 12 April 1927 Smetona dissolved the Third Seimas, and did not call new elections. He embarked on a long tour of the country to cement his authority, visiting synagogues and churches of all denominations. Rabbis in particular expressed confidence in him.

The Christian Democrats realised their mistake after a few months, and they became the president's most formidable foes. While Smetona was a practising Catholic and counted several priests as close friends, he refused to concede the hierarchy's demands for the exclusion of unbelieving teachers and anti-Catholic books from state schools. He proscribed Catholic youth and cultural organisations that mobilised support for the Christian Democrats. Catholic activists who broke the laws on public meetings were sentenced to forced labour.

Smetona had established his regime violently. For all his attempts to broaden his base of support, he had to maintain himself in power by force. The army suppressed a socialist rebellion in Tauragė on 8–9 September 1927. Among the 324 people arrested across the country, eight ringleaders were sentenced to death and shot. Other Social Democrats fled abroad.

The next major challenge came from the right. The Nationalists' own paramilitary wing, the Iron Wolf (Geležinas vilkas), was formed in 1927 to monitor and intimidate political opponents. By the summer of 1929 it had over four thousand members, most of them military veterans. Increasingly, however, they criticised Smetona for being 'soft' on national minorities and socialists. 'King of the Jews' was one sarcastic epithet. The president, fearing his prime minister was planning to oust him, pre-emptively sacked Voldemaras on 19 September 1929. However, most of the paramilitaries remained loyal Voldemarists (*voldemarininkai*). A bomb attack on the general staff in November 1930 provided the pretext to ban the Iron Wolf organisation, but the Voldemarists tried and failed four times in 1934–35 to topple Smetona. Voldemaras himself received a twelve-year sentence before being deported in 1938. The president made a point of commuting death sentences, but he also tried, not always successfully, to ensure senior military officers were loyal to himself. From 1935, military spending rose. Officers, who numbered 1,750 in an army of 25,000, enjoyed excellent housing, a luxurious club in Kaunas, and other privileges.

Smetona cemented his tenure of office through the May 1928 constitution. The executive president would be chosen by an electoral college appointed mainly by... the president. Smetona was unsurprisingly re-elected in 1931 and 1938. Despite censorship and harassment, opposition journalists and politicians continued their work, and political parties were delegalised only in 1936. Smetona then instituted an undemocratically elected, consultative Fourth Seimas that lasted until 1940. It approved the revised constitution of 1938, which referred to the sovereign nation, but no longer described Lithuania as 'democratic'.

Especially when speaking to foreign journalists, Smetona presented his rule as modelled on the strong American presidency, rather than the British parliamentary system. Like many international statesmen of his generation, Smetona admired Mussolini, but he did not share the *Duce*'s concept of the totalitarian, fascist state. In 1934, the year when Smetona foiled fascist-leaning attempts to take power in Lithuania, the leaders of Estonia and Latvia, Konstantin Päts and Kārlis Ulmanis, preempted comparable fascist movements and established their own variants of authoritarian rule. Writing in American exile in 1942, Smetona tried to contextualise his regime within the general crisis of democracy in interwar Europe. He compared the 'ultrademocratic constitutions' of 'the newly erected post-war states' to children's shoes that were 'several sizes too large' for them.[29]

Smetona's coup was preceded in May 1926 by Marshal Piłsudski's seizure of power in Poland. The similarities are striking. The victor over the Bolsheviks was denied the strong presidency he sought, as the 1921 constitution established a liberal parliamentary democracy. Piłsudski retreated from active politics, but built up his support in the army. Meanwhile proportional representation contributed to the difficulties in forming stable governments, but when the right wing seemed set to dominate the scene in 1926, Piłsudski and soldiers loyal to him violently overthrew the legitimate government. The 379 fatalities contrasted with the bloodless coup in Kaunas. He established an authoritarian, partly militarised regime, which sought the 'sanitisation' (*sanacja*) of corrupt and partisan politics. In 1930,

Piłsudski had his principal political opponents arrested, maltreated, and tried for sedition. Yet the opposition still criticised the regime in the sejm and in the press. The marshal himself usually took a backseat, concentrating on foreign and military policy, which culminated in non-aggression pacts with the Soviet Union in 1932 and Nazi Germany in 1934. His legacy was the constitution of 1935, which established a presidential system. Many Jews, who looked to Piłsudski to save them from the National Democrats, welcomed the 1926 coup. However, despite Piłsudski's rejection of exclusionary ethnic nationalism, his regime could not solve the problems of the marchlands.

The 1921 Treaty of Riga between Soviet Russia and the Republic of Poland partitioned the lands claimed by Belarusians and Ukrainians. Yet Poland's eastern border lay well to the west of the boundary of the Commonwealth before the first partition, and was not far from the line drawn by the second partition. The main difference was that the 1921 frontier bulged eastwards to maximise the strategic obstacle of the Prypiats´ marshes. The border agreed at Riga has sometimes been criticised as the worst of all possible outcomes for Poland: insufficiently far east as to ensure that the 'Second Republic' would operate as a multinational polity, but too far east to allow it to function as a cohesive nation-state. Piłsudski's supporters blamed the National Democrats for accepting less territory than the Soviets were prepared to concede. Although the negotiators in Riga exceeded their instructions, Andrzej Nowak has argued that Piłsudski regarded the outcome as acceptable in the circumstances. His plans for a federation lay in ruins, Poland needed peace, and his priority was to obtain the borders that could best secure Polish independence for a generation.[30]

Much of historical Lithuania thus became the north-eastern territories of Poland, contributing a quarter of its territory, but only an eighth of its population. The 1931 census was criticised by minority national activists at the time and later demographers as biased. Yet it reveals complex linguistic and religious demographics in the region. In the three north-eastern voivodships, 41 per cent of the population declared Polish as its native language, 9 per cent Yiddish, 2 per cent Lithuanian (half of them in the Švenčionys [Święcany] district), and 44 per cent either Belarusian, Ukrainian, or 'local' (*tutejszy*). The latter response dominated among the Poleshuks of the marshlands. This suggests not only resistance to all attempts to persuade them they belonged to a national community beyond their own horizons, but also a strategy for survival under rapidly changing regimes. It was not unwelcome to the Polish state, as it reduced the Belarusian and Ukrainian shares. By the less slippery criterion of religion, the results were 37 per cent Catholic, 9 per cent 'Mosaic', and 50 per cent Orthodox. Eighty-five per cent of the population lived in the countryside.

Without doubt the postwar economic challenges far exceeded the funds available for investment. Vilnius, Hrodna, and Brest were the only cities whose population exceeded 50,000. Most of the small and scattered towns were inadequately connected by roads of gravel, sand, and mud. Few landed estates were profitable in this era of low food prices, although more enterprising landowners diversified their business, including country-house tourism. Some high-earning professionals or officials in Warsaw or Vilnius used their ancestral homes or purchased manor houses as holiday homes. More radical land reforms might have increased the size of peasant farms and satisfied social expectations. As it was, the growth of the rural population produced further sub-division of plots. Most peasant households were largely self-sufficient. Modest earnings from hired labour or the sale of domestic products covered taxes and prized consumer goods. The rural population was hit hard by the miserably wet summer of 1928, followed by a snowy winter, and spring floods.

BREAKING EMPIRES, MAKING NATIONS?

It was inundated again in 1933. State-led and private investment in agriculture, infrastructure, industry, and services accelerated from 1935, but the tangible results were still modest.

The Polish state's policies towards the region's non-Polish inhabitants oscillated between promoting 'state patriotism', assimilation, and discrimination. Members of national minorities supposedly enjoyed equal individual rights as individual citizens, and state-supported education in their own language. In practice, the 'bilingual' elementary schools that almost entirely replaced Belarusian ones in the mid-1930s were intended to make peasants into Poles. Sometimes they succeeded, not least because Roman Catholics of Polish nationality were preferred for state employment and contracts. Although there were fewer cases here than further south, the Roman Catholic hierarchy pursued 'revindications' of Orthodox churches that had once been Uniate, while in the late 1930s the civil administration demolished allegedly 'abandoned' Orthodox churches.

Overlapping social, cultural, and political grievances helped the Belarusian Assembly of Peasants and Workers, known as the Hromada, to grow its membership to 100,000 by 1927. Its leaders looked across the Soviet border, where the first years of Soviet Belarus brought a spring bloom of Belarusian culture and education under the formula 'socialist in content, national in form'. From 1927 the Polish government cracked down against the conjoined communist and nationalist threat, banning the Hromada and imprisoning its leaders. The frontier ceased to be a destabilising factor after the Polish–Soviet non-aggression pact of 1932. During the 1930s, Stalin ruthlessly eliminated most of the Soviet Belarusian cultural and political elite, and completed the collectivisation of agriculture.

Some of the effects of Polish governance can be followed in Navahrudak, whose ruined castle inspired Mickiewicz to evoke the early Grand Dukes of Lithuania. Here the completion of a

LITHUANIA

mound dedicated to the Bard in 1931 was marked by galas attended by Vilnan and Varsovian literati. Between 1921 and 1939 the town was the seat of the Republic's least populous voivodship. Initially, out of a population of less than 6,500 people, there were about 3400 Jews, 1600 Catholics, 1,000 Orthodox, 300 Muslims, and a few dozen Protestants. By the end of the period, more than half the population of over 15,000 were Roman Catholics who declared themselves as Poles. The state and municipal offices moved from damp former monastic premises into purpose-built seats, while many officials lived in an attractive 'colony' of individual residences, built in the style of small manor houses, connected to locally generated electricity and modern sewerage. Pavements and flower-beds made strolls around the town centre pleasanter, while a cinema, amateur theatre, and a few restaurants and cafés offered entertainment. On the other hand, the town was linked only by a single-track narrow-gauge railway to the line that connected Vilnius and Lida with Baranavichy (Baranowicze), whence trains ran to Warsaw. The state of the roads prevented the bus service from operating between the first heavy snowfall and the spring thaw. The *Vilnan Courier* (*Kurier Wileński*) reported rather sarcastically in 1936:

> For some, Nowogródek is only the cradle of Mickiewicz, for others, it is 'Polish Siberia', the place of banishment for the grave sins of fathers (30 percent of the inhabitants are officials), for still others a place of quiet vegetation with the radio and a sentimental family, or on the contrary—where one joins with Bacchus and whistles at everything; for a few, fallow terrain for serious work for the state and society.[31]

The jewel in Piłsudski's crown remained Vilnius, regarding whose status he had neither any intention, nor any option of compromising. When Voldemaras explained Lithuania's position to the League of Nations in Geneva on 9 December 1927,

BREAKING EMPIRES, MAKING NATIONS?

Piłsudski accosted him and demanded to know if he wanted 'peace or war'. The flustered Voldemaras had to say 'peace', but this widely reported incident resolved nothing. Lithuanian organisations in Vilnius—schools, St Nicholas's Church, the bookstore, the theatre, and the press—experienced some harassment from the municipal and state authorities, especially after Smetona's 1928 constitution explicitly declared Vilnius to be Lithuania's capital. Earlier, however, Dr Basanavičius's seventy-fifth birthday on 23 November 1926 prompted a kind of truce. Prominent visitors also came from Kaunas for his funeral at the Rasos Cemetery a few months later. Lithuanians lionised 'the patriarch' for spending the last years of his life at his post. But inevitably Lithuanians, like Belarusians, became less numerous and less audible in the city than before the war.

The former capital of the Grand Duchy of Lithuania had to come to terms with its provincial and isolated location. Unemployment remained stubbornly high until the later 1930s. Vilnius received a modest share of state investment. The city council did what it could, but most dwellings remained beyond the reach of modern sewerage and electricity. Buses and taxis improved transportation. Several cinemas opened, and radio broadcasting began for those who could afford the sets. Some new buildings were erected, some of them in the modernist style, especially on the renamed Mickiewicz Avenue. Thankfully, the city's elites were concerned not to destroy its historic beauty. The Vilnan Baroque was studied and appreciated.

Vilnius's population slowly recovered, probably surpassing pre-war levels in the mid-1930s. The increase came mainly in Poles. Jewish numbers were depleted by wartime and postwar violence, malnutrition and emigration, and then by a falling birth rate. Jews had a declining share of trade, as elsewhere. Nevertheless, according to the 1931 census, Vilnius still had 55,000 Jewish residents (28 per cent), and Jews continued to sit on the city council. Jewish theatre, innumerable publications, and sports clubs all flourished. Yiddish remained in general use, but older Jews often spoke Russian, while many younger Jews learned Polish, so they could study and advance professionally. Too successfully, in the eyes of some Polish nationalists.

Piłsudski restored Vilnius University by decree on 28 August 1919, and named it after its royal founder, King Stephen Báthory. After ten years, student numbers rose above 3,000 and stabilised at that level. Depending on the year, between a tenth and a fifth of them were Jewish, whose situation worsened during the 1930s. Harassment mounted, leading to so-called ghetto-benches at the back of lecture halls. Despite some early efforts to find candidates, Stefan Batory University had no chair either of Lithuanian, Hebrew, Yiddish, or Belarusian studies. The first historian to be awarded a doctorate was Henryk Łowmiański who did pioneering research on early Lithuania. The best work in Jewish studies was conducted at the Jewish Scientific Institution (YIVO) which was founded 1925 and moved into a new modernist building in 1933.

The Polish-language literary scene was very lively. Stanisław 'Cat' Mackiewicz was an unconventional journalist who defies ideological classification. Another iconoclast was his younger brother Józef, who also wrote novels. An experimental, anti-establishment group of young poets named themselves after their journal *Żagary* (which in local parlance means dry twigs). Their most famous member is Czesław Miłosz. Born on a small family estate near Kaunas, he was educated in Vilnius, where he later worked for Polish radio.

Piłsudski died on 12 May 1935. His final journey took him to Kraków Cathedral, to rest alongside kings and queens, bards and heroes. But his body no longer contained his heart. In accordance with his will, it was removed and taken to Vilnius. On the first anniversary of his death, the urn holding his heart was solemnly re-interred, together with his mother Maria, at the Rossa (Rasos) Cemetery. The Soviet regime did not dare to destroy the monument, and it remains the first destination of many Polish pilgrimages to Vilnius. Lithuanians, understandably, do not share the enthusiasm, but at the time of his death, the Lithuanian press coverage was sober, even respectful. Römeris's verdict is instructive:

> If he had lived in 1863, perhaps he would have been the leader of the 'Reds' and his name might be recalled by Lithuanians with respect and affection—like those who during the uprising remembered about Lithuania's autonomy vis-à-vis Poland. There is no doubt that Józef Piłsudski had a sense of Lithuania's political distinctiveness from Poland; Lithuania and Lithuanians, and also Lithuanian Poles were to him different from Poland and ethnic Poles. By the Poles he might for this be described as a separatist and a Lithuanian, as indeed some of them still maintain. And he himself liked to call himself a Lithuanian. [...] However, times change. [...] The man who in 1863 would have been called a Lithuanian separatist today becomes, in the light of the ideals of Lithuania reborn as a nation, an enemy of this very same national Lithuania.[32]

In a speech delivered in 1938, Smetona expressed the binary character of modern nationalism: 'The old type of Polish Lithuanian, which the late Marshal Piłsudski represented—we hear he was not of Polish but of Lithuanian origin—is doomed to disappear. Today the time has come to say one or the other, and one cannot remain both.'[33]

Smetona cultivated a different style to Piłsudski. He preferred the image of a philosopher called from his library to the cares of state—more of a Marcus Aurelius than a Julius Caesar. However, his admirers began to cast him as a second Vytautas when the quincentenary of the Grand Duke's death was commemorated in 1930. Vytautas was acceptable to all sides, including as a protector of Jews, Tatars, and Karaites. He personified Lithuanian greatness as well as resistance to Polish perfidy. The monarch's portrait toured the country. Statues were unveiled, medallions, coins, and stamps were issued, and the university in Kaunas became the Vytautas Magnus University (Vytauto Didžiojo universitetas).

The Vytautas the Great War Museum was founded in Kaunas in 1921. Part of its imposing modernist building was opened in 1930, and it was completed six years later. It forms a square with the altar and Monument to the Fallen Soldiers in the Wars of Independence, as well as busts of the heroes of the national revival, and the bronze Freedom Statue by Juozas Zikaras. Mounted on a tall pedestal, this was unveiled on the tenth anniversary of independence in 1928. The Soviet occupants destroyed the monument in 1950, but the statue was restored in 1966, and the reconstructed monument was re-inaugurated on 16 February 1989. Daily ceremonies of remembrance and song took place there in the interwar period. Since independence was regained, they have been held there again.

In 1932, a large statue of Vytautas was unveiled in the grounds of the Military Academy. Destroyed during the Second World War, a replica now stands on Kaunas's main boulevard, Freedom Avenue (*Laisvės aleja*). Beneath the armoured hero with a fearsome two-handed sword, the pedestal crushes four enemy soldiers—a Teutonic Knight, a Tatar, a Muscovite, and... a Pole. The monument's original purpose was the one often manifested on placards during the quincentenary—'Vytautas, lead us to Vilnius!'[34]

As these examples indicate, the 'temporary capital' of Kaunas was a showpiece for the Lithuanian nation-state. In 1918 a population of just 18,000 inhabited its dingy buildings, but this figure mushroomed to 92,000 in 1923, and then grew steadily to 154,000 in 1939. By then, three-fifths of the city's population were ethnic Lithuanians. Those who came to live and work tended to be educated children of better-off farmers. Many of them enthusiastically participated in the Lithuanisation of formerly Jewish, Polish, or Russian spaces. Between 1921 and 1931, Kaunas was well governed by Jonas Vileišis as mayor, who had modern sewerage, three bridges, three new schools, and many new streets built, and introduced buses. Among the stars of its literary firmament was Sofija Kymantaitė-Čiurlionienė, who taught Lithuanian language and literature at Vytautas Magnus University and headed the Lithuanian girl scouts. Professor Vincas Krėvė-Mickevičius was not only an innovative writer in Lithuanian, but also an expert on Slavonic philology. Adolfas Šapoka graduated in history in 1929, honed his craft in Prague and Stockholm, and soon became Lithuania's foremost historian. He wrote enduringly important monographs on the sixteenth- and seventeenth-century unions and edited and co-authored the authorised synthesis of Lithuanian history (*Lietuvos istorija*, 1936), which sold 17,000 copies. Such was the pent-up demand for this legendary work, suppressed during the Soviet era, but venerated clandestinely and in emigration, that two editions in 1989 and 1990 between them sold over a quarter of a million copies.

Besides its university and other institutions of higher education, including a veterinary academy and a musical conservatory, Kaunas impressed visitors with stylish apartment buildings, villas, shops, cafés, restaurants, museums, art galleries, libraries, theatres, orchestras, cinemas, and the headquarters of Lithuanian radio. The building boom probably contributed to relatively high wages among construction workers compared to Riga and Tallinn. Neo-classicist designs were preferred for public buildings in the 1920s, but the 1930s saw modernist and Art Deco styles employed for the seats of ministries, schools, hospitals, and corporations, creating an architectural heritage listed by UNESCO among its world heritage sites in 2023. The most ambitious construction of all was the Church of Christ's Resurrection, perched on the 'green hill' (Žaliakalnis) north of the city centre. The bold design submitted in 1928 by an architect of Latvian origin, Kārlis Reisons, combined a soaring tower, modernist forms, and Lithuanian folk motifs. The work began in 1933, funded mainly by donations. The Soviet regime turned the not-quite-finished building into a radio factory. The Church was finally consecrated in 2004, and its roof terrace offers a panoramic view of Kaunas.

Lithuania's tragic, modern heroes were the pilots Steponas Darius and Stasys Girėnas. Both emigrated to the United States in their youth. On 15 July 1933, their aeroplane, the *Lituanica*, took off from New York. They successfully crossed the Atlantic Ocean, and 100,000 people waited at Kaunas to greet them on 17 July. Alas, having flown 6,411 kilometres non-stop in 37 hours and 11 minutes, their plane crashed in East Prussia, probably because of engine failure in poor weather. Their mausoleum in Kaunas was destroyed during the Soviet period, but their bodies were quietly reburied. The wreckage of the *Lituanica* may be seen at the Vytautas the Great War Museum, while a replica is in the Aviation Museum in Kaunas.

Basketball provided Lithuania with still more heroes: the men's team were European champions in 1937 and 1939. On the second occasion, when the championships were held in Kaunas, the women's team won the silver medal. Recreational exercise was also in vogue. Bernard Newman, who cycled around the Baltic in the summer of 1938, records how sea-bathing at Palanga was divided into three sections: mixed around the pier, men to the left, and women to the right. Not understanding the sign in Lithuanian, he blundered into the women, who were not wearing swimming costumes.[35]

The civilisational advances apparent by the late 1930s had been hard won. Smaller towns presented a duller prospect than Kaunas. Income per capita still trailed Poland and was only half that of Latvia or Finland. Nonetheless, Prime Minister Juozas Tūbelis saw Lithuania through the Great Depression. Appointed by his brother-in-law Smetona in 1929, Tūbelis remained in office, presiding over three cabinets of ministers, until 1938. His fiscally prudent, moderately *dirigiste* policies prioritised stability and solvency. Ambitious industrialisation remained a project for the 1940s, but leather goods and linen were manufactured at Šiauliai, and exported via the railway to Klaipėda opened in 1932. The need to prevent a balance-of-payments deficit entailed high tariffs and reduced imports. Agricultural exports rose. In 1924, Lithuania exported 542 tonnes of butter, in 1939—17,413 tonnes.[36] Great Britain was an increasingly important buyer, and by the late 1930s had become Lithuania's leading trading partner. However, low global commodity and food prices made some farms unviable, and the consequent sales at auction depressed the price of land. Emigration continued at a high level, much of it to South America after the United States closed its doors. The bitterest moment in the countryside came in 1935, when the Pieno centras agency slashed its purchase price for milk threefold. Striking dairy farmers in Suvalkija prevented deliveries to towns. Three protesters were shot, five of the eighteen death sentences were carried out, and 1,000 people were imprisoned or fined. The domestic foundations of Smetona's regime were beginning to crack, but external challenges would prove decisive.

iii. *Independence Lost*

Following Hitler's takeover of power in Germany in 1933, armed and uniformed Nazi formations began to parade through the streets of Klaipėda. Abuse of Lithuanians and attacks on Jews became more frequent. When the Lithuanian authorities discovered ample evidence of a plot early in 1934, they banned the organisations. After a nine-month trial in Kaunas, eighty-seven Nazi plotters were sentenced, four of them to death. Germany protested and halted imports of Lithuanian geese—a major source of foreign earnings. Smetona prudently commuted the death sentences, and later pardoned all those still imprisoned. There was an ominous analogy in the Saarland, where the local population, ruled by France since 1919, overwhelmingly voted to return to Germany in a plebiscite held in January 1935.

Lithuania was internationally isolated. Great Britain effectively withdrew from the Baltic Sea following the 1935 Anglo–German Naval Agreement. Latvia and Estonia prioritised their relations with Poland over ties with Lithuania. The mutual assistance treaty signed by the three Baltic states in 1934 excluded the questions of Vilnius and Klaipėda. Estonia and Latvia wished to preserve the status quo. So did Lithuania on Klaipėda, but the passionate desire to regain Vilnius might be compared to Hungarians' outrage at the 1920 Treaty of Trianon which had deprived them of two-thirds of their population and territory.

Lithuanian foreign minister Stasys Lozoraitis urged a pragmatic *modus vivendi* with Poland. However, after Piłsudski's death in 1935, the marshal's disoriented followers sought common ground with the resurgent National Democrats and hardened the Polish state's policies towards national minorities. Smetona, feeling pressure from the right, did not moderate his rhetoric on Vilnius. The shooting of a Polish border guard on 11 March 1938 gave Warsaw a pretext to issue an ultimatum for Lithuania to agree within forty-eight hours to restore diplomatic relations and open the border. Polish troops massed on the frontier, while demonstrators demanded a march on Kaunas. None of the great powers supported Lithuania, so having listened to his generals, Smetona bowed to the inevitable. Poland opened an embassy in Kaunas and Lithuania opened an embassy in Warsaw. However, the consulate in Vilnius, which local Lithuanians welcomed, only began to function fully ten days before the Red Army arrived in September 1939. The May 1938 constitution restated that Vilnius was the capital of Lithuania, but Smetona now had to avoid escalation. The Vilnius Liberation Union suspended its activities in November 1938. Because the regime had long prepared Lithuanian society to resist the Polish peril, it faced public outrage. Heads had to roll. Smetona replaced Tūbelis as prime minister with Father Vladas Mironas, a signatory of the 1918 Act. The career diplomat Juozas Urbšys became foreign minister.

Lithuania was just as vulnerable in Klaipėda. Even in the countryside, many Lithuanian-speaking farmers saw their future in Germany. The intensity of local Germans' desire to 'return to the Reich' overcame the economic benefits of 70 per cent of Lithuanian trade passing through the port. Having destroyed Czechoslovakia, Germany issued an ultimatum to Lithuania on 20 March 1939. Two days later Smetona agreed to cede Klaipėda, and on 23 March Hitler made a triumphal entry into the city. This second debacle further emboldened the president's critics. Smetona again restructured his government, appointing ministers from the Christian Democrats and Popular Peasants. General Jonas Černius became prime minister in place of Mironas.

Viacheslav Molotov and Joachim von Ribbentrop signed their infamous pact in Moscow on 23 August 1939. The Soviet side leaked to the governments of the Baltic states the supposedly secret clause that partitioned Eastern Europe between the two totalitarian empires, while also recognising 'Lithuania's interest in the Vilnius region'.[37] On 1 September Germany invaded Poland, and two days later Great Britain and France declared war on Germany. They did not launch an offensive, however. Despite encountering fierce resistance, the Germans overcame the outflanked, outnumbered, and outgunned Polish armies. On 17 September hundreds of thousands of Soviet troops invaded Poland from the east. On hearing the news, most of Poland's political and military leadership crossed the Romanian border. In the eastern marchlands, the collapse of state authority left landed

LITHUANIA

estates exposed. Some were looted and burned by Belarusian or Ukrainian villagers, but those proprietors who had lived well with their neighbours, such as Senator Tadeusz Giedroyć and his family, experienced kindness and protection before the Red Army and its commissars arrived and the arrests began. Among the larger towns, only Hrodna held out against the invaders between 20 and 22 September. Murderous Soviet reprisals against civilians and prisoners-of-war followed. The Germans reached Brest first, and on 22 September they marked the handover to the Red Army with a joint parade. The last regular Polish forces surrendered in Podlachia on 6 October.

The Lithuanian government refused German entreaties to march on Vilnius, fearing a declaration of war by Great Britain and France. On 17 September, in response to the Soviet invasion of Poland, Lithuania mobilised its reservists, bringing the army's strength to almost 90,000, but the Soviets took Vilnius from the Poles on 19 September. On 28 September, the day of the fall of Warsaw, the German and Soviet regimes adjusted their agreement. In exchange for a greater share of central Poland east of the River Vistula, Germany yielded up Lithuania to the Soviet sphere of influence. In the lands incorporated into the Belarusian and Ukrainian Soviet Socialist Republics, the new regime implemented a terrifying strategy of 'decapitation'—arresting, deporting, and often killing hundreds of thousands of people marked by their state service, relative wealth, or religious ministry as ideological or class enemies. By no means all the victims were Catholics and Poles. It should have been a warning for Lithuania.

Early in October, the Lithuanian army was partly demobilised, and foreign minister Urbšys obeyed a summons to Moscow. The Soviets demanded military bases in which they would station 50,000 soldiers (later reduced to 20,000). They had already imposed similar terms on Estonia and Latvia. For Lithuania, the carrot accompanying the stick was Vilnius, but refusal of the

BREAKING EMPIRES, MAKING NATIONS?

Soviet demands would mean its loss to the Belarusian SSR. The treaty of 10 October bought Lithuania 6,700 square kilometres of land inhabited by half a million people, of whom the great majority were Poles, Jews, and Belarusians. The demographic disproportion would have been still greater had the Soviets handed over all the territory they had offered back in 1920.

As usual, the Red Army looted Vilnius before leaving. Lithuanian troops paraded through the city and hoisted the tricolour over Gediminas's castle on 28 October 1939. Other units dismantled the demarcation line. Euphoric celebrations took place across the country, but as Römeris presciently observed, Lithuanians were 'laughing through tears'.[38] The Lithuanian state, which had mobilised the nation for almost two decades to regain Vilnius, had made no plans for what to do with the city if it were recovered. Soldiers, officials, pilgrims, and tourists, brought up in the sacred cause of Lithuania's capital, encountered an alien environment once they got there. Even in the surrounding villages, Lithuanian speakers were hard to find. Initially, much of the Polish population hoped that the Lithuanian 'occupation' would not last long before an Allied victory restored the city to Poland. Besides, as a Lithuanian colonel reported, 'they say that, for the moment, the Lithuanians are better than the Bolsheviks'. He believed that the city's Jews took the opposite view.[39] This was at best an approximation, not least because of Soviet hostility to Jewish religion and businesses, but the perception that the Jews had collectively welcomed the Red Army fed antisemitic agitation and violence in Vilnius during the autumn of 1939.

Pending the implementation of hastily ordained schemes of resettlement, the Lithuanian state tried to distinguish between, on the one hand, 'true Poles' who had settled in the Vilnius region since 1920, as well as wartime refugees, and on the other, 'Polonised Lithuanians' who were to be given citizenship and persuaded to declare Lithuanian nationality. However, the rapid

LITHUANIA

Lithuanisation of the city's spaces, symbols, schools, and institutions consolidated Polish hostility to the new order. Mickiewicz Avenue became Gediminas Avenue, and no fewer than 490 streets had been renamed by May 1940.[40] Stefan Batory University was shut down on 15 December (soon after the professors of the Jagiellonian University in Kraków had been incarcerated by Nazi Germany in Sachsenhausen). In January Vilnius University opened, with the teaching in Lithuanian. For the moment two faculties—Humanities and Law—were transplanted from Kaunas. Some of the students, who also moved from Kaunas, engaged in a new 'song war' in the city's churches. The new pope, Pius XII, refused to change ecclesiastical boundaries, but the Vatican did pressure Archbishop Jałbrzychowski into ordaining Lithuanian-language services alongside Polish ones. Lithuanian policies towards the region's Belarusians and Jews, potential allies against the Poles, remained inconsistent and hesitant. Having insisted that all official and legal business be conducted in Lithuanian, the government faced the practical problem of replacing administrators, teachers, and policemen. It also had to feed tens of thousands of unemployed people and 30,000 refugees, two-fifths of them Jews. Polish soldiers were disarmed and interned, but escapes were tolerated.[41] The Lithuanian press began to voice impatience for state institutions to move from the temporary to the true capital, but Smetona was in no hurry to move his residence and office to Vilnius. The feeling of unease was expressed in the ditty '*Vilnius mūsų, o mes—rusų*' (Vilnius is ours, but we are Russia's).

The Soviet Union attacked Finland at the end of November 1939. However, the Finns inflicted enormous casualties on the invaders during the 'Winter War', before a compromise peace treaty was agreed on 13 March 1940. This delay probably prolonged the semblance of neutral statehood for Lithuania, Latvia, and Estonia. In the meantime, the three governments made every

BREAKING EMPIRES, MAKING NATIONS?

effort to satisfy the Soviet military authorities. Meticulously kept records of incidents between Soviet military personnel and Lithuanian citizens show that the former were almost always responsible for altercations, but the slightest fracas or theft prompted the Soviets to complain. The three governments' desperation to avoid provoking Stalin at all costs, combined with wishful thinking that all might yet be well, in the face of mounting evidence to the contrary, is an instructive chapter in the textbook of appeasement.

Having learned lessons in Finland, the Soviet Union prepared to take over Lithuania, Latvia, and Estonia during the German conquests of Denmark, Norway, the Low Countries, and France in the spring of 1940. On 25 May, the Soviet authorities made another risible accusation, alleging that Soviet soldiers had been kidnapped outside their bases in Lithuania. Antanas Merkys, who had succeeded Černius as Lithuania's sixteenth prime minister in November, was summoned to Moscow, where Molotov morally broke him. As the Lithuanian government bent over backwards to cooperate, the Soviet demands escalated. The ultimatum delivered in Moscow to Juozas Urbšys on 14 June involved more troops, changes to the government, and putting the minister of the interior and the head of security on trial, but Molotov told Urbšys that the Red Army would invade anyway. The air and sea blockade of the three Baltic states had already started. Smetona argued for armed resistance, although he had no illusions about the outcome. Most of his ministers and generals told him that fighting was pointless. Lithuania's geostrategic situation was much less favourable than Finland's. Berlin encouraged the Lithuanian government to submit, which raised hopes that Germany would reverse the Soviet annexation. At 7 am on 15 June, Smetona handed over power to Merkys and left, repeatedly saying 'I do not intend to bolshevise Lithuania with my own hands'.[42]

LITHUANIA

Smetona and his family crossed the German border. They later moved to Switzerland, and then to the United States. He died in a fire at his residence in Cleveland in 1944, and his body remains in America. Had he stayed at his post, he would probably have died in Soviet captivity—the fate of his fellow presidents, Ulmanis and Päts. He is honoured in Lithuania today with a few streets and statues, but the destruction of Lithuania's parliamentary democracy weighs heavily on the debit side of his ledger. On the other hand, 'Smetona's times' enjoy an enduring reputation for prosperity, honesty, and law and order.

Lithuanian generals called on the Lithuanian army and population not to resist the Red Army. Commissar Vladimir Dekanozov came to Kaunas to form a puppet government. He installed Justas Paleckis, the son of a Telšiai blacksmith and a journalist with Communist connections, as prime minister and acting president. A few left-wing intellectuals, including Krėvė-Mickevičius, agreed to join the government. Nearly all Lithuanian Communists who had earlier fled to the USSR had fallen victim to Stalin's purges, but some local Communists had survived in Lithuanian prisons. At this time there were between 1,400 and 2,000 Communist party members, between a quarter and a third of them Jewish. This overrepresentation has encouraged antisemitic conspiracy theories, but it does not change the fact that most Communists were not Jews, and the overwhelming majority of Jews were not Communists.

On 5 July 1940 the new regime announced elections for 14–15 July. Unlike in Estonia and Latvia, where the presidents remained in post until after the elections, deportations of 'nationalists' and 'fascists' began earlier. The elections were rigged in almost every conceivable way. In each electoral district, all citizens had to vote for a single candidate endorsed by the so-called Lithuanian Union of Working People. Because not enough people voted on 14 July, the polling stations were kept open on 15 July as well. The counting was arbitrary. On 21 July the resulting 'People's Assembly' applied to join the USSR. The same day it banned the national anthem, flag, and coat of arms. On 30 July, a delegation asked the Supreme Soviet in Moscow to accept the application. The delegates included Antanas Sniečkus, who had embraced Communism during the First World War, led the Communist Party of Lithuania since 1927, and repeatedly been incarcerated by the independent Republic; General Vincas Vitkauskas; Paleckis; and a few left-wing writers. In this way, on 3 August Lithuania became the fourteenth republic of the union, soon followed by Latvia and Estonia. Paleckis took the largely decorative role of president of the Supreme Soviet of the Lithuanian Soviet Socialist Republic, while Mečys Gedvilas, a Communist member since 1934, chaired the Council of People's Commissars of Lithuania—the equivalent of prime minister. Moscow entrusted far more power to Sniečkus as First Secretary of the Lithuanian branch of the Communist Party of the Soviet Union. A typical Soviet republic's constitution was imposed on 16 August, including the usual fictitious assurances of civil rights and the supreme irony—its right to leave the USSR.

The consequences of Soviet rule for Lithuania would become apparent in the months that followed. Numbed shock turned to outrage and hatred. Smetona's regime had not kept the public informed of the nature of the Soviet threat, and there was no way for a democratic opposition to do so. Yet just as intense processes of memorialisation and militarisation had shaped the Lithuanian nation during independence, so they would contribute to its responses to imperial occupation.

6

HAMMER, SWASTIKA, AND SICKLE

(1940–1991)

In half a century, Lithuania experienced a Soviet occupation that lasted one year, a Nazi German occupation that lasted over three years, and a second Soviet occupation that lasted for forty-six years. The chronological asymmetry might suggest that the third of these occupations was far more important than the first two in shaping modern Lithuania. The second instalment of Soviet rule did indeed bring profound changes to Lithuania's society, economy, and landscape, and to the lives of its people. Particularly in the late 1940s and early 1950s, the Stalinist sickle reaped bodies and souls out of much of the countryside. Yet these transformations and traumas were conditioned first by the hammer-blows of the totalitarian Soviet revolution inflicted upon Lithuania in 1940–41, and then by the total war fought by Nazi Germany not only against its equally pitiless Soviet foe, but also against 'subhuman' races. Although the German occupants disappointed, exploited, and oppressed their Lithuanian subjects, leading some of them to resist, they succeeded in drawing some of them into the realisation of their murderous racial project, while leaving many more people with troubling memories of what they had witnessed, but not striven to prevent.

The wartime extermination of nearly all of the Jews, who for centuries had been part of the fabric of historical Lithuania, and the postwar expulsion of most of the Poles, with whom Lithuania's history had so long been entangled, enabled ethnic Lithuanians, despite Russophone immigration from elsewhere in the Soviet Union, to build the social and cultural foundations of a modern Lithuanian nation-state with its undisputed capital in Vilnius. Predominantly an urban society by the 1970s, Lithuanians continued to value their rural, linguistic, historical, and musical heritage in ways that helped them to assert their collective will, take advantage of the felicitous moment that began in the late 1980s, and win back their independence.

The independent Lithuania of the 1990s would draw deeply on a narrative of continuity with the interwar independent republic, in order to ease the strains of its transition from a Soviet republic to a functioning market economy, liberal society, and parliamentary democracy, ready to enter the European Union in 2004. The utter illegitimacy of the Soviet regime, obvious from the circumstances of its twofold imposition, has encouraged collective memories of repression and resistance. They were important, but the emphasis not only privileges the postwar decade, which was indeed marked by mass deportations and prolonged armed struggle, but also underplays the extent to which ordinary Lithuanians adapted to the brutal bulldozing of one world, and the breakneck building of another. As the historian Violeta Davoliūtė has demonstrated, the story of how 'the Soviet Lithuanian cultural mainstream' articulated these transformations is worth telling.[1] The poet Algimantas Baltakis put it nicely:

> We are the first generation from the plough.
> In us the earth remains unsettled
> Half city and half village.[2]

HAMMER, SWASTIKA, AND SICKLE

i. *Soviet and Nazi Occupations and the Holocaust*

The Sovietisation of Lithuania was underway even before the formal creation of the Lithuanian Soviet Socialist Republic (LSSR) on 3 August 1940. On 26 June, the interim regime abrogated the Concordat with the Vatican and went on to exclude religious teaching and publishing from public life. It nationalised no fewer than 1,600 larger enterprises and banks in July. Land was also nationalised, although for the moment, peasants were left to manage the farms they had once owned. Collectivisation remained a dark storm cloud on the horizon. In the ensuing redistribution, based on a new upper limit of thirty hectares, 70,000 farmers increased their holdings, while 24,000 lost some of their land. Because taxes were raised substantially on larger and middle-sized farms, several thousand peasants who had applied for more land changed their minds, and food production fell. Swingeing taxes and suffocating regulations forced most smaller firms out of business. The regime confiscated most savings as it imposed the ruble, crushing the commercial and professional classes.

Although the expropriation of businesses and bank deposits disproportionately affected Jewish people, many, perhaps most of them, greeted the Soviet takeover with relief. Even for older, wealthier, and more religious Jews, a regime that proclaimed equality for all nationalities was preferable to the prospect (sooner or later) of Nazi German rule. There were opportunities for Jews in schooling, higher education, and culture—but only on Soviet terms. Institutions and organs that were deemed hostile, such as the Yiddish-language newspaper *Vilnan Truth* (*Vilner emes*), were closed down. The regime promoted secular education in Yiddish, but discouraged religious education in Hebrew. The building of the Kaunas *yeshiva* was turned into a factory, and Saturday became a day of work.

LITHUANIA

Because the malicious stereotype of Jewish Bolshevism has levied so murderous a toll, it is worth re-emphasising that only a small minority of Lithuanian Jews actively supported the new order. A few Jews occupied prominent positions in the regime, including its security forces, but most of Lithuania's new rulers were not Jewish. Jews made up a fifth of the 5,000 or so members of the Lithuanian branch of the Communist Party of the Soviet Union in October 1940. This was two and a half times their share of the total population, but slightly less than their share of the urban population (boosted by Vilnius). As more Russians and ethnic Lithuanians joined the party, the proportion of Jews fell to about an eighth on the eve of the German invasion. In the higher echelons, it was even lower: there were five Jewish members of the party's central committee out of forty-seven. Four out of the seventy-nine members of the People's Assembly were Jews, while the government of the LSSR included two Jewish 'people's commissars' (ministers) and three deputy-commissars.[3] Of the 138 most senior officers of the People's Commissariat for Internal Affairs, better known as the NKVD (Narodnii komissariat vnutrennikh del) in the LSSR in May 1941, seventy-two were Russians, forty-three ethnic Lithuanians, and twenty-three Jews.[4]

The proportions of those arrested and imprisoned for political offences between July 1940 and May 1941 were rather different. Among more than 6,600 people, 58 per cent were Lithuanians; 25 per cent were Poles; 5 per cent were Jews; and 4 per cent were Russians. A total of 375 Lithuanian Jews arrested in this period subsequently died in Soviet labour camps, but by a twist of fate, many more owed their survival of the Holocaust to their deportation into the wintry fastnesses of the Arctic, Siberia, and Central Asia.[5] Among these survivors was Menachem Begin, arrested in Vilnius and sentenced to eight years' imprisonment in September 1940. He left the Soviet Union with the Polish army commanded by General Władysław Anders, from which he absconded (with his commander's connivance) in order to fight for a Jewish state in Palestine. He later became prime minister of Israel and made peace with Egypt.

All these repressions paled before the round-ups and mass deportations that took place between 14 and 19 June 1941. The NKVD planned to deport over 22,000 people, of whom almost two-thirds were family members of 'enemies of the people'. The records are incomplete, but in these few days the regime arrested and deported at least 17,000 people: 70 per cent of them Lithuanians; 18 per cent Poles; 9 per cent Jews; and 2 per cent Russians.[6] Cattle-trucks packed full of people left the station of Naujoji Vilnia on 19 June 1941. Among the deportees was First Secretary Antanas Sniečkus's own brother and his family, who farmed too many hectares for their own good. Doubtless this treatment contributed to the decision of their mother and five of their siblings to flee to the West in 1944.

Just three days later, on 22 June 1941, the massed forces of Nazi Germany invaded the Soviet Union. The following day a provisional Lithuanian government, dominated by Christian Democrats and Voldemarists, was formed in Kaunas. It broadcast a national uprising against the Soviets. Drawing on the experiences of those who had fought a generation earlier, partisans quickly took over most of the country. They attacked retreating convoys of Soviet officials and sympathisers, before the front moved north and east. Functionaries of the NKVD killed about a thousand more 'enemies of people' before fleeing. Their victims included seventy-three politicians, public servants, businessmen, teachers, and students who had been incarcerated at Telšiai. They were taken to the nearby Rainiai Forest, tortured, mutilated, and murdered. By 28 June, Soviet rule in Lithuania had ended. That same day the Germans disarmed Lithuanian partisans in Kaunas. The provisional Lithuanian government announced the formation of the National Labour Protection Battalion (Tautinio darbo apsaugos batalionas) as the nucleus of a future Lithuanian army. Many of its recruits had joined the uprising against the Soviets. The German authorities initially tolerated the activities of the provisional government (which included restoring private property, although not to Jews), but they refused to recognise its authority. Kazys Škirpa, the Lithuanian Ambassador to Germany, had formed the broad-based Lithuanian Activists' Front (Lietuvių Aktyvistų Frontas) in November 1940, but when the invasion began, he was kept in Berlin. The German military administration for the conquered Baltic states and much of Belarus was capped by the establishment on 25 July 1941 of the Reichskommissariat Ostland. The Lithuanian provisional government dissolved itself on 5 August. The Front was disbanded on 26 September. However, the German occupants could spare few men, and so were heavily reliant on ethnic Lithuanians to administer, tax, and police the country. Although hopes for Lithuania to be recognised as a state allied to Germany, comparable to Finland or Hungary, came to nothing, many individual Lithuanian citizens, some of whom had been prominent in the interwar republic, collaborated with the occupying regime in various ways and were complicit in its crimes. The hierarchy was clear. Below the Germans was the Lithuanian majority, which Nazi German racial theorists ranked below the Latvians, and well below the Estonians, because of a greater admixture of Slav blood. For both racial and political reasons, Poles were subject to harsher treatment than Lithuanians, but at the bottom were Jews and Roma.

Of the 42,000 people who departed with the Soviet authorities, fewer than 6,000 were Jewish.[7] Many Jews who tried to escape were turned back at the border of the Belarusian SSR. Death stalked those who remained in Lithuania. The notorious head of the German security forces, Reinhard Heydrich, ordered his *Einsatzgruppen* (operational groups) to eliminate Jews and Communists behind the advancing front. Franz Walter Stahlecker's

HAMMER, SWASTIKA, AND SICKLE

Operational Group A followed in the wake of Army Group North, heading through the Baltic states towards Leningrad. Stahlecker arrived in Tilsit on 22 June, and just two days later, the local Gestapo shot 201 Jewish men in Gargždai. He reached Kaunas on 25 June. He later reported: 'During the first hours following the invasion of the city, attempts were made to instigate Jewish pogroms, although difficulties were encountered in provoking local antisemitic forces.'[8] Those difficulties were soon overcome, with the help of the Voldemarist journalist turned paramilitary commander, Algirdas Klimaitis. Seared into Jewish collective memories and attested by witnesses is the murder of sixty-eight Jews in the Lietūkis Garage in Kaunas on 27 June. The photograph of a thug glorying in his butchery is often reproduced.

Stahlecker's summary of the first few months of the operation, dated 15 October 1940, makes it clear that he had sought to 'establish as unshakable and provable facts for the future that it was the liberated population itself which took the most severe measures, on its own initiative, against the Bolshevik and Jewish enemy, without any German instructions being evident'.[9] This admission casts some doubt on some of his claims, particularly regarding the numbers of people killed by locals acting on their own initiative. However, Holocaust survivors have testified to Lithuanian partisans' involvement in murders in many different locations during the first few days of the invasion. The controversies continue, but it seems reasonable to conclude that while some ethnic Lithuanians did begin to kill Jews and destroy or loot Jewish property before the arrival of German forces, they were not representative of the nation as a whole. On the other hand, few people took any action to protect Jews, either at the time or later. It would have been very dangerous for them to have done so. There is no compelling reason to doubt either the breadth or the sincerity of the welcome initially extended to the Germans as liberators of Lithuania from Soviet rule.

LITHUANIA

The killing of Jews became more systematic from July 1941 onwards, and the roles of German and Lithuanian forces became better defined. Under German supervision, units of the National Labour Protection Battalion would typically select, gather, and march the victims to killing sites outside towns, where they were shot into pits. They would then join German units in hunting down escapees. In the Vilnius region, which had a different command structure, the Germans made similar use of the mostly Lithuanian Special Squad (Sonderkommando, Ypatingasis būrys). The first mass killings of Vilnan Jews took place in the nearby Paneriai Forest in July. By the end of the year several tens of thousands of people had been murdered there, not all of them Jewish. The fortifications at Kaunas also served as killing grounds. On 4 July 1941, Karl Jäger, the commander of Einsatzkommando 3/A, ordered the National Labour Protection Battalion to kill 463 Jews in the Third Fort; and on 6 July, 2,514 more. On 29 October, he reported the killing of about 9,200 Jews, almost half of them children, at the Ninth Fort.

The National Labour Protection Battalion re-formed into two auxiliary police battalions on 7 August. These formations multiplied and in total about 20,000 men served in them. Several thousand policemen deserted, while several hundred were killed in action, mainly by Soviet and Polish partisans. Ten battalions were involved in the guarding, conveying, and killing of Jews in German-occupied Lithuania, Belarus, Ukraine, and Poland. Among the 2nd Battalion's war crimes was the mission, carried out jointly with German units, to eradicate Jews from western Belarus in the autumn of 1941, with the exception of those already confined in ghettoes. The operation culminated in the murder of most of the Jews of Slutsk on 27–28 October.

This particular killing spree was directed by Antanas Gečas vel Gecevičius, who had joined the Lithuanian army in 1937, but subsequently served the NKVD as an agent. He then offered his

HAMMER, SWASTIKA, AND SICKLE

service to the Germans, claiming to be descended from an old German family. Later, having surrendered to the Americans in October 1944, he declared himself Polish, and served in the Polish army in Italy. Decorated by both sides for bravery, he passed through the postwar Polish Resettlement Corps and settled in Edinburgh. It has been suspected he was protected by the British intelligence service MI6. Finally exposed as a war criminal in 1986, he lost a libel suit in 1992, but the Republic of Lithuania only issued a warrant for his extradition in 2001. Still denying his guilt, he died in Scotland before he could face trial.

The prevalence of children, women, and elderly and sick men among the Jews murdered in the summer and autumn of 1941 was deliberate. Noting the civil administration's reluctance to assist in organising mass executions, Stahlecker explained to his superiors why some Jews had to live a little longer:

> After the carrying out of the first large-scale executions in Lithuania and Latvia it already proved that the total elimination of the Jews is not possible there, at least not at the present time. As a large part of the skilled trades is in Jewish hands in Lithuania and Latvia, and some (glaziers, plumbers, stove-builders, shoemakers) are almost entirely Jewish, a large proportion of Jewish craftsmen are indispensable at present for the repair of essential installations, for the reconstruction of destroyed cities, and for work of military importance. Although the employers aim at replacing Jewish labor with Lithuanian or Latvian workers, it is not yet possible to replace all the Jews presently employed, particularly in the larger cities. In cooperation with the labor exchange offices, however, Jews who are no longer fit for work are picked up and will be executed shortly in small *Aktionen*.[10]

Jews who were still alive would therefore gradually be worked to death. Timothy Snyder has explained the workings of the wartime economy of starvation in Europe's 'Bloodlands': the survival-time of those incarcerated in both ghettoes and prisoner-of-war camps depended on the relative availability of food and labour, which either moderated or accentuated the imperatives of the racial ideology of extermination.[11]

Early in July 1941, the Jews of Vilnius were ordered to form a council or *Judenrat*, which would receive and carry out orders, and to wear a distinguishing yellow Star of David. They were banned from the main streets, trains, and even pavements, before the civil authorities under Mayor Karolis Dabulevičius helped the German military authorities to establish the larger and smaller ghettoes in September. Of the initial 58,000 Jews confined, about 20,000 remained alive at the end of the year. The instructions to establish the Kaunas ghetto were given on 10 July 1941 by Jurgis Bobelis, the military commandant, and Kazimieras Palčiauskas, the mayor. Of the 30,000 Jews crammed behind the barbed wire enclosing the Vilijampolė district in mid-August, only 17,500 were left in December. In Šiauliai, about 1,000 Jews were shot before the remaining 5,000 were concentrated in two ghettoes on 15 August. Švenčionys, where about 500 Jews were still alive, was the other only ghetto still existing at the end of 1941.[12] Fewer than one in twenty Jews survived the initial wave of killings and ghettoisation by escaping, hiding, or joining partisan groups.

Within the ghettoes, a significant number of healthy younger men survived the regime of backbreaking labour, minimal rations, and cruel punishments until the early spring of 1943. Many left the ghettoes for work and were escorted back, often by auxiliary policemen who also guarded the ghetto boundaries. The communities within administered and policed themselves under German supervision. Those Jews who held responsibility had to calculate the chances of communal survival by keeping the strongest workers alive longest, so they might be economically useful to the Germans. Despite everything, the ghettoes saw a rich cultural life, featuring lectures, lending libraries, theatrical performances, concerts, schools, and religious worship.

Resistance sometimes involved sabotage, whether in factories or in the transportation of materials. Abba Kovner issued a now-

HAMMER, SWASTIKA, AND SICKLE

famous proclamation in the Vilnius ghetto on 1 January 1942: 'Let us not be taken like lambs to the slaughter!'[13] The Anti-Fascist Struggle Organisation was formed in the Kaunas ghetto at the end of 1941. A United Partisan Organisation (Fareinigte partizaner organizacie) was formed in January 1942, led by Yosef Glazman. It grew to 300 members. Its five-man cells were organised into platoons and two battalions. They contacted Soviet partisans, stole weapons and smuggled them into the ghetto. However, its plan for a breakout early in 1943 was uncovered, and most of its members were killed, often after torture.

Liquidations of ghettoes and mass murders resumed in the spring of 1943 on Heinrich Himmler's orders. The Vilnius ghetto was destroyed in August and September of that year. Armed resistance to the deportation of the fittest to concentration camps in Estonia led to the detonating of buildings, killing hundreds under the rubble. On 14 September 1943, the Gestapo summoned Jakub Gens, a Lithuanian-speaking, former Lithuanian army officer, who headed the ghetto's administration, and murdered him. After the final liquidation on 23–24 September, the 3,500 weakest survivors were gassed in Auschwitz-Birkenau, while approximately 4,000 were assigned to forced labour in various places. About half of these people survived the war. About 360 resistance fighters from Vilnius escaped via the sewers to join Soviet partisans. A few survivors came out of hiding places in the ruins of the ghetto when the Germans were finally driven from the city in July 1944. Over 200 Jewish fighters escaped from Kaunas, including ninety-four from the infamous Ninth Fort. Sixty made it out of Šiauliai. In total, about 2,000 Jews fought with, or were sheltered by Soviet partisans.[14] They derailed trains, and blew up bridges, a factory, and a power station.

Fewer than 500 survived the Šiauliai ghetto, mostly in Dachau, where American soldiers liberated them. The Kaunas ghetto became a concentration camp. The remaining children, sick, and elderly persons were seized and probably sent to death camps by the SS (Schutzstaffel), assisted by Ukrainian policemen, on 26 March 1944. When the camp was liquidated and incinerated in July, the 7,000 inmates were either shot or transported. Men went to Dachau, women and children first to Stutthof, and then to Auschwitz-Birkenau. A few hundred escaped. Overall, about 2,400 of the original 30,000 inhabitants of the Kaunas ghetto survived the war. Among those who escaped was George Kadish, who returned to the ruins to recover his extraordinary collection of clandestine photographs of life, death, and destruction in the ghetto.[15]

The final toll will never be known exactly. Least studied is the fate of the thousand or so Roma of Lithuania, most of whom are presumed to have been killed by the *Einsatzgruppen* and their auxiliaries in 1941. The LSSR counted 208,000 Jews in 1941. Of these about 8,500 survived in the USSR, fewer than 3,000 survived in German concentration camps, and fewer than 2,000 escaped the ghettoes. About 195,000 Jewish people died.[16] That means that approximately 94 per cent of Jews in Lithuania were killed in the Holocaust. About four-fifths of them were already dead by the end of 1941. The death toll in western Belarus and Podlachia, annexed by the USSR from Poland in 1939, was similar in its proportions and timing. In eastern Belarus, more Jews fled before the Germans arrived, although many could not. This 'Holocaust by bullets' was a much more sudden process than the staged, industrialised process that predominated in German-occupied Europe west of the Molotov–Ribbentrop line. Was the different rate of extermination determined by the desire to create living space for the planned German colonisation of the Baltic region? Or because of the exigencies of a very rapid advance, resulting in a shortage of troops to occupy territory, when so many were needed at the front?

At least 2,300 Lithuanian families are known to have helped Jews.[17] By 1 January 2022, 923 Lithuanians had been recognised

HAMMER, SWASTIKA, AND SICKLE

by Yad Vashem as 'Righteous among the Nations' on the basis of available evidence.[18] Nevertheless, in the considered verdict of Arūnas Bubnys, 'although the Final Solution was initiated and organised by the Nazis, it would not have been implemented so rapidly and on such a scale without the active collaboration of the Lithuanian authorities and the local population'.[19] Below a thin crust of German senior officers and officials, ethnic Lithuanians administered the occupied territories. Besides the role of the auxiliary police battalions in organised killings, many opportunist killings and denunciations that led to executions—both of Jews in hiding and their rescuers—took place in the countryside. The proportions between those Gentiles who helped Jews, those who harmed them, and the passive majority can only be guessed at.

The Nazi-approved Lithuanian-language press conjured up a beguiling image of what Violeta Davoliūtė has called a 'dreamworld'. These journalists gloated at the change in the fortunes of the Jews after the departure of the Red Army. In their columns, well-spoken Lithuanians enjoyed the urban café scene, while Midsummer festivities and bountiful harvests marked an untainted, timeless idyll in the countryside. Reality was rather different. The German takeover may have brought back relative stability to small towns and villages, including religious freedom for Christians, but by the middle of 1943, the German occupation was as onerous as during the First World War. Rations of food and fuel were cut, and requisitions from farms reached enervating levels. The Germans closed down the universities in Vilnius and Kaunas, and sent dozens of activists to Stutthof. Up to 70,000 Lithuanians were rounded up and sent to Germany for forced labour. German colonial ambitions led to the settlement of 30,000 Germans on the land, often at Lithuanian expense, especially in the Suvalkija region annexed by Germany in 1939.

By the end of 1943, Germany's final defeat was no longer in doubt. Several resistance movements merged under the authority

LITHUANIA

of an underground government. The Supreme Committee for the Liberation of Lithuania (Vyriausiasis Lietuvos išlaisvinimo komitetas) was led by Social Democrat Steponas Kairys, who was later recognised with his wife as righteous among the nations for rescuing and caring for a Jewish girl. The committee called for a common struggle for a democratic Lithuania, and advocated passive resistance against Nazi Germany. It wished to avoid German reprisals and conserve forces for the future struggle against the Soviets.

Understandably, Soviet partisans had no such scruples. Following their assassination of German officials near Švenčionys on 19 May 1942, the German command immediately ordered the killing of 400 Poles from the town and the surrounding region. The Lithuanian civil administration selected the victims. The shootings were mainly carried out the following day by the Vilnius region Special Squad, in cooperation with the German Security Police and the Lithuanian auxiliary police. In command was Major Jonas Maciulevičius, who was later arrested in French-occupied Germany, and tried and executed in Poland in 1950. In a notorious incident in June 1944, the SS took revenge for an ambush by Soviet partisans of one of its convoys. It burned alive 119 ethnic Lithuanian villagers, including forty-nine children, at Pirčiupiai, south-west of Vilnius.

Soon afterwards the Red Army advanced swiftly across Belarusian and Polish territory, before halting in August at the River Vistula. The Polish Home Army (Armia Krajowa) began its long-planned operation to liberate Wilno (Vilnius) at dawn on 7 July 1944. Fifteen thousand Polish soldiers attacked the German garrison from the east and south-east, but they suffered heavy losses. Far more numerous units of the Red Army joined the fighting in the evening, initially cooperating with the Poles in driving back the defenders. On 13 July, the remaining Germans withdrew and the Polish flag briefly fluttered atop Gediminas's castle. However, the Soviet command ordered the Polish soldiers out of the city. General Ivan Cherniakhovskii tricked the Polish senior officers into a meeting and had them arrested. In what became a familiar pattern, the rank-and-file were then disarmed, interned, or re-conscripted, either into the Red Army or Polish formations under its command. Cherniakhovskii's 3rd Belorussian Front continued its advance, taking Šiauliai on 27 July and Kaunas on 1 August. It renewed its offensive in October and reached the Baltic Sea, while the Germans dug in at Memel (Klaipėda). They finally abandoned the city on 28 January 1945 and evacuated via the Curonian Spit. It was not only in districts inhabited predominantly by Germans that soldiers of the Red Army plundered, raped, and killed civilians. This was not a subject that could be talked about openly in Soviet Lithuania.

The 16th 'Lithuanian' Rifle Division of the Red Army, which had been created for propaganda purposes in December 1941, but whose personnel was mainly Russian, bolstered by Lithuanian Jewish refugees, entered Lithuanian territory in the summer of 1944. Supplemented by ethnic Lithuanian conscripts as the front advanced, it took part in the fighting for Šiauliai and Klaipėda, before being sent to Latvia. The division's record was notable more for heavy, disproportionately Jewish casualties, and for numerous desertions than for military success, but after the war it became part of the narrative of Soviet Lithuania. In all, more than 100,000 Lithuanian citizens were conscripted into the Red Army.

In contrast, efforts to organise a Lithuanian army under German command fell flat. A recruiting drive for a Waffen-SS force analogous to those formed in Latvia and Estonia was abandoned. General Povilas Plechavičius, who had begun his career in the Imperial Russian Army, distinguished himself in the wars of independence, and played a part in the 1926 coup, agreed to lead a Lithuanian Territorial Defence Force (Lietuvos vietinė rinktinė) on 1 February 1944. As the nucleus of a Lithuanian army, it was intended to fight both the approaching Red Army

LITHUANIA

and Poles. For several months before the battle for Vilnius, the Polish Home Army periodically controlled much of the countryside around the city. The Lithuanian Territorial Defence Force began its operations on 1 March, and rapidly recruited volunteers. It fought several engagements against the Home Army in the first half of May, generally coming off worse. Both sides—and their historians—have accused the other of terrorising villages and killing civilians of the other nationality. The best attested crimes are the 258th Auxiliary Police Battalion's killing of thirty-nine Polish civilians at Glitiškės (Glinciszki) on 20 June 1944, and the 5th Wilno Brigade of the Home Army's revenge killing of at least sixty-eight Lithuanian civilians in and around Dubingiai three days later.

The German command wanted cannon fodder, not competition. On 15 May Plechavičius was arrested, and his force disbanded. More than 100 soldiers were shot or despatched to concentration camps, and several thousand were conscripted into the German army or for forced labour. Some ended up fighting the Red Army in western Latvia until the end of the war. At least as many hid in the woods, whence they would join the armed resistance to the postwar Soviet regime. Other soldiers joined the exodus of tens of thousands of Lithuanians to the west, mainly via Germany. Farmers, professionals (teachers, engineers, lawyers, doctors), and students constituted the core of these émigrés. Their choice was justified by the nefarious activities of the NKVD as soon as the front moved on. The Supreme Committee for the Liberation of Lithuania was unable to unite with the diplomatic representatives of the pre-war state into a single government-in-exile.

ii. *Diplomats and Diasporas*

The United States of America refused to accept the legality of the Soviet annexation of the Baltic states. On 15 June 1940, the day after the Soviet ultimatum to Lithuania, President Franklin Roosevelt ordered the freezing of all Lithuanian, Latvian, and Estonian assets within the remit of the United States Treasury, just as the assets of Denmark and Norway had also been frozen after their occupation by Germany. Even before the rigged elections took place, the State Department announced the opposition of the United States to 'any form of intervention on the part of one state, however powerful, in the domestic concerns of any other sovereign state, however weak', and to 'any activities that were carried out by force or the threat of force.'[20] The Atlantic Charter agreed by the United States and Great Britain on 14 August 1941 envisaged the restoration of 'sovereign rights' to those 'forcibly deprived of them'.[21]

Lithuanian, Latvian, and Estonian diplomats abroad continued as their nations' official representatives, funded by a drip-feed from their countries' frozen assets. Smetona was paid a modest pension as 'constitutional president' until his death in 1944. The Lithuanian reserves ran out in 1980, but the wealthier Latvian Diplomatic Service stepped in with an interest-free loan, which was repaid by independent Lithuania in 2005. The long-serving first head of the Lithuanian Diplomatic Service was Stasys Lozoraitis Senior, formerly minister of foreign affairs, then ambassador to Italy, who moved into the Vatican City with his family after Mussolini's regime recognised the Soviet takeover of Lithuania. He was succeeded first by Stasys Bačkis who had earlier represented Lithuania in France, and then in 1987 by his son Stasys Lozoraitis Junior who had headed the mission in Rome. The legations thus maintained unbroken the legitimate thread of Lithuanian statehood throughout five decades of Soviet and Nazi occupation.

The Latvian historian Una Bergmane explains why the United States took this position: first, the principled rejection after the First World War of the assumption that 'might is right'; second, growing concern at the aggressive alliance between Nazi Germany and Soviet Russia; third, the fact that several policy-shapers in Washington DC had served in junior diplomatic roles in the Baltic states. The maintenance of this stance after the USA became an ally of the Soviet Union in December 1941, as well as after the war, when the Americans might have recognised de jure Soviet rule as part of a peace settlement, owed something to the cordial trust built up between leaders of the Baltic diasporas and dozens of senators and congressmen. There was no danger of such concessions during the icier phases of the Cold War, but the onset of *détente* prompted lobbying to persuade President Gerald Ford's administration not to concede the legality of Soviet rule in the Baltics as part of the 1975 Helsinki Accords.

Despite tensions between mostly older émigrés who rejected any contact with the Soviet authorities, and mostly younger people who were willing to bend a little in order to visit their homelands and cultivate relations with their compatriots, the three emigrant communities were held together by associations, publications, churches, Sunday schools, and national holidays and commemorations. The consoling idea of the ultimate reversal of the illegal occupation kept alive 'the myth of return', and motivated many to stay in touch with their roots. At the same time, most members of the diasporas integrated well into American society. Their incomes exceeded the national average.[22] Because of earlier migration, the Lithuanian community was by far the most numerous of the three. Among its best-known representatives in the postwar generation are the Chicago-born filmmaker Robert Zemeckis and the tennis champion Vitas (Vytautas) Gerulaitis. With his mane of blond hair, New York's glamorous 'Lithuanian lion' played a flamboyant game on and off court until his premature death in 1994.

Relations with Poles in exile varied. Although Smetona came round to the idea of reconciliation, from 1941 the Polish government-in-exile saw Nazi Germany as its principal enemy. The Soviet Union formally became its partner in the Allied coalition. Most Lithuanians unhesitatingly identified the USSR as their country's greatest foe. However, in 1943, after the revelation of the NKVD's murder of over 4,000 Polish officers at Katyń in 1940, the Soviet Union broke off relations with the Polish government-in-exile. After the Tehran Conference, it became obvious that Stalin intended to shift postwar Poland westwards, thereby creating the potential for Poles and Lithuanians to recognise each other as fellow victims of Soviet imperialism. However, mutual resentments from the interwar period remained too vivid, and Lithuanian nationalism was too fixated on the threat of Polonisation, to allow for much trust. After the war, most Polish émigrés in the West came from the territories lost to the USSR, many from the Vilnius region. The sine qua non for Lithuanian exiles was an unequivocally Lithuanian Vilnius, so for decades nothing was more likely to provoke an argument among émigrés. Descendants of nineteenth-century migrants sided with more recent arrivals.

By the same token, Lithuanian emigrants found they had much in common with Ukrainians in North America. The Ukrainians' relations with Poles were strained by the slaughter of Poles (and Ukrainians who helped them) at the hands of the Ukrainian Insurgent Army in Volhynia and eastern Galicia in 1943–44, as well as by postwar ethnic cleansing and the long shadow of earlier violence. Nevertheless, numerous Polish citizens of Lithuanian, Belarusian, or Ukrainian nationality were among those evacuated with General Anders's army on its trek from Soviet Central Asia to Iran, and thence to Palestine and Italy. Some joined at a later stage. From this milieu emerged people who bridged the gap, such as the engineer and Social Democratic politician of Tatar origin, Juozas Vilčinskas. His son Aleksas, after a successful professional career, would in the 1990s become the long-serving secretary of the British–Lithuanian Society.

LITHUANIA

The seeds of political reconciliation were sowed by Jerzy Giedroyc, born into that venerable, but impoverished princely family in Minsk in 1906, and the journalist Juliusz Mieroszewski. In the interwar period Giedroyc had articulated radical nationalist views, but they changed under the influence of Mieroszewski, whom he met in North Africa. From the 1950s onwards, Mieroszewski, writing in the columns of Giedroyc's Paris-based magazine *Kultura* as 'the Londoner', argued that Poles should accept the loss of their former territories in the east as the condition of reconciliation with Ukraine, Lithuania, and Belarus. In 1974, he and Giedroyc jointly expounded the concept that Poland's future independence would never be secure without the future independence of Ukraine, Lithuania, and Belarus from Soviet imperial rule, and vice versa. Most Lithuanian émigrés long remained mistrustful (not least because many of Mieroszewski's fellow-Londoners vehemently disagreed with him), but some found their interest piqued when *Kultura* began to publish news from Soviet-ruled Lithuania from the 1970s onwards.

iii. *Sovietisation and Lithuanisation*

The violent re-Sovietisation of Lithuania was violently contested. The Lithuanian Soviet Socialist Republic had never been abolished by its creators, so its structures, headed by Antanas Sniečkus as the chief of the local Communist Party, were simply re-imposed once the front had moved westwards, without any constitutional formalities. Elections were first held to the Supreme Soviet of the LSSR in 1946. They were predictably unfree and unfair, just like all subsequent elections until the late 1980s. The elimination of the regime's enemies began immediately. NKVD functionaries identified and arrested those who had worked in the wartime or even pre-war administration or police, had participated in non-Soviet partisan units, whether Polish or Lithuanian, had evaded the draft into the Red Army, or were merely suspected of hostility to the Soviet Union. By the middle of 1945 about 15,000 people had been seized. About 6,000 Russian-speaking officials took the places of those dismissed.

Farmsteads and villages burned as part of the repression, even during Christmas 1944. As younger men fled to the woods— 30,000 of them by May 1945—insurgent and counter-insurgent forces struggled for control of the countryside, and even the smaller towns. Known informally as the 'forest brothers' (*miško broliai*), the anti-Soviet partisans would be sustained for almost a decade by their almost messianic belief that a Third World War would break out between the Soviet Union and the Western Allies, and bring the liberation of Lithuania. Similar armed struggles took place in Estonia, Latvia, western Ukraine, Romania, and Poland, but the Lithuanian Partisan War exceeded them all in intensity and scale. A total of 50,000 people passed through the ranks, although never more than a quarter of that number at any one time. The fighting was vicious, and partisans' life expectancy was short, with up to 20,000 combatants killed in action. Infiltration was also endemic, and not everyone could withstand the physical and moral hardships.

For the first two years of the Lithuanian Partisan War, insurgent units of up to several hundred men fought the Soviet security forces in the open. They often scored morale-boosting successes such as freeing prisoners from gaol, but they suffered heavy casualties. Later the partisans' focus switched to ambushes carried out by smaller groups, and intimidating and punishing collaborators with the regime. Inevitably, mistakes were made and innocents perished. Without doubt, among the arboreal brethren who fought heroically against the second Soviet occupation of their country were some former auxiliary policemen who had committed war crimes. Partisans needed food, drink, clothing, and transportation. While many farming families gladly did all they could to help, willingly taking risks, others were coerced, and in effect, robbed, lending some credibility to the regime's propaganda against 'bandits'. A poem written by Justinas Marcinkevičius in 1966, '1946', captures an anxious teenager's perspective on how 'the forest' came to the cottage by night, and 'the city' by day. The Soviet terrorisation of rural communities even sank to the public display and desecration of decomposing partisans' corpses. Relatives who recognised their menfolk faced a traumatic dilemma: if they identified their menfolk for burial, they would be punished themselves.

In February 1949, the leaders of various partisan groups met underneath a homestead in the village of Minaičiai in central Lithuania. In 2010 President Dalia Grybauskaitė opened the reconstructed bunker as a museum. Here they created a united leadership for the Movement for the Struggle for Lithuanian Freedom (Lietuvos laisvės kovos sąjūdis). Their declaration proclaimed their ultimate goals of Lithuania's freedom from Soviet occupation, and democratic parliamentary elections. The seimas solemnly enacted the declaration into law on its fiftieth anniversary, 16 February 1999. The presidium of the Movement chose as its chairman Jonas Žemaitis, codenamed 'Vytautas'. One of the most talented officers of the pre-war army, he had joined the Lithuanian Territorial Defence Force before escaping to the forest, where he won respect for his skill and spirit as a leader. But as terror, infiltration, and exhaustion took their toll, the armed resistance weakened. Finally, Žemaitis was betrayed and captured in 1953. This blow ended the organised war, although some small groups and individuals held out until the next decade. Žemaitis was tortured in Moscow, interrogated by the notorious head of the security apparatus, Lavrenty Beria, and executed in 1954. In 2009, on the centenary of his birth, the seimas declared that he had performed the duties of the legitimate head of state between 1949 and 1954, effectively making him the 'fourth president' of Lithuania. The declaration emphasised that the 'continuity of the State of Lithuania was expressed, inter alia, by the self-defence of the Republic of Lithuania against the aggression of the USSR in 1944–1953'.[23]

In 2018, the seimas also posthumously recognised as acting head of state Žemaitis's successor, the American-born Adolfas Ramanauskas, code name Vanagas ('the hawk'), who was captured and tortured in 1956, and executed the following year. In 2018 his body was discovered and identified, and solemnly reburied at Antakalnis Cemetery. His alleged involvement in the murder of Jews in Druskininkai in 1941 continues to generate controversy.[24]

The Soviet regime's most effective response to the partisans' challenge was violently to transform rural society. Mass deportations were combined with the collectivisation of agriculture. Propaganda demonised the stereotypical figure of the relatively wealthy peasant or *kulak* (*buožė* in Lithuanian). The late wartime and early postwar deportations targeted sundry class enemies and the families of suspected partisans. Many more people were swept up by the much larger operations carried out in May 1948, March 1949, and the autumn of 1951. The first of these targeted almost 50,000 people for deportation, although as many as 10,000 may have been able to escape; the second targeted almost 29,000 people; the third over 20,000 people. In total, in 1941 and between 1944 and 1952, the Soviet occupants deported almost 130,000 Lithuanian citizens, 70 per cent of them women and children, from their homeland. Not all of them were ethnic Lithuanians. Between 4,000 and 5,000 were Poles. The logistics and conduct of these operations required almost as many personnel of the Ministry of State Security as the number of deportees, particularly in 1949, when mass deportations were carried out simultaneously in Estonia, Latvia, and Lithuania. The commanders of the operation received Soviet decorations for their 'heroism'.

LITHUANIA

Soldiers and functionaries would usually surround a house at night, and families would be ordered to pack. Resistance was met with violence. The victims would be taken to the train station, whence crowded and insanitary cattle trucks would carry them by fits and starts towards their distant destinations, taking weeks or months to arrive. Conditions and work varied, but most were forced to fell trees, or transport and process timber deep in the Tomsk, Krasnoyarsk, and Irkutsk regions of Siberia. The greatest danger to health was the intense winter cold, but spring and summer unleashed clouds of mosquitoes. Inadequately heated barracks or sheds, primitive medical care, and onerous labour quotas linked to rations of bread and broth all took their toll. About 28,000 deported people died in exile, a quarter of them children. Yet survivors have reported many instances of unexpected human kindness in adversity.

The intensification of deportations was part of the effort to uproot rural resistance. In the first few years after the war, agriculture was still dominated by individual farms. For those who surrendered their families' hard-won land, life and work in a collective farm (*kolkhoz*), enduring quotas, payments in kind, tiny personal plots, and restrictions on movement, had echoes of their not-so-distant ancestors' experience of serfdom. The mass deportations showed, as they were meant to, the consequences of resisting. During the decisive year of 1949, the proportion of agricultural households in collective farms jumped from 4 per cent to 60 per cent.[25] In 1953 the regime announced that the process was complete. In statistical terms it was, but this did not mean that the collective farms worked as intended. The disincentives to industriousness, initiative, and honesty initially reduced agricultural productivity. From the late 1950s, the impact of mechanisation and the heavy use of chemical fertilisers began to increase output at the expense of the natural environment. The long-term human legacy was social alienation and alcoholism.

HAMMER, SWASTIKA, AND SICKLE

The combination of war, terror, and collectivisation in the countryside encouraged younger people to migrate to the cities. Danger and divided loyalties contributed to the exodus, but so did the dismal prospect of a lifetime on a collective farm. Marcelijus Martinaitis, a peasant lad who later became a noted poet, recalled his father urging him 'there is nothing for you here, not even enough food, no future. Disappear from here'.[26] Comparable processes of displacement and homogenisation took place during the 1940s in other parts of the Soviet bloc, but each country had its own specific trajectory. Population losses were significantly greater in the towns and cities, often dramatically so, because of the Holocaust, but the population of interwar Lithuania was less urban than that of Latvia. There were many fewer civilian casualties in the countryside, where most ethnic Lithuanians still lived. The effect was that less than 15 per cent of the population of the LSSR lived in towns in 1946. This proportion rose to over half by the early 1970s. Even without the 5 per cent deported into the depths of the Soviet Union, more than half of the population was affected by displacement within a generation. Moreover, relatively fewer Lithuanians than Latvians and Estonians emigrated to the West at the end of the war. So plenty of ethnic Lithuanians were available to fill up the cities and work in the factories, many of which were dispersed across the country, in smaller towns such as Alytus and Utena. So there was less need for imported labour than in Latvia and Estonia, which were almost overwhelmed by Russophone immigrants.

This outcome also owed much to the policy adopted by ethnic Lithuanian Communists and the effectiveness of their lobbying. Antanas Sniečkus was one of the longest-serving and most successful leaders of any Soviet republic. In some respects, he was a pitiless hardliner who authorised terror against his compatriots. During the 'thaw' that began after Stalin's death, and accelerated after Nikita Khrushchev's partial denunciation of Stalin's crimes in 1956, Sniečkus strove to prevent, limit, or delay the return of deportees to Lithuania. After successive categories of exiles were amnestied (with those partisans still alive having to wait until 1963), the regime prohibited about 30,000 people from returning to Lithuania. The 60,000 who did return encountered suspicion and discrimination not only from the authorities, for example in employment and education, but also from their neighbours, some of whom had appropriated their property. Sniečkus, partly because he had the knack of anticipating orders to crack down from Moscow, won the trust of Stalin, Khrushchev, and Leonid Brezhnev in turn. He got on well with the formidable chairman of the Lithuanian Bureau of the Central Committee of the Communist Party of the Soviet Union, Mikhail Suslov. Suslov, who came from a peasant family in south-central Russia, acquired an encyclopaedic knowledge of the works of Marx, Lenin, and Stalin, made himself useful during the purges of the 1930s, and directed the postwar deportations. From the mid-1960s he was the Soviet Union's chief ideologue.

Having covered his back in this way, Sniečkus was able, with every alternate pulse of purge or expansion, gradually to increase the proportion of mostly youthful ethnic Lithuanians in the Lithuanian party apparatus. By the early 1970s, ethnic Russian and Jewish Communists had been marginalised, and with them the position of second secretary of the local party, supposedly a minder from Moscow. Whereas at the beginning of 1949 barely a fifth of the 24,500 members of the Communist Party of Lithuania were ethnic Lithuanians, by the start of 1970 they constituted two-thirds of the 116,600 members, and the proportion continued to rise.[27] Official requirements for officials to be able to communicate in Lithuanian as well as Russian were enforced by the later 1950s. Sniečkus encouraged Lithuanian institutions of higher education to over-produce qualified engineers and other technical specialists, thereby reducing the need for Russophone migrants.

HAMMER, SWASTIKA, AND SICKLE

Significant, but not overwhelming numbers of Russian-speaking migrants—workers, soldiers, officials, and their families—did move to the LSSR, particularly to Vilnius, Klaipėda, and other places of industrial and military significance. Nevertheless, the overall proportion of ethnic Lithuanians in the population remained stable, and ultimately rose a little, largely because of the falling proportion of Jews and Poles. Intermarriage contributed to these processes, as did the youthful demographic profile of the Lithuanians. Jews began returning from the depths of the USSR in the autumn of 1944. Together with survivors, their numbers reached 10,000 early in 1946.[28] They tended to congregate in larger towns and cities, and to look to the Soviet authorities for protection from Lithuanian and Polish partisans. Some participants and supporters of the resistance movement regarded Jews as collaborators with the Soviet occupants, whether or not they were Communist Party members.

The fragile renascent Jewish community suffered a further blow when Stalin blamed 'Zionist' doctors for the death of his cultural supremo, Andrei Zhdanov, in 1948. An antisemitic campaign clanked into gear and gained significant—although far from universal—popular support. Henceforth silence reigned on the Jewish victims of the Holocaust, entailing an attempt to erase the memory of the Jerusalem of the North. Even the saved materials from YIVO were pulped. The regime had the 1945 monument to the victims killed at Paneriai blown up in 1952, and replaced it with a more modest one that effaced anything specifically Jewish about the site. In 1948 the Jewish school in Vilnius closed, followed in 1950 by that in Kaunas. Many Jews emigrated. On the other hand, others arrived among the Russian-speaking immigrants from other Soviet republics.

Even among those who retained their Jewish identity, fluent command of Yiddish yielded first to habitual use of Russian, and only later and more rarely to Lithuanian. Nonetheless Yiddish-language cultural life survived via amateur theatre, concerts, and literature, grudgingly tolerated by the regime. Religious life restarted after the German retreat, but went underground between the late 1940s and mid-1950s. For a few years afterwards, the two permitted synagogues in Vilnius and Kaunas were overcrowded (requests from communities elsewhere for registration were denied). Jewish Lithuanians were disproportionately well educated, and tended to be employed in the state administration, despite barriers to their advance to the uppermost echelons. However, after this brief revival, Jewish communities aged and shrank. Between 1959 and 1989, the number of declared Jews in Lithuania halved from almost 25,000 to just over 12,000, corresponding respectively to 0.9 and 0.3 per cent of the general population. Even in Vilnius, the proportion of Jews fell from 6.9 to 1.6 per cent in the same period, despite immigration. Emigration was easier from the LSSR than from other republics. Between 1968 and 1979, 83 per cent of applications for visas were approved.[29] Yet despite everything, a modicum of Jewish communal life continued, and Jews participated in the Lithuanian movement for reform and independence at the end of the 1980s.

After the Holocaust, Poles were the predominant nationality in and around Vilnius. In July 1944, the NKVD estimated that the city was inhabited by 85,000 Poles and 8,000 Lithuanians. This meant that despite an almost tenfold increase in the proportion of Lithuanians since 1939, they were still outnumbered by more than ten to one.[30] Stalin had already decided to move populations to match borders, rather than the other way round. Whatever room for negotiation there was over the exact course of Poland's new eastern frontier, Vilnius would be beyond it. On 22 September 1944, the Soviet-sponsored, Communist-led committee that claimed to be Poland's provisional government agreed the principle of 'voluntary repatriation' with the restored LSSR. In practice, those identifying as Poles came under heavy pressure to go. The NKVD's arrest of at least 10,000 Poles by the beginning of 1945 concentrated minds. Minimal compensation was offered to those 'repatriated', leading to the sale of property at knock-down prices. Despite the proximity of the border, the journey was long and arduous. In total, about 170,000 left for Poland in 1945–46, of whom 80,000 were from the city of Vilnius. However, only another 10,000 left the Vilnius region.[31] Moreover, some Poles crossed the border from the Belarusian SSR to settle in the south-east of the LSSR, reducing the net losses. The regime correctly feared that few Lithuanians would wish to farm the region's generally low-quality land. Not all of those people who wished to leave were permitted to do so. Several thousand Jews and ethnic Lithuanians who had been citizens of the Second Polish Republic also preferred the prospect of Communist-ruled Poland to Soviet Lithuania (or its anti-Soviet resistance). For some Jews, Poland was a step towards Israel or the USA.

A second wave of 'repatriation' in 1956–59 saw a further 48,000 Poles leave. Among those that departed were the Kozakiewicz family, who left the village of Šalčininkėliai (Małe Soleczniki). The sporting facilities of the port city of Gdynia allowed Władysław Kozakiewicz to become a champion pole-vaulter. Famously, having twice broken the world record while overcoming cheating officials and the jeering crowd on his way to the gold medal at the Moscow Olympics in 1980, he twice gave 'the shaft' gesture, delighting his countrymen and angering the Kremlin. Perhaps, had this impoverished family stayed, the same chauvinist Muscovite crowd would have cheered on a victorious Soviet athlete. But this 'counter-factual' assumes that the LSSR would have noticed and nursed outstanding talent in such a backwater. Today the newly constructed sport and recreation facilities in the village of his birth bear his name.

A marked reversal of social and cultural status occurred. The country's educated elite was now predominantly Lithuanian, while

LITHUANIA

most remaining Poles belonged to the neglected rural population of the Vilnius region, or were low-skilled workers who moved into the city and its suburbs. All indicators of educational and professional attainment were lower than for ethnic Lithuanians. Possibly following pressure from Moscow, the LSSR established a network of Polish-language primary and secondary schools in the south-east of the country, at the expense of Lithuanian-language ones. These institutions taught Russian, rather than Lithuanian, as a second language. Despite this, some Polish parents preferred to send their children to Russian-language schools, for the better subsequent prospects. Either way, few Poles learned Lithuanian to a reasonable standard. The number of those declaring Polish nationality in censuses rose slowly from 230,000 in 1959 to 258,000 to 1989, while declining from 9.7 per cent to 7 per cent of the LSSR's population. However, a significant minority of these people gave Russian, rather than Polish, as their first language, while the rural 'simple speech' overlapped with north-western Belarusian dialects.

With the slaughter of the Jews and the departure of the great majority of Polish Vilnans, the city became, as Theodore Weeks puts it, almost 'a demographic tabula rasa'.[32] This shattering of continuity has been compared to the transformation of the Prussian and German cities of Königsberg and Memel into Soviet Russian Kaliningrad and Soviet Lithuanian Klaipėda respectively. Although Vilnius seemed a city of ghosts and ruins, with 40 per cent of homes seriously damaged, it was in better physical condition than Warsaw. Vilnius, like other Lithuanian cities, attracted many beggars from elsewhere in the Soviet Union. Ethnic Lithuanians were at first reluctant to settle in Vilnius, unless they were members of the *nomenklatura* (a list of vetted Communists who qualified for senior party or state positions), or else aspired to join this privileged class. Spacious apartments and even villas awaited this fortunate and favoured few.

Migration of ethnic Lithuanians to Vilnius increased dramatically from 1949, although it took more than three decades before they outnumbered the combined numbers of mostly Russian-speaking immigrants, who had provided much of the postwar city's industrial workforce at first, and local Poles. The regime attempted with mixed results to use the Soviet system of internal passports to manage migration to Vilnius. The 1959 census recorded a population of 236,000, of which 33 per cent declared Lithuanian nationality; that of 1970: 372,000, of which 43 per cent were Lithuanian; that of 1979: 476,000, of which 47 per cent were Lithuanian; and that of 1989: 577,000, of which 55 per cent were Lithuanian.[33] At some point during the 1980s, the old dream of Lithuanian nationalists was finally turned into reality by Lithuanian Communists.

Immediately after the war, the status of Vilnius briefly hung in the balance. The formal head of state, Justas Paleckis, insisted on turning the historical capital into the Soviet capital. Unusually, Stalin agreed with him, so Sniečkus, who was open to the pragmatic alternative of Kaunas, which emerged from the war almost intact, changed his mind. He repeatedly stated that Vilnius 'should become the largest industrial centre and the heart of [the] cultural life of Lithuania'.[34] Paleckis combined a medievalist strain of Romanticism with anti-clericalism and an exalted cult of youth. The first Soviet Lithuanian outdoor song festival, held in Vilnius on 13 July 1945, was supposed to be 'national in form and socialist in content', but it turned out to be quite nationalist in content as well.[35] The adjustment was made all the easier by associating 'feudal' and 'bourgeois' class enemies with the Poles. The LSSR's capital in Vilnius would be rebuilt to fit the presumed needs of the reforged *homo sovieticus*, 'Soviet man'. It should have suited 'Soviet woman', too, but despite her legal equality, she remained firmly in second place. However, the results of Sovietisation did not turn out quite as planned. This was partly because of the rapidity with which so many people from the countryside, uprooted from their ancestral farms, moved into Vilnius and other cities. As Davoliūtė puts it: 'the urbanisation of the nation amounted to the ruralisation of the city'.[36] Chickens long had the run of many a Vilnius courtyard, and of the buses in and out of the metropolis.

In the radiant vision of Soviet Lithuania, culture would replace religion. The regime pressed writers into service. Some, including Antanas Venclova, Juozas Baltušis, and Eduardas Mieželaitis, were left-wingers who had sat out the war in the Soviet Union. Others were on probation. For those writers compromised by work for the Nazi German occupants, the price of acceptance could be infiltration and betrayal of anti-Soviet partisans. The underground press condemned and threatened collaborating literati. Older writers recruited and mentored younger ones, offering both privileges and prestige. Student poets sought to impress girlfriends or boyfriends. Some of those traumatised by wartime experiences succumbed to crapulous debauchery. But those born in the 1930s could feel they had the world at their feet as they began their studies. Among those born in this generation were the poet Justinas Marcinkevičius, and the musicologist Vytautas Landsbergis. The latter's father was the architect Vytautas Landsbergis-Žemkalnis, who enjoyed continual professional success despite the many changes of regime during his 100-year-long life. Vilnius University reopened in 1945 with 800 students. Three quarters of the 3,000 students in 1950 were ethnic Lithuanians. Vilnius still looked shabby, drawing unfavourable comparisons with Kaunas, and Lithuanians were still a minority of the city's population, but these were challenges to be met head-on by fresh-faced youngsters in full cry. These young men and women left the troubled countryside behind, and embraced urban modernity.

The streets and institutions of Vilnius were marked by bilingual Lithuanian and Russian signs. Many of these commemorated Soviet heroes, such as Kapsukas, imposed on the University as its patron in 1955. Some Lithuanian national figures made the cut, including Jonas Basanavičius. Among the renamed thoroughfares, Calvary Street (*Kalvarijų gatvė*) became Dzerzhinskii Street in 1947, but Gediminas Avenue was renamed in honour of Stalin as late as 1952. This straight artery, with large squares at either end, provided the public space for the most important parades, held every 1 May (International Labour Day), 9 May (Victory Day), and 7 November (the anniversary of the 'October Revolution'). State holidays that marked anniversaries such as 16 February 1918 were replaced by more suitable ones, such as the anniversary of the establishment of the LSSR on 21 July 1940. These holidays were also occasions for rallies, lectures, films, and conferences, which were repeated, on a smaller scale, in other cities, towns, and villages. Even workers on collective farms had to be suitably edified. The regime selectively harvested the pre-Soviet past as it sought to create a coherent narrative that led from medieval Lithuania to the fulfilment of the Lithuanian nation's socialist and Soviet destiny. It duly inflated the significance of traces of proletarian revolutionary activity, such as the one night Lenin spent in Vilnius. A museum dedicated to Feliks Dzerzhinskii was opened in 1959. Statues were of course erected to Stalin, Lenin, and such like. Later they were joined by smaller monuments to Lithuanian national heroes and heroines, including the statue of Žemaitė unveiled in 1970.

The physical rebuilding that took place was significant, but fell well short of the grand Soviet schemes drawn up in 1941. The Green Bridge, detonated in 1944, was rebuilt in 1950 with muscular statues personifying the Red Army, study, industry, and agriculture. It was renamed after General Cherniakhovskii, who had been killed outside Königsberg in 1945. The railway station, also rebuilt in 1950, was a bombastic exercise in Stalinist classicism. Still more grandiose was the Central Library of the LSSR, opened in 1963.

LITHUANIA

The changes were greatest in the heart of former Jewish Vilnius, along German Street. The pillaged and roofless Great Synagogue could have been renovated, but despite appeals from the revived Jewish community, the building was blasted in 1947 and demolished between 1955 and 1957, to be replaced by a kindergarten. Sports facilities were built on the site of the Jewish cemetery on the north bank of the Neris. The grave of the Gaon was one of the few moved to a new site. Traces of Tatar Lukiškės were also buried. In contrast, from 1948 onwards most churches were closed or converted to other functions, but not demolished. Among those closed was the Catholic cathedral. A few were permitted to remain open as closely watched places of worship. The three crosses that had looked down on the city were blown up in 1950.

Nevertheless, for better or worse (for example regarding sanitation) much of the Old Town saw little alteration. This was due to a shortage of resources, combined with the planners' restraint. This relatively benign neglect, more like postwar L'viv than Minsk, made it possible for the city's architectural heritage to be studied, appreciated, and preserved. For decades, Vladas Drėma researched the legacy of early modern Vilnius, which fitted neither Soviet nor nationalist paradigms. He struggled against the 1960s mode for 'gothicisation', that is for stripping away render to expose the brickwork of old buildings. Architects who tried to reference the country's ecclesiastical baroque tradition as a source for the new Soviet architecture could expect stinging criticism. As late as 1985, the Communist ideologue Lionginas Šepetys questioned 'whether a masterpiece of Baroque would have been erected if the nobleman Pacas had not oppressed his serfs'.[37] Enthusiasts focused on the craftsmen rather than the patrons. There was scope among the thousands of stuccoed sculptures at Antakalnis to find some ordinary folk. Gradually restrictions on research loosened, and limited resources were made available for conservation. They came at an ideological price, though. St Casimir's Church was restored as a museum of atheism, opened in 1961.

Trakai Castle was a special case. In 1955 the modest postwar conservation works of the picturesque ruins on the island became a full-scale reconstruction of Vytautas's fortress and residence. Khrushchev belatedly criticised it as an example of misplaced priorities in 1960, when it was too late to reverse the project. Sniečkus explained to him that:

> in the rebuilt castle it was planned to open a museum in which it could be possible to represent the fight of the Lithuanian and Russian nations against crusaders, feudal lords, the bourgeoisie, and fascist invaders. Considering that very many tourists and guided tours visit Trakai Castle, this museum may play an important role in educating working people in the spirit of friendship of peoples and Soviet patriotism.[38]

The republic's quantum of fiscal autonomy allowed the work to continue at lower intensity until it was completed in the 1980s. Although the underfunded museum opened to the public in 1961 implied, rather than proclaimed, Lithuania's medieval greatness, the castle soon drew hundreds of thousands of visitors annually. Conveniently located for an excursion from Vilnius, it continues to be one of Lithuania's most popular tourist attractions.

Sniečkus discreetly encouraged the national component of Soviet Lithuania, even modernist artists berated by Khrushchev, as long as they were good Soviet Lithuanians. After the 'thaw', Lithuanian artists, architects, musicians, actors, directors, and writers began to achieve all-union recognition. In Vilnius, the Neringa Café on Lenin Avenue (no longer Stalin Avenue) opened in 1959 with frescoes that blended Lithuanian folk motifs into the modernist design. It became a favourite venue for members of the political and cultural elites, and for visitors from elsewhere in the USSR and abroad. They included the carefully monitored foreign tourists permitted to visit Vilnius and Kaunas. The intellectual establishment fêted Jean-Paul Sartre and Simone de Beauvoir in 1965, although it became painfully obvious that Sartre did not think Lithuanian writers could break through to a global audience if they continued to write in Lithuanian. Narratives of socialist success seemed plausible by the early 1960s, as the Soviet Union basked in its early lead in the Space Race.

1965 also saw the Order of Lenin collectively awarded to the model republic: the LSSR. By this time the economy had grown considerably. Early efforts concentrated on reconstructing and constructing factories, and meeting centrally set targets for providing produce to the rest of the union. From 1957 a degree of decentralisation in economic policy to the republics mitigated the inefficiencies and waste inherent in central planning. The LSSR developed an agro-industrial specialisation. These enterprises produced processed foodstuffs, animal feed, and chemical fertilisers. One of the largest capital investments was the hydroelectric power station at the dam on the Nemunas upriver from Kaunas, completed in 1960. The creation of the 'Kaunas Lagoon' (*Kauno marios*) inundated thirty-five villages.

Standards of living had also risen from their low postwar base, especially in the towns and cities. Prefabricated concrete blocks of cramped flats became ubiquitous, most of them three- to five-storey *khrushchevki* without lifts, many of which survive to this day. The Lazdynai suburb of Vilnius, designed in 1962, and built from 1969 onwards, was more ambitious. It won acclaim for its bold modernist architecture and careful landscaping, and is still regarded as a good place to live. Other high-rise housing estates, built in the larger towns in the 1970s and 1980s, were drearier. All were prodigious wasters of energy. In general, the years and decades from the late 1950s onwards brought most town-dwellers some kind of normalisation. True, the shortages, queues, coupons, waiting lists, and bureaucratic absurdities inseparable from a centrally planned economy continued to sap civic energy and initiative. Aspirations and achievements, hesitantly encouraged by Soviet-era advertising, focused on obtaining an apartment, and then a refrigerator, a washing machine, furniture, a telephone, and a car. The threat of repression, albeit less fatal than in the Stalinist period, hung over those who dared to voice criticism of the regime. For those prepared to conform to Soviet expectations and keep their heads down, it was possible to have a fulfilling private life—to study, fall in love, bring up a family, and go on modest holidays. Bitter memories of collectivisation and deportation were silenced, although not obliviated.

Most of the people who moved from the collectivised countryside to the towns perceived this everyday Soviet modernity as an improvement. Electricity and plumbing certainly made life easier. Nevertheless, the repeated tragedies of forced moves, first to collective farms and larger villages, then to towns and cities, as programmes of rural 'melioration' intensified in the later 1960s, contributed to a mounting sense of loss at a passing world. It began to be expressed in an ethnographic turn in culture. Violeta Davoliūtė traces this shift in the *oeuvre* of Justinas Marcinkevičius. His epic poem *The Twentieth Spring* (*Dvidešimtas pavasaris*, 1956), first brought him widespread official and popular recognition. It followed the path from the troubled, but traditionally evoked countryside to the radiant future in Soviet Lithuanian Vilnius. His next major work, *The Pine that Laughed* (*Pušis, kuri juokėsi*, 1961) has often been interpreted as a critique—or even attempted intimidation—of the circle of Tomas Venclova. Some readers have detected a resemblance between the privileged son of Antanas Venclova and the talented, but superficial Romas, the son of a professor. His fascination with Western philosophy is contrasted with the naïve wisdom and goodness of Gailiūnas, an art student from the countryside. Marcinkevičius's evolution continued with a trilogy of epic dramas—*Mindaugas* (1968), *Katedra*

(1971), and *Mažvydas* (1977)—set deep in the national past. The chanting in the third of these spectacles of the word 'Lithuania' in three equally stressed syllables—'*LIE-TU-VA*'—put audiences into a trance. Thus pronounced, the country's name would later resonate in the demonstrations and song festivals that helped to topple the Soviet empire. Marcinkevičius's poetry readings often reduced the mostly female audiences to tears. It has to be said that the male literary lions tended to deride female 'graphomaniacs'.

By the 1970s, the cult of Lithuania's primeval and rural past was burgeoning. The authenticity of folk performances by the elderly folk group 'Kupiškis Wedding' (Kupiškėnų vestuvės), compared to the slick Soviet dance troupe Lietuva, profoundly moved audiences, including those watching on television. Films, documentaries, and photographs explored the aesthetics of the vanishing rural past. This trend can be placed within the wider Soviet literary context of 'village prose', but unlike in other Soviet republics, it encountered little opposition from the oracles of orthodox Marxism-Leninism. Its most intelligent Lithuanian critic was the metropolitan liberal Tomas Venclova. But as the *enfant terrible* of the literary establishment, this founder-member of the Lithuanian Helsinki Group in 1976 was permitted to emigrate. He took up a post at Yale University the following year. Venclova conceived Lithuanian culture and identity far more broadly, taking in the artistic achievements of the Renaissance and Baroque, even when they were expressed in Polish, or for Polish-speaking patrons. These views helped him to enter into dialogue and become friends with an older, exiled Polonophone poet who proclaimed himself the last citizen of the Grand Duchy of Lithuania. Czesław Miłosz, who held a chair in Slavic Studies at Berkeley, embarrassed Poland's Communist rulers when he won the Nobel Prize for Literature in 1980. Venclova's blunt comments made in emigration that writers' 'search for ethical or aesthetic values in the village' seemed 'pointless' and were 'a disease' upset Lithuanian Americans, most of whom still treasured an idyllic rural vision of their ancestral land.[39] He and two slightly older academics in American exile, the sociologist Vytautas Kavolis and the political scientist Aleksandras Štromas, developed a liberal, progressive strain of Lithuanian nationalism or patriotism, open to dialogue with Poles, Jews, and Russians, as opposed to integrist ethno-linguistic nationalism.

Although the ethnographic turn in Lithuanian culture was not always as anti-Soviet as it was later represented, it contributed to the unbottling of anti-Soviet memories and to the ultimate rejection of Soviet Lithuania as fundamentally illegitimate. Popular culture, tradition, faith, and defiance all merged at the Hill of the Crosses. The site is an ancient hillfort, which rises modestly out of the Samogitian plain near Šiauliai. After the Uprisings of 1831 and 1863–64, families commemorated fallen insurgents whose bodies could not be recovered by placing crosses here. The landmark became a place of pilgrimage, and the number of crosses reached 400 in 1938. The growing number of crosses irritated the Soviet regime which in 1961 destroyed 5,000 of them. But they kept being placed there at night. By the early 1970s, the authorities were destroying hundreds of crosses every year and regularly bulldozing the site. After the signing by the Soviet Union and its satellites on 1 August 1975 of the Helsinki Accords, which recognised postwar frontiers but also affirmed the principle of national self-determination and enshrined basic human rights, including freedom of religion, in international law, the embarrassed LSSR changed tactics. Expedients included roadblocks because of alleged epidemics, removal of crosses supposedly without artistic value, and even flooding the area. Nonetheless, the phenomenon proved unstoppable. The harassment ended in 1988, and by 1990, there were 55,000 crosses on or around the Hill, of which more than 1,000 were over 3 metres high. Most are made of wood; some are of metal or stone. While some are simply created from two twigs tied together with grass, others are elaborately carved. Many carry rosaries. Pope John Paul II celebrated Mass here before a huge congregation on 7 September 1993. The numbers of crosses, pilgrims, and tourists continue to grow.[40]

From the re-establishment of the LSSR in 1944, the Catholic Church was targeted as an obstacle to Sovietisation. Although the constitution guaranteed the right to practise religion, many churches were soon closed, as were as all monasteries, friaries, and convents. The system of registration allowed the authorities to control parishes and their clergy, and facilitated the punishment of priests who attempted to instruct children in the faith after school. The sole remaining seminary, in Kaunas, was deprived of its property and most of its students. Attempts to communicate with the Vatican risked charges of spying and draconian punishments. The regime reacted with fury to clerical evasion of orders to urge the partisans to disband, and to covert succour to the cause of independence. About a third of all priests were arrested, imprisoned, or deported between 1944 and 1953.

Bishops led by example. Vincentas Borisevičius, bishop of Telšiai, was tried for treason and executed in 1946. Teofilius Matulionis had been incarcerated by the Bolsheviks twice before the war, before he returned to Lithuania as bishop of Kaišiadorys in 1943. Imprisoned for a further decade in 1946, he spent the remainder of his life under house arrest, before officers of the KGB (Committee for State Security, Komitet gosudarstvennoi bezopasnosti) killed him with poison in 1962. He was beatified in 2017. Mečislovas Reinys, briefly minister of foreign affairs in 1925–26, and administrator of the archdiocese of Vilnius from 1940, was sentenced to seven years' imprisonment for anti-Soviet activities in 1947. He died a prisoner in 1953. By 1949, three prelates administered six dioceses under the strict control of the state.

The Soviet regime failed either to destroy religion altogether, or to promote Orthodoxy at the expense of Catholicism. The much smaller communities of Old Believers, Lutherans, and other Protestants were hard pressed to survive at all. From the mid-1950s the regime's policies shifted to the invigilation, infiltration, and division of Catholic clergy and laity alike. Church closures were paused, limited publication of prayer books and calendars were permitted, two approved bishops were consecrated, and many priests returned from exile. However, harassment continued spasmodically, including renewed church closures, in response to manifestations of mass religiosity. So did the efforts to propagate atheism. Urbanisation took its toll, as traditional religious practices were harder to uproot in the countryside. While 82 per cent of infants were baptised in 1957, by 1970 the proportion had slipped to 45 per cent.[41]

The reforms of the Second Vatican Council of 1962–65 brought both opportunities and challenges for the Soviet regime. On the one hand, the hierarchy and older believers might be portrayed as reactionaries opposed to progressive changes. On the other hand, the regime feared lay initiatives, as well as the Lithuanian liturgy, introduced in 1970. It also became increasingly nervous about being exposed abroad for persecuting people for their faith. An important role here was played by the Centre for the Study of Religion and Communism, founded in 1969 by an Anglican priest, Canon Michael Bourdeaux. Later renamed the Keston Institute after its London premises, it meticulously documented cases of religious persecution in the Soviet bloc and intervened on behalf of repressed believers. It rapidly won a reputation for accuracy and persistence. The institute's immense archive contained a petition for religious freedom signed by 17,000 Lithuanians in 1972. In 2007 Bourdeaux personally returned it to the archbishop of Kaunas. This was Sigitas Tamkevičius, who as a young priest had clandestinely become a Jesuit. He founded and edited the underground *Chronicle of the Catholic Church in Lithuania* (*Lietuvos katalikų bažnyčios kronika*)

LITHUANIA

which ran from 1972 until 1989. In 1978 he and two other priests openly told foreign journalists in Moscow that they had formed the Catholic Committee for the Defence of Believers' Rights in Lithuania. It was active for five years before Tamkevičius was sent to a labour camp. Undeterred, rising numbers of clergy and believers signed petitions and protest letters, participated in illegal processions and meetings, and openly taught the faith. The election of Karol Wojtyła as Pope John Paul II brought to the Holy See a religious leader who had the measure of Soviet Communism. He toughened up his predecessors' *Ostpolitik*, and infused the bloc's Catholics with a new confidence.

The last two decades of Soviet Lithuania saw the cause of religious freedom interact with other forms of protest. At noon on 14 May 1972, a long-haired, religiously inclined nineteen-year-old hippy called Romas Kalanta set himself alight in the centre of Kaunas, and died of his injuries during the night. Although his brief suicide note ('blame only the regime for my death') was only discovered in the archive of the KGB after Lithuania regained its independence, news of the event sparked serious rioting that took two days to quell, and a spate of suicides by self-immolation. The regime falsely portrayed Kalanta as a schizophrenic. Sniečkus reassured the Kremlin that he had the situation under control, and blamed the influence of Western radio broadcasts. But the attractions of Western music and clothes, especially denim jeans, could not be overcome. Unlike in the West, however, non-conformism was not primarily about lifestyles and hairstyles, but encompassed protest against the repressive Soviet system.

The veteran party boss died two years later, and his successor as first secretary, the mediocre Petras Griškevičius, was less able and less inclined to resist pressure from Moscow. One of the ways in which he sought to compensate for his lack of authority was by using hunting for game to bond with members of the *nomenklatura*. The stifling but sclerotic central leadership, headed by the ageing sybarite Leonid Brezhnev from 1964 until 1982, pressed the republics to promote Russian as the common language of *homo sovieticus*, and to erode national differences and traditions. The use of Russian gained somewhat at the expense of Lithuanian in transport facilities, the police, state offices, and larger enterprises, as well as in the Party itself. By then, however, the national character of Soviet Lithuania seemed ineradicable, in contrast to the situation in Estonia, Latvia, or most of Ukraine. Lithuanian held its own as the principal language of higher education, not only in the humanities. Griškevičius and his colleagues pursued an inconsistent policy towards dissenters in the LSSR, reflecting that in the Soviet Union as a whole. Repression alternated with concessions.

The Lithuanian Helsinki Group publicly announced its existence in Moscow in the autumn of 1976. It communicated with other groups in the Soviet bloc and informed the world about breaches of human rights. Besides Venclova, the founders included the teacher and poetess Ona Lukauskaitė-Poškienė, who had earlier spent seven years in a labour camp in the Arctic, the Jewish physicist Eitan Finkelstein, the Jesuit Karolis Garuckas, and the Catholic intellectual Viktoras Petkus. He paid the highest price with a seven-year prison sentence in 1978, followed by internal exile, before being permitted to return to Lithuania in 1988.

Whereas the Helsinki Group operated openly, acting as if Soviet constitutional guarantees applied in reality, the Lithuanian Liberty League (Lietuvos laisvės lyga) was an underground organisation. Founded in 1978, it sought the restoration of Lithuanian independence by peaceful means. Its leader, Antanas Terleckas had already been twice imprisoned for anti-Soviet activities. On the fortieth anniversary of the Molotov-Ribbentrop Pact he was one of the forty-five Baltic citizens (thirty-five of them Lithuanians), supported by eleven Russian dissidents, who addressed a memorandum to the signatory states of the Atlantic Charter and the secretary-general of the United Nations. It called on the Soviet Union to publish the secret protocols of the pact, to denounce it as null and void, and to withdraw foreign troops from the three Baltic states. Two months later Terleckas was arrested and sentenced to three years' imprisonment followed by four years' internal exile.

The years 1980–81 brought Lithuanian opponents of the Soviet regime the inspiring example of the 'Solidarity' mass movement in Poland: this independent, self-governing trade union of almost 10 million workers ripped the façade from the so-called workers' state as nothing else could. The temporary breakdown of censorship in Poland permitted taboo subjects in history—such as the Katyń massacre and the Molotov–Ribbentrop Pact—to be raised and discussed in a way that ensured that they could never again be denied completely. The Polish press became highly interesting to Lithuanian intellectuals, many of whom knew the language well. However, the militarised Polish regime's violent suppression of 'Solidarity' through the imposition of martial law in December 1981 brought great relief to the Lithuanian and central Soviet leaderships. The latter decayed into a risible gerontocracy. Brezhnev's demise in 1982 was swiftly followed by the deaths of Yurii Andropov in 1984 and Konstantin Chernenko in 1985, but the prospects for political change seemed as dismal as the funereal grimaces of the elderly members of the Politburo, as they shuffled behind the latest coffin destined for the Kremlin wall.

iv. *Independence Regained*

The Soviet empire ended far more suddenly than anyone anticipated. Indelible images include President Ronald Reagan demanding 'Mr Gorbachev, tear down this wall!' in front of the Brandenburg Gate on 12 June 1987 (provoking derision from Western European intellectuals) and the celebrations when the Berlin Wall was breached on 9 November 1989. That year, Poland led the satellite states out of their orbits around Moscow. The Soviet Union itself ceased to exist on 26 December 1991. Lithuanians, Latvians, and Estonians played a highly visible and audible part in its collapse. Most of this book has emphasised the distinctiveness of Lithuanian history, but for these few crucial years, the three nations usually acted together, aware that they could achieve much more by cooperating than by going it alone. From the perspective of the Baltic nations, the story remains, as the Swedish social scientist Stefan Hedlund put it, that 'of David rising to fight Goliath, with a shrewd deployment of soft power as the legendary sling stone'.[42] That 'soft power' included the revelation of historical truth and the civic energy unleashed by three 'Singing Revolutions'. The Baltic states were the first to leave the Soviet Union, but their departure did not in itself destroy it. The secession of Ukraine, combined with power struggles in the Russian Soviet Socialist Federal Republic (RSFSR) itself, dealt the USSR its coup de grâce. None of this would have happened as quickly as it did, in the way that it did, had it not been for Mikhail Sergeievich Gorbachev.

Gorbachev played a unique part in global and Lithuanian history. His ambitions to build friendly relations with the West in 'a common European home' ultimately proved incompatible with the violent crackdown to which he resorted in seeking to shore up the crumbling Soviet Union. Nevertheless, his vision and character were moulded by his own career as a model *apparatchik*. He rose from his mixed ethnic Russian and ethnic Ukrainian background on a collective farm in the North Caucasus. His Stakhanovite feats on a combine harvester helped him to study law at Moscow State University as a member of the Communist

Party of the Soviet Union. His long and exemplary record administering his native Stavropol region gave him a rarely matched grasp of provincial realities in the Khrushchev and Brezhnev eras, and also cleared him to go on mind-opening trips to the West. Both these factors would affect his later attitude to the Baltic republics. Appointed a secretary of the party's Central Committee with responsibility for agriculture in 1978, he advanced rapidly. He was promoted to the Politburo in 1980, where Andropov groomed him for greater things. Although he had to wait for Chernenko's death on 10 March 1985 before becoming general secretary, he had already been marked out by Margaret Thatcher: 'I like Mr Gorbachev. We can do business together'.[43]

Gorbachev's slogans and policies of *uskorenie* (acceleration), *glasnost'* (openness or transparency), *perestroika* (restructuring), and *demokratizatsiia* (which gains nothing in translation) had unintended consequences in the Baltics. His cult of 'Europeanness' aligned with the Western outlook of these three republics. He looked to them to blaze the trails for his reforms, imagining them to be privileged, prosperous, happy, and fundamentally on his side. Underestimating the power of history and song, his optimism turned to bewilderment, irritation, and a sense of betrayal by the 'radicals' who defied his efforts to save the union.

In retrospect, not least in Gorbachev's own view, the beginning of the end was the disaster of 26 April 1986. A reactor exploded at the Chernobyl nuclear power plant, located on the Prypiat' River near Ukraine's border with Belarus. The Soviet authorities' reflexive denials and inadequate reactions exposed many people to intense radiation. The radioactive cloud drifted northwest over the Belarusian SSR and the Baltic republics before it triggered alarms in Sweden. The widespread protests against the low value placed by the Soviet system on human life and health, and its comparable lack of concern for the natural environment, had particular resonance in Lithuania. The Ignalina nuclear power plant, which had opened in 1983 next to the newly constructed town of Sniečkus (renamed Visaginas in 1992), was of similar design. Its reactor had already revealed the flaw that was to prove fatal at Chernobyl. Ignalina's engineers informed other power stations in the USSR, which failed to act on the warning. Professional concerns and public demonstrations delayed the commissioning of the second reactor and led to the cancellation of the third.

The next warning signal concerned history. Antanas Terleckas returned to Lithuania from his exile in eastern Siberia in 1987. In Vilnius on 23 August 1987, he and several hundred supporters of the Lithuanian Liberty League protested against the Molotov–Ribbentrop Pact at the statue of Adam Mickiewicz (erected in 1984 next to St Anne's church). The security forces filmed and photographed this demonstration, but did not break it up. Anniversary protests also took place that day in Riga and Tallinn.

Petras Griškevičius died in November 1987. The next first secretary of the Lithuanian party was another veteran Communist. Like Gorbachev, Ringaudas Songaila had a background in agricultural affairs but was endowed with less imagination. He struck Gorbachev as a laggard in the urgent task of restructuring the stagnant Soviet economy. This perception helps to explain why the formation on 3 June 1988, at the seat of the Lithuanian Academy of Sciences in Vilnius, of a committee charged with creating the Lithuanian Popular Front did not disturb Gorbachev. Like the Popular Front of Estonia, founded in April 1988, the Lithuanian committee of thirty-five intellectuals, most of them Communist Party members, endorsed Gorbachev's own slogans. Insofar as he increased the republics' economic autonomy, his own aims coincided with those of the Baltic reformers, and they could be regarded as useful allies. His chief ally in the Politburo, Aleksandr Yakovlev, brought back favourable impressions from a visit to Vilnius on 11–12 August. However, their references to 'sovereignty', even when confined to economic matters, were heavily freighted with nationalism. A sanctioned meeting in the Vingis Park in Vilnius drew up to 100,000 people on the presumed anniversary of King Mindaugas's coronation on 6 July. The movement's leaders announced their intention to legalise the banned national anthem and flag, and those wishes were granted later that summer.

A still larger meeting took place in the Vingis Park on the forty-ninth anniversary of the Molotov–Ribbentrop Pact on 23 August. About a quarter of a million people participated in the greatest song festival yet seen in Lithuania. The movement's leaders also involved themselves with the spontaneous, youthful 'rock march' (*roko maršas*) phenomenon that had developed since 1987. These events combined concerts with political speeches and national symbols. Songs such as Antis's 'Zombies' (*Zombiai*) surreptitiously mocked the Soviet Army. The Lithuanian Liberty League went much further in its demands. On 28 September 1988, its demonstration at Cathedral Square was violently broken up on Songaila's orders. The militia's flailing batons prompted a wit to dub the event 'the ball of the bananas'. Facing a backlash, even within the ranks of the Communist Party, Songaila stepped aside. Algirdas Brazauskas became first secretary of the Party on 20 October. This tall, imposing, and (by party standards) charismatic civil engineer and economist had risen through the ranks since the 1960s. He would now seize his historical moment.

So would his near contemporary, Professor Vytautas Landsbergis, chosen as the chairman of the Reform Movement of Lithuania (Lietuvos Persitvarkymo Sąjūdis) at its constituent congress in Vilnius held on 22–23 October. The delegates comprised 980 ethnic Lithuanians, nine Poles, eight Russians, and six Jews. Coordinating meetings were also held in smaller cities such as Šiauliai. Sąjūdis had 200,000 members within a year. It benefited from the existence of the Lithuanian Liberty League as a reminder to the regime of its own relative moderation, but unlike its counterparts in Estonia and Latvia, this broadly-based reform movement was not seriously challenged for support from the radical nationalist flank.

Sąjūdis also benefited from the lesser appeal, again compared to the equivalents in Estonia and Latvia, of the Yedinstvo (Unity) movement. This was backed by the regime's hardliners and attracted some support among the Russian- and Polish-language minorities. Yedinstvo not only opposed independence, but also criticised *perestroika*, which prolonged Gorbachev's tolerance of Sąjūdis. All three Baltic popular movements' choice of non-violence piled pressure on Gorbachev not to use force. This was also a refrain of American diplomacy, backed by economic leverage. The popular mood changed fast, and by end of 1988 the atmosphere in the three capitals horrified Gorbachev's envoys. His closest aide, Anatolii Cherniaev, concluded that the scenarios were either Czechoslovakia in 1968 (the violent restoration of orthodoxy) or Finland in 1918 (the letting go of a peripheral imperial province).

Gorbachev announced plans for a partly elected, all-union Congress of Peoples' Deputies on 22 October 1988. Two weeks later, the leaders of the three popular movements discussed them in Riga. They agreed to oppose any new all-union powers by invoking the supremacy of the republics' own laws. The Estonian Supreme Soviet was the first legislature to assert sovereignty on 16 November 1988. When, for the moment, its Latvian and Lithuanian counterparts declined to follow suit, Sąjūdis protested. The USSR's constitutions of 1924, 1936, and 1977 theoretically allowed republics to leave the union, but no mechanism for their doing so existed in law. Matters drifted and the last moment to agree a new union treaty passed. By the start of 1989, Gorbachev's room for manoeuvre was shrinking fast. He faced severe economic and fiscal problems, opposition from

LITHUANIA

within the party and state bureaucracy to his reforms, ethnic violence between Armenians and Azeris in the disputed region of Nagorno-Karabakh, and a new American administration. George H. W. Bush had not shared Reagan's genial repartee with Gorbachev, and his secretary of state, James Baker, decided to review relations with the USSR. The year 1989 would bring the loss of the wider empire, which Gorbachev and his allies could not and would not prevent.

The leaders of Poland's 'Solidarity' movement, who took up some of the reins of power in September 1989, sympathised with the cause of Lithuanian independence. They refused to support the autonomist aspirations of Polish minority leaders in the LSSR. At this point we must backtrack a little. The Lithuanian Supreme Soviet's decision on 8 October 1988 to make Lithuanian the sole official language of the republic, followed by the language law of 25 January 1989, caused much alarm. After a two-year transition period, all court proceedings, for example, would have to be conducted in Lithuanian. Thirty local authorities covering most of the south-east of the country declared themselves Polish national municipalities. In May 1989, the inaugural congress of the Union of Poles in Lithuania initiated a path towards a Polish autonomous region within the LSSR. Its projected boundaries encircled Vilnius by at least a dozen kilometres on every side. Polish and Lithuanian were to be its official languages, and Russian that of mutual communication. In September, two of these local authorities, both led by Communist activists, declared themselves Polish National–Territorial Districts. The Lithuanian Supreme Soviet declared these moves unconstitutional, but the stand-off continued until September 1991.

Gorbachev's policy of *glasnost'* enabled the 'return' of memory to contribute to the fall of the Soviet regime in Lithuania, Latvia, and Estonia. Memoirs of the deported and displaced, as well as detailed accounts of the fall of the interwar republics, became widely available from 1987 onwards. They included, in 1988, the second version of the memoirs of Dalia Grinkevičiūtė. She had published them anonymously in Russian in an underground (*samizdat*) journal in 1979. Born in 1927, this well-educated daughter of a high-ranking state official and member of Smetona's Nationalist Union was deported with her mother and brother to the desolate Trofimovsk Island in the delta of the River Lena in northeastern Siberia in June 1941. They survived the first winter and moved to Yakutsk. Having returned illegally to Kaunas in 1949, the mother died and was buried in the cellar of their old house in which they were hiding. Rearrested, Dalia was sent back to Siberia. Freed during the 'thaw', she studied and practised medicine, but remained under suspicion, and was periodically interrogated, for the rest of her life. Shortly before she died in 1987, she passed her manuscript to Justinas Marcinkevičius. The famous poet broke through the barrier of censorship when he quoted her memoirs in an article about their meeting and his reading of her text. It was then openly published in instalments in 1988. She had written an unfinished Lithuanian version in 1949–50 and buried it. This was rediscovered in 1991 and published in 1996.

The publication did more than mobilise public anger at the Soviet regime's manifold crimes against humanity. It bridged the chasm between the intelligentsia and the regime's victims. Grinkevičiūtė's consigning of her legacy to Marcinkevičius conferred legitimacy on intellectuals who had enjoyed a comfortable life in the LSSR and might otherwise have experienced greater resentment from victims or indeed, less privileged conformists. A backlash did tarnish the unrepentantly pro-Soviet Baltušis and Mieželaitis. But few followed their examples. Polished writers had the ability eloquently to express what hundreds of thousands of people wished to hear or read. In this way, the trauma of deportation and repression became a collective memory, even among those who had not directly experienced it themselves. Soviet deportations were linked to earlier expulsions by the Teutonic Knights and the tsarist empire. Poems of deportees were 'emerging from oblivion and desecration like white bones from the land of eternal frost', wrote the literary critic Viktorija Daujotytė in 1988.[44] Exhumations, repatriations, and reburials of the Siberian dead followed. Relics of displacement and deportation became art forms. These performances and pilgrimages had their roots in the ethnographic turn of the 1970s. The collective memory of deportation encompassed people's displacement from the countryside to the towns. Landsbergis claimed in May 1990 that 'we were deported not only from our homeland but from our language, customs, religion, respect for ourselves and our earth'.[45] As Davoliūtė argues, the 'return of memory', experienced by the masses and articulated by the elites, helped give the movement for reform and independence cohesion, when the potential for recrimination was high. The shared commemoration of the victims of Stalinism became an utter rejection of the Soviet empire.

The practice of history involves, among other things, the rigorous study of sources to establish as far as possible, a full and accurate record of what happened at crucial junctures in the past. Understood thus, 'History proved a robust weapon of the weak'.[46] One source in particular—the secret protocol of the Molotov–Ribbentrop pact—was crucial to the status of the three Baltic countries. From 1987, pressure mounted on the Soviet leadership to admit its existence and content. The problem was not only that drawing attention to the alliance between Stalin and Hitler, contracted in 1939, would undermine the Soviet myth of 'the Great Patriotic War' against Nazi Germany that had begun in 1941. Full acknowledgement would expose the fundamental illegitimacy of the Soviet annexation of Lithuania, Latvia, and Estonia. It would demonstrate that their independent statehood could be restored, and would not have to be created anew. The secret protocol was already known from the German version, which in 1988 was published in translation in all three Baltic republics. The Soviet side had long denounced it as a forgery. The original Russian-language version was kept in a sealed envelope in the Politburo archive in Kremlin. Gorbachev was aware of its explosive contents by 1987, but he continued to assert that its existence was uncertain, for example in his speech to open the Congress of Peoples' Deputies on 25 May 1989.

Partly free elections to this huge, 2,250-member assembly had taken place two months earlier. Sąjūdis candidates won thirty-six of the forty-two mandates they were allowed to contest, with slightly less overwhelming victories achieved by the popular movements in Estonia and Latvia. On 14 July 1989, the Estonian Popular Front leader Edgar Savisaar proposed the 'Baltic Way' to his Latvian and Lithuanian counterparts. Thanks to a marvel of logistics, facilitated by the state authorities of all three republics, but to a great degree improvised by informal networks, on 23 August 2 million people linked hands for 670 kilometres from Tallinn to Vilnius. Symbolic arrangements of coffins, flags, and the date all underlined to the massed Western media that the Nazi–Soviet pact was a crime against human rights and against Europe. Drawing attention to the illegal nature of the secret protocol under international law also helped to bring onside many Western intellectuals. Progressives' ingrained hostility to nationalism and their unwillingness to contemplate frontier changes worked in practice against the rights of smaller nations to self-determination. In Washington DC, the conservative Senator Jesse Helms had no such qualms when he quoted the Balts' 'Appeal to the nations of the world': 'Have you not noticed our absence?'[47]

On 27 August the Central Committee of the Communist Party of the Soviet Union threatened that 'the very viability of

LITHUANIA

the Baltic nations could be called into question' by 'nationalist hysteria'. Gorbachev doubled down on 19 September 1989, claiming that 'there is no basis for questioning the decision made by the Baltic republics to join the USSR and the choice made by the people there to be part of the Soviet Union'. The right of self-determination, he went on, could only be exercised within the union.[48] Nevertheless, a commission headed by Yakovlev got to work, and on 24 December 1989 the Congress of People's Deputies recognised and condemned the secret protocol by a vote of 1,435 to 251, without noting the implications for the annexations. The same day Brazauskas and his Lithuanian comrades voted to split from the Communist Party of the Soviet Union.

After almost a year in office, the Bush administration had decided to work with Gorbachev, fearing his replacement by a hardline regime in Moscow. The White House was prepared to put pressure on him to achieve a united Germany in NATO, but it would not take risks for the cause of the Baltic states' independence, and it opposed the independence of other republics. On the other hand, the diasporas and their numerous allies on both sides of both houses in Congress kept up the pressure, and the administration could not abandon the non-recognition of the three states' annexation in 1940. These factors, combined with the 'red line' against the use of force, ensured that the White House was in practice less hostile to the Baltic cause than the openly transactional West German chancellor, Helmut Kohl. President François Mitterrand let slip the long-term effects of French intellectuals' *mirage russe* by opining that 'historically, these areas had been part of Russia'.[49] The summit between Bush and Gorbachev in Malta on 2–3 December 1989 left the Soviet side with the impression that the USA would not expand NATO beyond Germany or encourage the secession of the Baltic states from the USSR. But the Americans made no written promise of either kind. The uncertainty created a window of opportunity that the leaders of the Baltic nations and their international supporters could exploit.

Gorbachev visited Lithuania between 11 and 13 January 1990. He was shaken to discover that it was too late for enhanced autonomy within the union, but he offered no alternative to his mantra about the 'Soviet constitution'. He hinted that he could support territorial autonomy, and perhaps frontier changes as well (Klaipėda bordered the Kaliningrad district of the RSFSR, while areas with a Polish majority bordered the Belarusian SSR). Some of the Communist Polish activists were prepared to take the bait, but in general, the gambit backfired. In the elections to the Lithuanian Supreme Soviet on 24 February, Sąjūdis-supported candidates won ninety-four of the 133 seats after running a campaign to restore full independence. Brazauskas's Communist Party of Lithuania was more circumspect, advocating 'a step-by-step approach'.[50]

On the second day of the assembly's deliberations, at 10.44 pm on 11 March, 124 deputies joyfully voted for the Act of the Re-Establishment of the State of Lithuania, with only six abstentions and none against. The deputies asserted the underlying continuity of the sovereign Republic of Lithuania, once again able to exercise its independence, and restored the Vytis as the emblem of statehood. Invoking the abstract right of national self-determination could have tied up the matter in Soviet constitutional law for years. Smetona's 1938 constitution was therefore restored for half an hour, before the Provisional Basic Law introduced democratic and civil rights into the structures of the Soviet republic. The legislature, called the Supreme Council (Aukščiausioji Taryba) as well as the Reconstituent Seimas, would supervise the executive and judicial powers. Landsbergis was elected as chairman of the Supreme Council and acting head-of-state. On 17 March the economist Kazimira Prunskienė became prime minister. The NKVD had killed her father, a forest ranger, in 1944.

LITHUANIA

The Congress of Peoples' Deputies reacted by declaring Lithuanian independence null and void on 15 March 1990. The secession law it adopted on 3 April made the process onerous and uncertain. Meanwhile, the popular movements of Latvia and Estonia won their respective elections, and signalled their intention to follow the Lithuanian example when the time was right. Gorbachev refused to negotiate with the Lithuanians unless they annulled their declaration and accepted the Soviet constitution. At the start of April, he became ambivalent on the use of force, and made threats via the newspapers and diplomatic channels concerning Lithuania's national minorities and frontiers. Tensions rose over conscription into the Soviet army, which Lithuanians rejected. Soviet soldiers occupied some public buildings. On 17 April Moscow implemented an economic blockade of Lithuania, resulting in severe cuts to fuel, heating, and employment. In such circumstances, the US Congress would not finalise the trade agreement that Gorbachev needed.

Independent Lithuania now needed international recognition. The Americans covertly pressured the Lithuanians to suspend their declaration. Mitterrand and Kohl did so overtly, but their joint letter to Landsbergis on 25 April did at least boost his status. Prunskienė toured Sweden, Norway, Denmark, Canada, the USA, Great Britain, France, and Germany, with mixed results. Kohl delivered the bluntest rejection. Members of the Lithuanian diaspora warmly greeted her and helped to keep the cause on the international agenda. For example, the distinguished translator Romas Kinka coordinated the meeting with Margaret Thatcher, represented Sąjūdis in Britain until independence was secured, and then joined Lithuania's foreign ministry as its spokesman before returning to London. The Lithuanian seimas remained in contact with the more cautious Supreme Soviets of Latvia and Estonia. On 17 May Gorbachev finally met Prunskienė. Five days later, he met the respective leaders of the Latvian and Estonian

Supreme Soviets, Anatolijs Gorbunovs and Arnold Rüütel. After the Soviet-American trade agreement had been signed in Washington, but not yet approved by Congress, on 13 June Prunskienė met the Soviet prime minister Nikolai Ryzhkov in Moscow and agreed to suspend the law re-establishing statehood. At the end of June the USSR lifted the blockade.

The Iraqi invasion of Kuwait on 2 August 1990 and the resultant preparations for the First Gulf War further distracted the West, which was already focused on Germany. But the Baltic states pushed at the limits of diplomatic protocol to make themselves visible. Besides their friends in the US Congress, they gained significant support from Poland, Denmark, Sweden, Norway, and Iceland. After a row, in which they had been asked to leave a summit of the Conference for Security and Cooperation in Europe in Paris in November 1990, Gorbachev denounced the 'militant nationalism and mindless separatism' that threatened 'Balkanization, and what is worse, Lebanization'.[51] He was now on borrowed time, caught between hardliners who wanted to use force to crush the Baltic revolt, and the challenge of the charismatic Boris Yeltsin. The latter became chairman of the Supreme Soviet of the RSFSR in May 1990, and vigorously rocked the Soviet boat. Yeltsin met Landsbergis, Gorbunovs, and Rüütel at Jūrmala on 27 July 1990.

The dénouement came in the New Year. On 2 January 1991 special forces of the Soviet interior ministry seized the buildings of the Lithuanian Communist Party in Vilnius as well as the Press House in Riga, and more Soviet troops moved into all three countries. Soon afterwards Prunskienė resigned over food prices. The economist Albertas Šimėnas took over with a largely unchanged cabinet. On 10 January Gorbachev seized what seemed a good moment to demand Lithuania's compliance with the Soviet constitution. Motorised units moved into Vilnius the next day, and also secured military sites in other towns. As crowds began to muster at key sites in Vilnius, KGB forces and units of the Pskov Airborne Division launched an attack on the Television Tower. By the time they had taken it on 13 January, thirteen people were dead. Another man died later. Five hundred and eighty people needed medical attention for wounds and injuries of varying severity. But broadcasts from Sitkūnai near Kaunas reached the nation and the world.

At this critical juncture, Prime Minister Šimėnas disappeared (to Druskininkai, it later transpired). The seimas summoned him, and when he could not be found, dismissed him and installed Gediminas Vagnorius as premier on 13 January. In the early hours of that decisive day, all three popular movements called on their compatriots to defend their parliaments. They came in their tens of thousands. In Vilnius Landsbergis urged them on: 'Singing has helped us; it has helped us for hundreds of years. [...] Let's ignore the shooting and let's sing!'[52] Some Polish parliamentarians arrived at the seimas and declared their willingness to die together. For the moment the Soviet forces decided not to attack.

A huge crowd of 600,000 people demonstrated in solidarity in Riga on 14 January. Major protests also took place in Leningrad, Moscow, L'viv, Tbilisi, and Chișinău, as well as outside the Soviet embassy in Warsaw and the consulates in Gdańsk and Kraków. Yeltsin flew to Tallinn on 14 January, and called for Gorbachev's resignation on 19 January. Even Patriarch Aleksei II called the use of force an error and a sin. The cautious official American, French, and German reactions were stiffened by responses from Congress and northern Europe. Iceland's outspoken foreign minister Jón Baldvin Hannibalson announced that his country was considering full recognition. Iceland was the first state to recognise Lithuanian independence on 11 February, although the establishment of diplomatic relations had to wait. Gorbachev pulled back from the brink in the face of citizens' mass mobilisation, and stinging criticism both at home and abroad. He knew that storming parliament buildings in the Baltic would result in bloodbaths. His public relations disaster was completed by the funeral of twelve of the fourteen victims of the Soviet attack on the Television Tower. Enormous crowds gathered in Cathedral Square and along the route to Antakalnis Cemetery.

Towards the end of January, Gorbachev backtracked, blaming everyone but himself. The soldiers left early in February. Had the crackdown succeeded, Gorbachev would have taken full advantage of it. His vehement denials of responsibility for the bloodshed are implausible. He had already authorised violence in Tbilisi in April 1989 (when twenty people were killed) and Baku in January 1990 (when over 140 died). Five more people were killed when Soviet troops attacked the ministry of the interior in Riga on 20 January. Those carrying out the attacks in Vilnius stated that their orders came from the head of the KGB Vladimir Kriuchkov and the interior minister Boris Pugo. Gorbachev approved the build-up of troops and only distanced himself after deciding not to proceed.

Instead of participating in Gorbachev's referendum on the renewal of the union, which most republics held on 17 March, the three Baltic states held their own votes on independence. Lithuania went first, on 9 February. With an 84 per cent turnout, 91 per cent voted in favour, meaning that over 76 per cent of those entitled to vote had chosen independence. Czechoslovak President Václav Havel hailed the 'expression of the authentic will of the Lithuanian nation'.[53] On 15 February, at a gala to mark the following day's anniversary of the establishment of Lithuanian statehood in 1918, Brazauskas called on Lithuanians 'to celebrate the most important date in our history', but also expressed remorse for it being forgotten for so long.[54] Latvia and Estonia voted on 3 March. It turned out that many Russian speakers also wanted to leave the Soviet Union. In Latvia, with an 88 per cent turnout, 74 per cent voted in favour; in Estonia, with an 83 per cent turnout, 78 per cent voted in favour.

LITHUANIA

The analysis of the results in Lithuania showed that the turnout was low in the Vilnius district (surrounding the city) at just 42 per cent, although 57 per cent of the votes cast were for independence. In the Šalčininkai district, the turnout was lower still, at 25 per cent, although 53 per cent voted 'yes'. Polish voters' evident passivity drew much comment in Lithuania and abroad. Denials by local Communists that they had encouraged a boycott may be evaluated in the light of the decision (following a meeting with Politburo member Oleg Shenin) of the local councils of the Vilnius and Šalčininkai districts to hold Gorbachev's all-union referendum on 17 March. Besides the fact that the referendum was illegal under Lithuanian law, the voting arrangements were irregular. But it does seem that most of the population of the two districts voted, and of those that did, nearly all preferred to remain in the Soviet Union. Amidst accusations of disloyalty levelled at the Polish minority, the Union of Poles in Lithuania repeatedly expressed its support for Lithuanian independence, but it also expected far-reaching autonomy. On 22 May its second congress approved a project for an autonomous Polish national-territorial region, surrounding Vilnius, in which about two-thirds of the inhabitants were Poles. The Lithuanian authorities were, for the moment, prepared to make some linguistic, cultural, and educational concessions in this part of the country, euphemistically summed up as respect for 'the Slavonic ethno-cultural image of Lithuania',[55] but not to undermine the state's territorial and political unity. Communications were kept open between the Union of Poles and Sąjūdis, but no agreement was reached.

Massive demonstrations in Moscow in March frustrated Gorbachev's attempt to remove Yeltsin as chairman of the Russian Supreme Soviet. With the White House worried by scenarios of Soviet collapse, Bush received Yeltsin as President of the RSFSR (the result of an additional question in the Russian referendum on the union) on 12 June 1990. A treaty between the RSFSR and Lithuania signed on 29 July was a step towards Russian recognition of Lithuanian independence. The Americans now sought to convince Soviet leadership that the Baltic states' independence was better than any alternative. The union might yet survive without them. Ukraine and other republics were a different matter. After signing a treaty on nuclear arms reduction at the Moscow summit of 30–31 July, Bush made his 'chicken Kiev' speech to the Ukrainian Supreme Soviet on 1 August. He warned that 'freedom is not the same as independence', and America would 'not aid those who promote a suicidal nationalism based on ethnic hatred'.[56]

Gorbachev was stunned to learn from Bush that on 31 July paramilitaries acting for the Soviet interior ministry had killed seven Lithuanian border guards at the Medininkai customs post with the Belarusian SSR. The loss of the outer empire, the weakening of the party's leading role, and the threat to the further existence of the union all angered Gorbachev's hardline critics. Plotters led by Pugo, Kriuchkov, Defence Minister Dmitrii Yazov, Prime Minister Valentin Pavlov, and Vice-President Gennadii Yanaiev planned to take control of Moscow and Leningrad and to impose direct presidential rule on the more truculent republics. They had Gorbachev arrested in Crimea on 19 August. Again, the American response was cautious until it was clear that the coup would fail. Yeltsin's heroics at the Russian parliament building exposed the plotters' poor planning and weak base of support, especially in the military. The putsch collapsed on 21 August. A shaken Gorbachev returned to Moscow, where he realised how dependent he was on Yeltsin.

In the Baltic states, Soviet troops seized some key communications buildings. Crowds again defended the Vilnius seimas, and soldiers again retreated on 19 August. In his diary Bush expressed his anxiety that Landsbergis, 'this hardliner in Lithuania', 'may

LITHUANIA

end up calling for troops'.[57] On 21 August a further move against the parliament building failed, but paratroopers killed a Lithuanian guard. On 20 and 21 August the Estonian and Latvian Supreme Soviets respectively proclaimed their countries' independence. On 23 August (the fifty-second anniversary of the infamous pact) Yeltsin recognised Estonian, Latvian, and Lithuanian independence on behalf of the RSFSR. The previous day Iceland announced its recognition and full diplomatic relations with all three states. The member states of the European Community did likewise on 27 August, the USA followed suit on 2 September, and the Soviet State Council conceded recognition on 6 September. President Bush welcomed all three acting heads-of-state on 18 September, when they came to New York to join the United Nations.

The Baltic states showed other Soviet republics that independence could be achieved by a combination of will, skill, and luck. Ukraine's Supreme Council declared independence on 24 August, and its citizens overwhelmingly approved the decision in the referendum held on 1 December. On a turnout of 84 per cent, 92 per cent voted 'yes'. Even in Crimea, most votes were cast for independence. Following a deal reached between the leaders of Russia, Ukraine, and Belarus in the Belavezha Forest (where Grand Dukes of Lithuania and Russian tsars had once hunted bison), the Soviet Union was wound up. Russia claimed most of its legal, diplomatic, and military inheritance. A generation would pass before a Russian dictator would try to rebuild the empire, and, in that time, Lithuania would transform itself again.

7

A COUNTRY IN EUROPE

(1991–2024)

The Republic of Lithuania established in 1918 has, in its two incarnations, already exercised its independence for longer than the combined Soviet and Nazi German occupations. More than a generation of Lithuanian citizens has now been born and brought up in independent Lithuania. This history cannot end in 1991, or even in 2004, when Lithuania joined the European Union (EU) and the North Atlantic Treaty Organization (NATO). Yet few historians have contested the academic terrain staked out by economists, political scientists, sociologists, and cultural anthropologists. This final chapter will be more provisional in its conclusions than the others. As Zhou Enlai answered when asked in 1972 about the French Revolution, it's 'too early to say'.*
The first part of the chapter will summarise the constitution agreed and introduced in 1992 and then chart the country's changing political and economic fortunes against the shifting

---

* The world's media assumed he meant the revolution of 1789, but his conversation with Henry Kissinger concerned the events of 1968.

background of international events. The second part will offer reflections on demographic, social, and cultural changes since the early 1990s. The final section of the book is a vignette from the edge of Lithuania in 2024.

Nostalgia for the Soviet or Communist era has affected, in some degree, all the former Soviet republics and satellite states. The 1990s brought dislocation and despair to many people whose stable existence was overturned. Some states, such as Belarus under Aleksandr Lukashenko from 1995, turned away at an early stage from the transition to a market economy, civil society, and political democracy. Other countries tried out variants that sought to mitigate the human and consequent political costs. The rejection by most Lithuanians of Soviet rule as oppressive and illegitimate, even if this involved some selective memorisation, helped to preserve national cohesion amidst the strains of a relatively rapid transition. Much the same can be said about Estonia and Latvia, although there, the far greater numbers of Russophone immigrants created larger pools of nostalgia for Soviet times, while sharpening the threat felt by ethnic Estonians and Latvians. It helped all three Baltic states that their experience of the USSR was shorter by a generation than that of most of the other republics. Interwar independence was a living memory for those born before the mid-1930s. Other factors included the relatively high numbers of returning émigrés, untainted by post-Soviet style dependencies and bringing valuable know-how and contacts. The principal Lithuanian example is former President Valdas Adamkus. These advantages made the three countries more akin to the former satellite states than, say, Kazakhstan, Armenia, or most of Ukraine. This widely perceived difference facilitated their acceptance into the supranational structures of the West in 2004—often tendentiously described as their 'return to Europe'. The fleeting opportunity to escape the Russian orbit motivated the Baltic elites to seize their moment and press forward, rather than postpone hard decisions.

A COUNTRY IN EUROPE

Lithuanians, Latvians, and Estonians have never taken their hard-won independence for granted. Gravitating towards the USA, they have often been stereotyped in Western Europe as paranoid Cold Warriors and Russophobes. Some of the harsher expressions of their respective ethno-linguistic nationalisms have played into their critics' hands. The attempts of Vladimir Putin's regime to haul former Soviet republics, especially Ukraine, back into a renewed Russian empire, as well as the 'hybrid war' waged against the West for the past two decades, have—at last—vindicated the Baltic and Polish warnings. Since 2022, some former sceptics, not least in Germany and France, have admitted as much. Lithuania has been placed in the West's new front-line, 1,000 kilometres east of the previous one, by the so-called 'return of history' to Europe (as if history ever went away...). The geographical centre of the European sub-continent, located by French geographers in 1989 at Girija, north of Vilnius, has for centuries been far from Europe's political, economic, and cultural centres of gravity. No longer. Nordic and Baltic countries now set multiple examples to the founding six of the European Community. Lithuania, today more than ever, is a country in Europe.

i. *A Democratic Republic*

One of the most important tasks facing independent Lithuania was to turn its Provisional Basic Law into a fully-fledged constitution. Constitutional experts worked through the country's defence of its independence in 1990–91, and in October 1992 the seimas approved the final draft. A majority of the electorate (three quarters of the three quarters who voted) approved the constitution in the referendum held on 25 October 1992. Vytautas Landsbergis, as head of state, promulgated the constitution on 6 November 1992.

The 154 articles are arranged in fifteen chapters: 'The State'; 'The Human Being and the State'; 'Society and the State';

LITHUANIA

'National Economy and Labour'; 'The Seimas'; 'The President of the Republic'; 'The Government of the Republic of Lithuania'; 'The Constitutional Court'; 'The Court'; 'Local Self-Government and Governance'; 'Finances and the State Budget'; 'National Audit Office'; 'Foreign Policy and National Defence'; 'Alteration of the Constitution'; and 'Final Provisions'.

The preamble founds the constitution in the will and cultural continuity of the nation, the historical continuity of the state, and the highest civic and democratic standards:

> The Lithuanian Nation, having created the State of Lithuania many centuries ago, having based its legal foundations on the Lithuanian Statutes and the Constitutions of the Republic of Lithuania, having for centuries staunchly defended its freedom and independence, having preserved its spirit, native language, writing, and customs, embodying the innate right of the human being and the Nation to live and create freely in the land of their fathers and forefathers—in the independent State of Lithuania, fostering national concord in the land of Lithuania, striving for an open, just, and harmonious civil society and State under the rule of law, by the will of the citizens of the reborn State of Lithuania, adopts and proclaims this Constitution.[1]

The first chapter spells out that 'The State of Lithuania shall be an independent democratic republic' (Article 1), and that 'The Nation shall execute its supreme sovereign power either directly or through its democratically elected representatives' (Article 4).

Among the enumerated human rights are 'Freedom of thought, conscience and religion' (Article 26). State education shall be secular, but religion may be taught in schools 'at the request of parents' (Article 40). All citizens have the right to free education until they reach sixteen years of age, while those with the requisite abilities are also guaranteed free higher education (Article 41). 'The family shall be the basis of society and the State. Family, motherhood, fatherhood and childhood shall be under the protection and care of the State. Marriage shall be concluded upon the free mutual consent of man and woman,' and it may be registered in churches. Parents are expected to take care of their children, and children of their parents in old age (Article 38). The State's support for citizens in unemployment, ill health, old age, and maternity does not entail state socialism: 'Lithuania's economy shall be based on the right of private ownership, freedom of individual economic activity and initiative' (Article 46).

In keeping with the concept of the nation elaborated in the preamble, 'Lithuanian shall be the State language' (Article 14). The constitution speaks of 'ethnic communities' rather than national minorities: 'Citizens belonging to ethnic communities shall have the right to foster their language, culture, and customs' (Article 37) and 'Ethnic communities of citizens shall independently manage the affairs of their ethnic culture, education, charity, and mutual assistance. Ethnic communities shall be provided support by the State' (Article 45). Unlike Latvia and Estonia, with their much larger populations of Russian-speaking postwar immigrants, Lithuania did not restrict its citizenship to persons, and their descendants, who had lived in the country before 1940. Such a step would not have disqualified much of the Polish minority.

The experience of the struggle for independence is reflected in the incorporation as a constitutional act of the prohibition on 8 June 1992 of membership in post-Soviet alliances (Article 150). Moreover, 'there may not be any weapons of mass destruction and foreign military bases on the territory of the Republic of Lithuania' (Article 137). Those who had sought territorial autonomy for the Polish minority are rebuked: 'The territory of the State of Lithuania shall be integral and shall not be divided into any State-like formations' (Article 10).

The constitution contains safeguards against the concentration of power in the same hands. The only public offices open to members of parliament are those of prime minister and cabinet-level ministers. One effect of this provision has been that junior ministers have generally been highly qualified and relatively young experts in their fields of responsibility. The unicameral seimas is elected for four-year-terms with 141 members, who must be at least twenty-five years old. Seventy-one of these are directly elected for single-member constituencies, and seventy are chosen by proportional representation from party lists (with a 5 per cent threshold). This was a compromise between the post-Communists' preference for proportional representation, and Sąjūdis's wish for single-member constituencies (optimistically counting on the prominence and popularity of its leaders). The president, government, members of the seimas, and citizens (with a threshold of 50,000 signatures) all have the right of legislative initiative. The passing of a constitutional law requires the support of at least three fifths (eighty-five) of the 141 members, but changes to the most fundamental questions, including the entire first chapter of the constitution, are reserved for referendums.

The executive branch consists of the president, prime minister, and the government (defined as the cabinet of ministers). The nation chooses the president in a two-stage election for a five-year term, and no one may serve for more than two terms. The president designates the prime minister and government, but they must secure parliamentary support. The presidential veto may be overridden by an absolute majority of the seimas (at least seventy-one members), and presidential decrees may also be overturned by the legislature. The president's ability to dissolve the seimas and call new elections largely depends on whether parliament can pass a state budget. The president 'shall decide the basic issues of foreign policy and, together with the Government, conduct foreign policy' (Article 84), and nominates diplomats. She or he is also commander-in-chief of the armed forces.

The independent judiciary holds the ring between the executive and legislative powers, with the constitutional court and the

A COUNTRY IN EUROPE

supreme court of appeal at the apex of the judicial structure. The president nominates all the judges to the supreme court, and three of the nine judges to the constitutional court (including the chief justice). Three more are nominated by the parliamentary speaker, and three by the chief justice of the supreme court. All serve for a single nine-year term.

The form of government merged two visions. One, supported by Sąjūdis, gave a greater role to the directly elected president, no doubt in anticipation that the presidency would be won by one of its own. The other, strictly parliamentary, was favoured by the post-Communist formation led by Algirdas Brazauskas. The resultant compromise placed Lithuania's democracy somewhere between those of France and Poland (which replaced its interim constitution with a full version in 1997). The Estonian constitution, approved in June 1992, and the Latvian constitution of 1922, amended in 1993, provide for the election of the largely representational president by proportionally elected parliaments. In general, the Lithuanian constitution met the standards of its time as a liberal and democratic foundation for a sovereign polity. Its emphasis on the ethnic and linguistic character of the nation is so rooted in Herder's ideas as to evoke the national 'spirit' in the preamble. But the preamble of the Latvian constitution is still more didactic:

> Since ancient times, the identity of Latvia in the European cultural space has been shaped by Latvian and Liv traditions, Latvian folk wisdom, the Latvian language, universal human and Christian values. Loyalty to Latvia, the Latvian language as the only official language, freedom, equality, solidarity, justice, honesty, work ethic and family are the foundations of a cohesive society.[2]

The experience of the Soviet economic blockade of Lithuania in the spring and summer of 1991 probably eased the political challenge of hauling the Lithuanian economy out of the Soviet rut. The government led by the youthful Gediminas Vagnorius began privatisation and reformed the interim coupons (talonai) that had restricted demand, making them independent from the ruble, which was in free fall. This helped to curb very high inflation. However, the coherence of the broad-based Sąjūdis movement fractured as the social costs of fast-rising unemployment and fuel shortages bit deep. Vagnorius's replacement as prime minister, Aleksandras Abišala, doubled down on austerity measures, including cuts in state spending and salary freezes.

The referendum on the constitution held on 25 October 1992 was combined with parliamentary elections. The victory of Brazauskas's post-Communist Democratic Labour Party of Lithuania with 44 per cent of the proportional vote, and an overall majority of seventy-three seats in the seimas, is still an unmatched result for any free election held in Lithuania since 1920. Sąjūdis and its partners won just thirty seats. The post-Communists were able to persuade voters that they did not threaten Lithuania's sovereignty, independence, or democracy, but they would implement necessary reforms less harshly than Sąjūdis. Brazauskas became speaker of the seimas and acting head of state, while the chemical engineer Bronislovas Lubys took over as prime minister.

Brazauskas won the first presidential elections on 14 February 1993. He gained 61 per cent of the votes in the first round, including almost all those cast by members of the Polish and Russian minorities. He beat Stasys Lozoraitis Junior, who had preserved the continuity of the interwar Republic as the head of its diplomatic service-in-exile. Brazauskas presented himself as pragmatic and moderate. He resigned, as the constitution required, from the Democratic Labour Party, and distanced himself from the government. The double post-Communist victory in Lithuania was the first in any of the states of the former bloc; it was followed by Poland (in 1993 and 1995) and elsewhere.

A COUNTRY IN EUROPE

Reeling in shock, Sąjūdis reformed into the centre-right Homeland Union or 'Conservatives' in May 1993.

Soon after the presidential elections, Lubys resigned and went into business; he became one of Lithuania's richest men, as head of the agricultural fertiliser company Achema. The next prime minister was a former manager of a state dairy enterprise, Adolfas Šleževičius. Inflation came down, partly through parsimonious public-sector pay rises, partly because of a monetary squeeze by the Bank of Lithuania. This enabled the long-awaited reintroduction of an independent and permanent currency on 25 June 1993. Each litas was worth 100 talonai. These coupons, decorated with Lithuanian fauna, were recycled into toilet paper. The exchange rate, initially set at five litai to the American dollar, was finally fixed at 3.9 litai in 1994. Lithuania's monetary and fiscal stability, reinforced by the introduction of Value Added Tax, began to attract significant foreign investment.

Institutions envisaged by the constitution, such as the constitutional court, were established, and local government structures were reformed, making them more democratic and accountable. Lithuania formally applied to join NATO at the start of 1994 and the EU at the end of 1995. The former seemed a particularly distant prospect. In the optimistic aftermath of the Cold War, there was little appetite in the West to risk cordial relations with Yeltsin's Russia for the sake of the former satellite states' long-term security, and still less for the 'indefensible' Baltic states. Although the last Russian soldiers left Lithuania just before midnight on 31 August 1993 after a telephone conversation between Yeltsin and Brazauskas, Russo–Lithuanian relations remained fraught. Special arrangements for extra-territorial transportation between the Kaliningrad exclave and Belarus enabled the Russians to depict technical difficulties as Lithuanian obstruction. Latvia and Estonia, which had larger Russian minorities, and worse relations with Russia, seemed to prioritise entry into the EU. Vilnius persuaded Riga and Tallinn to pursue a joint path to NATO, which would greatly increase their visibility and audibility in the negotiations.

Lithuania's entry into NATO also depended on good relations with Poland, which was on a faster track and joined the organisation in 1999. The main obstacle was the situation of the Polish minority. Immediately after Lithuania had secured its independence in August 1991, the gloves came off towards the local authorities that had declared autonomy and cooperated with Moscow in 1989–91. Although on 3 September 1991 the Šalčininkai district council dismissed its chairman, Czesław Wysocki, who had openly supported the putsch, the following day the seimas voted to dissolve the councils of the Šalčininkai and Vilnius districts, as well as the municipality of Sniečkus (now Visaginas) which was dominated by Russian-speakers. Some local activists faced criminal investigations, and a few were tried and sentenced to brief terms in prison. Local Poles complained that the ensuing direct rule by ethnic Lithuanian commissioners facilitated an unfair redistribution of land. Under the reprivatisation legislation, it was possible, for example, to obtain the 'equivalent' of good agricultural land in Samogitia in lower-quality, and therefore more extensive, land in the south-east. However, land located within easy reach of Vilnius was much more valuable, and Poles who had lost their property in 1940, or their heirs, were rarely able to recover it. The city boundaries of Vilnius were extended, while pre-war Polish documents were initially rejected as illegal. Some of the ethnic Lithuanians who have acquired land near Vilnius have prided themselves on their patriotism in helping to re-Lithuanise the region. That said, Lithuanian government submissions to the Council of Europe have insisted that the law takes no account of ethnicity, and that economic forces have driven changes in landownership in the suburbs and environs of the city.

A COUNTRY IN EUROPE

Public opinion in Poland had little sympathy with pro-Soviet Communist activists, but it was receptive to complaints of discrimination against ordinary Poles, particularly concerning the spelling of personal names. Language legislation required names to be written in identity cards and passports in the Lithuanian alphabet, so that the aforementioned felon was officially Česlav Vysocki. The longstanding Lithuanian nationalist conviction that people who declared themselves Poles were 'really' slavicised Lithuanians who should be reclaimed for the nation gained traction through the perception of their disloyalty to the state. Moreover, because Poles still formed the majority in the Vilnius district, the question also aggravated historical Lithuanian sensitivities about the city itself.

According to the seventeenth article of the constitution, 'The capital of the State of Lithuania shall be the city of Vilnius, the long-standing historical capital of Lithuania'. In accordance with the Giedroyc–Mieroszewski doctrine, which became a guiding principle of Polish foreign policy in the 1990s, independent Poland was willing to recognise its territorial losses in the east, and to acknowledge Vilnius as Lithuania's capital. However, Lithuanian expectations that Poland apologise for its 'occupation' of the city and its environs in the interwar period met with a firm refusal. The standoff led to a segment of Polish opinion demanding that recognition of the frontier be traded for better treatment of the Polish minority. In the end, on 26 April 1994, Presidents Algirdas Brazauskas and Lech Wałęsa signed the treaty of 'friendly relations and good-neighbourly cooperation' in Vilnius (an important condition for the Lithuanian side). This regretted historical conflicts in a generalised way, recognised the frontier as inviolable, and promised reciprocal respect for national minorities.[3] The agreement by no means ended controversies over language and land rights, and the relationship has since passed through warmer and cooler phases. Nevertheless, it has provided a firm foundation for the strategic cooperation between the two countries, including Poland's advocacy of Lithuania's entry into NATO.

Meanwhile, complaints mounted about the slow pace and chaotic implementation of privatisation and re-privatisation. Late in 1995, the Lithuanian Joint-Stock Innovation Bank (Lietuvos akcinis inovacinis bankas), founded in 1988, collapsed. It transpired that Prime Minister Šleževičius had withdrawn his shares the day before. Although the Democratic Labour Party expressed its continued confidence in him, President Brazauskas demanded his resignation, which was then forced by a parliamentary vote of no confidence in February 1996. Šleževičius was never convicted. Like his predecessor, he went into business. He was succeeded by a veteran economist, Laurynas Stankevičius, until the parliamentary election in the autumn of 1996. The turn-out fell sharply to 53 per cent. The Democratic Labour Party was reduced to just 10 per cent and twelve seats. The post-Sąjūdis Homeland Union took 33 per cent of the vote and, with a strong showing in single-member constituencies, won seventy seats. It formed a government with the Christian Democrats, with sixteen seats, so this coalition had the power, if it could agree to do so, to overturn presidential vetoes and even amend the constitution. Landsbergis returned as speaker, and Vagnorius as prime minister.

Brazauskas decided not to contest the 1998 presidential election. The lawyer he endorsed, Artūras Paulauskas, faced Valdas Adamkus. The latter, born Voldemaras Adamkavičius in Kaunas in 1926, had fought the Red Army in 1944 before emigrating via Germany to the USA. A civil engineer active in the Lithuanian diaspora, he distinguished himself working for the American Environmental Protection Agency before retiring in 1997. He renounced his American citizenship and narrowly won the election in the run-off.

The centre-right coalition splintered amidst policy disagreements and personality clashes. In May 1999, Vagnorius resigned,

A COUNTRY IN EUROPE

and after a brief interlude under Irena Degutienė as acting prime minister, he was succeeded by one of the most recognisable politicians of the second era of independence. Rolandas Paksas had been a Soviet aerobatics champion before making his fortune in the construction industry. He switched loyalties from the Democratic Labour Party before becoming mayor of Vilnius in 1997. He resigned the premiership within six months, protesting against the sale of an oil refinery to an American firm. Andrius Kubilius, a physicist, took over as prime minister until parliamentary elections in the autumn of 2000.

The centre-right cabinets of 1996–2000 addressed the challenge of meeting the formidable entry requirements of the EU. These were set out, perhaps more to deter than to encourage potential members, in 1993 and 1995. Candidate countries would have to demonstrate their institutions were stable, and capable of assuring democracy, the rule of law, human rights, and protection for minorities. They would also have to show that their functioning market economies could cope with the competitive pressures of the EU's Single Market. They would need to implement the entire *acquis communautaire* of European law, and sign up to the goals of monetary, economic, and political union. In practice, among other things, these criteria led to tightening up the investigation and prosecution of corruption, and to more transparent procedures for state contracts. Privatisation accelerated and included larger enterprises and utilities. Some sales proved controversial, especially when foreign buyers were involved. Although standards of living were improving by 1998, a crisis in Russia plunged the Lithuanian economy into a brief recession in 1999. The 2000 election left the Homeland Union and Christian Democrats with just ten seats between them. The Social Democratic Coalition held together by Brazauskas won fifty-one seats, but did not enter government, until an unstable, nominally centrist and liberal coalition formed by Paksas's and

LITHUANIA

Paulauskas's parties fell apart. Paksas became prime minister again, but in the summer of 2001 Paulauskas reached a deal with Brazauskas who returned to front-line politics as prime minister. He also became leader of the Social Democratic Party of Lithuania, created by the merger of the Democratic Labour Party and the Social Democrats. The stable centre-left government benefited from a pronounced economic upturn and continued to prepare Lithuania for entry into the EU and NATO.

In both cases, negotiations formally began in 1999 and successfully concluded in 2002. The EU invited Lithuania and nine other countries to join at its summit in Copenhagen in December 2002. Constitutional legislation and a referendum were required. The threshold of the latter was lowered to a minimum turnout of 50 per cent and a simple majority of votes cast. The concern was not about 'no' votes, but about apathy. To ensure an adequate turnout, postal voting was enabled and polling stations opened on both Saturday 10 and Sunday 11 May 2003. In the end appeals from the prime minister and president (who had earlier repeated his aerobatic stunts as part of the campaign), encouragement from priests at Sunday Mass, and even supermarket discounts for voters, helped to push the turnout to over 63 per cent. Of the valid votes cast, 91 per cent endorsed 'Lithuania's membership of the European Union', and only 9 per cent opposed it. The celebrations of the result were repeated on 1 May 2004, when the EU enlargement took effect. On 21 December 2007, routine controls ceased at the borders with Latvia and Poland, when the three countries joined the Schengen Area of free movement.

When Poland, Czechia, and Hungary became members of NATO in 1999, Lithuania received little encouragement. The following year, Lithuania proactively organised the 'Vilnius Ten' with nine other states kept in NATO's waiting room. Following the terrorist attacks of 11 September 2001, and the American

A COUNTRY IN EUROPE

invocation of Article Five of the North Atlantic Treaty ('an armed attack against one or more of them in Europe or North America shall be considered an attack against them all'), the 'Vilnius Ten' expressed their willingness to join the common cause, for example by making their airspace available to the USA. Success came at NATO's summit in Prague on 21–22 November 2002. Seven of the 'Vilnius Ten' received invitations to join the alliance: Bulgaria, Estonia, Latvia, Lithuania, Romania, Slovakia, and Slovenia. (Croatia and Albania had to wait until 2009, and North Macedonia until 2020.) President George W. Bush then flew to Vilnius and declared: 'Anyone who would choose Lithuania as an enemy has also made an enemy of the United States of America'. Lithuania's then foreign minister, Antanas Valionis, recalls: 'For a nation that had suffered for centuries from eastern expansion, President Bush's words that from now on those who are Lithuania's enemies will also be the enemies of the US, guaranteed existential security'.[4]

Political drama surrounded the presidency. Paksas unexpectedly beat the incumbent Adamkus in the second round of the election held in January 2003. To his populist slogans he added stunts, such as flying himself from one election rally to another in a helicopter. He even flew an aeroplane under a bridge. The following year, he was shown to have granted Lithuanian citizenship to the Russian oligarch Yurii Borisov in return for a campaign donation of US$400,000. The seimas impeached Paksas. Removed from office on 6 April 2004, he announced his intention to run again for the presidency but was promptly banned from doing so by a constitutional amendment. The constitutional court overturned this expedient and ruled instead that persons who violated the constitution or their oath of office were barred from public office. Paulauskas acted as head of state until Adamkus was elected president for a second time on 27 June 2004 and sworn in on 6 July.

LITHUANIA

The Paksas scandal clouded some of the joy at Lithuania's entry into the EU and NATO, but his impeachment probably strengthened the state's credentials regarding the rule of law. Adamkus returned to the highest office in time to participate in NATO's Istanbul Summit on 28–29 June 2004. However, despite the booming economy (growth topped 10.5 per cent in 2003), Lithuania's first European parliamentary elections, held in 2004, produced a shock. The newly formed Labour Party led by Viktor Uspaskich, who had come to the LSSR in the mid-1980s, became a Lithuanian citizen in 1991, and made his fortune in the energy industry, won 30 per cent of the votes, and sent five MEPs to Brussels and Strasbourg. This Labour Party did almost as well in the elections to the seimas in October 2004, again garnering most of its support in small towns. Its populist recipes included simultaneously reducing prices and increasing minimum wages and old age pensions. Brazauskas was able to patch together a weakened coalition government and remain as prime minister. Uspaskich became minister for the economy, but he and the speaker, Paulauskas, faced accusations of fraudulent accounting in 2006. The Labour Party was put on trial and Uspaskich fled to Moscow. The coalition broke up, Brazauskas announced his retirement, and Social Democrat Gediminas Kirkilas, formerly defence minister, took the helm of a minority government. As growth soared over 11 per cent in 2007, this government was criticised for its loose fiscal discipline.

The parliamentary elections of 2008 yielded victory for the centre-right. Kubilius's Homeland Union won 20 per cent of the vote and forty-five seats; the newly formed National Resurrection Party (containing some celebrities), gained 15 per cent and sixteen seats; and two centrist liberal movements a total of 11 per cent and nineteen seats between them. This coalition enabled Kubilius to serve a full term as prime minister. He immediately had to deal with the global financial crisis precipitated by irresponsible American bankers. Lithuania's GDP fell by almost 15 per cent in 2009, and unemployment climbed to over 15 per cent of the workforce. Finance minister Ingrida Šimonytė implemented unpopular decisions, such as raising indirect and company taxes, and cutting public-sector salaries and pensions. Winning plaudits from the ratings institutions, the Lithuanian economy entered a long stretch of export-led growth, but its days of double-digit expansion were over.

The end of the decade brought the satisfying celebrations of Lithuania's millennium (the first mention of '*Litua*' in a historical source) and a generational changing of the guard. Valdas Adamkus, who brought moral authority to the presidency, stepped down at the end of his second term in 2009. Taking a lead in foreign policy, his mediation contributed to the success of the 2004 Orange Revolution in Ukraine. In August 2008, he joined the presidents of Poland, Ukraine, and Estonia, and the prime minister of Latvia, in a mission of solidarity to Georgia, which had just been invaded by Russia. In Tbilisi, Lech Kaczyński asked rhetorically if after Georgia, it would be Ukraine's turn to face Russian aggression, and then Poland's. Adamkus's friendship with Kaczyński warmed the two countries' relations.

The vicious Chechen wars of the 1990s should have been heeded as an early warning that even Yeltsin's Russia had not forsaken its claims to the former empire. Instead, defence budgets were slashed across Western Europe, while the Baltic states had little to spend anyway. Despite incidents such as the assassination in England of Aleksandr Litvinenko in 2006, most opinion-formers in the West still preferred to hope for the best, even after the Russian seizure of Crimea in 2014 laid bare the neo-imperial ambitions that Vladimir Putin had already revealed in his rant to the 2007 Munich security conference. Germany benefited from cheap gas from Russia after the Nord Stream 1 pipeline went operational in 2011.

LITHUANIA

After the shutting down of the Ignalina nuclear power plant in 2009 (a condition of EU membership) and facing multiple obstacles to a new nuclear facility, Lithuania's long road to energy security has led via the gas terminal at Klaipėda opened in 2014; a gas pipeline from Poland, opened in 2022; and electric interconnections with Poland, Sweden, Finland, and Estonia. The security imperative has merged with that presented by global warming and Lithuania's consequent international obligations. Wind turbines have multiplied across the landscape, and two huge offshore wind farms are to be constructed near Palanga. The country has an ambitious plan to generate 90 per cent of its energy from renewable sources by 2030. The number of electric and hybrid vehicles quintupled between 2020 and 2024 to about 25,000.

The 2009 presidential elections brought a comfortable victory in the first round to Dalia Grybauskaitė. She gained her doctorate in economics in Moscow in 1988 and later served as finance minister in the Brazauskas government, until she was nominated as Lithuania's European commissioner. Given responsibility for EU finance, in the teeth of French opposition she shifted the budget's emphasis away from agricultural subsidies towards growth and employment, driven by investment in research and development. Competence was the core of her appeal, but her reputation for toughness (underlined by her black belt in karate) also helped her cause. She only banked half of her presidential salary and made a point of flying with low-cost airlines. Grybauskaitė also made assertive use of her presidential powers. She soon realised that a reset with Russia was impossible, and, like her predecessor, became one of Putin's sternest critics.

Grybauskaitė mourned her 'teacher and mentor' in a graveside address. Algirdas Brazauskas died of lymphatic cancer on 26 June 2010. Condolences poured in from world leaders, and thousands filed past his coffin as it lay in state for two days in the presidential palace. Still larger crowds bade him farewell on 1 July, as a military escort accompanied the gun-carriage bearing his coffin to the Antakalnis cemetery. In attendance were presidents: Toomas Ilves of Estonia, Valdis Zatlers of Latvia, Mikheil Saakashvili of Georgia; and former presidents: Martti Ahtisaari of Finland, Arnold Rüütel of Estonia, Guntis Ulmanis of Latvia, Leonid Kuchma of Ukraine, and Lech Wałęsa and Aleksander Kwaśniewski of Poland. The latter, a close friend with a similar political background, hailed Brazauskas as 'a great Lithuanian and a wonderful European'. The occasion was marred by the tone-deaf decision of the cardinal-archbishop of Vilnius, Audrys Bačkis, not to allow the coffin inside the cathedral during the Requiem Mass. The various reasons advanced included Brazauskas's divorce and re-marriage to a divorced woman, and the Communist persecutions of the Church. Grybauskaitė, Adamkus, and Landsbergis all criticised the decision. Relatively few people attended the Mass in Vilnius, whereas the earlier Mass at the cathedral in Kaišiadorys, where he grew up, was packed. The celebrant, Father Algirdas Jurevičius, compared the deceased statesman's deals to Grand Duke Vytautas's negotiations with the Teutonic Order.[5] Brazauskas, like his medieval hero, adored hunting. His most visible legacy is the rebuilt Palace of the Grand Dukes of Lithuania next to Vilnius Cathedral.

The price of austerity was the Kubilius government's defeat at the 2012 elections. However, his Homeland Union did better than expected, with 16 per cent of the vote and thirty-three seats. A coalition government was formed between Social Democrats, Uspaskich's Labour Party, Paksas's new 'Order and Justice' formation, and for the first time, the Electoral Action of Poles in Lithuania, led by Waldemar Tomaszewski (then officially Valdemar Tomaševski). The latter party withdrew from the government in 2014 following a series of controversies regarding its autocratic leader's manifest support for Russia, even after its annexation of Crimea. He wore a ribbon of St George at the Victory Day parade in Vilnius on 9 May 2014. The government's co-habitation with President Grybauskaitė proved bumpy (she even examined candidates for ministers on their command of English). The cabinet led by the engineer and economist Algirdas Butkevičius served a full term, a sign of a maturing parliamentary democracy. Steady economic growth continued, and the chief achievement of the government was the introduction of the Euro in 2015. However, the accompanying price rises cost the government much support in the parliamentary elections of 2016.

The Social Democrats lost their lead late in the campaign both to the Homeland Union, now led by Gabrielius Landsbergis, the grandson of Vytautas; and to a formation that emerged out of relative obscurity, renamed the Lithuanian Farmers and Greens Union (Lietuvos valstiečių ir žaliųjų sąjunga). This party campaigned on a mixture of anti-establishment, socially conservative, economically left-wing, and environmentalist slogans. Its leader is a wealthy businessman (the owner of Agrokoncernas founded in 1993), Ramūnas Karbauskis. Two contrasting aspects of his persona may particularly interest the historian. One is his association with neo-paganism. The other is his support for temperance—the cause of Bishop Valančius. The Homeland Union rejected a broad coalition including the Social Democrats, so the latter entered a coalition with the Farmers and Greens Union. A popular former police officer, who had served as the minister of interior in the previous government, Saulius Skvernelis, became prime minister. His government also served a full term, despite becoming a minority government for much of the parliamentary term. It later gained support from Paksas's Order and Justice, as well as from the expanded Polish and Russian formation now called the Electoral Alliance of Poles–Christian Families Alliance. The economic outlook continued to be favourable, enabling the government to cut some taxes, raise public-sector pay, and introduce child benefit. The presidential election of 2019 saw Gitanas Nausėda, a banker with a blurred political profile, win a decisive second-round victory against Ingrida Šimonytė, who was endorsed by the Homeland Union.

Relations with Moscow deteriorated further, following the 2016–19 trial of sixty-seven former Soviet officials and military officers, including former Minister of Defence Dmitrii Yazov for the war crimes committed in 1991. All but one of them were found guilty and sentenced in absentia to ten years' imprisonment. The Russian government reacted with predictable outrage and threatened the judges. The Baltic states had begun to improve their military and political readiness after the Russian seizure of Crimea in 2014. Lithuania reintroduced conscription in 2015. Donald Trump, elected to the American presidency in 2016, called into question the USA's commitment to NATO. His threats did at least prompt increases in defence spending among Europe's laggards.

The spring of 2020 brought the COVID-19 pandemic from Wuhan to Lithuania. The initial quarantine, which lasted from March to June 2020, was replaced by graded risk zones, before another lockdown took effect in November. Vaccination began towards the end of the year and ultimately covered 73 per cent of the adult population. Restrictions were gradually removed between March and July 2021. By that time, the total number of confirmed cases had reached nearly 283,000, but this climbed beyond a million the following March, when the total number of deaths attributed to the coronavirus reached 8,750.

The parliamentary elections held during the pandemic in October 2020 featured extended voting times and facilities for self-isolating voters. The Homeland Union improved its voting share to 26 per cent and won fifty seats. It formed a coalition with the Liberal Movement and its splinter, the Freedom Party, with Šimonytė as prime minister. Almost half her cabinet were women. Its priorities were education, the quality of public services, including digitisation of the state, as well as infrastructure and energy. Foreign minister Landsbergis led a charge of the Lithuanian light brigade against the massed cannons of Communist China, riding well in front of the timorous ranks of the EU. The government counted on Taiwanese investment compensating for the relatively modest trading relations with China. However, the results of the pro-Taiwan policy remain uncertain.

Šimonytė's government also had to deal with the Belarusian regime's violent suppression of pro-democracy protests. Lithuania extended its protection to many Belarusian exiles including Sviatlana Tsikhanouskaia, who would almost certainly have beaten Aleksandr Lukashenko in the 2020 presidential election, had the count not been falsified. One of the most visible and audible features of the protests was the Pahonia, in the forms of the chasing knight and the patriotic song with words written by Maksim Bahdanovich in 1916. Lukashenko's desperate struggle to cling to power saw him finally turn against any expression of the legacy of the Grand Duchy of Lithuania. In response to the succour offered to his opponents by Lithuania, Poland, and Latvia, the Belarusian dictator exploited the desire of many people from war-torn countries in Asia and Africa to settle in Europe. Flights and visas were laid on, and migrants and refugees bussed to the state's western frontiers. The three NATO allies guarded and fortified their eastern borders, as the Belarusian regime encouraged, indeed forced migrants to breach the fences.

On 24 February 2022, Russia escalated its hybrid war against Ukraine into a full-scale invasion. Like their Baltic and Polish neighbours, Lithuanians unhesitatingly came to Ukraine's aid. They manifested their solidarity through demonstrations, taking in refugees, and crowd-funding drones. Braving Russian threats, Lithuania blocked, as far as EU laws permitted, the transit of Russian goods to Kaliningrad, banned Russian-language broadcasting, and at every stage argued for stiffer economic sanctions

A COUNTRY IN EUROPE

and looser conditions on military aid. By the middle of 2024, the total value of Lithuanian military, financial, and humanitarian aid to Ukraine, bilaterally and via the EU, exceeded 1 billion euros, equivalent to 2 per cent of GDP.

Few Lithuanians doubt that if Ukraine falls to neo-imperial Russia, Lithuania and its neighbours will be next in line. However, the country's security has significantly improved in important respects. NATO belatedly agreed a 'tripwire' in the east in 2016. Great Britain now leads the multinational NATO battlegroup deployed in Estonia; France the one in Latvia; Germany the one in Lithuania; and the USA that in Poland. Since 2022, not only have most European members of NATO significantly increased defence spending, with Poland leading the way, but Finland and Sweden have joined the Atlantic alliance. Their entry has not suddenly turned the Baltic Sea into a 'NATO lake', but reinforcement of the Baltic states has become much easier. The build-up of Russian nuclear, chemical, and conventional weaponry in the Kaliningrad region threatens Lithuania and Poland, but by the same token, Russian shipping is vulnerable. Planners and journalists fixate on scenarios of the Kremlin manipulating Russian speakers in Latvia or Estonia into revolt and then seeking to close the 'Suwałki gap'. This is where the Polish-Lithuanian borderland (called Suvalkija in Lithuanian ethnography) is squeezed by Russian and Belarusian territory. However, that post-glacial landscape is far easier to defend than to attack.

The geopolitical and ideological continuities evident in the current situation reach back, if not to the last ice age, then to the epic conflicts between Muscovite tsars and Grand Dukes of Lithuania—not least in Putin's twisted narratives. Not unlike Catherine II's Russian empire faced by the reforming Polish–Lithuanian Commonwealth, Putin's incarnation of empire cannot tolerate the dangerous example of a vibrant, democratic neighbouring state to the south-west choosing a different path than that of the corrupt mire of dependency on the Kremlin. So when manipulation and intimidation failed, the Russian regime resorted to amputation, destruction, abduction, torture, rape, and murder, accompanied by re-heated claims that Ukraine has no authentic existence as a state, a nation, or a culture. At stake, among other things, are the history and legacies of the Grand Duchy of Lithuania and the Polish–Lithuanian Commonwealth. As in the nineteenth-century theories of Official Nationality, Moscow pays them a back-handed compliment, by denouncing their seduction of Ukraine away from its Russian destiny.

ii. *Social Transformations*

More than three decades of independence have allowed ordinary Lithuanian citizens to enjoy unprecedented personal freedoms. Some have treated liberty as licence. The corruption scandals mentioned above were merely the tip of an iceberg. The early 1990s saw the police unable to cope with the rapid rise in organised violent crime. The tide turned with the convictions of the Kaunas mafioso Henrikas Daktaras, and the Vilnius boss Boris Dekanidze. In 1995, the latter was the last of the seven men executed (by a single bullet to the back of the head) in independent Lithuania. The constitutional court ruled capital punishment unconstitutional in 1998, although opinion polls indicate considerable support among the public for its restoration. Lithuania adopted a new criminal code in 2000, moving on from Soviet and post-Soviet syndromes in the judicial and penal system.

People inured to the restrictions and shortages of Soviet life, in which private enterprise was officially denounced as capitalist exploitation, suddenly experienced bewildering freedom to travel and trade. Flea markets taught the laws of supply and demand. Lithuanians ventured abroad in large numbers, at first more to buy and sell all manner of products than as tourists. The resourcefulness and persistence needed to live tolerably within the Soviet system provided the initial business model. Small firms mushroomed, meeting all manner of real and imagined needs. Many went bust, but the hardest working, luckiest, and most unscrupulous entrepreneurs became very rich. The Vilnius stock exchange opened in 1993. Supermarket shopping, free of the elaborate Soviet system of queues and coupons, soon caught on, and the Maxima network, owned by Nerijus Numavičius, soon covered the country. The appearance of Western television shows, whether via Lithuanian- and Russian-language stations, or via satellite dishes and later cable connections, promoted a vast range of useful and useless products as part of a glamorous and comfortable lifestyle. Of course, only a small minority could purchase most of what they desired. Many bought cars, although many owners could not afford much fuel, and so kept their pride and joy in large car parks at some distance from their apartments.

The social costs of the transformation to a market economy were borne by those less able to take advantage of new opportunities. Many pensioners reverted to survival mode. Low-skilled workers in factories that lost old clients and could not find new ones found themselves unemployed. Much Lithuanian industry had been dispersed beyond the major cities, so the closure of unprofitable factories could devastate small towns for years. When collective farms and their assets were broken up, most of the workforce could adapt neither to individual nor to cooperative farming. The misery that afflicted smaller communities all over the country exacerbated the problems of alcoholism and suicide, already at high levels in the Soviet era, especially among men. Meanwhile, the nimbler *kolkhoz* managers and some former *apparatchik*s bought up tracts of high-quality farmland. As the careers of prominent politicians suggest, the agro-industrial sector has remained a key part of the Lithuanian economy. The privatisation process inevitably favoured those with the earliest and priviest access to information about decisions, which mattered much more in the age before the internet.

On the other hand, the pain has not been without gain. Lithuania's low-regulation, low-tax, low-borrowing approach, maintained (with a few hiccups) by successive governments, has brought Lithuania an enviable reputation among foreign investors. Between 1996 and 2013, seven free economic zones were opened in different parts of the country. They offer firms tax incentives, services, and infrastructure. The strongest manufacturing sectors are biotechnology and biopharmaceutics, food processing, laser technology, furniture, and logistics. A well-educated workforce (more than half of young Lithuanians go on to higher or further education) has helped to keep productivity high, as real wages have gradually risen. EU structural funds have generally been well invested in education, research and development, and infrastructure. Despite the downturns of 1998, 2009, and 2020, Lithuania's gross domestic product has, after adjusting for inflation, more than tripled since the low point of 1995. Measured per capita, it has moved past Latvia and is closing on Estonia. As prosperity spread, many Lithuanians took to shopping in malls by the 2000s, and on the internet by the 2010s. Spending on recreation has climbed as well. Lively Palanga draws the holiday crowds as much as it ever did during the Soviet era, but the guest houses and boutique hotels at Nida on the Curonian Spit have gone upmarket. Vilnan elites often socialise there in July and August, alongside appreciative foreign visitors. All-inclusive packages in Turkey or Egypt are now within the reach of moderately wealthy families, and are widely advertised.

Freedom of travel, however, has had its downside. The emigration in search of work of so many Lithuanian citizens, disproportionately young and well educated, has been responsible for much of the ongoing demographic crisis. After an initial wave of departures to Russia, the main direction has been westwards. Between 17,000 and 28,000 people left every year in the decade after 1992. Numbers spiked from 2004, when Lithuania entered the EU. Great Britain and Ireland, which opened their labour markets, were the first destinations of choice. The peak year for emigration followed the drastic shrinkage after the financial crisis: more than 83,000 people left in 2010. Net emigration remained high until 2017, but in 2019 Lithuania became a country of net immigration. Some were re-migrants from post-Brexit Britain, but the 2020s have seen tens of thousands of mostly Russian-speaking Belarusian and Ukrainian refugees settle in Lithuania. Their influx has changed the soundscape of Vilnius. However, the first three decades of independence saw the continuing Lithuanisation of the population. Between the censuses of 1989 and 2021, the proportion declaring Lithuanian nationality rose from 80 per cent to 85 per cent. Those declaring Polish nationality fell slightly, from 7 per cent to 6.5 per cent, indicating a comparable level of emigration, while those declaring Russian nationality declined more steeply, from 9 per cent to 5 per cent.

Lithuania's current welcome of immigrants of working age is partly a consequence of its persistently low birthrate. The number of live births has plummeted to less than 21,000 in 2023. The fertility rate of just 1.18 is far below the 2.1 needed for population replacement. This figure was last achieved in 1987, when more than 59,000 live births were recorded. The combination of a shortage of children and unprecedented emigration (exceeding that to the New World in the late nineteenth and early twentieth centuries) has led to a greater demographic contraction than during the Second World War. From a peak of over 3,700,000 in 1991, the country's population slid to just over 2,800,000 in 2022, a fall of almost a quarter. By way of comparison, Latvia lost almost 30 per cent of its population, and Estonia 13 per cent, in approximately the same period, with the fall disproportionately affecting ethnic Russians.

LITHUANIA

Rising life expectancy, especially among women, has not compensated for the dearth of babies, but it has exacerbated the problem of an ageing population. Vilnius is the only city in Lithuania to have generally maintained, and recently increased its population—it probably topped 600,000 in 2024. Despite the large number of students, the population of Kaunas fell from 422,000 in 1989 to below 299,000 in 2021, and those of other cities have shrunk in proportion. In smaller towns and villages, the shortage of children has forced school mergers. On the other hand, funds transferred by emigrants of working age to their families in Lithuania have softened the impact of the economic transition. Moreover, in contrast to previous waves of emigration, travel for family reunions has become much easier thanks to budget airlines serving Vilnius, Kaunas, Palanga, and Riga, as well as cheap coach tickets. Many Lithuanian citizens have embraced hybrid lifestyles, spending part of each year abroad, but gladly returning home. Instead of 'letters from America' arriving at intervals of several months or years, communication in the smartphone age is instantaneous and ubiquitous.

Emigration and falling rates of marriage and baptism are among the challenges that have confronted mainstream religions. During and immediately after the 'Singing Revolution', churches benefited greatly from religious freedom. With the Soviet-era restrictions lifted, many new churches were built, paid for by willing congregations. John Paul II drew huge crowds during his pilgrimage to Lithuania in 1993. The association of Lithuanian national identity with Roman Catholicism came naturally to many conservative politicians, while many former Communist Party members hurriedly burnished their religious credentials. However, disputes over the restitution of property left a bad taste. Rumours of sexual abuse by members of the clergy could no longer be swept under the carpet as the 2010s neared their close, and the Catholic Church now faces a reckoning like that in Ireland.

A COUNTRY IN EUROPE

Traditional Catholic teaching on marriage, sex, contraception, abortion, and child-rearing is increasingly ignored or rejected, partly because many younger Lithuanians have embraced an ever-expanding range of sexual and gender identities. On the other hand, a recurring component of populist politics has been homophobic discourse. This has been linked (not least by the Kremlin's online trolls) to stories that the European Union is determined to impose a 'gender ideology' noxious to the constitutionally enshrined model of the Christian family. Questions such as civil partnerships, same-sex marriage, and adoption by same-sex couples now divide public opinion. President Nausėda takes ambivalent positions.

The Lutheran and Reformed Churches, the Armenian Apostolic Church, as well as Old Believers, all cling on with dwindling congregations. The number of self-identifying Jews stands at a historic low of about 2,250, of whom fewer than half worship in synagogues. There are a similar number of Tatars, while immigration from Muslim countries has stayed at extremely low levels. The 2021 census counted just 192 Karaites. Following decades of contraction, the ranks of the Greek Catholic and Orthodox Churches have recently been swelled by refugees from Belarus and Ukraine. The latter have prompted the Orthodox Church to transfer its allegiance from the Moscow Patriarchate to the Ecumenical Patriarchate in Constantinople. Neo-pagan movements revived after being suppressed in the Soviet Union. By far the best organised of them, Romuva, seeks to recreate the religious rituals and belief-system of pre-Christian Lithuanians. Critics' arguments that these are now unknowable cut little ice with the movement's enthusiastic followers. Among them are both environmentalists and ethnic nationalists, especially among the young, increasingly alienated from conventional Catholicism. The fastest growing group are those who declare no religion at all.

LITHUANIA

Independence enabled Lithuanian society to address the Holocaust. During the Soviet period, the genocide of Lithuanian Jews was subsumed into the category of Nazi German crimes against Soviet citizens during the 'Great Patriotic War', which is to say that it was effectively ignored. Since 1989 it has been possible to commemorate the specifically Jewish victims. Among the Sąjūdis leaders was the Jewish academic Emanuelis Zingeris who chaired the foreign affairs commission in the Reconstituent Seimas, but some Jews remained sceptical. The Vilna Gaon Lithuanian State Jewish Museum was established as early as 1989, and his statue was unveiled close to the site of the Great Synagogue in 1997.

Considerably more sensitive has been the question of the complicity of ethnic Lithuanians in the Holocaust, not least because some American critics used the problem to oppose the swift recognition of Lithuanian independence. As early as March 1989, Landsbergis made a speech on behalf of Sąjūdis to the Constituent Congress of the Lithuanian Jewish Cultural Association. He acknowledged and lamented individual Lithuanians' undoubted criminal participation in the Holocaust, but he rejected collective national responsibility. He noted the involvement of some Jews in Stalinist repression, which, when exaggerated by Nazi propaganda, created conditions for fanaticism and cruelty to manifest themselves. He also reminded his audience that 'the victims of the anti-Lithuanian genocide also rest in unknown graves, scattered from the undergrowth in Lithuania to islands in the Arctic Ocean'.[6] It was a start, and among Lithuanian historians are now several eminent specialists on the history of Jews in Lithuania, Lithuanian Jews, and Jewish Lithuanians—the concepts are not identical. Efforts at Lithuanian–Jewish dialogue continue despite controversies and backlashes. Problems have arisen from the simplified procedures to restore civic rights to the victims of Soviet repression, which left open the possibility of perpetrators of crimes

A COUNTRY IN EUROPE

against Jews being rehabilitated. Addressing the Israeli parliament, the Knesset, in 1995, President Brazauskas acknowledged the involvement of Lithuanians in the Holocaust, promised to bring surviving perpetrators to justice, and asked for forgiveness. In 1998 President Adamkus founded the International Commission for the Evaluation of the Crimes of the Nazi and Soviet Occupation Regimes. These efforts have been difficult, however, to square with the widespread conviction that Lithuanians were victims, but not perpetrators or bystanders of genocide.

Research on the atrocities committed by the Soviet occupants, and on Lithuanian freedom fighters' resistance, has been pursued by historians employed by various academic institutions, but in particular by the Genocide and Resistance Research Centre of Lithuania (Lietuvos gyventojų genocido ir rezistencijos tyrimo centras) founded in 1992. The centre's mission encompasses the commemoration of freedom fighters and victims, and it runs the Museum of Occupations and Freedom Fights (Okupacijų ir laisvės kovų muziejus) located in the former Gestapo and KGB headquarters opposite Lukiškės Square, where Murav'ev presided over hangings in 1863–64. Visitors experience the cells, interrogation rooms, and torture and execution chambers. The regime killed more than 1,000 prisoners here between 1944 and the early 1960s. There are also exhibitions on the Forest Brothers and the *Shoah*. Their respective proportions have attracted criticism, especially in the USA.

The 1994 treaty with Poland largely left history to historians. Since then, Lithuanian and Polish academics have engaged in generally open-minded and often cordial cooperation about all periods of the shared past. Noted Lithuanian professors, such as the media-friendly Alfredas Bumblauskas, the long-serving director of the Lithuanian Institute of History, Alvydas Nikžentaitis, and the youthful rector of Vilnius University, Rimvydas Petrauskas, have sometimes spoken out to calm periodic squalls in the

Lithuanian–Polish relationship. The tongue-in-cheek subtitle of the book *Before Falling into the Twilight. Lithuania in the Eighteenth Century: When Both Poland and Warsaw were Ours*, published by the military historian turned conservative politician Valdas Rakutis in 2022, may herald a readiness to address the history of the entire Commonwealth, instead of fencing off the history of the Grand Duchy of Lithuania.[7] The phenomenal sales of Kristina Sabaliauskaitė's *Silva Rerum*, a critically acclaimed tetralogy of historical novels set in seventeenth- and eighteenth-century Vilnius, have revealed a hitherto unsuspected public appetite for the Polish–Lithuanian past.

Tomas Venclova's harsh critique in 2010 of 'a primitive, unthinking nationalism', and of 'isolation and provinciality' among his compatriots sparked counterblasts against his supposed arrogance and elitism.[8] But the characteristics he identified flourish at the edges of the Lithuanian political scene. The latest populist party, called the Dawn of Nemunas (Nemuno aušra), is led by Remigijus Žemaitaitis, who has been accused of antisemitic insinuations. He won over 9 per cent of the vote in the first round of the 2024 presidential election.

That said, by no means all expressions of Lithuanian nationalism could be described as primitive and unthinking. The centenary of Lithuanian independent statehood celebrated in 2018 spread a warm glow of national achievement, heightened by the contrast with the fortunes of Belarus and Ukraine. Both in 1918–20 and in 1989–91, the nation's leaders had seized the moment. Interest grew in the signatories of the declaration of independent statehood. It did not escape notice that one of them signed himself Stanisław Narutowicz, and not Stanislovas Narutavičius—what document could be more official than the act of 16 February 1918? Four years later the seimas finally passed a law that allowed members of ethnic minorities, whose ancestors had used the name, to use the foreign letters q, w, and x in the spelling of their names in official documents. This does not include foreign diacritics (which in Polish are the letters ą, ć, ę, ł, ś, ź, and ż). So far, very few of Lithuania's Poles have taken advantage of the possibility.

The centennial celebrations were marked by a work of art that succeeded in making the distant and dusty figure of the 'patriarch', Jonas Basanavičius, more accessible. The opera *Post Futurum* premièred in Vilnius on 2 March 2018. Composed by Gintaras Sodeika and written by Sigitas Parulskis, it depicts Basanavičius in 1918 as a vulnerable widower, tempted by Satan with the return of his wife Gabriela Eleonora. He is shown the tragic sufferings of Lithuanians in the twentieth century, and—knowing Lithuania will one day be free—he signs the declaration of independence anyway.

iii. *26 May 2024*

Just under half of the Lithuanian electorate chooses to exercise its democratic rights in the second round of the presidential election. The incumbent, Gitanas Nausėda, is favourite, having won 45 per cent of the votes in the first round. As in 2019, he faces Ingrida Šimonytė, who since 2020 has been prime minister. Her cabinet is the eighteenth government since 1990. Neither is an ideologue; both candidates made their reputations as economists. But Nausėda appeals to a wider spectrum of voters, especially in the smaller towns and villages, than the head of the fiscally conservative, socially liberal government. The result is a landslide: 74 per cent to 24 per cent. Even in Vilnius, where the prime minister topped the first-round poll, the president wins 56 per cent of the votes in the run-off. In the Šalčininkai district, three quarters of whose population is still Polish, his victory is overwhelming: 95 per cent. Nausėda is no less hostile to Putin's Russia than Šimonytė. Yet in this district, as in Visaginas with its large ethnic Russian population, the most popular candidate in the first round was Eduardas Vaitkus. This professor of medical science from Kaunas is notorious for his conspiracy theories: anti-vaccination, anti-Western, and anti-Ukrainian. During the campaign he promised a 'dictatorship of law', withdrawal from the EU and NATO, and separate 'negotiations' with Russia. Once again, these marginal regions trouble Lithuanian mainstream opinion, but we shall follow the road south from Vilnius on this warm, cloudless Sunday.

Once past the airport, views open up over fields and forests. The road crosses the meandering River Merkys at Jašiūnai (Jaszuny), where on 8 October 1920 General Żeligowski's forces took two hours to defeat the Lithuanian soldiers who blocked the way to Vilnius. The Calvinist church founded here by the Radziwiłłs is long gone, but in the 1820s, the Baliński family hosted Jan Śniadecki and other aristocratic and intellectual guests in the neo-classical palace and landscaped park. Further south, Šalčininkai (Soleczniki) presents itself sprucely. There is no litter or graffiti, but plenty of flowers. On the main square, the statue of a youthful and optimistic Adam Mickiewicz tells us—in Lithuanian and Polish—to 'have a heart, and look into the heart'. Meanwhile, the trilingual monument to Kastus' Kalinoŭski/Konstanty Kalinowski/Konstantinas Kalinauskas shows him contemplating an insurgent's broken scythe. Just to the south is one of only two border crossings with Belarus still operational at the time of writing.

From Šalčininkai the road east leads into an 'appendix' of Lithuanian territory almost surrounded by Belarus. The ageing, shrinking population is mostly Polish. Locals spin a yarn that it owes its shape to Stalin's pipe, placed on the map before he left the room during border negotiations between the Belarusian and Lithuanian SSRs in 1940. Much of this salient forms a regional historical park, noted for its brightly painted wooden houses with

A COUNTRY IN EUROPE

flowering gardens and orchards. Dieveniškės (Dziewieniszki) is a quiet, well maintained small town with an attractive wooden church from 1783. The Jewish cemetery silently recalls the once-flourishing, mostly Yiddish-speaking community of Devenishok, which was forced into a ghetto and murdered by the Nazis. Today the grass is freshly mown. Pebbles placed on surviving gravestones pay respect to the dead.

A few kilometres northeast is Norviliškės (Narwiliszki). An immaculate small shop offers a modest selection of food and a somewhat wider choice of alcohol. Towards the end of the village stands the castle, a former Franciscan monastery suppressed by the Russian Empire. It was restored—or, more accurately, reconstructed—with EU funds after 2005, and became a hotel and restaurant. Between 2007 and 2010, the spacious meadow in front of the arcaded façade hosted the Be2gether Festival, held under the slogan 'music opens borders'. Attendance peaked at over 10,000 people. Today, no one disturbs the violet lupins that grow here in profusion. The castle is closed. Beyond it lies the green-painted wooden church, consecrated in 1929, and beyond that, the well-kept cemetery. Cars drive up every now and then, as graves are tidied, flowers placed, and candles lit. The gravestones hint at the interwoven stories of local families. Some tell of long lives—spanning the Russian Empire, independent Poland, Soviet and German occupations, and independent Lithuania. Others record lives cut tragically short. Many monuments have been inscribed by hand into wet concrete. Spelling, grammar, and even letters of the alphabet all reflect the local patterns of speech.

Norviliškės cemetery long served a large parish of many villages and hamlets, which is now split by the frontier. Smallholdings and collective farms crossed the boundary between the two Soviet socialist republics: it is said locally that a walk from the cottage to the privy could involve a trip abroad. In practice, the strip of

LITHUANIA

ploughed land, punctuated by pairs of marker posts, remained easy to cross until Lithuania's entry into the Schengen Zone in 2007 brought more expensive visas, higher customs duties, and tighter controls at the designated crossing points. A bilateral agreement signed in 2006 preventively alleviated these rigours for inhabitants of the border region. Divided families and neighbours could stay in touch. It is said that at Norviliškės, communion wafers were handed over the fence, while coffins occasionally went under it (in the other direction). Nor was the fence an effective barrier to cigarettes and other contraband. Until the late 2010s, many inhabitants of nearby Belarusian villages would make long round trips via the Lithuanian consulates in Hrodna or Minsk to visit the graves of their loved ones at Christmas, Easter, and All Saints' Day. Then Lukashenko's regime began to weaponise migration into the EU. In 2021 vigorous protests prevented the opening of a facility to house and process 500 unauthorised migrants in nearby Dieveniškės. Nowadays, villagers on the Belarusian side merely approach the upgraded fence, topped with cameras and concertina wire, to pray for their deceased relatives. Cigarette smugglers use drones. On this afternoon, a muscular young man in civilian clothes, who appears to be reading the inscriptions, discreetly follows historians around the cemetery. As they drive back towards Vilnius, a patrol stops them and, having asked politely, inspects the car boot.

Europe's fortified frontier bisects the heartlands of historical Lithuania. For now.

FAMILY TREE OF THE GEDIMINID–JAGIELLONIAN DYNASTY*

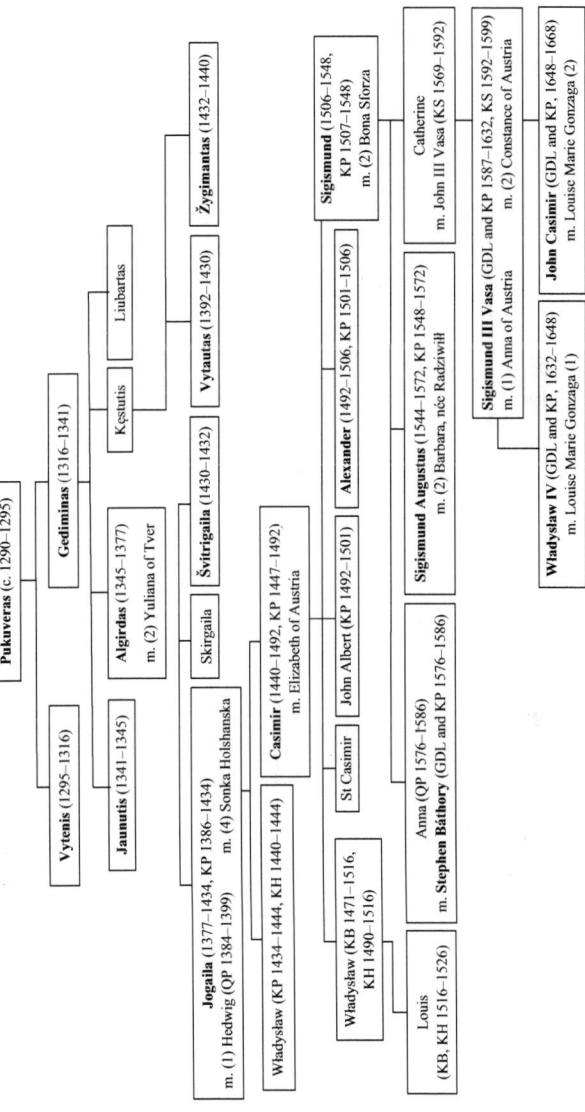

* Regnal dates are as **Grand Duke of Lithuania**, unless stated as King or Queen regnant of Poland, Hungary, Bohemia, or Sweden.

ACKNOWLEDGEMENTS

I first wish to express my gratitude to Michael Dwyer for inviting me to write this book, and to Lara Weisweiller-Wu and Daisy Leitch who have patiently seen it through to publication, along with all their colleagues at Hurst. I thank the anonymous reviewers whose suggestions and corrections have greatly improved the book. I am solely responsible for its remaining faults.

Humility behoves outsiders who seek to convey the history of another country. In my attempts to understand Lithuania—old and new—I have for over a quarter of century benefited from the generosity and support of many individuals and institutions. The latter include the BIP–Institute of Law, the British Academy, the British-Lithuanian Society, the Embassy of the Republic of Lithuania to the United Kingdom, the Francis Skaryna Belarusian Library and Museum, the Lithuanian Academy of Sciences, the Lithuanian Institute of History, the National Museum–Palace of the Grand Dukes of Lithuania, the Polish Academy of Sciences, the Royal Irish Academy, the UCL School of Slavonic and East European Studies, Vilnius University, Vytautas Magnus University, and the Wróblewski Library of the Lithuanian Academy of Sciences. Alongside the written corpus of scholarship, the opportunity to converse at length is rightly valued by most historians. I would like to thank Rasa Banytė-Rowell, Darius Baronas,

ACKNOWLEDGEMENTS

Jakub Beneš, Rima Cicėnienė, Jarosław Czubaty, Simon Dixon, Peter Duncan, Vydas Dolinskas, Karin Friedrich, Robert Frost, Joanna Gierowska-Kałłaur, Rebecca Haynes, Andrei Ianushkevich, Regina Jakubėnas, Robertas Jurgaitis, Vaida Kamuntavičienė, Rūstis Kamuntavičius, Zigmas Kiaupa, Jūratė Kiaupienė, Romas Kinka, Jan Malicki, Andrei Matsuk, Sigitas Mitkus, Sigitas Narbutas, Alvydas Nikžentaitis, Daiva Parulskienė, Rimvydas Petrauskas, Antony Polonsky, Andrzej Pukszto, Stephen Rowell, Jurgita Šiaučiūnaitė-Verbickienė, Asta Skaisgirytė-Liauškienė, Magdalena Ślusarska, Ramunė Šmigelskytė-Stukienė, Darius Staliūnas, Neil Taylor, Artūras Vasiliauskas, Aleksas Vilčinskas, Theodore Weeks, Henryk Wisner, Adam Zamoyski, Andrzej Zakrzewski, and Hubert Zawadzki. I am particularly grateful to Thomas Lorman, with whom I have long shared the teaching of the course 'Poland and Lithuania Transformed, 1569–1923' at UCL, and who read much of the book, to its advantage.

My parents have unceasingly encouraged me, as have my friends Lynda and Ian. As ever, I owe most of all, including a deeper understanding of Lithuania, to Wioletta.

LIST OF MAPS AND ILLUSTRATIONS

Map 1: Lithuania, its neighbours, and the five ethnographic regions—Aukštaitija, Dzūkija, Suvalkija, Mažoji Lietuva, and Žemaitija. 14
Map 2: Lithuanian expansion from the thirteenth to the fifteenth centuries. 47
Map 3: The contraction of the Grand Duchy of Lithuania, 1487–1569. 48
Map 4: The Commonwealth's territorial gains and losses, 1582–1699. 96
Map 5: The partitions of the Commonwealth, 1772–95. 177
Map 6: The lands of the former Polish–Lithuanian Commonwealth, 1795–1846. 178
Map 7: Actual and claimed Lithuanian territory, 1918–40. 244

* * *

1. Monument to Gediminas and Palace of the Grand Dukes of Lithuania, Vilnius. Photograph by Editorpsl via Wikimedia Commons (CC BY-SA 4.0).
2. Zygmunt Vogel, *The Church and Monastery of the Priests of the Mission*, Vilnius, c. 1800. Lithograph featured in *Albums of Vilnius* (Wilczyński, 1845). Public domain / Polish National Library.

LIST OF MAPS AND ILLUSTRATIONS

3. Jan Matejko, *The Battle of Grunwald*, 1878. Oil on canvas. Public domain / National Museum in Warsaw.
4. Interior of the Church of Saints Peter and Paul, Antakalnis, Vilnius. Photograph by Kontis Šatūnas via Wikimedia Commons (public domain).
5. Franciszek Smuglewicz, *The Interior of the Great Synagogue*, Vilnius, 1785–86. Watercolour featured in *Vilnius 100 Years Ago in Watercolours* (Zahorski, 1912). Public domain / Polish National Library.
6. Anonymous painter, *Nobles in the Uniforms of their Palatinates*, 1790s. Oil on canvas. Public domain / National Museum of Poland, Kraków.
7. Mikalojus Konstantinas Čiurlionis, *Samogitian Cemetery*, 1909. Tempera on cardboard. ARTGEN / Alamy Stock Photo.
8. Artur Grottger, *Lithuania: The Forest*. Pencil drawing. Public domain / Polish National Library.
9. Artur Grottger, *Lithuania: The Sign*. Pencil drawing. Public domain / Polish National Library.
10. Artur Grottger, *Lithuania: The Oath*. Pencil drawing. Public domain / Polish National Library.
11. Artur Grottger, *Lithuania: The Battle*. Pencil drawing. Public domain / Polish National Library.
12. Artur Grottger, *Lithuania: The Ghost*. Pencil drawing. Public domain / Polish National Library.
13. Artur Grottger, *Lithuania: The Apparition*. Pencil drawing. Public domain / Polish National Library.
14. Petras Rimša, model for the *Lithuanian School*, 1906. Gypsum sculpture. Reproduced with kind permission of the M. K. Čiurlionis National Museum of Art, Kaunas.
15. First issue of *Nasza Niwa*, 1906. Public domain via Wikimedia Commons.
16. Jan Bułhak, *Vilnius: the Bernardine Alley at Night*, 1912.

LIST OF MAPS AND ILLUSTRATIONS

Photographic print. Public domain / National Museum of Poland, Warsaw.
17. Jan Bułhak, *Vilnius: General View*, 1912–16. Photographic print. Public domain / Museum of Art in Łódź.
18. The Council of Lithuania (*Lietuvos Taryba*) that later declared independent statehood. Photograph by Aleksandra Jurašaitytė (later Vailokaitienė) via Vilnius University Library.
19. Deputies to the Constituent Seimas, 1920. Photographer unknown. Reproduced with kind permission of the Maironis Lithuanian Literature Museum.
20. Pieno Centras building (1931–34), 1938. Photographer unknown. Public domain / Trakai History Museum (CC BY 4.0).
21. Stasys Girėnas, Steponas Darius and the *Lituanica*, 1933. Photographer unknown. Historic Images / Alamy Stock Photo.
22. George Kadish, *The body is gone*, 1943. Public domain / United States Holocaust Memorial Museum, courtesy of George Kadish / Zvi Kadushin.
23. Jewish cemetery at Dieveniškės, 2024. Photograph by Wioletta Pawlikowska.
24. Lithuanian partisans of the Vytautas military district, 1947. Photograph by Juozas Karla. Reproduced with kind permission of the Museum of Occupation and Freedom Struggles, Vilnius.
25. Hill of the Crosses. Ana Flašker / Alamy Stock Photo.
26. Postcard of the Lazdynai estate, Vilnius, 1974. Creator unknown.
27. Trakai Castle, 2021. Photograph by Augustas Didžgalvis via Wikimedia Commons (CC BY-SA 4.0).
28. The Baltic Way in Šiauliai, 23 August 1989. Photograph by Rimantas Lazdynas via Wikimedia Commons (CC BY-SA 3.0).

LIST OF MAPS AND ILLUSTRATIONS

29. Defending the Seimas, 13–14 January 1991. Photograph by Algimantas Žižiūnas. Public domain / Lithuanian Central State Archives.
30. Cemetery at Norviliškės, 2024. Photograph by Wioletta Pawlikowska.
31. Gravestone at Norviliškės, 2024. Photograph by Wioletta Pawlikowska.

NOTES

INTRODUCTION

1. Some of Lithuania's finest historians have collaborated on the as yet uncompleted twelve-volume, multi-part *Lietuvos istorija*, published in Vilnius by Baltos lankos since 2005. For single-volume histories, see the section on further reading.
2. This is essentially the same approach as that taken by the longer, more academic history by Matthias Niendorf: *Geschichte Litauens. Regionen, Reiche, Republiken, 1009–2009*, Wiesbaden: Harrassowitz, 2022, p. 5.

1. THE RISE OF AN EMPIRE (TO 1386)

1. Rasa Mažeika, 'The Grand Duchy Rejoins Europe: Post-Soviet Developments in the Historiography of Medieval Lithuania', *Journal of Medieval History*, 21, 1995, pp. 289–303 (at p. 302).
2. Marija Gimbutas, *The Prehistory of Eastern Europe*, Part 1: *Mesolithic, Neolithic and Copper Age Cultures in Russia and the Baltic Area*, Cambridge, MA: Peabody Museum, 1956; eadem, 'The Indo-Europeans: Archaeological Problems', *American Anthropologist*, 65, 1963, pp. 815–36; eadem, *The Balts*, London: Thames and Hudson, 1963.
3. Mara Kalnins, *Latvia: A Short History*, London: Hurst, 2015, pp. xxvii, 204.
4. Marija Gimbutas, *The Civilization of the Goddess: The World of Old Europe*, San Francisco: Harper, 1991; Charlene Spretnak, 'Anatomy of a Backlash: Concerning the Work of Marija Gimbutas', *Journal of Archaeomythology*, 7, 2011, pp. 1–27.
5. Darius Baronas and S. C. Rowell, *The Conversion of Lithuania: From Pagan Barbarians to Late Medieval Christians*, Vilnius: Institute of Lithuanian Literature and Folklore, 2015, pp. 27–30.

6. Rasa Banytė-Rowell, 'Brides for the Afterlife? Some Considerations on Female Burials from West Lithuania in the Third Century CE', *Wiadomości Archeologiczne*, 73, 2022, pp. 109–30.
7. Gimbutas, *The Balts*, p. 155.
8. Baronas and Rowell, *Conversion*, pp. 34, 49–53.
9. Darius Baronas, 'The Year 1009: St Bruno of Querfurt between Poland and Rus", *Journal of Medieval History*, 34:1, 2008, pp. 1–22.
10. Tomas Baranauskas, 'On the Origin of the Name of Lithuania', *Lituanus*, 55:3, 2009 (http://www.lituanus.org/2009/09_3_02%20Baranauskas.html); Baronas and Rowell, *Conversion*, pp. 67–71.
11. Baronas and Rowell, *Conversion*, pp. 72–73, 77.
12. Tomas Baranauskas, *Lietuvos valstybės ištakos*, Vilnius: Vaga, 2000.
13. Quoted after Andrzej B. Zakrzewski, *Wielkie Księstwo Litewskie. Prawo-ustrój–społeczeństwo*, Warsaw: Campidoglio, 2013, p. 88.
14. Baronas and Rowell, *Conversion*, pp. 155–60. Cf. Dariusz Kołodziejczyk, *The Crimean Khanate and Poland-Lithuania: International Diplomacy on the European Periphery (15th–18th Century). A Study Followed by an Annotated Edition of Relevant Documents*, Leiden: Brill, 2011, pp. 3–7, 14–16.
15. Baronas and Rowell, *Conversion*, p. 316.
16. The term was used by S. C. Rowell, *Lithuania Ascending: A Pagan Empire within East-Central Europe, 1295–1345*, Cambridge: Cambridge University Press, 1994, but a more complex argument is made by Zenonas Norkus, *An Unproclaimed Empire: The Grand Duchy of Lithuania from the Viewpoint of the Comparative Sociology of Empires*, New York: Routledge, 2019. Cf. Susan Reynolds, 'Empires: A Problem of Comparative History', *Historical Research*, 79, 2006, pp. 151–65.
17. Baronas and Rowell, *Conversion*, p. 246.
18. Ibid., pp. 249–56.
19. Robert Frost, *The Oxford History of Poland-Lithuania*, vol. 1: *The Making of the Polish-Lithuanian Union, 1385–1569*, Oxford: Oxford University Press, 2015, pp. 3–4, 34, 47–57.

2. FORGING A UNION (1386–1569)

1. Alfonas Eidintas, Alfredas Bumblauskas, Antanas Kulakauskas, and Mindaugas Tamošaitis, *The History of Lithuania*, Vilnius: Eugrimas, 2013, p.44; cf. Edvardas Gudavičius, 'Lithuania's Road to Europe', *LHS*, 2, 1997, pp. 15–27, Jūratė Kiaupienė, 'The Grand Duchy of Lithuania in East Central

Europe, or Once Again about the Lithuanian-Polish Union', *LHS*, 2, 1997, pp. 56–71.
2. Darius Staliūnas, 'From Ethnocentric to Civic History: Changes in Contemporary Lithuanian Historical Studies', in Kimitaki Matsuzato (ed.), *Emerging Meso-Areas in the Former Socialist Countries: Histories Revived or Improvised?*, Hokkaido: Hokkaido University, 2005, pp. 311–31 (at p. 331).
3. Rūstis Kamuntavičius, *Gudijos istorija: Baltarusijos istorija*, Vilnius: Mokslo ir encyklopedijų leidybos centras and Lietuvos Didžiosios Kunigaikštytės institutas, 2021; idem, 'Whose Grand Duchy? Contesting the Multicultural Past in Lithuania and Belarus', in Stanley Bill and Simon Lewis (eds), *Multicultural Commonwealth: Poland-Lithuania and Its Afterlives*, Pittsburgh: University of Pittsburgh Press, 2023, pp. 205–19.
4. Frost, *Oxford History*, vol. 1, pp. 61, 67, 199–200, and passim; cf. S. C. Rowell, 'Forging a Union? Some Reflections on the Early Jagiellonian Monarchy', *LHS*, 1, 1996, pp. 6–21; Jūratė Kiaupienė, *Between Rome and Byzantium: The Golden Age of the Grand Duchy of Lithuania's Political Culture*, Boston, MA: Academic Studies Press, 2019, pp. 41–2 and passim.
5. *Sources on Jewish Self-Government in the Polish Lands from Its Inception until the Present*, ed. François Guesnet and Jerzy Tomaszewski z"l, Leiden: Brill, 2022, pp. 19–23, 27–8 (quotation at pp. 21, 22).
6. Baronas and Rowell, *Conversion*, pp. 261–78, 309–15 (quotation at p. 277).
7. Marek Daniel Kowalski, 'Nieznany dokument papieski dla Andrzeja, pierwszego biskupa Seretu i Wilna, i powstanie biskupstwa wileńskiego', *Studia Źródłoznawcze*, 53, 2015, pp. 123–34.
8. Baronas and Rowell, *Conversion*, pp. 293–309; Rimvydas Petrauskas, 'Noble Names: Changes in Lithuanian Aristocratic Name-Giving During the Late Fourteenth and Fifteenth Centuries', in Richard Butterwick and Wioletta Pawlikowska (eds), *Social and Cultural Relations in the Grand Duchy of Lithuania: Microhistories*, New York: Routledge, 2019, pp. 91–104 (at pp. 93–5).
9. Sven Ekdahl, 'The Turning Point in the Battle of Tannenberg (Grunwald/Žalgiris)', *Lituanus*, 56:2, 2010 (https://www.lituanus.org/2010/10_2_06%20Ekdahl.html); Frost, *Oxford History*, vol. 1, pp. 103–07. Remembrance of the battle is analysed by Dangiras Mačiulis, Rimvydas Petrauskas, and Darius Staliūnas, *Kas laimėjo Žalgirio mūšį? Istorinio paveldo dalybos Vidurio ir Rytų Europoje*, Vilnius: Vaga, 2012; in Polish: *Kto wygrał bitwę pod Grunwaldem?*, Warsaw: Instytut Pamięci Narodowej and Lietuvos institutas istorijos, 2015.

10. Recent research is gathered in Jūratė Kiaupienė and Lidia Korczak, et al. (eds), *1413 m. Horodlės aktai (dokumentai ir tyrinėjimai)/Akta Horodelskie z 1413 roku (dokumenty i studia)*, Vilnius: Lietuvos istorijos institutas, 2013; cf. Frost, *Oxford History*, vol. 1, pp. 109–21. On the coats of arms, see Edmundas Rimša, *Heraldry Past to Present*, Vilnius: Versus aureus, 2005.
11. Baronas and Rowell, *Conversion*, pp. 327–78.
12. Frost, *Oxford History*, vol. 1, pp. 131–48 (quotation at p. 143); Rimvydas Petrauskas, 'Valdovas ir jo karūna: neįvykusios Vytauto karūnacijos aplinkybės', *Lietuvos istorijos metraštis*, 2, 2009, pp. 57–72; *idem*, 'Korona Witolda: niedoszła koronacja i jej późniejsza legenda historyczna', in Urszula Augustyniak (ed.), *Tradycja—metoda przekazywania i formy upamiętnienia w państwie polsko-litewskim, XV—pierwsza połowa XIX wieku*, Warsaw: Neriton, 2011, pp. 13–23, debunks the 'theft' of the crown, and explains the development of the legend.
13. Rimvydas Petrauskas, 'The Lithuanian Nobility in the Late Fourteenth- and Fifteenth Centuries: Composition and Structure', *LHS*, 7, 2002, pp. 1–22; *idem*, 'Noble Names'.
14. Jūratė Kiaupienė, *Between Rome and Byzantium: The Golden Age of the Grand Duchy of Lithuania's Political Culture*, Boston, MA: Academic Studies Press, 2019, pp. xvii–xviii.
15. Frost, *Oxford History*, vol. 1, pp. 308, 315, 337–43, 346–9 (quotation at p. 342); Rimvydas Petrauskas, 'Wielkie Księstwo Litewskie a Unia Mielnicka', in Lidia Korczak et al. (eds), *Akty unii wileńskiej i mielnickiej (1499–1501). Dokumenty i studia*, Kraków and Vilnius: Polska Akademia Umiejętności and Lietuvos institutas istorijos, 2022, pp. 177–98 (at pp. 196–7); cf. Jūratė Kiaupienė, 'Funkcjonowanie zapisów unii z lat 1499 i 1501 w Wielkim Księstwie Litewskim i Królestwie Polskim', ibid., pp. 199–234.
16. Frost, *Oxford History*, vol. 1, pp. 349–53 (quotation at p. 349).
17. See 'The Grand Hetman Kostiantyn Ostrogski Lithuanian-Polish-Ukrainian Brigade', https://litpolukrbrig.wp.pl/en.
18. S. C. Rowell, 'Was Fifteenth-Century Lithuanian Catholicism as Lukewarm as Sixteenth-Century Reformers Would Have Us Believe?', *Central Europe*, 8:2, 2010, pp. 86–106; Baronas and Rowell, *Conversion*, pp. 3–6, 18–19, 459–517, 521–4 (quotation at p. 524).
19. Wioletta Pawlikowska-Butterwick, 'A Foreign Elite? The Territorial Origins of the Canons and Prelates of Vilna in the Second Half of the Sixteenth

Century', *Slavonic and East European Review*, 92:1, 2014, pp. 44–80; *eadem*, 'Regarding the Sixteenth-Century Statutes of the Chapters of Vilna and Samogitia', in Wioletta Pawlikowska-Butterwick and Liudas Jovaiša (eds), *Vilniaus ir Žemaičių katedrų kapitulų Statutai / The Statutes of the Chapters of Vilna and Samogitia*, Vilnius: Lietuvių katalikų mokslo akademija, 2015, pp. 113–213 (at pp. 117–18, 124–6, 143, 156, 176, 195).
20. Quoted after Zakrzewski, *Wielkie Księstwo Litewskie*, p. 50.
21. Andrei Ianushkevich, *Vialikae Kniastva Litoŭskae i Infliantskaia voina 1558–1570 hh.*, Minsk: Medisont, 2007, pp. 292–97; Jūratė Kiaupienė, 'The Grand Duchy of Lithuania and the Grand Dukes of Lithuania in the Sixteenth Century: Reflections on the Lithuanian Political Nation and the Union of Lublin', in Richard Butterwick (ed.), *The Polish-Lithuanian Monarchy in European Context, c. 1500–1795*, Basingstoke: Palgrave, 2001, pp. 82–92; *eadem*, *Between Rome and Byzantium*, pp. 97–8; Frost, *Oxford History*, vol. 1, pp. 446–53 (quotation at p. 448).
22. *Akta unji Polski z Litwą 1385–1791*, ed. Stanisław Kutrzeba and Władysław Semkowicz, Kraków: Polska Akademja Umiejętności and Towarzystwo Naukowe Warszawskie, 1932, nos. 136 and 138, pp. 302, 313. Natalia Iakovenko, *Ukraïns'ka shliakhta z kintsia XIV do seredyny XVII stolitiia (Volyn' i Tsentral'na Ukraïna)*, Kyiv: Naukova Dumka, 1993, transformed understanding of the princely and noble elites of southern Rus'.
23. Quoted after Henryk Lulewicz, *Gniewów o unię ciąg dalszy. Stosunki polsko-litewskie w latach 1569–1588*, Warsaw: Neriton, 2002, p. 24.
24. Kutrzeba and Semkowicz (eds.), *Akta unji Polski z Litwą*, no. 149, p. 358; Frost, *Oxford History*, vol. 1, pp. 492–4.

3. A COMMONWEALTH OF TWO NATIONS? (1569–1795)

1. Quoted after Lulewicz, *Gniewów o unię ciąg dalszy*, p. 152.
2. Ibid., p. 335.
3. Zakrzewski, *Wielkie Księstwo Litewskie*, pp. 103–17; Andrzej Rachuba, *Wielkie Księstwo Litewskie w systemie parlamentarnym Rzeczypospolitej w latach 1569–1763*, Warsaw: Wydawnictwo Sejmowe, 2002.
4. Robert I. Frost, *The Northern Wars: War, State and Society in Northeastern Europe, 1558–1721*, Harlow: Longman, 2000, pp. 150–1.
5. *Triumfo diena/Dies Triumfi/Days of Triumph*, ed. Eugenija Ulčinaitė and Eugenijas Saviščevas, Vilnius: Nacionalinis muziejus Lietuvos Didžiosios Kunigaikštytės valdovų rūmai, 2011.

6. Quoted after Frost, *The Northern Wars*, p. 147.
7. Ibid., pp. 150–1.
8. Karin Friedrich, 'Political Loyalties in the Commonwealth's Borderlands: Bogusław Radziwiłł (1620–1669) and the Problem of Treason', in Yvonne Kleinmann et al. (eds), *Imaginations and Configurations of Polish Society: From the Middle Ages through the 20th Century*, Göttingen: Wallstein Verlag, 2017, pp. 143–73.
9. Artūras Vasiliauskas, 'The Practice of Citizenship among the Lithuanian Nobility, ca. 1580–1630', in Karin Friedrich and Barbara M. Pendzich (eds), *Citizenship and Identity in a Multinational Commonwealth. Poland–Lithuania in Context, 1550–1772*, Leiden: Brill, 2009, pp. 71–102; idem, 'Noble Community and Local Politics in the Wilkomierz District During the Reign of Sigismund Vasa (1587–1632)', in Richard Butterwick and Wioletta Pawlikowska (eds), *Social and Cultural Relations in the Grand Duchy of Lithuania: Microhistories*, New York: Routledge, 2019, pp. 132–47.
10. Wioletta Pawlikowska-Butterwick, 'Property and Personal Relations in the Jurydyka of the Vilna Cathedral Chapter in the Sixteenth and Early Seventeenth Century (with Particular Reference to the Scandalous and Suspicious Misdeeds of Canon Isaac Fechtinus)', *Wschodni Rocznik Humanistyczny*, 13, 2016, pp. 53–82; Wioletta Pawlikowska, 'The Challenge of Trent and the Renewal of the Catholic Church in the Grand Duchy of Lithuania: The Higher Clergy of Vilnius and the Problems of Plural Benefices and Residence in the Sixteenth Century', *Bažnyčios Istorijos Studijos*, 4, 2011, pp. 37–56.
11. Wioletta Pawlikowska-Butterwick, '"Lithuanians", "Foreigners" and Ecclesiastical Office: Law and Practice in the Grand Duchy of Lithuania', *Journal of Ecclesiastical History*, 68:2, 2017, pp. 285–305.
12. Personal communication from Robert Frost in advance of his *Oxford History of Poland-Lithuania*, vol. 2: *The Making of the Polish–Lithuanian Republic, 1569–1648* (forthcoming).
13. I have learned much from the research of Alesia Mankouskaya.
14. Quoted after Robert Frost, *After the Deluge: Poland–Lithuania and the Second Northern War, 1655–1660*, Cambridge: Cambridge University Press, 1993, p. 50.
15. *XVII a. vidurio Maskvos okupacijos Lietuvoje šaltiniai*, vol. 1: *1657–1662 m. Vilniaus miesto tarybos knyga*, ed. Elmantas Meilus, Vilnius: LII, 2011, p. 684.

16. Henadz Sahanovich, *Nieviadomaja vajna, 1654–1667*, Minsk: Navuka i technika, 1995.
17. Wioletta Pawlikowska, 'Marriage or Mitre? The Careers of Bishops from the Pac Family in the Grand Duchy of Lithuania during the Reformation and Counter-Reformation', *Slavonic and East European Review*, 99:4, 2021, pp. 700–27 (at pp. 721–2).
18. Mindaugas Šapoka, *War, Loyalty, and Rebellion: The Grand Duchy of Lithuania and the Great Northern War, 1709–1717*, London and New York: Routledge, 2018.
19. Zigmantas Kiaupa, *Trumpasis XVIII amžius (1733–1795 m.)*, vol. vii/1 of *Lietuvos istorija*, Vilnius: Baltos lankos, 2012, pp. 253–4.
20. Cezary Kuklo, *Demografia Rzeczypospolitej przedrozbiorowej*, Warsaw: DiG, 2009, pp. 210–16; Kiaupa, *Trumpasis XVIII amžius*, vol. vii/1, p. 255; cf. Emanuel Rostworowski, 'Ilu było w Rzeczypospolitej obywateli szlachty?', *Kwartalnik Historyczny*, 94:3, 1987, pp. 3–40.
21. Raimonda Ragauskienė, *Vilniaus 'aukso amžius'. Miesto gyventojai ir svečiai XVI a. 6–7-ajame deš. (Vilniaus vietininko teismo knygų duomenimis)*, Vilnius: Lietuvos istorijos institutas, 2021, p. 133.
22. *Mowa Jego Krolewskiey Mci Na Seymie 1766. dnia 11 Octobris miana.*
23. Agnius Urbanavičius, *Vilniaus naujieji miestiečiai 1661–1795 metais. Sąrašas*, Vilnius: Lietuvos istorijos instituto leidykla, 2009, pp. 522–9.
24. Mindaugas Klovas, Elmantas Meilus, Antoni K. Urmański, and Oksana Valionienė, *Vilniaus sociotopografijos metmenys XIV–XVIII a.*, Vilnius: Lietuvos istorijos institutas, 2021, p. 93.
25. Kiaupa, *Trumpasis XVIII amžiaus*, vol. vii/1, pp. 180–1; cf. Kuklo, *Demografia Rzeczypospolitej*, p. 234.
26. Ramunė Šmigelskytė-Stukienė, *Michał Kleofas Ogiński. Politician, Diplomat and Minister (1786–1794)*, Vilnius: Petro ofsetas, 2015. On administration: Ramunė Šmigelskytė-Stukienė, Eduardas Brusokas, Liudas Glemža, Robertas Jurgaitis, and Valdas Rakutis, *Modernios administracijos tapsmas Lietuvoje: valstybės institucijų raida 1764–1794 metais*, Vilnius: Petro ofsetas, 2014.
27. Stanisław Kościałkowski, *Antoni Tyzenhauz. Podskarbi nadworny litewski*, 2 vols, London: Wydawnictwo Społeczności Akademickiej Uniwersytetu Stefana Batorego w Londynie, 1970–1971.
28. Stanisław August to Augustyn Deboli, 3 May 1788, quoted after Emanuel Rostworowski, *Sprawa aukcji wojska na tle sytuacji politycznej przed Sejmem Czteroletnim*, Warsaw: PWN, 1957, p. 224.

29. Adolfas Šapoka, *Raštai*, vol. 2: *Lietuva reformų seimo metų. Iki 1791 m. gegužės 3 d. Konstitucijos*, Vilnius: Vilniaus pedagoginio universiteto leidykla, 2008, pp. 444–6; idem, 'Gegužės 3 d. konstitucija ir Lietuva', in *Lietuvos praeitis*, vol. 1, part 1, Kaunas, 1940, pp. 137–210.
30. Quoted after Jerzy Michalski, 'Zagadnienie unii polsko-litewskiej w czasach Stanisława Augusta', in idem, *Studia historyczne z XVIII i XIX wieku*, vol. 1: *Polityka i społeczeństwo*, Warsaw: Stentor, 2007, pp. 44–73 (at p. 64).
31. Richard Butterwick, 'Zaręczenie Obojga Narodów. Analiza języka politycznego', *XVIII amžiaus studijos*, 9, 2023, pp. 190–203.
32. Ramunė Šmigelskytė-Stukienė, *Lietuvos Didžiosios Kunigaikštystės konfederacijos susidarymas ir veikla 1792–1793*, Vilnius: LII Leidykla, 2003.
33. Richard Butterwick, *The Polish-Lithuanian Commonwealth 1733–1795: Light and Flame*, New Haven, CT: Yale University Press, 2020, p. 385.

4. UNDER IMPERIAL RULE (1795–1914)

1. Miroslav Hroch, *Social Preconditions of National Revival in Europe: A Comparative Analysis of the Social Composition of Patriotic Groups Among the Smaller European Nations*, Cambridge: Cambridge University Press, 1985.
2. Theodore R. Weeks, *Vilnius Between Nations 1795–2000*, DeKalb, IL: Northern Illinois University Press, 2015, p. 95.
3. Jerzy Ochmański, *Historia Litwy*, 3rd edn, Wrocław: Zakład Narodowy im. Ossolińskich, 1990, p. 184.
4. Antony Polonsky, *The Jews in Poland and Russia*, vol. 1: *1350 to 1881*, Oxford: The Littman Library of Jewish Civilization, 2010, pp. 323–3.
5. Ochmański, *Historia Litwy*, p. 190.
6. 'To Litwinka, dziewica-bohater, Wódz Powstańców—Emilija Plater!'.
7. *Naujas istatimas Jezaus Christaus wieszpaties musu lietuwiszku liežuwiu iszgulditas par Jozapa Arnulpa kunigaykszti Giedrayti wiskupa žiemayciu, ženklinika S. Stanislowo*, Iszpautas Kunigus Missionorius, Wilniuje 1816.
8. Ochmański, *Historia Litwy*, p. 194.
9. Polonsky, *The Jews in Poland and Russia*, vol. 1, p. 354.
10. Quoted ibid., vol. 1, p. 368.
11. Quoted after Egidijus Aleksandravičius and Antanas Kulakauskas, *Pod władzą carów. Litwa w XIX wieku*, Kraków: Universitas, 2003, p. 87. Lithuanian original: *Carų valdžioje. Lietuva XIX amžiuje*, Vilnius: Baltos lankos, 1996.
12. Quoted after Aleksandravičius and Kulakauskas, *Pod władzą carów*, p. 155.

NOTES   pp. [204–231]

13. Quoted after Mikołaj Gliński, 'Kastuś Kalinoŭski and the Rise of the Political Idea of Belarus', *culture.pl*, 2023 (https://culture.pl/en/article/kastus-kalinouski-the-rise-of-the-political-idea-of-belarus).
14. Aleksandravičius and Kulakauskas, *Pod władzą carów*, pp. 199, 310.
15. Zbysław Wojtkowiak, 'Bractwa trzeźwości na Żmudzi w połowie XIX wieku', in *Litwini—historia i kultura. Sesja naukowa. Szreniawa, 28–29 czerwca 2008*, ed. Krzysztof Pietkiewicz, Szreniawa: Muzeum Narodowe Rolnictwa i Przemysłu Rolno-Spożywczego, 2009, pp. 81–7 (at p. 83).
16. Aleksandravičius and Kulakauskas, *Pod władzą carów*, pp. 297–8, 303–04.
17. Ibid., pp. 310–12. Ochmański, *Historia Litwy*, p. 234.
18. For the tabulated results of answers to the language question (*Tablitsa XIII. Raspredelenie naseleniia po rodnomu iazyku*), in *Pervaia Vseobshchaia perepis' naseleniia Rossiiskoi Imperii 1897 g.*, 50 vols, St Petersburg, 1903–05, see: www.demoscope.ru/weekly/ssp/rus_lan_97_uezd_eng.php?reg=91. Cf. Weeks, *Vilnius Between Nations*, p. 61.
19. See: https://lnm.lt/en/museums/jonas-basanavicius-birthplace/.
20. Tomas Balkelis, *The Making of Modern Lithuania*, London and New York: Routledge, 2009, p. 32.
21. Quoted ibid., p. 27.
22. Quoted after Timothy Snyder, *The Reconstruction of Nations: Poland, Ukraine, Lithuania, Belarus, 1569–1999*, New Haven, CT: Yale University Press, 2003, p. 39.
23. Juozas Tumas-Vaižgantas, 'Lietuvai mestusose', *Tevynės sargas*, 1899, no. 10, quoted after Dangiras Mačiulis and Darius Staliūnas, *Lithuanian Nationalism and the Vilnius Question, 1883–1940*, Marburg: Verlag Herder-Institut, 2015, p. 8.
24. Quoted after Balkelis, *The Making of Modern Lithuania*, pp. 24, 70–72.
25. Quoted in Rimantas Miknys, 'Decisions of the Lithuanian Assembly (the Great Seimas of Vilnius) of 4–5 December 1905', *LHS*, 10, 2005, pp. 145–54 (p. 152). The word *lytis* could also be translated as 'sex', which better fits the conceptual horizons of the time.
26. Quoted after Miknys, 'Decisions of the Lithuanian Assembly', p. 153.
27. Quoted after Balkelis, *The Making of Modern Lithuania*, p. 64.
28. Aleksandravičius and Kulakauskas, *Pod władzą carów*, p. 113.
29. Quoted after Balkelis, *The Making of Modern Lithuania*, p. 78.
30. Quoted ibid., p. 93.
31. Mečislovas Davainis-Silvestraitis, *Tevynainiu giesme* (1884), quoted after

Mačiulis and Staliūnas, *Lithuanian Nationalism and the Vilnius Question*, pp. 6–7.

32. Antanas Smetona, 'Kur Lietuvos centras?', *Viltis*, 16 December 1910, quoted after Mačiulis and Staliūnas, *Lithuanian Nationalism and the Vilnius Question*, p. 14.
33. Jonathan Steinberg, *Bismarck: A Life*, Oxford: Oxford University Press, 2011, p. 394.
34. *Nasza Niwa*, 10/23 November 1906, no. 1. Cf. the translation in Per Anders Rudling, *The Rise and Fall of Belarusian Nationalism 1906–1931*, Pittsburgh: University of Pittsburgh Press, 2015, p. 54.
35. Bohdan Cywiński, *Szańce kultur. Szkice z dziejów narodów Europy wschodniej*, Warsaw: Centrum Europejskie Natolin-Wydawnictwo Trio, 2013, p. 230.
36. Snyder, *The Reconstruction of Nations*, pp. 43–44, 282.
37. Quoted after Rudling, *The Rise and Fall of Belarusian Nationalism*, p. 47.
38. Darius Staliūnas, 'An Awkward City: Vilnius as a Regional Centre in Russian Nationality Policy (ca 1860–1914)', in Andrzej Nowak (ed), *Russia and Eastern Europe: Applied 'Imperiology'*, Warsaw: Instytut Historii PAN, 2006, pp. 222–43.
39. Mindaugas Kvietkauskas, *Vilniaus literatūrų kontrapunktai: Ankstyvasis modernizmas 1904–1915*, Vilnius: Lietuvos rašytojų sąjungos leidykla, 2007.
40. Tomas Venclova, *Opisać Wilno*, Warsaw: Zeszyty Literackie, 2006, p. 144.
41. Quoted after Balkelis, *The Making of Modern Lithuania*, p. 25.

5. BREAKING EMPIRES, MAKING NATIONS? (1914–1940)

1. Tomas Balkelis, *War, Revolution, and Nation-Making in Lithuania, 1914–1923*, Oxford: Oxford University Press, 2018, p. 158.
2. Quoted ibid., pp. 36–7.
3. Quoted after Balkelis, *The Making of Modern Lithuania*, p. 105.
4. Quoted after Weeks, *Vilnius Between Nations*, p. 100.
5. Alexander Watson, *Ring of Steel: Germany and Austria-Hungary at War 1914–1918*, London: Allen Lane, 2014, pp. 394–403.
6. Vejas Liulevicius, *War Land on the Eastern Front: Culture, National Identity and German Occupation in World War I*, Cambridge: Cambridge University Press, 2000, pp. 125–8.
7. Erich Ludendorff, *My War Memories 1914–1918*, 2 vols, London: Hutchinson, 1919, vol. 1, p. 178–9.

8. Ibid., vol. 1, pp. 187–8.
9. Aleksander Szklennik, *'Wspomnienia o wydarzeniach w Wilnie i w kraju'. Dziennik*, ed. Joanna Gierowska-Kałłaur, 2 vols, Warsaw: Instytut Historii PAN, 2018–19, vol. 1, p. 214.
10. Andrzej Pukszto, *Między stołecznością a partykularyzmem. Wielonarodowościowe społeczeństwo Wilna w latach 1915–1920*, Toruń: Europejskie Centrum Edukacyjne, 2006, pp. 25–6.
11. Quoted after Weeks, *Vilnius Between Nations*, p. 102.
12. Ludwik Abramowicz, 'Polska a Litwa', quoted after Pukszto, *Między stołecznością a partykularyzmem*, p. 36.
13. Ludendorff, *My War Memories*, vol. 2, p. 470.
14. Quoted after Pukszto, *Między stołecznością a partykularyzmem*, pp. 45, 53.
15. Balkelis, *The Making of Modern Lithuania*, p. 108.
16. *Lietuvos valstybės tarybos protokolai 1917–1918*, ed. Alfonsas Eidintas, Raimundas Lopata, Vilnius: Lietuvos Istorijos institutas, 1991, pp. 18–79.
17. The text is available for example at: https://www.archives.gov/milestone-documents/president-woodrow-wilsons-14-points.
18. Quoted after: http://viduramziu.istorija.net/etno/vasario16-en.htm.
19. The proclamation in all four languages is printed as the endpapers of Joanna Gierowska-Kałłaur, *Józef Piłsudski wobec kwestii białoruskiej (1918–1920)*, Warsaw: Instytut Historii PAN, 2023.
20. Balkelis, *War, Revolution, and Nation-building*, pp. 136–7.
21. Ibid., p. 145.
22. Ibid., p. 149.
23. Ibid., p. 127.
24. Mačiulis and Staliūnas, *Lithuanian Nationalism and the Vilnius Question*, p. 127.
25. Balkelis, *War, Revolution, and Nation-building*, p. 157.
26. Alfred Erich Senn, *The Emergence of Modern Lithuania*, New York: Columbia University Press, 1959, pp. 231–2.
27. Eidintas et al., *The History of Lithuania*, p. 193.
28. Quoted after Eidintas, *Antanas Smetona*, p. 155.
29. Quoted ibid., p. 161.
30. Andrzej Nowak, 'Józef Piłsudski: a Federalist or an Imperialist?', in *idem*, *History and Geopolitics: A Contest for Eastern Europe*, Warsaw: Polish Institute of International Affairs, 2008, pp. 169–86.
31. Quoted after Włodzimierz Mędrzecki, *Kresowy kalejdoskop. Wędrówki przez*

ziemie wschodnie Drugiej Rzeczypospolitej 1918–1939, Kraków: Wydawnictwo Literackie, 2018, p. 326.
32. Quoted after Aleksandravičius and Kulakauskas, *Pod władzą carów*, p. 175.
33. Quoted after Eidintas, *Antanas Smetona*, p. 285.
34. Quoted after Mačiulis and Staliūnas, *Lithuanian Nationalism and the Vilnius Question*, p. 147.
35. Bernard Newman, *Baltic Roundabout*, 2nd edn, London: Herbert Jenkins, 1940.
36. Eidintas et al., *The History of Lithuania*, p. 193.
37. Quoted after Mačiulis and Staliūnas, *Lithuanian Nationalism and the Vilnius Question*, p. 171.
38. Quoted ibid., p. 175.
39. Quoted after Šarūnas Liekis, *1939: The Year that Changed Everything in Lithuania's History*, Amsterdam: Rodopi, 2010, p. 171.
40. Weeks, *Vilnius Between Nations*, p. 160.
41. Tomas Balkelis, 'War, State, Ethnic Conflict and the Refugee Crisis in Lithuania, 1939–1940', *Contemporary European History*, 16:4, 2007.
42. Quoted after Eidintas, *Antanas Smetona*, p. 377.

6. HAMMER, SWASTIKA, AND SICKLE (1940–1991)

1. Violeta Davoliūtė, *The Making and Breaking of Soviet Lithuania: Memory and Modernity in the Wake of War*, London and New York: Routledge, 2013. p. xvi.
2. Quoted ibid., p. 114.
3. Arūnas Bubnys, 'Jews in Soviet Lithuania in 1940–1941', in Vladas Sirutavičius, Jurgita Šiaučiūnaitė-Verbickienė, and Darius Staliūnas (eds), *The History of the Jews in Lithuania: From the Middle Ages to the 1990s*, Leiden: Brill, 2020, pp. 386–90.
4. Niendorf, *Geschichte Litauens*, p. 247.
5. Bubnys, 'Jews in Soviet Lithuania', p. 393.
6. Davoliūtė, *The Making and Breaking of Soviet Lithuania*, p. 38.
7. Ibid.
8. Quoted after Arūnas Bubnys, 'The Holocaust in Lithuania in 1940–1941', in Vladas Sirutavičius, Jurgita Šiaučiūnaitė-Verbickienė, and Darius Staliūnas (eds), *The History of the Jews in Lithuania: From the Middle Ages to the 1990s*, Leiden: Brill, 2020, p. 398.
9. Report by *Einsatzgruppe A* in the Baltic countries, 15 October 1941, jewish

NOTES

virtual library.org, https://www.jewishvirtuallibrary.org/report-by-einsatzgruppe-a-in-the-baltic-countries-october-1941?utm_content=cmp-true.
10. Ibid.
11. Timothy Snyder, *Bloodlands: Europe Between Hitler and Stalin*, London: The Bodley Head, 2010, p. 263 and passim.
12. Bubnys, 'The Holocaust', pp. 403–05.
13. Quoted after Arūnas Bubnys, 'The Jewish Anti-Nazi Resistance', in Vladas Sirutavičius, Jurgita Šiaučiūnaitė-Verbickienė, and Darius Staliūnas (eds), *The History of the Jews in Lithuania: From the Middle Ages to the 1990s*, Leiden: Brill, 2020, p. 419.
14. Ibid., pp. 426–7.
15. 'George Kadish', Holocaust Encyclopedia, United States Holocaust Memorial Museum, https://encyclopedia.ushmm.org/content/en/article/george-kadish.
16. Bubnys, 'The Holocaust', p. 418.
17. Ibid., p. 417.
18. Names of Righteous by Country, https://www.yadvashem.org/righteous/statistics.html.
19. Bubnys, 'The Holocaust', p. 417.
20. Sumner Welles, 23 July 1940, quoted after Una Bergmane, *Politics of Uncertainty: The United States, the Baltic Question, and the Collapse of the Soviet Union*, New York: Oxford University Press, 2023, p. 18.
21. Quoted ibid., p. 19.
22. Ibid., pp. 24–6.
23. https://e-seimas.lrs.lt/portal/legalAct/lt/TAD/TAIS.339103.
24. See Evaldas Balčiūnas, 'More Evidence: Did Adolfas Ramanauskas Lead a Hitlerist Militia in the Early Days of the Lithuanian Holocaust?', *Defending History*, 2019, https://defendinghistory.com/more-evidence-of-adolfas-ramanauskass-leading-a-hitlerist-militia-in-early-days-of-lithuanian-holocaust/99094.
25. Davoliūtė, *The Making and Breaking of Soviet Lithuania*, p. 49.
26. Quoted ibid., p. 50.
27. Samuel Barnai, 'Jews in Soviet Lithuania: The Revival after the Holocaust', in Vladas Sirutavičius, Jurgita Šiaučiūnaitė-Verbickienė, and Darius Staliūnas (eds), *The History of the Jews in Lithuania: From the Middle Ages to the 1990s*, Leiden: Brill, 2020, p. 443.
28. Ibid., p. 432.

29. Ibid., pp. 438, 450.
30. Davoliūtė, *The Making and Breaking of Soviet Lithuania*, p. 39.
31. Theodore Weeks, 'Repopulating Vilnius, 1939–1949', in Tomas Balkelis and Violeta Davoliūtė (eds), *Population Displacement in the Twentieth Century: Experiences, Identities and Legacies*, Leiden: Brill Rodopi, 2016, pp. 135–59; cf. Vitalija Stravinskienė, 'Between Poland and Lithuania: Repatriation of Poles from Lithuania, 1944–47', in Balkelis and Davoliūtė (eds), *Population Displacement*, pp. 160–78.
32. Weeks, *Vilnius Between Nations*, p. 156.
33. Davoliūtė, *The Making and Breaking of Soviet Lithuania*, p. 44.
34. Quoted after Živilė Mikailienė, 'Soviet Vilnius: Ideology and the Formation of Identity', *LHS*, 15, 2010, p. 183.
35. Quoted after Davoliūtė, *The Making and Breaking of Soviet Lithuania*, p. 69.
36. Ibid., p. 3.
37. Quoted after Marija Drėmaitė, '"Vilnius. A Baroque City": Changing Perceptions of Baroque Heritage during the Twentieth Century', *RIHA Journal*, 0212, June 2019, p. 18.
38. Quoted after Eglė Rindzevičiūtė, 'Imagining the Grand Duchy of Lithuania: The Politics and Economics of the Rebuilding of Trakai Castle and the "Palace of Sovereigns" in Vilnius', *Central Europe*, 8:2, 2010, p. 188, corrected, following a suggestion from one of the reviewers, after Vytautas Tininis, *Sniečkus. 33 metai valdžioje*, Vilnius: self-published, 2000, pp. 168–69, which reveals that 'of peoples' is intended rather than 'national'.
39. Davoliūtė, *The Making and Breaking of Soviet Lithuania*, p. 135.
40. Statistics from: https://kryziukalnas.lt/?id=44.
41. Arūnas Streikus, 'Christianity in Lithuania in the 20th Century', in Darius Baronas et al., *Christianity in Lithuania*, Vilnius: Aidai, 2002, pp. 127–62 (at p. 150).
42. Stefan Hedlund, 'The Mice That Roared', in Charles Clarke (ed.), *Understanding the Baltic States: Estonia, Latvia and Lithuania since 1991*, London: Hurst, 2023, pp. 75–90 (p. 76).
43. Charles Moore, *Margaret Thatcher: The Authorized Biography*, vol. 2: *Everything She Wants*, London: Allen Lane, 2015, pp. 240–1, discusses the parentage of the phrase.
44. Quoted after Davoliūtė, *The Making and Breaking of Soviet Lithuania*, p. 165.
45. Ibid., p. 165.
46. Karel Piirimäe, 'Contributions of the Baltic Independence Campaigns to

Soviet Collapse', in Clarke (ed.), *Understanding the Baltic States*, pp. 91–106 (at p. 93).
47. Quoted after Bergmane, *Politics of Uncertainty*, p. 60.
48. Quoted ibid., p. 60–62.
49. Quoted ibid., p. 65.
50. Quoted after Eidintas, Bumblauskas, Kulakauskas, and Tamošaitis, *The History of Lithuania*, p. 273.
51. Quoted after Bergmane, *Politics of Uncertainty*, p. 112.
52. Quoted after Eidintas, Bumblauskas, Kulakauskas, and Tamošaitis, *The History of Lithuania*, p. 280.
53. Quoted after Bergmane, *Politics of Uncertainty*, p. 143.
54. Quoted after Dominik Wilczewski, *Litwa po litewsku*, Sękowa: Wydawnictwo Czarne, 2024, p. 141.
55. Quoted after Vladas Sirutavičius, 'On the Polish National and Territorial Autonomy in Lithuania (the Spring–Summer of 1991)', *Studia z Dziejów Rosji i Europy Środkowo-Wschodniej*, 52, 2018, special issue (1), pp. 163–95 (p. 190).
56. Quoted after Bergmane, *Politics of Uncertainty*, p. 151.
57. Quoted ibid., p. 154.

7. A COUNTRY IN EUROPE (1991–2024)

1. Constitution of the Republic of Lithuania, https://e-seimas.lrs.lt/portal/legalAct/lt/TAD/TAIS.21892.
2. https://www.saeima.lv/en/legislative-process/constitution.
3. Traktat między Rzecząpospolitą Polską a Republiką Litewską o przyjaznych stosunkach i dobrosąsiedzkiej współpracy, sporządzony w Wilnie dnia 26 kwietnia 1994 r.; Lietuvos Respublikos ir Lenkijos Respublikos draugiškų santykių ir gero kaimyninio bendradarbiavimo sutartis, State Gazette, 16 December 1994.
4. https://www.lrt.lt/en/news-in-english/19/2238006/red-line-and-turning-point-lithuania-s-path-to-joining-nato-20-years-ago.
5. https://www.baltictimes.com/news/articles/26513/.
6. Vladas Sirutavičius, 'Perestroika, Sąjūdis, 11 March 1990, and the Lithuanian Jews', in Vladas Sirutavičius, Jurgita Šiaučiūnaitė-Verbickienė, and Darius Staliūnas (eds), *The History of the Jews in Lithuania: From the Middle Ages to the 1990s*, Leiden: Brill, 2020, pp. 460–1.

p. [392]

7. Valdas Rakutis, *Prieš panyrant į sutemas. Lietuva XVIII amžiuje: kai ir Lenkija, ir Varšuva buvo mūsų*, Vilnius: Alma Littera, 2022.
8. Quoted after Davoliūtė, *The Making and Breaking of Soviet Lithuania*, pp. 175–6.

FURTHER READING

Endnotes have been kept to a minimum, largely restricted to references for quotations and statistics that are not widely available and uncontested. Few readers would benefit from an attempt to provide a long multilingual bibliography, but the selection of works that follow show much recent research has been made available in English, not least in the open-access journal *Lithuanian Historical Studies*, abbreviated as *LHS*.

General

Arloŭ, Uladzimir and Zmicier Hierasimovič, *Belarus. The Epoch of the Grand Duchy of Lithuania: An Illustrated History*, Minsk: Technalohija, 2018.

Baronas, Darius, Liudas Jovaiša, Mindaugas Paknys, Eligijus Raila, and Arūnas Streikas, *Christianity in Lithuania*, Vilnius: Aidai, 2002.

Bill, Stanley and Simon Lewis (eds), *Multicultural Commonwealth: Poland–Lithuania and Its Afterlives*, Pittsburgh: University of Pittsburgh Press 2023.

Briedis, Laimonas, *Vilnius: City of Strangers*, Budapest: Central European University Press, 2009.

Davies, Norman, *Vanished Kingdoms: The History of Half-Forgotten Europe*, London: Allen Lane, 2011.

Eidintas, Alfonsas, Alfredas Bumblauskas, Antanas Kulakauskas, Mindaugas Tamošaitis, *The History of Lithuania*, Vilnius: Eugrimas, 2013.

Frost, Robert, 'Ordering the Kaleidoscope: The Construction of Identities in the Lands of the Polish-Lithuanian Commonwealth since 1569', in Len Scales and Oliver Zimmer (eds), *Power and the Nation in European History*, Cambridge: Cambridge University Press, 2005, pp. 212–31.

Guesnet, François and Jerzy Tomaszewski z"l (eds), *Sources on Jewish Self-Government in the Polish Lands from Its Inception until the Present*, Leiden: Brill, 2022.

Hosking, Geoffrey, *Russia: People and Empire, 1552–1917*, London: Harper Collins, 1997.

Janonienė, Rūta, Tojana Račiūnaitė, Marius Iršėnas, and Adomas Butrimas (eds), *The Lithuanian Millennium: History, Art and Culture*, Vilnius: Vilnius Academy of Arts Press, 2015.

Kalnins, Mara, *Latvia: A Short History*, London: Hurst, 2015.

Kasekamp, Andres, *A History of the Baltic States*, Basingstoke: Palgrave Macmillan, 2010.

Kiaupa, Zigmantas, *The History of Lithuania*, 2nd edn, Vilnius: Baltos lankos, 2004.

Kiaupa, Zigmantas, Jūratė Kiaupienė, and Albinas Kuncevičius, *The History of Lithuania before 1795*, Vilnius: Lithuanian Institute of History, 2000.

Liekis, Šarūnas, Antony Polonsky, and Chaeran Freeze (eds), *Jews in the Former Grand Duchy of Lithuania since 1772*, vol. 25 of *Polin: Studies in Polish Jewry*, Oxford: Littman Library of Jewish Civilization, 2013.

Lieven, Anatol, *The Baltic Revolution: Estonia, Latvia, Lithuania and the Path to Independence*, New Haven: Yale University Press, 1993.

Mickūnaitė, Giedrė, *Making a Great Ruler: Grand Duke Vytautas of Lithuania*, Budapest: Central European University Press, 2006.

Nikžentaitis, Alvydas, Stefan Schreiner, and Darius Staliūnas (eds), *The Vanished World of Lithuanian Jews*, Amsterdam: Rodopi, 2004.

Nowak, Andrzej, *History and Geopolitics: A Contest for Eastern Europe*, Warsaw: Polish Institute of International Affairs, 2008.

O'Connor, Kevin C., *The History of the Baltic States*, 2nd edn, Santa Barbara, CA: Greenwood, 2015.

Ochmański, Jerzy, 'The National Idea in Lithuania from the 16th to the First Half of the 19th Century: The Problem of Cultural-Linguistic Differentiation', *Harvard Ukrainian Studies*, 10:3/4, 1986, pp. 301–15.

Plakans, Andrejs, *A Concise History of the Baltic States*, Cambridge: Cambridge University Press, 2011.

FURTHER READING

Plokhy, Serhii, *The Origins of the Slavic Nations: Premodern Identities in Russia, Ukraine and Belarus*, Cambridge: Cambridge University Press, 2006.

Polonsky, Antony, *The Jews in Poland and Russia*, 3 vols, Oxford: The Littman Library of Jewish Civilisation, 2010–12.

Potašenko, Grigorijus (ed.), *The Peoples of the Grand Duchy of Lithuania*, Vilnius: Aidai, 2002.

Sirutavičius, Vladas, Jurgita Šiaučiūnaitė-Verbickienė, and Darius Staliūnas (eds), *The History of the Jews in Lithuania: From the Middle Ages to the 1990s*, Leiden: Brill, 2020.

Snyder, Timothy, *The Reconstruction of Nations: Poland, Ukraine, Lithuania, Belarus, 1569–1999*, New Haven, CT: Yale University Press, 2003.

Taylor, Neil, *Estonia: A Modern History*, 3rd edn, London: Hurst, 2025.

Vardys, V. Stanley and Judith B. Sedaitis, *Lithuania: The Rebel Nation*, Boulder, CO: Westview Press, 1997.

Venclova, Tomas, *Vilnius: A Personal History*, Riverdale-on-Hudson: Sheep Meadow Press, 2009.

Weeks, Theodore R., *Vilnius Between Nations 1795–2000*, DeKalb, IL: Northern Illinois University Press, 2015.

Chapter 1
The Rise of an Empire

Banytė-Rowell, Rasa, 'Brides for the Afterlife? Some Considerations on Female Burials from West Lithuania in the Third Century CE', *Wiadomości Archeologiczne*, 73, 2022, pp. 109–30.

Baranauskas, Tomas, 'On the Origin of the Name of Lithuania', *Lituanus*, 55:3, 2009, pp. 28–36.

Baronas, Darius, 'The Encounter between Forest Lithuanians and Steppe Tatars in the Time of Mindaugas', *LHS*, 11, 2006, pp. 1–16.

Baronas, Darius, 'The Year 1009: St Bruno of Querfurt between Poland and Rus'', *Journal of Medieval History*, 34:1, 2008, pp. 1–22.

Baronas, Darius and Rowell, S. C., *The Conversion of Lithuania: From Pagan Barbarians to Late Medieval Christians*, Vilnius: Institute of Lithuanian Literature and Folklore, 2015.

FURTHER READING

Berend, Nora (ed.), *Christianization and the Rise of Christian Monarchy: Scandinavia, Central Europe and Rus'*, Cambridge: Cambridge University Press, 2007.

Biermann, Felix, Christofer Hermann, Arkadiusz Koperkiewicz, and Edvinas Ubis, 'Burning Alt-Wartenburg. Archaeological Evidence for the conflicts between Teutonic Order and Grand Duchy of Lithuania from the deserted medieval town near Barczewko (Warmia, Poland)', *Lietuvos Archeologija*, 45, 2019, pp. 265–93.

Christiansen, Eric, *The Northern Crusades*, 2nd edn, London: Penguin, 1997.

Duczko, Władysław, *Viking Rus: Studies on the Presence of Scandinavians in Eastern Europe*, Leiden: Brill, 2004.

Franklin, Simon and Jonathan Shepard, *The Emergence of Rus 750–1200*, London and New York: Routledge, 2013.

Giedroyć, Michał, The Arrival of Christianity in Lithuania: Early Contacts (Thirteenth Century)', *Oxford Slavonic Papers*, new series, 18, 1985, pp. 1–30.

Giedroyć, Michał, 'The Arrival of Christianity in Lithuania: Between Rome and Byzantium, 1281–1341', *Oxford Slavonic Papers*, new series, 20, 1987, pp. 1–33.

Giedroyć, Michał, 'The Arrival of Christianity in Lithuania: Baptism and Survival, 1341–1387', *Oxford Slavonic Papers*, new series, 22, 1989, pp. 34–57.

Gimbutas, Marija, *The Prehistory of Eastern Europe*, part 1: *Mesolithic, Neolithic and Copper Age Cultures in Russia and the Baltic Area*, Cambridge, MA: Peabody Museum, 1956.

Gimbutas, Marija, *The Balts*, London: Thames and Hudson, 1963.

Gimbutas, Marija, 'The Indo-Europeans: Archaeological Problems', *American Anthropologist*, 65, 1963, pp. 815–36.

Gimbutas, Marija, *The Civilization of the Goddess: The World of Old Europe*, San Francisco: Harper, 1991.

Haak, Wolfgang, et al., 'Massive Migration from the Steppe is a Source for Indo-European Languages in Europe', *Nature*, 522, 2015, pp. 207–11.

Heather, Peter, *Empires and Barbarians: The Fall of Rome and the Birth of Europe*, Oxford: Oxford University Press, 2009.

FURTHER READING

Heather, Peter, 'Race, Migration and National Origins', in *History, Memory and Public Life: The Past in the Present*, ed. Anna Maerker, Simon Sleight, and Adam Sutcliffe, London: Routledge, 2018, pp. 80–100.

Kalnins, Mara, *The Ancient Amber Routes: Travels from Rīga to Byzantium*, Riga: Pētergailis Press, 2013.

Lasberg, Katrin, *Chronology of the Weichselian Glaciation in the South-Eastern Sector of the Scandinavian Ice Sheet*, Tartu: University of Tartu Press, 2014.

Mažeika, Rasa, 'Was Grand Prince Algirdas a Greek Orthodox Christian?', *Lituanus*, 33, 1987, pp. 35–55.

Mažeika, Rasa, 'The Grand Duchy Rejoins Europe: Post-Soviet Developments in the Historiography of Medieval Lithuania', *Journal of Medieval History*, 21, 1995, pp. 289–303.

Michałowski, Roman, *The Gniezno Summit: The Religious Premises of the Founding of the Archbishopric of Gniezno*, Leiden: Brill, 2016.

Mittnik, Alissa, et al., 'The Genetic Prehistory of the Baltic Sea Region', *Nature Communications*, 9, 2018, p. 442.

Petrauskas, Rimvydas, 'The Gediminids, the Algirdids and the Jagiellonians: *stirps regia* in the Grand Duchy of Lithuania', in Eugenijas Saviščevas and Marijus Uzorka (eds), *Lithuania—Poland—Sweden: European Dynastic Unions and Historical-Cultural Ties*, Vilnius: National Museum–Palace of the Grand Dukes of Lithuania, 2014, pp. 35–49.

Reynolds, Susan, 'Empires: A Problem of Comparative History', *Historical Research*, 79, 2006, pp. 151–65.

Rowell, S. C., 'Between Lithuania and Rus´: Dovmont-Timofey of Pskov, His Life and Cult', *Oxford Slavonic Papers*, new series, 25, 1992, pp. 1–33.

Rowell, S. C., 'Pious Princesses or Daughters of Belial? Pagan Lithuanian Dynastic Diplomacy, 1279–1423', *Medieval Prosopography*, 15:1, 1994, pp. 3–79.

Rowell, S. C., *Lithuania Ascending: A Pagan Empire within East-Central Europe, 1295–1345*, Cambridge: Cambridge University Press, 1994.

Rowell, S. C., 'Baltic Europe', in *The New Cambridge Medieval History*, vol. 6: *c. 1300–c. 1415*, ed. Michael Jones, Cambridge: Cambridge University Press, 2000, pp. 697–734.

Rowell, S. C., '1386: The Marriage of Jogaila and Jadwiga Embodies the Union of Lithuania and Poland', *LHS*, 11, 2006, pp. 137–44.

FURTHER READING

Spretnak, Charlene, 'Anatomy of a Backlash: Concerning the Work of Marija Gimbutas', *Journal of Archaeomythology*, 7, 2011, pp. 1–27.

Verkholantsev, Julia, 'Ruthenia (Lithuania-Rus)', in David Wallace (ed.), *Europe: A Literary History, 1348–1418*, Oxford: Oxford University Press, 2016, vol. 2, pp. 420–39.

Vitkūnas, Manvydas, and Gintautas Zabiela, *Baltic Hillforts: Unknown Heritage*, Vilnius: Society of the Lithuanian Archaeology, 2017.

CHAPTER 2
FORGING A UNION

Backus, Oswald P., *Motives of West Russian Nobles in Deserting Lithuania for Moscow, 1377–1514*, Lawrence: University of Kansas Press, 1957.

Dubonis, Artūras, Darius Antanavičius, Raimonda Ragauskienė, and Ramunė Šmigelskytė-Stukienė, *The Lithuanian Metrica: History and Research*, Boston: Academic Studies Press, 2020.

Ekdahl, Sven, 'The Turning Point in the Battle of Tannenberg (Grunwald/Žalgiris)', *Lituanus*, 56:2, 2010.

Frost, Robert, *The Oxford History of Poland-Lithuania*, vol. 1: *The Making of the Polish-Lithuanian Union 1385–1569*, Oxford: Oxford University Press, 2015.

Gudavičius, Edvardas, 'Lithuania's Road to Europe', *LHS*, 2, 1997, pp. 15–27.

Kiaupienė, Jūratė, 'The Grand Duchy of Lithuania in East Central Europe, or Once Again about the Lithuanian-Polish Union', *LHS*, 2, 1997, pp. 56–71.

Kiaupienė, Jūratė, 'The Grand Duchy of Lithuania and the Grand Dukes of Lithuania in the Sixteenth Century: Reflections on the Lithuanian Political Nation and the Union of Lublin', in Richard Butterwick (ed.), *The Polish-Lithuanian Monarchy in European Context, c. 1500–1795*, Basingstoke: Palgrave, 2001, pp. 82–92.

Kiaupienė, Jūratė, *Between Rome and Byzantium: The Golden Age of the Grand Duchy of Lithuania's Political Culture*, Boston, MA: Academic Studies Press, 2019.

Kołodziejczyk, Dariusz, *The Crimean Khanate and Poland-Lithuania: International Diplomacy on the European Periphery (15th–18th Century)*,

FURTHER READING

A Study of Peace Treaties Followed by an Annotated Edition of Relevant Documents, Leiden: Brill, 2011.

Kriegseisen, Wojciech, *Between State and Church: Confessional Relations from Reformation to Enlightenment: Poland—Lithuania—Germany—Netherlands*, Frankfurt-am-Main: Peter Lang, 2016.

Mickūnaitė, Giedrė, *Maniera Greca in Europe's Catholic East: On Identities of Images in Lithuania and Poland (1380s–1720s)*, Amsterdam: Amsterdam University Press, 2023.

Norkus, Zenonas, *An Unproclaimed Empire: The Grand Duchy of Lithuania from the Viewpoint of the Comparative Sociology of Empires*, New York: Routledge, 2020.

Nowakowska, Natalia, *Church, State and Dynasty in Renaissance Poland: The Career of Cardinal Fryderyk Jagiellon (1468–1503)*, Aldershot: Ashgate, 2017.

Nowakowska, Natalia, *King Sigismund of Poland and Martin Luther: The Reformation before Confessionalization*, Oxford: Oxford University Press, 2018.

Nowakowska, Natalia (ed.), *Remembering the Jagiellonians*, London: Routledge, 2018.

Padalinski, Uladzimir, 'The Representation of the Grand Duchy of Lithuania in the Final Stage of the Seym of Lublin (June to August 1569)', *Zapiski Historyczne*, 79:4, 2014, pp. 27–51.

Pawlikowska, Wioletta, 'The Challenge of Trent and the Renewal of the Catholic Church in the Grand Duchy of Lithuania: The Higher Clergy of Vilnius and the Problems of Plural Benefices and Residence in the Sixteenth Century', *Bažnyčios Istorijos Studijos*, 4, 2011, pp. 37–56.

Pawlikowska, Wioletta, 'Marriage or Mitre? The Careers of Bishops from the Pac Family in the Grand Duchy of Lithuania during the Reformation and Counter-Reformation', *Slavonic and East European Review*, 99:4, 2021, pp. 700–27.

Pawlikowska-Butterwick, Wioletta, 'A Foreign Elite? The Territorial Origins of the Canons and Prelates of Vilna in the Second Half of the Sixteenth Century', *Slavonic and East European Review*, 92:1, 2014, pp. 44–80.

Pawlikowska-Butterwick, Wioletta, 'Regarding the Sixteenth-Century Statutes of the Chapters of Vilna and Samogitia', in Wioletta Pawlikowska-

FURTHER READING

Butterwick and Liudas Jovaiša (eds), *Vilniaus ir Žemaičių katedrų kapitulų Statutai / The Statutes of the Chapters of Vilna and Samogitia*, Vilnius: Lietuvių katalikų mokslo akademija, 2015, pp. 113–213.

Pawlikowska-Butterwick, Wioletta, 'Property and Personal Relations in the Jurydyka of the Vilna Cathedral Chapter in the Sixteenth and Early Seventeenth Century (with Particular Reference to the Scandalous and Suspicious Misdeeds of Canon Isaac Fechtinus)', *Wschodni Rocznik Humanistyczny*, 13, 2016, pp. 53–82.

Petrauskas, Rimvydas, 'The Lithuanian Nobility in the Late Fourteenth- and Fifteenth Centuries: Composition and Structure', *LHS*, 7, 2002, pp. 1–22.

Rowell, S. C., 'Forging a Union? Some Reflections on the Early Jagiellonian Monarchy', *LHS*, 1, 1996, pp. 6–21.

Rowell, S. C., 'Bears and Traitors or: Political Tensions in the Grand Duchy, c.a. 1440–1481', *LHS*, 2, 1997, pp. 28–55.

Rowell, S. C., 'Casimir Jagiellończyk and the Polish Gamble', *LHS*, 4, 1999, pp. 7–39.

Rowell, S. C., '1446 and All That', in Irena Valikonytė (ed.), *Lietuva ir jos kaimynai: Nuo normanų iki Napoleono*, Vilnius: Lietuvos istorijos institutas, 2001, pp. 188–277.

Rowell, S. C., 'Dynastic Bluff? The Road to Mielnik, 1385–1501', *LHS*, 6, 2001, pp. 1–22.

Rowell, S. C., 'The Joyous Entry of Casimir I and IV into Lithuanian and Polish Cities', *LHS*, 11, 2006, pp. 89–106.

Rowell, S. C., 'Was Fifteenth-Century Lithuanian Catholicism as Lukewarm as Sixteenth-Century Reformers Would Have Us Believe?', *Central Europe*, 8:2, 2010, pp. 86–106.

Vilimas, Darius, 'The Formation of the Land Court System in the Grand Duchy of Lithuania (1564–1588)', *LHS*, 10, 2005, pp. 1–28.

Chapter 3
A Commonwealth of Two Nations?

Ambroziak, Tomasz, 'The Necessity to Reexamine the Question of Lithuanian Particularism during the Reign of Sigismund III and Władysław IV', *Zapiski Historyczne*, 79:4, 2014, pp. 89–109.

FURTHER READING

Augustyniak, Urszula, *History of the Polish-Lithuanian Commonwealth: Society—State—Culture*, Frankfurt-am-Main: Peter Lang, 2015.

Bardach, Juliusz, 'The Constitution of 3 May and the Mutual Guarantee of the Two Nations', in Samuel Fiszman (ed.), *Constitution and Reform in Eighteenth-Century Poland: The Constitution of 3 May 1791*, Bloomington, IN: Indiana University Press, pp. 357–78.

Bem, Kazimierz, *Calvinism in the Polish Lithuanian Commonwealth 1548–1648: The Churches and the Faithful*, Leiden: Brill, 2020.

Blanning, Tim, *Augustus the Strong: A Study in Artistic Greatness and Political Fiasco*, London: Allen Lane, 2024.

Butterwick, Richard, *Poland's Last King and English Culture: Stanisław August Poniatowski, 1732–1798*, Oxford: Clarendon Press, 1998.

Butterwick, Richard, 'Catholicism and Enlightenment in Poland-Lithuania', in Ulrich L. Lehner and Michael Printy (eds), *A Companion to the Catholic Enlightenment in Europe*, Leiden: Brill, 2010, pp. 297–358.

Butterwick, Richard, *The Polish Revolution and the Catholic Church 1788–1792: A Political History*, Oxford: Oxford University Press, 2012.

Butterwick, Richard, *The Polish-Lithuanian Commonwealth 1733–1795: Light and Flame*, New Haven, CT: Yale University Press, 2020.

Butterwick, Richard, and Wioletta Pawlikowska (eds), *Social and Cultural Relations in the Grand Duchy of Lithuania: Microhistories*, New York: Routledge, 2019.

Butterwick-Pawlikowski, Richard, 'Before and After Suppression: Jesuits and Former Jesuits in the Polish-Lithuanian Commonwealth, c. 1750–1795', in Robert A. Maryks and Jonathan Wright (ed.), *Jesuit Survival and Restoration: A Global History, 1773–1900*, Leiden: Brill, 2015, pp. 51–66.

Constitution of 3 May 1791. English Translation from 1791 by Franciszek Bukaty, foreword Anna Grześkowiak-Krwawicz, Warsaw: Muzeum Łazienki Królewskie and Archiwum Główne Akt Dawnych, 2018.

Dukwicz, Dorota, 'The Internal Situation in the Polish-Lithuanian Commonwealth (1769–1771) and the Origins of the First Partition (in the Light of Russian Sources)', *Acta Poloniae Historica*, 103, 2011, pp. 67–84.

Filipczak-Kocur, Anna, 'Poland-Lithuania before Partition' in Richard

FURTHER READING

Bonney (ed.), *The Rise of the Fiscal State in Europe c. 1200–1815*, pp. 443–79.

Frick, David, *Meletij Smotryc′kyj*, Cambridge, MA: Harvard Ukrainian Research Institute, 1995.

Frick, David, *Kith, Kin, and Neighbors: Communities and Confessions in Seventeenth-Century Wilno*, Ithaca, NY: Cornell University Press, 2013.

Friedrich, Karin, 'Polish-Lithuanian Political Thought, 1450–1700', in Howell Lloyd et al. (eds), *History of European Political Thought, 1450–1700*, New Haven, CT: Yale University Press, 2007, pp. 409–47.

Friedrich, Karin, 'Noble Power Brokerage in the Polish-Lithuanian Commonwealth: The Case of Bogusław Radziwiłł', in Jakub Basista, Adam Kaźmierczyk, Mariusz Markiewicz, and Dominika Oliwa (eds), *Miscellanea res Polonorum, Brittanorum ac Judaeorum illustrantia*, Kraków: Historia Iagellonica, 2015, pp. 13–26.

Friedrich, Karin, 'Political Loyalties in the Commonwealth's Borderlands: Bogusław Radziwiłł (1620–1669) and the Problem of Treason', in Yvonne Kleinmann et al. (eds), *Imaginations and Configurations of Polish Society: From the Middle Ages through the 20th Century*, Göttingen: Wallstein Verlag, 2017 pp. 143–73.

Friedrich, Karin, and Barbara Pendzich (eds), *Citizenship and Identity in a Multinational Commonwealth: Poland-Lithuania in Context, 1550–1772*, Leiden: Brill, 2009.

Frost, Robert, *After the Deluge: Poland-Lithuania and the Second Northern War 1655–1660*, Cambridge: Cambridge University Press, 1993.

Frost, Robert, 'The Nobility of Poland-Lithuania, 1569–1795', in H. M. Scott (ed.), *The European Nobilities in the Seventeenth and Eighteenth Centuries*, 1st edn, Harlow: Longman, 1995, vol. 2, pp. 183–222.

Frost, Robert, *The Northern Wars: War, State and Society in Northeastern Europe, 1558–1721*, Harlow: Longman, 2000.

Frost, Robert, '"Everyone Understood what it Meant": The Impact of the Battle of Poltava on the Polish-Lithuanian Commonwealth', *Harvard Ukrainian Studies*, 31:1, 2009, pp. 159–76.

Frost, Robert, 'The Ethiopian and the Elephant? Queen Louise Marie Gonzaga and Queenship in an Elective Monarchy, 1645–1667', *Slavonic and East European Review*, 91:4, 2013, pp. 787–817.

FURTHER READING

Grześkowiak-Krwawicz, Anna, *The Political Discourse of the Polish-Lithuanian Commonwealth: Concepts and Ideas*, New York: Routledge, 2020.

Guesnet, François, 'The Jews of Poland-Lithuania (1650–1815)', in *The Cambridge History of Judaism*, vol. 7: *The Early Modern World, 1500–1815*, ed. J. Karp and A. Sutcliffe, Cambridge: Cambridge University Press, 2018, pp. 798–830.

Hundert, Gershon D., *Jews in Poland-Lithuania in the Eighteenth Century*, Berkeley, CA: University of California Press, 2004.

Jones, Robert E., 'Runaway Peasants and Russian Motives for the Partitions of Poland', in Hugh Ragsdale (ed.), *Imperial Russian Foreign Policy*, Cambridge: Cambridge University Press, 1993, pp. 103–16.

Kempa, Tomasz, 'The Issue Regarding "the Reform of the Union" of Lublin in Lithuanian Policy in the Period of the Three Interregna following the Death of King Sigismund Augustus (1572–1588)', *Zapiski Historyczne*, 79:4, 2014, pp. 53–88.

Kempa, Tomasz, 'Religious Tolerance and Intolerance in Vilnius in the Sixteenth and Seventeenth Centuries', in Andrzej Chwalba and Krzysztof Zamorski (eds), *The Polish-Lithuanian Commonwealth: History, Memory, Legacy*, New York: Routledge, 2021, pp. 138–55.

Kopczyński, Michał, and Wojciech Tygielski (eds), *Under a Common Sky: Ethnic Groups of the Commonwealth of Poland and Lithuania*, Warsaw: Polish History Museum, 2017.

Kotljarchuk, Andrej, 'Ruthenian Protestants of the Grand Duchy of Lithuania and their relationship with Orthodoxy, 1569–1767', *LHS*, 12, 2007, pp. 41–62.

Lewitter, L. R., 'Russia, Poland and the Baltic, 1697–1721', *Historical Journal*, 11:1, 1968, pp. 3–34.

Litwin, Henryk, 'Catholicisation among the Ruthenian Nobility and Assimilation Processes in the Ukraine during the years 1569–1648', *Acta Poloniae Historica*, 55, 1987, pp. 57–83.

Lord, Robert Howard, *The Second Partition of Poland: A Study in Diplomatic History*, Cambridge, MA: Harvard University Press, 1915.

Lukowski, Jerzy, 'The Papacy, Poland, Russia and Religious Reform, 1764–8', *Journal of Ecclesiastical History*, 39:1, 1988, pp. 66–92.

FURTHER READING

Lukowski, Jerzy, *Liberty's Folly: The Polish-Lithuanian Commonwealth in the Eighteenth Century*, London: Routledge, 1991.

Lukowski, Jerzy, *The Partitions of Poland: 1772, 1793, 1795*, Harlow: Longman, 1999.

Lukowski, Jerzy, *Disorderly Liberty: The Political Culture of the Polish-Lithuanian Commonwealth in the Eighteenth Century*, London: Continuum, 2010.

Maciejko, Paweł, *The Mixed Multitude: Jacob Frank and the Frankist Movement, 1755–1816*, Philadelphia, PA: University of Pennsylvania Press, 2011.

Madariaga, Isabel de, *Russia in the Age of Catherine the Great*, New Haven, CT: Yale University Press, 1981.

Meilus, Elmantas, 'The Jews of Lithuania during the Muscovite Occupation (1655–1660)', *LHS*, 14, 2009, pp. 53–70.

Michalski, Jerzy, *Rousseau and Polish Republicanism*, Warsaw: Instytut Historii PAN, 2015.

Michałowska-Mycielska, Anna, *The Council of Lithuanian Jews, 1623–1764*, Warsaw: Dialog, 2016.

Pawlikowska, Wioletta, '*Politiques* or *Zélés*? The Lithuanian Bishops and the Confederation of Warsaw (1573–1615)', in Robert Tomczak and Darius von Güttner-Sporzyński (eds), *Interregnum. Between Hereditary and Elective Monarchy*, Turnhout: Brepols, 2025 (forthcoming).

Pawlikowska-Butterwick, Wioletta, '"Lithuanians", "Foreigners" and Ecclesiastical Office: Law and Practice in the Grand Duchy of Lithuania', *Journal of Ecclesiastical History*, 68:2, 2017, pp. 285–305.

Plokhy, Serhii, *The Cossacks and Religion in Early Modern Ukraine*, Oxford: Oxford University Press, 2001

Rosman, Moshe J., *The Lord's Jews: Magnate-Jewish Relations in the Polish-Lithuanian Commonwealth during the 18th Century*, Cambridge, MA: Center for Jewish Studies and the Harvard Ukrainian Research Institute, 1990.

Roşu, Felicia, *Elective Monarchy in Transylvania and Poland-Lithuania, 1569–1587*, Oxford: Oxford University Press, 2017

Šapoka, Mindaugas, *War, Loyalty, and Rebellion: The Grand Duchy of Lithuania and the Great Northern War, 1709–1717*, London and New York: Routledge, 2018.

FURTHER READING

Šiaučiūnaitė-Verbickienė, Jurgita, 'The Social and Legal Status of Jews in the Grand Duchy of Lithuania and its Influence on the Status of Tatars and Karaites', *Central Europe*, 8:2, 2010, pp. 68–85.

Šiaučiūnaitė-Verbickienė, Jurgita, 'The Bankruptcy of the Vilnius Jewish Community in the Second Half of the 18th Century. The Structure of the Debts and the Process of their Repayment', *LHS*, 26, 2022, pp. 29–61.

Šiaučiūnaitė-Verbickienė, Jurgita, 'Was the Lithuanian Va'ad Abolished? Some Remarks on the History of Jewish Self-Government in the Grand Duchy of Lithuania', *Jewish Culture and History*, 24:3, 2023, pp. 293–312.

Skinner, Barbara, *The Western Front of the Eastern Church: Uniate and Orthodox Conflict in Eighteenth-Century Poland, Ukraine, Belarus, and Russia*, DeKalb, IL: Northern Illinois University Press, 2009.

Sliesoriūnas, Gintautas, 'Changes in Attitudes Towards Russia Among the Lithuanian-Polish Elite at the Turn of the Seventeenth and Eighteenth Centuries', *LHS*, 9, 2004, pp. 1–18.

Sliesoriūnas, Gintautas, 'The First Occupation of Vilnius During the Great Northern War (April–May 1702)', *LHS*, 14, 2009, pp. 71–104.

Šmigelskytė-Stukienė, Ramunė, '*Les Sujets mixtes*: The Problem of Double Subordination in the Period of the Partition of the Polish-Lithuanian Commonwealth, and the Case of Mykolas Kleopas Oginskis', *LHS*, 19, 2014, pp. 111–34.

Šmigelskytė-Stukienė, Ramunė, *Michał Kleofas Ogiński. Politician, Diplomat and Minister (1786–1794)*, Vilnius: Petro ofsetas, 2015.

Šmigelskytė-Stukienė, Ramunė, 'The Modernisation of the Court System in the Grand Duchy of Lithuania: Changes to the Organisation of the Local District Courts and Regulation of Judges' Duties in 1764–1793', *LHS*, 21, 2017, pp. 1–30.

Sysyn, Frank, 'Orthodoxy and Revolt: The Role of Religion in the Seventeenth-Century Ukrainian Uprising against the Polish-Lithuanian Commonwealth', in James D. Tracy and Marguerite Ragnow (eds), *Religion and the Early Modern State*, Cambridge: Cambridge University Press, 2004, pp. 154–84.

Teller, Adam, *Money, Power and Influence in Eighteenth-Century Lithuania:*

FURTHER READING

The Jews on the Radziwiłł Estates, Stanford, CA: Stanford University Press, 2016.

Teter, Magda, 'Jewish Conversions to Catholicism in the Polish-Lithuanian Commonwealth of the Seventeenth and Eighteenth Centuries', *Jewish History*, 17:3, 2003, pp. 257–83.

Zamoyski, Adam, *The Last King of Poland*, London: Weidenfeld and Nicolson, 1992.

Zujienė, Gitana, 'Witchcraft Court Cases in the Grand Duchy of Lithuania in the Sixteenth to Eighteenth Centuries', *LHS*, 20, 2015, pp. 79–125.

Chapter 4
Under Imperial Rule

Aleksandravičius, Egidijus, 'Political Goals of Lithuanians, 1883–1918', *Journal of Baltic Studies*, 23:3, 1992, pp. 227–38.

Aoshima, Yoko, and Darius Staliūnas (eds), *The Tsar, the Empire, and the Nation: Dilemmas of Nationalization in Russia's Western Borderlands, 1905–1915*, Budapest: Central European University Press, 2021.

Baar, Monika, *Historians and Nationalism: East-Central Europe in the Nineteenth Century*, Oxford: Oxford University Press, 2010.

Balkelis, Tomas, *The Making of Modern Lithuania*, London and New York: Routledge, 2009.

Blobaum, Robert, *Feliks Dzierżyński and the SDKPiL: A Study of the Origins of Polish Communism*, Boulder: Columbia University Press, 1984.

Czubaty, Jarosław, '"What is to be Done when the Motherland has Died?", The Moods and Attitudes of Poles after the Third Partition 1795–1806', *Central Europe*, 7:2, 2009, pp. 95–109.

Dixon, Simon, *The Modernisation of Russia 1676–1825*, Cambridge: Cambridge University Press, 1999.

Hroch, Miroslav, *Social Preconditions of National Revival in Europe: A Comparative Analysis of the Social Composition of Patriotic Groups Among the Smaller European Nations*, Cambridge: Cambridge University Press, 1985.

Inglot, Marek, 'The Society of Jesus in the Russian Empire (1772–1820) and the Restoration of the Order', in Robert A. Maryks and Jonathan

FURTHER READING

Wright (eds), *Jesuit Survival and Restoration: A Global History, 1773–1900*, Leiden: Brill, 2015, pp. 67–82.

Kamuntavičienė, Vaida, 'The Last Decades of the Existence of the Kaunas Bernardine Nuns (1842–1864)', *LHS*, 25, 2021, pp. 31–58.

Katilius, Algimantas, 'Memorandum of the Governor-General of the Vilna Gubernia Sviatopolk-Mirskii on the Lithuanian Latin Alphabet', *LHS*, 9, 2004, pp. 89–104.

Klier, John D., *Russia Gathers Her Jews: The Origins of the 'Jewish Question' in Russia, 1772–1825*, De Kalb, IL: Northern Illinois University Press, 1986.

Łossowski, Piotr, 'Russian Authorities' Policies towards National Minorities: Prohibition of Lithuanian Publications, 1864–1904', *Acta Poloniae Historica*, 88, 2003, pp. 65–84.

Mačiulis, Dangiras, 'The Commemoration of the 40th Anniversary of the Kražiai Massacre in Lithuania and Poland', *LHS*, 26, 2022, pp. 63–95.

Mačiulis, Dangiras and Darius Staliūnas, *Lithuanian Nationalism and the Vilnius Question, 1883–1940*, Marburg: Verlag Herder-Institut, 2015.

Merkys, Vytautas, 'Bishop Motiejus Valančius, Catholic Universalism and Nationalism', *LHS*, 6, 2001, pp. 69–88.

Miknys, Rimantas, 'Vilnius and the Problem of Modern Lithuanian Statehood in the Early Twentieth Century', *LHS*, 2, 1997, pp. 108–20.

Miknys, Rimantas, 'Decisions of the Lithuanian Assembly (the Great Seimas of Vilnius) of 4–5 December 1905', *LHS*, 10, 2005, pp. 145–54.

Motieka, Egidijus, 'The Great Assembly of Vilnius, 1905', *LHS*, 1, 1996, pp. 84–96.

Sirutavičius, Vladas and Darius Staliūnas (eds), *A Pragmatic Alliance: Jewish-Lithuanian Political Cooperation at the Beginning of the 20th Century*, Budapest: Central European University Press, 2011.

Skrupskelis, Ignas K., *Emancipating Lithuania: The Early Years of President Grinius*, Kaunas: Vytautas Magnus University, 2020.

Staliūnas, Darius, '"The Pole" in the Policy of the Russian Government: Semantics and Praxis in the Mid-Nineteenth Century', *LHS*, 5, 2000, pp. 45–67.

Staliūnas, Darius, 'An Awkward City: Vilnius as a Regional Centre in Russian Nationality Policy (ca 1860–1914)', in Andrzej Nowak (ed),

FURTHER READING

Russia and Eastern Europe: Applied 'Imperiology', Warsaw: Instytut Historii PAN, 2006, pp. 222–43.

Staliūnas, Darius, 'Between Russification and Divide and Rule: Russian Nationality Policy in the Western Borderlands in mid-19th Century', *Jahrbücher für Geschichte Osteuropas*, 55:3, 2007, pp. 357–373.

Staliūnas, Darius, *Making Russians: Meaning and Practice of Russification in Lithuania and Belarus after 1863*, Amsterdam: Rodopi, 2007.

Staliūnas, Darius, 'Hybrid Identities in the Era of Ethno-Nationalism: The Case of the *Krajowcy* in Lithuania', *Acta Baltico-Slavica*, 42, 2018, pp. 253–70.

Urbaniak, George, 'Lithomania versus Panpolonism: The Roots of the Polish-Lithuanian Conflict Before 1914', *Canadian Slavonic Papers*, 31:2, 1989, pp. 107–27.

Weeks, Theodore D., 'Defining Us and Them: Poles and Russians in the "Western Provinces," 1863–1914', *Slavic Review*, 53:1, 1994, pp. 26–40.

Weeks, Theodore D., *Nation and State in Late Imperial Russia: Nationalism and Russification on the Western Frontier, 1863–1914*, DeKalb, IL: Northern Illinois University Press, 1996.

Weeks, Theodore D., 'Russification and the Lithuanians, 1863–1905', *Slavic Review*, 60:1, 2001, pp. 96–114.

Zamoyski, Adam, *1812: Napoleon's Fatal March on Moscow*, London: Harper Collins, 2004.

Zawadzki, Hubert, *A Man of Honour: Adam Czartoryski as a Statesman of Russia and Poland, 1795–1831*, Oxford: Oxford University Press, 1993.

Chapter 5
Breaking Empires, Making Nations?

Balkelis, Tomas, 'War, State, Ethnic Conflict and the Refugee Crisis in Lithuania, 1939–1940', *Contemporary European History* 16:4, 2007, pp. 461–77.

Balkelis, Tomas, *War, Revolution, and Nation-Making in Lithuania, 1914–1923*, Oxford: Oxford University Press, 2018.

Bendikaitė, Eglė, 'The Zionist Press on Lithuanian-Jewish Economic Rivalry in the 1930s', *LHS*, 10, 2005, pp. 121–44.

Böhler, Jochen, *Civil War in Central Europe, 1918–1921: The Reconstruction of Poland*, Oxford: Oxford University Press, 2018.

FURTHER READING

Eidintas, Alfonsas, *Antanas Smetona and His Lithuania: From the National Liberation Movement to an Authoritarian Regime (1893–1940)*, Leiden: Brill, 2015.

Giedroyć, Michał, *Crater's Edge: A Family's Epic Journey through Wartime Russia*, London: Bene Factum Publishing, 2010.

Gierowska-Kałłaur, Joanna, 'Death-Agony and Birth-Pangs: Inheritors of the Grand Duchy of Lithuania under German Occupation 1915–1918', *Central Europe*, 17:2, 2019, pp. 110–25.

Griffante, Andrea, *Children, Poverty and Nationalism in Lithuania, 1900–1940*, Cham: Palgrave, 2019.

Jokubauskas, Vytautas and Hektoras Vitkus, 'Jews as Lithuanian Army Soldiers in 1918–1940 (a Quantitative Analysis)', *LHS*, 25, 2021, pp. 99–133.

Gimžauskas, Edmundas, 'The Belorussian Factor in the Genesis of the Modern Lithuanian State, 1915–1917', *LHS*, 6:1, 2001, pp. 107–26.

Laurinavičius, Česlovas, 'On the Political Power of the Act of 16 February 1918', *LHS*, 4, 1999, pp. 138–42.

Laurinavičius, Česlovas, 'Once Again on Soviet Statehood in Lithuania in 1918–1919', *LHS*, 13, 2008, pp. 179–90.

Liekis, Šarūnas, *A State within a State: Jewish Autonomy in Lithuania 1918–1925*, Vilnius: Versus aureus, 2003.

Liekis, Šarūnas, *1939: The Year that Changed Everything in Lithuania's History*, Amsterdam: Rodopi, 2010.

Liulevicius, Vejas, *War Land on the Eastern Front: Culture, National Identity and German Occupation in World War I*, Cambridge: Cambridge University Press, 2000.

Nowak, Andrzej, 'Reborn Poland or Reconstructed Empire? Questions on the Course and Results of Polish Eastern Policy (1918–1921)', *LHS*, 13, 2008, pp. 127–50.

Norkus, Zenonas, Aelita Ambruliviciute, and Jurgita Markeviciute, 'Real Wages of Lithuanian Construction Workers from 1913 to 1939 (Measured in Subsistence and Welfare Ratios) in a Cross-National Comparison', *LHS*, 23, 2019, pp. 25–57.

Pease, Neal, 'God's Patriot: Jerzy Matulewicz as Bishop of Vilna, 1918–25', *East Central Europe*, 18:1, 1991, pp. 69–79.

FURTHER READING

Pease, Neal, *Rome's Most Faithful Daughter: The Catholic Church and Independent Poland, 1914–1939*, Athens, OH: Ohio University Press, 2009.

Richter, Klaus, *Fragmentation in East-Central Europe: Poland and the Baltics, 1915–1929*, Oxford: Oxford University Press, 2020.

Rudling, Per Anders, *The Rise and Fall of Belarusian Nationalism 1906–1931*, Pittsburgh: University of Pittsburgh Press, 2015.

Senn, Alfred Erich, *The Emergence of Modern Lithuania*, New York: Columbia University Press, 1959.

Senn, Alfred Erich, *The Great Powers, Lithuania and the Vilna Question, 1920–1928*, Leiden: Brill, 1966.

Senn, Alfred Erich, *Lithuania 1940: Revolution from Above*. Amsterdam: Rodopi, 2007.

Stravinskienė, Vitalija, 'Ethnic-Demographic Changes in the Data of the Statistical Sources of the City of Vilnius (1920–1939)', *LHS*, 17, 2012, pp. 125–46.

Stravinskienė, Vitalija, 'I Cannot Find Any Work or Service ...' The Unemployed in Vilnius in 1920–1939', *LHS*, 21, 2017, pp. 107–36.

Tauber, Joachim, 'German Eastern Policy, 1917–1918', *LHS*, 13, 2008, pp. 67–74.

Zimmerman, Joshua D., *Jozef Pilsudski: Founding Father of Modern Poland*, Cambridge, MA: Harvard University Press, 2022.

CHAPTER 6
HAMMER, SWASTIKA, AND SICKLE

Bergmane, Una, *Politics of Uncertainty: The United States, the Baltic Question, and the Collapse of the Soviet Union*, New York: Oxford University Press, 2023.

Brandišauskas, Valentinas, 'The June Uprising of 1941', *LHS*, 3, 1998, pp. 49–72.

Christie, Paula, 'The Baltic Chain: A Study of the Organisation Facets of Large-Scale Protest from a Micro-level Perspective', *LHS*, 20, 2015, pp. 183–211.

Davoliūtė, Violeta, *The Making and Breaking of Soviet Lithuania: Memory and Modernity in the Wake of War*, London and New York: Routledge, 2013.

FURTHER READING

Dean, Martin C., *Collaboration in the Holocaust: Crimes of the Local Police in Belorussia and Ukraine, 1941–1944*, New York: St Martin's Press, 2000.

Donskis, Leonidas, *Identity and Freedom: Mapping Nationalism and Social Criticism in Twentieth-Century Lithuania*, London: Routledge, 2001.

Grinkevičiūtė, Dalia, *Shadows on the Tundra*, trans. Delija Valiukenas, Bath: Peirene, 2018.

Grybkauskas, Saulius, 'The Second Party Secretary and his Personal Networks in Soviet Lithuania after 1964: Towards the Localisation of the "Second"', *LHS*, 15, 2010, pp. 27–49.

Grybkauskas, Saulius, 'The Hunting Club of Petras Griškevičius and the Consolidation of the Lithuanian Nomenklatura', *LHS*, 18, 2013, pp. 123–46.

Grybkauskas, Saulius, 'Soviet Modernisation, Atheism and Insular Lithuanian Society', *LHS*, 20, 2015, pp. 213–31.

Grybkauskas, Saulius, 'The Making of the Titular Nation Engineers in Soviet Lithuania and Latvia (from the End of the 1940s to the mid-1950s)', *LHS*, 22, 2018, pp. 137–60.

Hedlund, Stefan, 'The Mice That Roared', in Charles Clarke (ed.), *Understanding the Baltic States: Estonia, Latvia and Lithuania since 1991*, London: Hurst, 2023, pp. 75–90.

Hiden, John, Vahur Made, and David J. Smith (eds), *The Baltic Question during the Cold War*, London: Routledge, 2008.

Ivanauskas, Vilius, 'Lithuanian Writers and the Establishment during Late Socialism: The Writers Union as a Place for Conformism or Escape', *LHS*, 15, 2010, pp. 51–78.

Kaszeta, Dan, *The Forest Brotherhood: Baltic Resistance against the Nazis and Soviets*, London: Hurst, 2023.

Laukaitytė, Regina, 'A Postwar Social Crisis: The Flood of Beggars into Lithuania in 1944–1947', *LHS*, 26, 2022, pp. 129–54.

Mikailienė, Živilė, 'Soviet Vilnius: Ideology and the Formation of Identity', *LHS*, 15, 2010, pp. 171–89.

Miłosz, Czesław, *Native Realm: A Search for Self-Definition*, London: Penguin, 2014.

Misiunas, Romuald J., and Rein Taagepera, *The Baltic States: Years of*

FURTHER READING

Dependence, 1940–1980, Berkeley and Los Angeles: University of California Press, 1983.

Moorhouse, Roger, *The Devils' Alliance: Hitler's Pact with Stalin, 1939–1941*, London: The Bodley Head, 2014.

Rindzevičiūtė, Eglė, 'Imagining the Grand Duchy of Lithuania: The Politics and Economics of the Rebuilding of Trakai Castle and the "Palace of Sovereigns" in Vilnius', *Central Europe*, 8:2, 2010, pp. 181–203.

Senn, Alfred Erich, *Gorbachev's Failure in Lithuania*. New York: St. Martin's Press, 1995.

Shapiro, Paul A., and Carl J. Reins (eds), *Lithuania and the Jews: The Holocaust Chapter*, Washington D.C.: United States Holocaust Memorial Museum, 2004.

Sirutavičius, Vladas, 'On the Polish National and Territorial Autonomy in Lithuania (the Spring-Summer of 1991)', *Studia z Dziejów Rosji i Europy Środkowo-Wschodniej*, 52, 2018, special issue (1), pp. 163–95.

Sirutavičius, Vladas, 'Between National and Indigenous Communism. Some Broad Brushtrokes in the Political Biography of Justas Paleckis: 1944–1953', *LHS*, 23, 2019, pp. 85–116.

Snyder, Timothy, *Bloodlands: Europe Between Hitler and Stalin*, London: The Bodley Head, 2010.

Stasiulis, Stanislovas, 'The Holocaust in Lithuania: The Key Characteristics of Its History, and the Key Issues in Historiography and Cultural Memory', *East European Politics and Society: and Cultures*, 34:1, 2020, pp. 261–79.

Stravinskienė, Vitalija, 'Soviet Passports and Their Implementation in East and Southeast Lithuania (1944–1989)', *LHS*, 23, 2019, pp. 117–43.

Terleckas, Antanas, 'The Sovietisation of Rural Areas of Lithuania: A Case Study of the Lenin's Way Kolkhoz in Deltuva (1948–1957)', *LHS*, 25, 2021, pp. 135–73.

Tranavičiūtė, Brigita, 'Soviet Consumer Goods Advertising: Propaganda and Consumption in the 1950s–1980s in Lithuania', *LHS*, 22, 2018, pp. 111–35.

Weeks, Theodore, 'Repopulating Vilnius, 1939–1949', in Tomas Balkelis and Violeta Davoliūtė (eds), *Population Displacement in the Twentieth Century: Experiences, Identities and Legacies*, Leiden: Brill Rodopi, 2016, pp. 135–59.

FURTHER READING

Chapter 7
A Country in Europe

Burant, Stephen R., 'Overcoming the Past: Polish-Lithuanian Relations, 1990–1995', *Journal of Baltic Studies*, 27:4, 1996, pp. 309–29.

Clarke, Charles, (ed.), *Understanding the Baltic States: Estonia, Latvia and Lithuania since 1991*, London: Hurst, 2023.

Kuczyńska-Zonik, Aleksandra and Andrzej Pukszto (eds), *Unique Treaty: Relations between the Republic of Poland and the Republic of Lithuania (1994–2024)*, Lublin: Instytut Europy Środkowej, 2024.

Mole, Richard C. M., *The Baltic States from the Soviet Union to the European Union: Identity, Discourse and Power in the Post-Communist Transition of Estonia, Latvia and Lithuania*, New York: Routledge, 2012.

Rogers, Monika, 'Law, Crime, and the Criminal Justice System's Transformation in Post-Soviet Lithuania: Some Trends and Functioning', *LHS*, 27, 2023, pp. 161–96.

Staliūnas, Darius, 'From Ethnocentric to Civic History: Changes in Contemporary Lithuanian Historical Studies', in Kimitaki Matsuzato (ed.), *Emerging Meso-Areas in the Former Socialist Countries: Histories Revived or Improvised?*, Hokkaido: Hokkaido University, 2005, pp. 311–31.

Švedas, Aurimas, 'Has the Soviet Experiment Truly Come to an End? Historiography, Places of Memory and the Political Elite', *LHS*, 15, 2010, pp. 157–70.

Wilson, Andrew, *Belarus: The Last European Dictatorship*, New Haven, CT: Yale University Press, 2011.

INDEX

B. Belarusian, Cz. Czech, Geo. Georgian, G. German, H. Hungarian I. Italian, L. Lithuanian, Lat. Latin, Latg. Latgalian, Latv. Latvian, P. Polish, R. Russian, Sam. Samogitian, U. Ukrainian, Y. Yiddish.

Abišala, Aleksandras (b. 1955), 368
Abramowicz, Ludwik (1879–1939), 253
Academy of Sciences of the Lithuanian SSR, 233–4, 327
Adalbert, Saint (Cz. Vojtěch, P. Wojciech, c.956–97), 24–5
Adam of Bremen (d. 1081/85), 21
Adamkus, Valdas (b. 1926 as Voldemaras Adamkavičius), 362, 372, 375, 377, 379, 391
Aestii, 21
Ahtisaari, Martti (1937–2023), 379
Åland Islands, 201
Albania, 259, 375
Albert, Bishop of Riga, 27
Albert II, King of Germany, 71
Albrecht von Hohenzollern, Duke of Prussia (1490–1568), 80–1
Aldona (baptised Anna, 1311/13–39), 43
Aleksandr Nevskii, film, 33

Aleksei II, Patriarch of Moscow (1929–2008), 356
Aleksei Mikhailovich, Tsar of Muscovy (1629–76), 122–3, 126
Alexander I, Emperor of Russia (1777–1825), 183, 186–9, 193, 196
Alexander II, Emperor of Russia (1818–81), 201–2, 206, 239
Alexander III, Emperor of Russia (1845–94), 220
Alexander V, Pope/Antipope (c.1339–1410), 44
Alexander, Grand Duke of Lithuania and King of Poland (1461–1506), 72, 76–9, 397
Alfred the Great, King of Wessex, 21
Algirdas, Grand Duke of Lithuania (c.1304–77), 5, 38–41, 43–4, 397
alphabets, Cyrillic and Latin, 25, 86, 191, 204, 209–11, 239, 262

INDEX

Alytus (P. Olita), 323
Amber 8, 16, 20–21
'Amber Declaration', 248
Ambraziejus, Juozapas (1855–1915), 221
America in the Bathhouse (Amerika pirtyje) (Antanas and Juozas Vilkutaitis), 216
Anders, Władysław (1892–1970), 302–3, 317
Andrei of Polatsk (L. Andrius Algirdaitis, c.1325–99), 41
Andropov, Yurii (1914–84), 342, 344
Anna Ivanovna, Empress of Russia (1693–1740), 151
Anna Jagiellon, Grand Duchess of Lithuania and Queen Regnant of Poland (1523–96), 102, 397
Anna Vasilovna (c.1393–1417), 63
Anti-Fascist Struggle Organisation, 309
antisemitism, 225, 235–6, 240, 262, 272, 277, 284, 293, 309, 325, 392
Anti-Trinitarians, 85, 120
Aragón, 86
Arctic, 15, 302
Armenia, 348, 362
Armenian Apostolic Church, 389
Ashmiany (L. Ašmena, P. Oszmiany), 69, 268
Astikas (baptised Cristinus, 1363–1443), 67
Astrava (P. Ostrowo), 54
Athos, Mount, 32
Atlantic Charter, 315, 342
Atlantic Ocean, 16, 17, 159, 288
Augustów, governorate, 217

Augustus II, Grand Duke of Lithuania and King of Poland, Friedrich August I Wettin, Elector of Saxony (1670–1733), 135–41, 143
Augustus III, Grand Duke of Lithuania and King of Poland, Friedrich August II Wettin, Elector of Saxony (1696–1763), 143–4, 151–2, 154, 168
Aukštaitija, 29, 4, 36–7, 242
Auschwitz-Birkenau, 309–10
Austria, 45, 233, see also Habsburg dynasty and monarchy
  Austrian monarchy (to 1804) 100, 135, 152, 158, 164, 173, 175
  Austrian Empire (1804–67), 45, 135, 157–8, 164, 198, 203, 238
  Austria-Hungary (1867–1918), 39, 181, 253, 256
Avignon, 62

Bačkis, Audrys, Cardinal, Archbishop of Vilnius (b. 1938), 379
Bačkis, Stasys (1906–99), 315
Bahdanovich, Maksim (1891–1917), 237, 382
Baker, James (b. 1930), 348
Baku, 357
Baliński family, 394
Baliński, Michał (1794–1864), 192
Balkelis, Tomas (b. 1970), 247
Baltakis, Algimantas (1930–2022), 300–1
Baltic languages, 2, 17–19, 22–4, 54, 81
Baltic peoples, 18–20, 22–4, 35–6, 81

INDEX

Baltic provinces, see Estonia, Latvia, and Livonia
Baltic Sea, 3, 5, 15–16, 20–1, 23–4, 27, 29, 109, 161, 201, 216, 249, 253, 288, 290, 313, 383
Baltic states, 'Baltics', 1–3, 24, 261–2, 290–1, 295, 304–5, 314–15, 341–5, 350–60, 362–3, 369, 377, 381–3, see also Estonia, Latvia, Lithuania
'Baltic Unity Day', 28
'Baltic Way', 1, 351
Baltušis, Juozas (1909–91), 330, 349
Bar, Confederation of (1768–72), 157
Baranauskas, Antanas, Bishop of Sejny (1835–1902), 221
Baranauskas, Tomas (b. 1973), 29
Baranavichy (P. Baranowicze), 282
Barbara, née Radziwiłł, Grand Duchess of Lithuania and Queen of Poland (L. Barbora Radvilaitė, c.1520–51), 6, 10–11, 86–7, 397
Baronas, Darius (b. 1973), 39, 42, 57, 63, 83
Basanavičius, Jonas (1851–1927), 217–18, 226–7, 248–9, 255–8, 264, 283, 331, 393
Basketball, 288
Bastuny (L. Bastūnai), 267
Batakietis, Jonas (P. Jan Batocki, d. 1558), 84
'Battle of the Sun' (Saulė, 1236), 28
Be2gether Festival, 395
Beauvoir, Simone de (1908–86), 334
Begin, Menachem (1913–92), 302
Belarus, 11, 15, 26, 45, 59, 105, 310, see also Rusˊ

in the Grand Duchy of Lithuania (to 1795), 29, 39, 50, 79, 107, 118, 125, 158, 173
in the Russian Empire (1795–1918) 179–91, 197–207, 212, 222–6, 234–42
in the Republic of Poland (1918–39) 279–83, 292
Belarusian People's Republic (Belaruskaia Narodnaia Respublika, 1918), 247, 259–60
Belarusian Soviet Socialist Republic (BSSR, 1920–91), 144, 266, 275, 281, 292–3, 304, 312, 318, 327, 344, 353, 359–60, 394–6
Under German occupation (1941–44) 304, 306, 310
Republic of (1991–), 3, 4, 50, 65, 197, 204–5, 362, 369, 382–3, 387, 392, 394–6
Belarusian Assembly of Peasants and Workers (Hromada), 281
Belarusian language, 10, 17, 50, 190–1, 200, 204–5, 207, 212, 222, 232, 234–9, 251–2, 262, 280–81, 284, 328, see also *ruski*
Belarusian Socialist Assembly, 224, 236–7
Belarusians 10, 50, 97, 113, 129, 156, 180, 182, 205, 229, 234, 237–9, 247–53, 259–63, 279–83, 292–4, 317, 382, 387, 389
Belgium, 248, 263
Bell, The (Varpas), 218–23, 228, 275
Bender (now Tighina, Moldova), 140
Benedict XV, Pope (1854–1922), 254

445

INDEX

Beraz'vechcha (P. Berezwecz), 144
Bergmane, Una, 315–16
Beria, Lavrenty (1899–1953), 320–1
Berkeley, University of California at, 336
Berlin, 84, 157, 183–4, 258, 260, 304
Berlin Wall, 343
Bermondt-Avalov, Pavel (1877–1973), 265
Bethmann-Hollweg, Theobald von (1856–1921), 253
Białowieża (B. Belavezha) Forest, 250, 360
Białystok (B. Belastok, R. Belostok, Y. Byalistok), 259, 266
Biarezina, river (P./R. Berezyna), 124, 187
Biron, Ernst, Duke of Courland (G. Ernst von Bühren, 1690–1772), 151–2
Biržiška, Mykolas (1882–1962), 256, 264
Black Sea, 5, 17, 22, 23, 54, 74, 153, 161, 201, 249
Blake, William (1757–1827), 188
Bobelis, Jurgis (1895–1954), 308
Bodin, Jean (c.1530–96), 101
Bohemia, 24, 36, 61, 64, 72–3, 81, 196
Bohusz, Ksawery (L. Ksaveras Bohušas, 1746–1820), 192
Bolesław the Valiant, King of Poland (P. Chrobry, c.967–1025), 24–5
Bolingbroke, see Henry IV
Bolivia, 216
Bona Sforza, Grand Duchess of Lithuania and Queen of Poland (1494–1557), 81, 86–8, 397
Borisevičius, Vincentas, Bishop of Telšiai (1887–1946), 338
Borisov, Yurii (L. Jurijus Borisovas, b. 1956), 375
Borodino, Battle of (1812), 187, 205
Bourdeaux, Michael (1934–2021), 339
Brandenburg, 113, 126, see also Prussia
Branicki, Jan Klemens (1689–1771), 155
Branicki, Ksawery (c.1730–1819), 165, 171
Braslaŭ (P. Brasław, L. Breslauja), 266
Brazauskas, Algirdas (1932–2010), 346, 352–3, 357, 367–9, 371–80
Brest (P. Brześć), 55, 85, 147, 280, 292
  palatinate, 156
  Treaty of Brest-Litovsk (1918), 256, 259
  Union of (1596), 121–2, 127, 198, see also Uniate Church
Bretke, Johannes (L. Jonas Bretkūnas, 1536–1602), 84
Brezhnev, Leonid (1906–82), 324, 341, 342, 344
Briansk, principality, 39
British-Lithuanian Society, 317
Bronze Age, 19–20
Bruno of Querfurt, Saint, 25
Brzostowski, Konstanty, Bishop of Vilnius (1644–1722), 132
Bubnys, Arūnas (b. 1961), 311
Bug, river (U. Zakhidnyi Buh,

INDEX

B. Zakhodni Buh), 61, 171–2, 253
Bulgaria, 70, 218, 375
Bułhak, Jan (1876–1950), 241–2
Bumblauskas, Alfredas (b. 1956), 391
Bund (Algemeyner Yidisher Arbeter-bund in Lite, Poyln un Rusland), 224
Burke, Edmund (1729–97), 168
Bush, George H. W. (1924–2018), 348, 352, 358–60
Bush, George W. (b. 1946), 375
Butkevičius, Algirdas (b. 1958) 380
Butvydas, see Pukuveras
Byzantine empire, 35, 39, 44, 58, 75, 76

Caffa (U. Feodosiia), 54
California, 17
Calvin, Jean (1509–64), 85
Calvinism, 10, 85, 101, 112–14, 116, 118, 120, 130, 156, 183, 389, 394
Canada, 19, 354
Carpathian Mountains, 22, 37, 69–70
Casimir, Saint (1458–84), 3, 72, 397
Casimir the Great, King of Poland (1310–70), 43–4
Casimir Jagiellon, Grand Duke of Lithuania and King of Poland (1427–92), 64, 70–6, 99, 397
Caspian Sea, 17
Catherine Jagiellon, Queen of Sweden (1526–83) 106, 397
Catherine II the Great, Empress of Russia (1729–96), 154–9, 163–4, 171, 173, 175, 183–4, 199, 383
statue in Vilnius, 241, 248
Catholicism, Roman Catholic Church, 107, 109, 114, 117, 121, 124, 155, 238, 338
conversions of pagans to 3–5, 7, 24–5, 27, 30–2, 43–6, 49, 56–7, 229
in the Grand Duchy of Lithuania (to 1569), 5, 33–4, 51, 53, 57–61, 65–7, 69, 83–6, 90
in the Grand Duchy of Lithuania (to 1795), 104–5, 112, 118–20, 128, 130–2, 144, 157, 160
and Jews, 146–7, 148, 150
in Poland, 43, 52, 99, 125, 157
conversions of Orthodox and Protestants to, 114, 121, 124, 136, 156, 238
Counter-Reformation, 114–19
and Enlightenment, 155–6, 163, 167–8
in the Russian Empire (1795–1915), 183–4, 194, 198, 207, 218, 220
and temperance, 208–9
and literacy in Lithuanian, 193, 208, 209–10, 214
and Lithuanian nationalism, 216, 218–19, 221, 226–8, 230–2, 238, 242
and Polish nationalism, 236, 238–9
in the Republic of Lithuania (1918–40, 1990–), 4, 266, 274–7, 388–9
in the Republic of Poland (1918–39) 274, 280–2
in the USSR (1940–41, 1944–90), 144, 292, 332, 337–41

INDEX

Černius, Jonas (1898–1977), 291, 295
Charlemagne (748–814), 21
Charles IX Vasa, King of Sweden (1550–1611), 107–8
Charles X Gustavus Vasa, King of Sweden (1622–60), 124–6
Charles XII Vasa, King of Sweden (1682–1718), 138–40, 150
Chashniki, Battle of (1564), 89–90
Chełm (U. Kholm), 198
Chernenko, Konstantin (1911–85), 342, 344
Cherniaev, Anatolii (1921–2017), 347
Cherniakhovskii, Ivan (1907–45), 313, 331
Chernobyl nuclear power plant, 344–5
Chicago, 213, 316
China, 382
Chişinău, 356
Chlewiński, Antoni (d. 1800), 174
Chodakauskaitė-Smetonienė, Sofija (P. Zofia Chodakowska, 1885–1968), 223
Chodkiewicz family (L. Chodkevičius, B. Khodkevich), 91, 113
Chodkiewicz, Jan (B. Ivan Khodkevich (c.1537–79), 93
Chodkiewicz, Jan Karol (c.1561–1621), 108, 112
Chojnice (G. Konitz), Battle of (1454), 74
Christendom, 24, 30–2, 36–7, 41, 52, 61–3, 84, 114
Christian Families Alliance, 380
Christian, Bishop, 31
Christianity, see Christendom, Catholicism, Orthodoxy, Protestantism
Christina Vasa, Queen Regnant of Sweden (1626–89), 124
Chronicle of the Grand Duchy of Lithuania and Samogitia, 81–2
Cieplak, Jan, Archbishop of Vilnius (1857–1926), 274
Čiurlionis, Mikalojus Konstantinas (P. Mikołaj Konstanty Czurlanis, 1875–1911), 229–30, 242
Civil Administration of the Eastern Lands (Zarząd Cywilny Ziem Wschodnich), 263
Claudius Ptolemy (c.100–c.170), 21
Clement XIV, Pope (1705–74), 162
Cleveland, Ohio, 296
Columbus, Christopher (1451–1506), 72
Communist Party of Lithuania/LSSR, 296–7, 302, 318, 324–5, 328, 340–1, 345–6, 352–3, 355, 359, 388
Communist Party of the Soviet Union, 297, 302, 324, 343–4, 348, 351–2
Politburo, 342, 344–5, 351, 358
confederations, 100–1, 126, 129, 136, 141, 157–9, 164–5, 168, 171–3
Conference for Security and Cooperation in Europe, 355
Conrad, Duke of Mazovia (c.1187–1247), 28
Constance (G. Konstanz), Council of (1414–18), 62–3

INDEX

Constantine, Roman Emperor, 3
Constantinople, 5, 24, 39, 57, 63, 74, 389
Constitution of 3 May 1791, 166–71
Constitution of 1922, 271
Constitution of 1928, 277, 283
Constitution of 1938, 278, 290, 353
Constitution of 1992, 363–8, 369, 371, 372, 374, 375, 384, 389
Constitution of the LSSR (1940), 297, 338, 341
Constitution of Estonia, 367
Constitution of Pylyp Orlyk (1709), 140
Constitution of Latvia, 367
Constitution of the USA, 167
Constitutions of the Republic of Poland (1921, 1935, 1997), 278, 279, 367
Constitutions of the USSR (1924, 1936, 1977), 347–8, 353–5
'Constitution' of Užupis, 7
Conti, Prince François-Louis de Bourbon- (1664–1709), 135–6
Copenhagen, 374
Council of Europe, 370
Council of Lords, 66, 70–1, 73, 77–81, 87, 91, 98–9, 105–6
Courland, governorate, 178, 182, 221, 225
Courland and Semigallia, Duchy of (1558–1795), 89, 125, 138, 151–2, 174–5
COVID-19 pandemic, 381
Crécy, Battle of (1346), 36
Crimea, 50, 54–5, 74, 123, 164, 184, 359, 360, 377, 379, 381

Crimean War (1853–56), 201
crusades, 3–4, 27–8, 36–7, 41, 60, 333, see also Livonia, Prussia
Curonia, 27–8, 31
Curonian Spit (L. Neringa), 193, 313, 386
Curonians, 23, 28, 35
Curzon Line, 265, 266
Czartoryski family 151–2, 155
Czartoryska, Izabela née Flemming (1745–1835), 165, 171
Czartoryska, Zofia née Sieniawska (1699–1771), 151
Czartoryski, Adam Jerzy (1770–1861), 183, 188–9
Czartoryski, Adam Kazimierz (1734–1821), 156, 165, 171
Czartoryski, August (1697–1782), 151
Czartoryski, Michał (1696–1775), 151, 165
Czech language, 196, 219
Czechia, 374
Czechoslovakia, 291, 347
Częstochowa, 150

Dabulevičius, Karolis (1898–1988), 308
Dachau, 309–10
Daktaras, Henrikas (b. 1957), 384
Dambrauskas, Aleksandras ('Adomas Jakštas', 1860–1938), 222, 254
Danish Straits, 16
Danylo I, Prince of Halych and Volhynia, King of Rus' (1201–64), 30–2
Darius, Steponas (1896–1933), 288

INDEX

'Dark Ages', 22
Daugava, river (G. Düna,
　P. Dźwina, B. Zakhodniaia
　Dzvina, R. Zapadnaia Dvina), 16,
　18, 23, 27, 89, 125, 265
Daugavpils (Latg. Daugpiļs,
　Y. Denenburg, G. Dünaburg,
　R. Dvinsk, P. Dyneburg,
　B. Dzvinsk), 265
Daujotytė, Viktorija (b. 1945), 350
Daukantas, Simonas (P. Szymon
　Dowkont, 1793–1864), 195, 218
Daumantas, Prince of Pskov
　(R. Dovmont, baptised Timofei,
　d. 1299), 31–2
Daumantas, ruler of Lithuania (d.
　1285), 34
Davoliūtė, Violeta, 300, 311, 330,
　350
Dawn of Nemunas, 392
Dawn, The (*Auszra*, later written
　Aušra), 216–19, 221
Degutienė, Irena (b. 1949), 373
Dekanidze, Boris (1962–95), 384
Dekanozov, Vladimir (1898–1953),
　296
Democratic Labour Party of
　Lithuania, 368, 372–4
Denmark, 23, 138, 295, 354–5
deportations, 9, 198, 206, 299–303,
　307–11, 314, 319–22, 324, 326–7,
　338, 341, 348–50
Dieveniškės (Y. Devenishok,
　P. Dziewieniszki), 395
Długosz, Jan (1415–80), 57, 60, 63
Dmitrii Donskoi, Grand Duke of
　Moscow (1350–89), 40–2
Dmitrii of Briansk (d. 1399), 41

Dmitrii, first False, Tsar of
　Muscovy (d. 1606), 109
Dmitrii, second False, Tsar of
　Muscovy (d. 1610), 109
Dmowski, Roman (1864–1939),
　234–5
Dniapro, river (Lat. Borysthenes,
　R. Dnepr, U. Dnipro), 124, 128,
　129, 164, 187, 238
Dolabella, Tommaso (1570–1650),
　110
Dominicans, 30
Donelaitis, Kristijonas (Lat.
　Christian Donalitius, 1720–78),
　194
Drėma, Vladas (1910–95), 332
Dresden, 141, 152
Druskininkai (P. Druskieniki,
　Y. Druzgenik), 230, 321, 356
Dubienka, Battle of (1792), 172
Dubingiai, 314
Dubnow, Simon (1860–1941), 240
Dunin-Marcinkiewicz, Wincenty
　(B. Vintsent Dunin-
　Martsinkevich, 1808–80), 191,
　237
Durbė, Lake, 31
Dutch Republic (United Provinces),
　111, 164
Dzierżyński, Feliks (R. Feliks
　Dzerzhinskii, 1877–1926), 224,
　266, 331
Dzūkija, 14

Echo of Lithuania (Lietuvos aidas),
　258
Edinburgh, 307
Egypt, 303, 386

INDEX

Einhard (c.775–840), 21
Eisenstein, Sergei (1898–1948), 33
Elbe, river, 22
Electoral Alliance of Poles(-Christian Families Alliance), 379–80
Elizabeth of Austria, Grand Duchess of Lithuania and Queen of Poland (c.1436–1505), 71–2, 76, 397
Elizabeth of Austria, Grand Duchess of Lithuania and Queen of Poland (c.1526–45), 86–7
Elizabeth of Bosnia, Queen of Hungary and Poland (c.1339–87), 45
emigration, 199, 213–18, 223, 239, 248, 255, 272, 288–9, 304, 314–18, 323, 325–7, 386–8
England, 25–6, 36, 111, 154, 175, 377, see also Great Britain
English language, 101, 120, 154, 216, 380
Erik XIV, King of Sweden (1533–77), 89
Ernest of Austria (1553–95), 99
Estonia, 1–4, 9, 11–12, 33, 102, 108
  in the Russian Empire (1721–1918), 182, 210, 250, 253
  Republic of (1918–40), 258, 261, 270, 273, 278, 290, 292, 294–6, 315
  German-occupied (1941–44), 304, 309, 313, 323
  Estonian SSR (1940–41, 1944–91), 297, 319, 321, 341–57
  Republic of (1991–), 360, 362–70, 375–9, 383, 386–7
Estonian language 9, 18, 19, 24, 210, 362
Estonian Popular Front, 351
Estonian Supreme Soviet, 347
Europe, 2, 12, 19–20, 29, 49, 158, 263, 267, 343–4, 351, 362, 363, 367, 375, 379, 381–3, 396
  Eastern and Central, 1, 3–4, 19–20, 23, 58, 103, 245–6, 270, 291, 307
  Western, 52, 103, 110, 153, 342, 363, 377
  medieval, 29, 35, 39, 61
  Jagiellonian, 72
  early modern, 79, 81, 83, 100, 116–17, 119, 120, 144
  nineteenth-century (1795–1914), 176, 180, 183, 186, 202, 235, 240, 243
  twentieth-century (1914–2004), 257, 278, 310, 356
Euro, 380
European Community (1957–92), 360, 363
European Union (EU) (1993–), 2, 9, 300, 361, 363, 369–70, 373–6, 382–3, 387, 389, 394, 396

Familia, see Czartoryski family
Farmer, The (Ūkininkas), 219
fascism, 276, 278
Faustina Kowalska, Saint (1905–38), 275
Fedor I, Tsar of Muscovy (1557–98), 109
Finkelstein, Eitan (b. 1942), 341
Finland, 3, 263, 288, 294–5, 304, 347, 378, 379, 383

451

INDEX

First World War (1914–18), 2, 182, 245–60, 269, 297, 311, 315
Foch, Ferdinand (1851–1929), 265
Ford, Gerald (1913–2006), 316
France 153, 352
   Kingdom of (843–1792, 1814–48), 101–2, 123, 129–30, 133–6, 151, 154, 156, 159, 164
   I Republic (1792–1804, 1870–), 173, 175, 181
   I Empire (1804–14), 185–7
   II Empire (1851–70) 201, 203
   III Republic (1870–1940) 235, 248, 255, 258–9, 270, 272–3, 291–2, 295, 314
   IV Republic (1944–58) 312
   V Republic (1958–) 354, 356, 363, 367, 378, 383
Franciscans, 7, 30, 44, 58, 395
Frank, Jacob (1726–90), 150
Frankists, 150, 185
Franklin, Benjamin (1706–90), 159
Frederick Augustus III/I, Elector, later King of Saxony and Duke of Warsaw (1750–1827), 168
Frederick II the Great, King of Prussia (1712–86), 156–7, 164
Frederick Jagiellon, Cardinal Archbishop of Gniezno (1468–1503), 72
Frederick William II, King of Prussia (1744–97), 164
Frederick William the Great Elector, Duke of Prussia (1620–88), 113, 126–7
Freedom (Laisvė), 266
Freedom Party, 381
French language, 120

French revolutions, 173, 361
Friedrich, Karin (b. 1963), 113
Frost, Robert (b. 1958), 51, 89, 111

Galicia, see also Halych
   Kingdom of Galicia and Lodomeria, (1772–1918), 37, 158, 238–9
   eastern, 266, 317
Galvanauskas, Ernestas (1882–1967), 270
Ganges, river, 17
Gaon of Vilnius, Eliyahu ben Shelomoh Zalman (1720–97), 149, 332, 390
Gargždai (G. Garsden, P. Gorżdy. Y. Gorzhd), 305
Garibaldi, Giuseppe (1807–82), 203
Garuckas, Karolis (1908–79), 341
Gaudemunda (d. 1288), 33
Gdańsk (G. Danzig), 136, 157–8, 173, 356
Gdynia, 327
Gečas vel Gecevičius, Antanas (1916–2001), 306–7
Gediminas, Grand Duke of Lithuania (c.1275–1341), 5–6, 34–5, 38–40, 43–4, 293, 312–13, 397
Gediminid dynasty and ancestry, 38–41, 56, 65–6, 90, 131, 151, 397
Gedvilas, Mečys (1901–81), 297
Geneva, 282–3
Genghis Khan (d. 1227), 40
Gens, Jakub (L. Jakubas Gencas, 1903–43), 309
George II Rákóczi, Prince of Transylvania (1621–60), 126
Georgia, 221, 377

INDEX

German language, 4, 10, 35, 85, 120, 174, 179, 194, 196, 212, 251
German settlement, 5, 27, 34, 249, 270–1, 275, 310–11
Germany, 11, 186, 328, 354
  Holy Roman Empire (800–1806), 25, 28, 31, 52, 64, 71, 115, 135–6
  German Empire (1871–1918), 179, 235–6, 240, 245, 247–60
  German Empire (Weimar Republic, 1918–33), 260–70
  German Empire (Nazi Germany, 1933–45), 245, 247, 279, 289–317, 326, 330, 350–1, 361, 372, 390
  Federal Republic of Germany (1949–), 352, 354–6, 363, 377, 383
Gerulaitis, Vitas (Vytautas) (1954–94), 316
Gestapo, 305, 309, 391
Giedraičiai
  First Battle of (1919), 264
  Second Battle of (1920), 264
Giedroyc, Jerzy (1906–2000), 318, 371
Giedroyć, Józef Arnulf, Bishop of Samogitia (L. Juozapas Arnulfas Giedraitis, 1754–1838), 193
Giedroyć, Melchior, Bishop of Samogitia (L. Merkelis Giedraitis, 1536–1609), 115
Giedroyć, Romuald (L. Romualdas Giedraitis, 1750–1824), 174
Giedroyć, Tadeusz (1888–1941), 292
Giełgud, Antoni (L. Antanas Gelgaudas, 1792–1831), 197

Gielgud, Sir John (1904–2000), 197
Gimbutas, Marija (L. Gimbutienė, 1921–94), 17–19
Girėnas, Stasys (1893–1933), 288
Girija, the geographical centre of Europe, 363
Glaubitz, Johann Christian (d. 1767), 144, 198
Glazman, Yosef (1913–43), 309
Glitiškės (P. Glinciszki), 314
Gniezno, archbishopric and metropolitan province, 25, 52, 72, 115
Golden Horde, 37–8, 54–5, see also Tatars
Gorbachev, Mikhail Sergeievich (1931–2022), 1, 343–59
Gorbunovs, Anatolijs (b. 1942), 355
Gosiewski, Wincenty (c.1620–62), 129
Goštautas family (P. Gasztołd), 67, 80, 86
Goštautas (baptised Andreas, d. 1408), 67
Goštautas, Albertas (P. Olbracht Gasztołd, c.1480–1539), 79, 81–2
Goštautas, Jonas (c.1383–1458), 70
Goštautas, Stanislovas (P. Stanisław Gasztołd, c.1507–42), 86
Great Britain, United Kingdom of (and Ireland/Northern Ireland), 141, 164, 168, 181, 186, 201, 203, 235, 245, 250, 278
  and the Baltic states 265–6, 270, 289–92, 307, 315, 354, 383
  emigration to and from 307, 387
Great Depression, 288–9
Great Northern War (1700–21), 138–41, 144

INDEX

Greater Poland (P. Wielkopolska), 90, 125, 139, 147, 167, 172, 173, 191, 236
Greek language, 18, 35, 39, 117
Greek Catholic Church, see Uniate Church
Gregory XVI, Pope (1765–1846), 198
Grinius, Kazys (1866–1950), 223, 275–6
Grinkevičiūtė, Dalia (1927–87), 349
Griškevičius, Petras (1924–87), 340–1, 345
Grottger, Artur (1837–1867), 205
Grunwald-Tannenberg, Battle of (1410, L. Žalgiris), 60–1, 248
Grybauskaitė, Dalia (b. 1956), 12, 320, 378–80
Guardian of the Fatherland (Tėvynės sargas), 219
Gucewicz, Wawrzyniec, b. Laurynas Masiulis (L. Laurynas Stuoka-Gucevičius, 1753–98), 160–1
Gulf of Finland, 3
Gulf of Riga, 27
Gulf War (I), 355
Gustavus II Adolphus, King of Sweden (1594–1632), 108

Habsburg dynasty, 71, 79, 81, 99, 100, 102, 106, 111, 135, 196
Habsburg monarchy, 181, 196, 245, see also Austria
Hadiach (P. Hadziacz), Union of (1658), 127
Halshanski, Ivan (U. Ivan Hol'shans'kyi, P. Iwan Holszański, L. Jonas Alšėniškis, d. 1402), 64, 66

Halych, principality, 29–33, 37–8, 41
Hannibalson, Jón Baldvin (b. 1939), 356
Hanover, 141
Hanseatic League, 27
Harvard University, 17
Hasidism, 149, 200
Havel, Václav (1936–2011), 357
Hebrew language, 240
Hedlund, Stefan (b. 1953), 343
Hedwig, Queen Regnant of Poland and Saint (P. Jadwiga, c.1373–99), 45–6, 53–4, 59, 397
Helena, Grand Duchess of Lithuania and Queen of Poland (1476–1513), 77
Helena, Saint (d. c.328), 3
Helms, Jesse (1921–2008), 351
Helsinki, 3
Helsinki Accords (1975), 316, 337
Helsinki Group, 336, 341
Henrician Articles, 100, 102
Henry, Grand Duke of Lithuania, King of Poland and France (Fr. Henri III Valois, 1551–89), 100–2
Henry IV, King of England (1367–1413), 36
Herbačiauskas, Juozas Albinas (P. Józef Albin Herbaczewski, 1876–1944), 264
Herder, Johann Gottfried (1744–1803), 18–19, 193, 367
Herodotus (c.484–c.425 BCE), 20
Herzl, Theodor (1860–1904), 240
Heydrich, Reinhard (1904–42), 304–5
Hill of the Crosses (L. Kryžių Kalnas), 337–8

INDEX

Himmler, Heinrich (1900–45), 309
Hindenburg, Paul von (1847–1934), 248
historians and history, 49–51, 97, 112–13, 120, 195–6, 284, 287, 350, 361, 390–2
Hitler, Adolf (1889–1945), 245, 289, 291, 350
Hoffman, Jerzy (b. 1932), 125–6
Hohenzollern dynasty 72, 81, 113, 245, 258
Holy See, 30, 59, 121, 274, 340, see also Catholicism, Rome, Vatican
Home Army (Armia Krajowa), 247, 312–14
Homel', 79
Homeland Union, 369, 372–3, 376–7, 379–82
Homelanders (*krajowcy*), 232–4
Homer, 190
Hope (Viltis), 230
Horodło, Union of (1413), 61–2, 70, 77, 82, 90
Hroch, Miroslav (b. 1932), 180
Hrodna (L. Gardinas, P./R./Y. Grodno), 29, 53, 72, 76, 83, 105, 147, 162, 170, 184, 212, 265, 266, 268, 280, 292, 396
governorate, 180, 199, 204, 206
sejms, 134, 161, 173
Huguenots, 101
Hungary, 24, 37, 41, 44–5, 52–3, 61, 64, 69–70, 72–4, 81, 133, 181, 304, 374
Huns, 22
Hussite revolution, 196
Hymans, Paul, 268

Iceland, 355–6, 360

Igelström, Otto (1737–1823), 173
Ignalina nuclear power plant, 10, 344–5, 378
Ignatius Loyola, Saint (1491–1556), 117
Illyria, 186
Ilūkste (G. Illuxt, L. Ilūkšta, P. Iłukszta), 265, 269
Ilves, Toomas Hendrik (b. 1953), 379
Indies, the 72
Indo-European languages, 17–20
Innocent III, Pope (1161–1216), 27
Innocent IV, Pope (c.1195–1254), 4, 30–1
Iran, 317
Iraq, 355
Ireland, 15, 245, 387, 388
Irkutsk, 322
Israel, 240, 303, 327, 391
Istanbul, 150, 376
Italian language, 120
Italy, 72, 103, 154, 181, 186, 197, 307, 315, 317
Ivan III, Tsar of Muscovy (1440–1505), 75–7
Ivan IV the Terrible, Tsar of Muscovy (1530–84), 79, 88–90, 99, 102–3, 108–9, 114
Ivanauskas, Tadas (P. Tadeusz Iwanowski, 1882–1970), 246
Ivanoŭski, Vatslaŭ (P. Wacław Iwanowski, 1880–1943), 247
Iwanowska, Sabina, née Jaczynowska (1877–1954), 247
Iwanowski family, 246
Iwanowski, Jerzy (1878–1965), 246
Iwanowski, Leonard (1845–1919), 246

INDEX

Iwanowski, Stanisław, 246

Jablonskis, Jonas (1860–1930), 211, 223, 255
Jäger, Karl (1888–1959), 306
Jagiellons, Jagiellonian dynasty, 64, 69–76, 78–83, 86–8, 90, 99, 102, 106, 397
Jałbrzychowski, Romuald, Archbishop of Vilnius (1876–1955), 274–5, 294
Jasiński, Jakub (1761–94), 174
Jašiūnai (P. Jaszuny), 394
Jastrzębiec, Andrzej, Bishop of Vilnius (d. 1398), 58
Jauniūnai, 28
Jefferson, Thomas (1743–1826), 172
Jerusalem, 27, 28
  'of the North/Lithuania', 8, 149, 325
  Patriarch of, 121
Jesuits, 27, 116–23, 130, 155, 162–3, 166, 184, 189, 339, 341
Jews, see also Hebrew language, Israel, Judaism, Yiddish language, Zionism
  settlement, 34, 54, 145, 160
  expulsions and deportations of, 76, 248, 302–3
  population, 144–5, 148, 160, 184–5, 239–40, 252, 272, 283, 293, 325–6, 389
  economic roles, 76, 113, 143, 145–6, 185, 187, 201, 212, 216, 224, 237, 240, 272
  self-government, 54, 146–9, 184–5, 200, 272
  relations with Christians, 54, 145–6, 150, 200
  violence against, 89, 123, 128, 163, 174, 225, 262, 283, 289
Jewish Enlightenment (*Haskalah*), 149, 200, 240
  schools, 149, 200, 240, 251, 272, 301, 325
  and uprisings, 174–5, 203
  in the Russian Empire, 180, 182, 184–5, 199–201, 212, 224 224–6, 229, 232, 237
  during the First World War, 248, 251–3, 262
  and socialism, 224–6, 240
  and Communism, 261–2, 293, 296, 301–2, 324, 326
  in the Republic of Lithuania (1918–40), 271–2, 275, 277, 285–7, 293–4
  in the Republic of Poland (1918–39) 262, 279, 282–4
  Holocaust (*Shoah*), 10, 247, 300, 304–11, 321, 325, 328, 390–1, 395
  partisans and soldiers, 309, 313
  in the LSSR (1940–1, 1944–90), 325–7, 332, 337, 341, 346
  in the Republic of Lithuania (1990–), 389–91
  cemeteries, 10, 332, 395
Jewish Scientific Institution (YIVO), 284, 325
Jogaila, Supreme Duke of Lithuania and King of Poland (P. Władysław II Jagiełło, 1351/52–1434), 5, 41–5, 51–65, 68–9, 76, 195, 397
John I Albert, King of Poland (1459–1501), 72, 76–7, 397
John I, King of Bohemia (1296–1346), 36

INDEX

John II Casimir Vasa, Grand Duke of Lithuania and King of Poland (1609–72), 123, 126, 129–31, 397

John III, King of Sweden (1537–92), 106, 397

John III Sobieski, Grand Duke of Lithuania and King of Poland (1629–96), 132–5

John Paul II, Saint and Pope (1920–2005), 53, 274, 338, 340, 388

Jonas Macys, 222–3

Jordanes, 21

Joselewicz, Berek (1764–1809), 175

Joseph II, Holy Roman Emperor (1741–1790), 158, 164

Judaism, 149–50, 200, 240–41, 326, 389

Julius Caesar, 285

Jurašaitytė-Vailokaitienė, Aleksandra (1895–1957), 256

Jurevičius, Algirdas, Bishop of Telšiai (b. 1972), 379

Jūrmala, 355

Kaczyński, Lech (1949–2010), 377

Kadish, George (Zvi Kadushin, 1910–97), 310

Kairys, Steponas (1879–1964), 256, 312

Kaišiadorys, 379

Kalanta, Romas (1953–72), 340

Kaliningrad, 12, 194, 328, 353, 369, 382–3, see also Königsberg

Kalinowski, Konstanty (B. Kastus' Kalinoŭski, L. Konstantinas Kalinauskas, 1838–64), 204–5, 237, 394

Kalnins, Mara (b. 1945), 18

Kalvarija (P. Kalwaria), 194–5

Kamuntavičius, Rūstis (b. 1975), 50

Kapčiamiestis (P. Kopciowo), 197–8

Karbauskis, Ramūnas (b. 1969), 380

Kaributas (baptised Dmitrii, d. after 1404), 42, 131

Karosas, Antanas, Bishop of Vilkaviškis (1856–1947), 274

Karpowicz, Michał Franciszek (L. Mykolas Prančiskus Karpavičius, 1744–1803), 163, 170, 174

Karuse, Battle of (1270), 33

Karvaičiai (G. Karwaiten), 193

Katyń massacre (1940), 317, 342

Kaunas (G. Kauen, Y. Kovne, R. Kovno, P. Kowno), 43, 124, 189, 197, 219, 228, 248, 251, 260, 266–8, 275, 334, 340, 349, 384, 388

alternative to Vilnius as capital, 231, 286, 329–30

Archbishopric, 274, 339–40

architecture, 287–8

Church of the Assumption of the Blessed Virgin Mary, 58–9

demographics, 160, 213, 251, 286–7, 293–4, 387–8

district sejmik, 152

government, seat of, 261, 264, 271, 289, 290, 296, 303, 329

governorate, 199, 208, 210, 213, 220, 222, 227, 229

House of Perkūnas, 120

Jews in, 240, 272, 301, 305–10, 325–6

Lagoon (Kauno marios), 334, 384

monuments 269, 286

INDEX

museums, 230, 246–7, 286, 288
Officers' Club, 277
Napoleon's Hill, 186
seminary, 338
University, 264, 273, 286–7, 294
Kavolis, Vytautas (1930–86), 337
Kazakhstan, 362
Kėdainiai (P. Kiejdany), 10–11, 229
Kėdainiai Union (1655), 125–6
Kėkštas (Jonas Mačys, 1867–1902), 222
Kernavė, 26, 33
Kęsgaila (baptised Michael, d. c.1450), 67
Kęsgaila family, 67, 80
Keston Institute, 339
Kęstutis (c.1308–82), 5, 40, 42–3, 397
Kettler, Gotthard von, Duke of Courland and Semigallia (1517–87), 89
KGB (Committee for State Security, Komitet gosudarstvennoi bezopasnosti), 338, 340, 356–7, 391
Kharkiv (R. Kharkov) University, 224
Kherson, 54
Khmel′nyts′kyi, Bohdan (P. Bohdan Chmielnicki, 1595–1657), 122–3, 126–7
Khotyn (P. Chocim)
Battle of (1621), 108
Battle of (1673), 132
Khrushchev, Nikita (1894–1971), 323–4, 333, 344
Kiaupienė, Jūratė (b. 1947), 71
Kinka, Romas (b. 1942), 354

Kircholm (Latv. Salaspils), Battle of (1605), 108
Kirkilas, Gediminas (1951–2024), 376
Klaipėda (G. Memel), 10, 31, 270–1, 275, 289–91, 313, 325, 328, 353, 378
Klimaitis, Algirdas (1910–88), 305
Klimas, Petras (1891–1969), 258
Klushino (P. Kłuszyn), Battle of (1610), 109
Kniprode, Winrich von (1310–82), 41
Knyszyn, 98–9
Kohl, Helmut (1930–2017), 352, 354
Kojelavičius-Vijūkas, Albertas (P. Wojciech Wijuk Kojałowicz, 1609–77), 120
Kołłątaj, Hugo (1750–1812), 163, 166, 168–9
Konarski, Stanisław (1700–73), 155–6
Königsberg, 12, 328, 331, see also Kaliningrad
Albertina University, 84, 115, 183–4, 193–4
Konotop, Battle of (1659), 127
Korwin-Milewski, Hipolit (1848–1932), 232–3, 241
Kościałkowski, Stanisław (1881–1960), 161–2
Kościałkowski, Tadeusz (b. c.1750), 166
Kościuszko, Tadeusz (L. Tadas Kosciuška, B. Tadevush Kastiushka, 1746–1817), 156, 159, 172–5, 185, 204, 217

INDEX

Kossakowski, Józef, Bishop of Livonia (L. Juozapas Kosakovskis, 1738–94) 171, 173

Kossakowski, Szymon (L. Simonas Kosakovskis, 1741–94), 157, 171, 173–4

Kovner, Abba (1918–87), 308–9

Kozakiewicz, Władysław (b. 1953), 327

Krajowcy, see homelanders

Kraków, 173, 356
  Academy/University, 59, 118, 163, 233, 264, 294
  (Arch)bishopric, 64, 72, 116, 274
  capital of the Kingdom of Poland, 5, 45–6, 53, 56, 59, 68–9, 77, 81
  coronations in, 45–6, 71, 87, 94, 101, 136
  Wawel Cathedral, 45, 76, 101–2, 284

Krasnoyarsk, 322

Kražiai (P. Kroże), 192, 208, 220

Kretinga, 194–5

Kreva (L. Krėva, P. Krewo), 42
  Union of (1385), 45

Krėvė-Mickevičius, Vincas (1882–1954), 287, 296

Kristiņa, Grizelda Marija (1910–2013), 19

Kriuchkov, Vladimir (1924–2007), 357, 359

Krivichi, 23, 239

Krupavičius, Mykolas (1885–1970), 276

Kubilius, Andrius (b. 1956), 373, 376, 379

Kuchma, Leonid (b. 1938), 379

Kudirka, Vincas (1858–99), 218–19, 221, 223

Kulikovo, Battle of (1380), 43

Kultura (magazine), 318

Kulvietis, Abraomas (c.1510–45), 84

'Kupiškis Wedding' (Kupiškėnų vestuvės), 336

Kuwait, 355

Kvietkauskas, Mindaugas (b. 1976), 242

Kwaśniewski, Aleksander (b. 1954), 379

Kyiv (R. Kiev), 24–5, 74, 123, 129, 199, 223, 229, 266
  Archbishopric and Metropolitanate, 75, 122
  palatinate, 91–2
  principality/duchy, 38–9, 54, 66
  Roman Catholic diocese, 90–1, 115

Kyivan Rus´, 24–5, 37

Kymantaitė-Čiurlionienė, Sofija (1886–1958), 228, 230, 255, 264, 287

L´viv (G. Lemberg, Y. Lemberik, Lat. Leopolis, P. Lwów), 92, 232, 233, 332, 356

Landsbergis, Gabrielius (b. 1982), 380, 382

Landsbergis, Vytautas (b. 1932), 330, 346, 350, 353–6, 359–60, 363, 372, 379, 380, 390

Landsbergis-Žemkalnis, Vytautas (1893–1993), 330

Łaski, Jan (1456–1531), 78

Lastoŭski, Vatslaŭ (P. Wacław Lastowski, 1883–1938), 239, 249

INDEX

Latgale (Latg. Latgola), 4, 265
Latgalian language/dialect, 17–18, 20
Latin language, 18, 25, 35, 54, 85, 101, 190, 195, 220
   official documents in, 5, 35, 86, 93, 135, 140
   literature in, 119–20, 217
   teaching of, 117, 163, 189
   translations into, 82, 106
Latin rite, see Catholicism
Latvia, 1–5, 9, 11–12, 15, 18, 27, 31, 108, 158, see also Courland, Livonia
   in the Russian Empire (1721/72/95–1915/18) 182, 210, 212, 223, 250
   German-occupied (1915–18, 1941–44) 251, 253, 304, 307, 313–14
   Republic of (1918–40), 4, 261, 265–6, 270, 273, 278, 288, 290, 292, 294–6
   Latvian Soviet Socialist Republic (1940–41, 1944–91), 297, 318–53, 341, 343, 347, 350–7
   Republic of (1991–), 28, 353–360, 362–9, 374–9, 382–3, 386–7
Latvian Diplomatic Service, 315
Latvian language, 2, 9, 17–18, 23, 174, 193, 195, 210, 212, 251
Leipzig, 230
Leita, river, 26
Lelewel, Joachim (1786–1861), 188–9
Lena, river, 349
Lenin, Vladimir Iliich Ulianov (1870–1924), 261, 324, 331
Leningrad, 305, 356, 359
Lesser Poland (P. Małopolska), 90, 125–7, 139
Lettgallians, 35
Levinas, Emmanuel (1906–95), 272–3
Liberal Movement, 381
liberum veto, 133–4, 137, 152, 155–7, 158, 168
Lida (L. Lyda), 246, 266, 282
Liepāja (G. Libau), 31
Lietava, river, 26
Lippomano, Luigi (1496–1559), 85
LitBel (Socialist Soviet Republic of Lithuania and Belarus, 1919–20), 261, 266
Lithuania (L. Lietuva, Y. Lite, B./R. Litva, P. Litwa)
   name 25–26, 336
   'Greater Lithuania', 23, 226
   King of (1253–63) 4, 29–31, 37, 258–9, 346
   Grand Duchy and Grand Dukes of (to 1569), 6, 11–12, 26–94
   Grand Duchy of (1569–1795), 97–177, see also Polish-Lithuanian Commonwealth
   political nation of the Grand Duchy of, 51, 68, 71, 76, 86, 93–4, 107, 141
   Grand Duchy of (afterlife) 179–81, 186, 190–1, 195–6, 205, 217–18, 226, 231–3, 236, 253, 260–3, 283, 336, 382, 384, 392
   in the Russian Empire (1795–1915), 179–248
   German-occupied (1915–18, 1941–44/5), 245–60, 301–14

INDEX

Lithuanian Soviet Republic (1918), 261
Republic of (1918–40, (1990–), 245, 257–78, 282, 285–97, 353–96
'Republic of Central Lithuania' (1920–22), 267–8
Lithuanian Soviet Socialist Republic (LSSR, 1940–41, 1944–90), 297, 299–303, 310, 313–14, 318–53, 376, 385–6, 394–5
Lithuania minor (L. Mažoji Lietuva), 3, 179–80, 269–70
Lithuania propria, 29, 39, 41, 54, 57, 63, 65–6, 69, 91, 125, 128
Lithuanian Activists' Front, 304
Lithuanian Art Society, 230
Lithuanian Democratic Party, 218
Lithuanian Diplomatic Service, 315
Lithuanian Farmers and Greens Union, 380
Lithuanian Institute of History, 391
Lithuanian Jewish Cultural Association, 390
Lithuanian Joint-Stock Innovation Bank, 372
Lithuanian language 2, 9–12, 17–23, 49, 58, 190, 192–6, 211–12, 218, 251–2, 261, 287
   in the Grand Duchy of Lithuania, 41, 85, 115, 119, 174, 184
   in Prussia, 84, 179, 193–4, 211–12, 216, 218
   in the Russian Empire, 181, 188, 193, 196, 200–1, 203, 208–23, 226–8, 230–2, 238–9
Lithuanian language policies, 264, 272, 328, 341, 348, 364–5, 371, 392–3
Lithuanian Liberty League, 341, 345–7
Lithuanian National Democratic Party, 227
Lithuanian News (Lietuvos žinios), 230, 242
Lithuanian nobility, 66–8
Lithuanian Partisan War, 318–23, 391
Lithuanian Peasant Union, 227
Lithuanian Popular Front, 345
Lithuanian Provincial Committee, 203
Lithuanian Riflemen's Union, 265
Lithuanian Scientific Society, 230–1
Lithuanian Social Democratic Party, 223–4
Lithuanian Special Squad, 306
Lithuanian Statute, First (1529) 82
Lithuanian Statute, Second (1566), 86, 91–2, 93
Lithuanian Statute, Third (1588), 105–6, 135, 147, 150, 183, 199
Lithuanian Statutes, 191, 364
Lithuanian Territorial Defence Force, 313–14
Lithuanian Union of Working People, 296–7
Lithuanian War Relief Committee, 255
Lithuano–Polish–Ukrainian brigade, 79
Litvaks, see Jews
Litvinenko, Aleksandr (1962–2006), 377

INDEX

Liubartas, Duke of Luts'k (baptised Dmitrii, c.1300–83), 38, 41, 397
Liubeshiv (P. Lubieszów), 156
Liulevicius, Vejas (b. 1966), 251
Livonia, see also Estonia, Latvia
  Bishopric, 27, 33, 171
  Livonian Order (1202/37–1561), 27–28, 30–33, 69, 74, 88–9
  Polish-Lithuanian (1561–1629/1772), 89–90, 102, 107–8, 125, 129, 133, 143, 144
  Swedish (c.1620–1721), 108, 125, 126, 138–9
  in the Russian Empire (1721–1917), 182, 225
Livs, 27
Łomża, diocese, 274
London, 161–2, 318, 339, 354
Louis I the Great, King of Hungary and Poland (1326–82), 41, 44–5, 52
Louis II/I Jagiellon, King of Hungary and Bohemia (H. II. Lajos, Cz. Ludvik I Jagellonský) 1506–26), 81, 397
Louis XIV, King of France (1638–1715), 135
Louis XV, King of France (1710–74), 151
Louise-Marie Gonzaga, Grand Duchess of Lithuania and Queen of Poland (1611–67), 123, 397
Łowmiański, Henryk (1898–1984), 284
Lozoraitis, Stasys (1898–1983), 290, 315
Lozoraitis, Stasys (1924–94), 315, 368

Lublin, 45
  Union of (1569), 51, 92–4, 98, 105
Lubomirska, Ludwika, née Sosnowska (1751–1836), 159
Lubomirski, Jerzy (1616–67), 129–30
Lubys, Bronislovas (1938–2011), 368–9
Ludendorff, Erich (1865–1937), 248–52, 254
Ludwig, Duke of Württemberg (1756–1817), 171
Ludwika Karolina, née Radziwiłł, Princess of Neuburg (1667–95), 132
Lukashenko, Aleksandr (B. Aliaksandr Lukashenka, b. 1954), 50, 204–5, 362, 382, 396
Lukauskaitė-Poškienė, Ona (1906–83), 341
Luts'k (P. Łuck), 38, 54, 55, 64, 69, 92, 115
Luther, Martin (1483–1546), 83
Lutheranism, 4, 81, 83–84, 107, 136, 144, 155, 160, 193, 270, 339, 389
Lutskevich, Anton (1884–1942), 249
Lutskevich, Ivan (1881–1919), 249
Lutterberg, Otto von (d. 1270), 33

Maciejowice, Battle of (1794), 175
Maciejowski, Bernard, Bishop of Kraków (1548–1608), 116
Mačiulevičius, Jonas (d. 1950), 312
Mackevičius, Antanas (P. Antoni Mackiewicz, 1828–63), 203–5

INDEX

Mackiewicz, Józef (1902–85), 284
Mackiewicz, Stanisław 'Cat' (1896–1966), 284
Magdeburg Law, 58
Mahileŭ (P. Mohylew, Y./R. Mogilev), 128
governorate, 178, 180, 206
Maironis (Jonas Mačiulis, 1862–1932), 221–2
Małachowski, Stanisław (1736–1809), 165
Malta summit (1989), 352
Mapu, Abraham (1808–67), 240
Marcinkevičius, Justinas (1930–2011), 320, 330, 335–6, 349
Marcus Aurelius, Roman Emperor, 285
Maria Theresa, Queen Regnant of Hungary and Bohemia, Empress (1717–80), 158
Marienburg, the (P. Malbork), 36, 44, 61
Marijampolė, 211, 217, 219, 228, 254
Martinaitis, Marcelijus (1936–2013), 323
Marx, Karl (1818–83), 324
Marxism-Leninism, 88, 336
Mary, Queen Regnant of Hungary (1371–95), 45
maskilim, 149, 240
Massalski, Ignacy, Bishop of Vilnius (L. Ignotas Masalskis, 1726–94), 160, 163, 184
Matejko, Jan (1838–93), 61
Matulaitis, Blessed Jurgis, Bishop of Vilnius (P. Jerzy Matulewicz, 1871–1927), 254, 274

Matulionis, Blessed Teofilius, Bishop of Kaišiadorys (1873–1962), 338
Maximilian II, Holy Roman Emperor (1527–76), 99, 102, 106
Maximilian of Austria (1558–1618), 106
Mazepa, Ivan (1639–1709), 140
Mažoji Lietuva, see Lithuania minor
Mazovia (P. Mazowsze), 99, 118, 119
Duchy (–1529), 28, 33, 44, 51, 81
Mažvydas, Martynas (c.1520–63), 84, 333
Mažylis, Liudas (b. 1954), 258
Mazyr (P. Mozyrz), 160
Mazzini, Giuseppe (1805–72), 203
Medininkai, 359, see also Varniai
Memel, see Klaipėda
Meračoŭshchyna (P. Mereczowszczyzna), 156
Merkinė (P. Merecz), 123
Merkys, Antanas (1887–1955), 295
Merkys, River, 394
Michał Korybut Wiśniowiecki, Grand Duke of Lithuania and King of Poland (1640–73), 131, 134
Michalkiewicz, Kazimierz (1865–1940), 221, 254
Mickevičius-Kapsukas, Vincas (1880–1935), 261, 331
Mickiewicz, Adam (B. Adam Mitskevich, L. Adomas Mickevičius, 1798–1855), 185, 188–92, 195, 217, 219, 263, 281–2
Death of the Colonel (*Śmierć pułkownika*), 190, 198

463

INDEX

Grażyna, 190
Konrad Wallenrod, 189
Pan Tadeusz, 154, 171, 185, 190–1
statues, 345, 394
Mielnik, Treaty of (1501), 78
Mieroszewski, Juliusz (1906–76), 318
Mieželaitis, Eduardas (1919–97), 330, 349
Mikhail Romanov, Tsar of Muscovy (1596–1645), 110–11
'Military Revolution', 103
Miłosz, Czesław (1911–2004), 273, 284, 336
Minaičiai, 320
Mindaugas II, see Urach, Wilhelm von
Mindaugas, King of Lithuania (c.1203–63), 4–5, 29–32, 37, 335, 346
Minsk, 9, 124, 191, 225, 236–7, 259, 263, 318, 332, 396
governorate, 178, 180
Mir, Battle of (1792), 171
Mironas, Vladas (1880–1953), 291
Misnagdim, 149
Mitau (now Latv. Jelgava), 216, 223
Mitterand, François (1916–96), 354
Mizrachi movement, 240
Mniszech, Maryna, Tsarina of Muscovy (1588–1614), 109
Mohács, Battle of (1526), 81
Mohl-Basanavičienė, Gabriela Eleonora (1861–89), 393
Moldavia (Rom. Moldova), Principality of, 74, 77, 122
Molière, Jean-Baptiste Poquelin (1622–73), 152

Molotov, Viacheslav (1890–1986), 291, 295
Molotov–Ribbentrop pact (1939), 1, 8, 291, 310, 341–2, 345, 346, 350–1
Mongols, 30, 37, 239, see also Tatars
Moniuszko, Stanisław (1819–72), 191
Morta (c.1210–1262), 30
Moscow, 43, 50, 75, 109–10, 124, 138–9, 187, 189, 223, 261
capital of the USSR, 291, 292, 295, 297, 320, 324, 328, 340–1, 352, 354–6, 358–9, 370
capital of the Russian Federation, 370, 381, 384
Grand Duchy/Tsardom of (to 1721), see Muscovy
Olympics (1980), 327
Patriarchate, 389
universities, 199, 211, 217, 343–4, 378
Movement for the Struggle for Lithuanian Freedom (Lietuvos laisvės kovos sąjūdis), 320
Mstsislaŭ (P. Mścisław, R. Mstislavl), 240
Munich Security Conference (2007), 377
Muraškaitė-Račiukaitienė, Ona (1896–1985), 271
Murav˙ev, Mikhail (1796–1866), 205–9, 241, 391
Muscovy
autocracy, 75, 98, 204–5, 229
claims to Rus', 35, 38, 43, 74–5, 239, 383
principality/Grand Duchy, 35,

INDEX

38, 40–43, 50–1, 63–4, 70, 74–5
Tsardom, 75–7, 79–81, 88–90, 98–9, 102–4, 107–11, 114, 122–30, 138–41, 145, 185
Mussolini, Benito (1883–1945), 276, 278, 315
Mutual Pledge of the Two Nations (1791), 170
Mykolas Kęsgailaitis (d. 1476), 73
Mykolas Žygimantaitis (c.1406–52), 71
Myshetskii, Daniil (d. 1661), 128

Nagorno-Karabakh, 348
Napoleon I Bonaparte, Emperor of the French (1769–1821), 179, 183, 185–9
Napoleon III Bonaparte, Emperor of the French (1808–73), 203
Narbutt, Teodor (L. Teodoras Narbutas, 1784–1864), 195–6
Narutowicz, Gabriel (1865–1922), 246, 275
Narutowicz, Stanisław (L. Stanislovas Narutavičius, 1862–1932), 246, 255–6, 264, 392
National Democratic Party, 234–6
National Labour Protection Battalion, 303–6
nationalism, 2, 11–12, 176, 180–1, 224–43, 245–6, 250–7, 279, 285, 317, 337, 346, 351–2, 355, 359, 363, 392
Naujoji Vilnia, 303
Nausėda, Gitanas (b. 1964), 381, 389, 393
Navahrudak (Y. Navaradok, L. Naugardukas, R. Novogrudok, P. Nowogródek), 29, 185, 281–2
district, 154, 158, 190–1
palatinate, 126
Nemunas, river (B./R. Neman, P. Niemen), 16, 29, 59, 123, 130, 161, 171, 175, 179–80, 186–8, 171, 198, 202, 238, 267, 334
Neris, river (B. Viliia, P. Wilia), 7–8, 9, 29, 33, 233, 332
Nethimer, 25
New York, 288, 316, 360
Newman, Bernard (1897–1968), 269, 288
Newton, Isaac (1643–1727), 189
Niasvizh (P. Nieśwież), 118–19, 152
Nicholas I, Emperor of Russia (1796–1855), 189, 199–201, 206
Nicholas II, Emperor of Russia (1868–1918), 211, 225
Nida (G. Nidden), 386
Nihil Novi statute (1505), 78
Nikžentaitis, Alvydas (b. 1961), 391
NKVD (Narodnii komissariat vnutrennikh del), 302–3, 306, 314, 317, 318, 326–7, 353
Nord-Stream 1 pipeline 377
North Africa, 318
North America, 211, 216, 317, 375
North Atlantic Treaty Organization (NATO), 2, 352, 361, 369–76, 381–3, 394
North Caucasus, 343
North Macedonia, 375
North Sea, 23
Norviliškės (P. Narwiliszki), 395–6
Norway, 295, 315, 354–5
Novgorod, 24, 40, 64, 75

465

INDEX

Novhorod-Siverskyi (R. Novgorod Severskii), 39, 42, 54
Nowak, Andrzej (b. 1960), 279
Numavičius, Nerijus (b. 1967), 385

Ober Ost, 249–52, 258
Oder, river (P. Odra), 18
Odesa (R. Odessa), 84
Ogiński, Michał Kleofas (1765–1833), 161
Ogiński, Mikołaj Michał (1849–1902), 230
Okelkovych family, 80
Oleśnicki, Zbigniew, Cardinal, Bishop of Kraków (1389–1455), 61, 64, 69
Orange Revolution (2004), 377
'Order and Justice', 379
Orlyk, Pylyp (P. Filip Orlik, 1672–1742), 140
Orsha (P. Orsza) Battle of (1514), 79
Orthodoxy
   in the Grand Duchy of Lithuania, 5, 29–34, 37–44, 50–1, 53, 57–8, 62–3, 66, 68–70, 75–9, 82, 90, 92, 104–5, 120–2, 127–8, 144, 156–7
   in the Russian Empire, 155, 184, 198, 200, 206–7, 229, 238–9, 241
   after 1918, 280–2, 338, 389
Ostmark, 273
Ostrogski, Konstanty Wasyl (U. Kostiantyn Vasyl' Ostroz'kyi, 1526–1608), 121
Ostroz'kyi family (P. Ostrogski), 80
Ostroz'kyi Kostiantyn (B. Kanstantyn Astroski, L. Konstantinas Ostrogiškis P. Konstanty Ostrogski, c. 1460–1530), 79
Otto III, Holy Roman Emperor (980–1002), 25
Ottoman Empire, 50, 70, 74, 77, 81, 100, 140–1, 153, 157, 163–4, 171, 173
   Polish-Lithuanian Commonwealth's wars with, 107–8, 111, 132–5, 137
Our Fate (Nasha Dolia), 236–7
Our Field (Nasha Niva), 237
Ožkabaliai, 217

Pabaiskas, Battle of (1435), 69
Pac (L. Pacas, B. Patsevich) family, 130–2, 137
Pac, Krzysztof (1621–84), 130
Pac, Michał Kazimierz (1624–82), 130–2
Pac, Mikołaj (L. Mikalojus Pacas, c.1527–85), 90–1
Pac, Mikołaj Stefan, Bishop of Vilnius (c.1623–84), 130
Padua, 62
Pahonia, 59, 204, 382
Paksas, Rolandas (b. 1956), 373–6, 379
Palacký, František (1798–1876), 196
Palanga (P. Połąga), 23, 161, 216, 223, 266, 269–70, 288, 378, 386, 388
Palčiauskas, Kazimieras (1907–92), 308
Paleckis, Justas (1899–1980), 296–7, 329

466

INDEX

Palemon (L. Palemonas), 81, 153
Palestine, 240, 272, 303, 317
Paneriai Forest, 306, 325
Panevėžys, 160–1
Pannonia, 21
Paris, 130, 156, 355
Paris, Treaty of (1856), 201
Parulskis, Sigitas (b. 1965), 393
Paszkiewicz, Dionizy (L. Dionizas Poška, 1764–1830), 192
Päts, Konstantin (1874–1956), 278, 296
Paul I, Emperor of Russia (1754–1801), 183
Paulauskas, Artūras (b. 1953), 372, 374–6
Pavlov, Valentin (1937–2003), 359
Pawlikowska, Wioletta, 115, 116
Pažaislis (P. Pozajście), 130–1, 194
Peasant Truth (Mużyckaja Prauda), 204
Pechenegs, 25
Peipus, Lake, 33
People's Will (Narodnaia Wola), 224
Pereiaslav, Treaty of (1654), 123
Peter, Saint, 62
Peter I the Great, Emperor of Russia (1672–1725), 35, 98, 110, 138–41, 229
Peter III, Emperor of Russia (1728–62), 154
Petkevičaitė-Bitė, Gabrielė (1861–1943), 223, 228, 247, 271
Petkus, Viktoras (1928–2012), 341
Petliura, Symon (1879–1926), 266
Petras Mangirdaitis (d. 1459), 67
Petrauskas, Rimvydas (b. 1972), 66–7, 391–2

Petro Mohyla, Metropolitan of Kyiv (Rom. Petru Movilă, P. Piotr Mohyła, 1596–1647), 122
Pfeil, Traugott von (1860–1920), 249
Philargis, Petros, see Alexander V
Piast dynasty 72, 81
Piłsudska, Maria, née Billewicz (1842–84), 285
Piłsudski family, 223–4, 266–8
Piłsudski, Józef (1867–1935), 224–5, 235, 246
  head of state of the Republic of Poland (1918–22), 260, 262–4, 266–70, 274, 279, 284
  de facto ruler of Poland (1926–35), 278–83, 284–5, 290
Pinsk, 32, 39, 118, 147, 262, 263
Pirčiupiai, 312
Pisa, 62
Pius XI, Pope (1857–1939), 274
Pius XII, Pope (1876–1958), 294
Plater, Emilia Broel- (1806–31), 190, 197
Plater, Jerzy Broel- (L. Jurgis Pliateris, 1810–36), 192–3
Plater, Konstanty Broel- (1749–1807), 169
Plechavičius, Povilas (1890–1973), 313–14
Plichta, Jakub, Bishop of Vilnius (d. 1407), 58
Pliny the Younger (61–c.113), 20–1
Plungė, 215, 230
Pociej, Ludwik (1664–1730), 141
Poczobut, Marcin (1728–1810), 162–3, 188
Podlachia (B. Padliashsha,

467

INDEX

L. Palenkė, U. Pidlashshia, P. Podlasie), 54, 78, 86, 92, 98, 106, 126, 147, 204, 292, 310

Podolia (U. Podillia, P. Podole, Y. Podolie), 39, 68, 71, 135, 149–50, 157, 205

Poland, 7, 10–11, 24–5, 61, 110, 125, 136, 185, 190–1, 235, 256–7, 342

   Kingdom of (1025–1385), 5, 38, 41–5, 51–2

   Crown of the Kingdom of (1385–1795), 45–6, 48–105, 108, 111–13, 119, 121–42, 147–65, 169–76, 186, 190–1

   Kingdom of (1815–1915), 179–80, 188, 196–8, 201–5, 211, 217–19, 225, 236

   German-occupied (1915–18), 249, 253–4

   Republic of (1918–39), 245–7, 260–70, 272–5, 278–85, 288, 290–2, 395

   German- and Soviet-occupied (1939–45), 291–4, 306, 309–10, 314–18

   Polish People's Republic (1944–89), 259–60, 319, 326–7, 336, 342–3, 348

   Republic of (1990–), 3, 6, 49, 79, 158, 204, 355–6, 363, 367, 370–2, 374, 377–9, 382–3, 391–2

Poland–Lithuania, see Polish-Lithuanian Commonwealth

Połaniec, 173

Polatsk (P. Połock, R. Polotsk), 41–2, 70, 89–90, 102, 122, 198

   Archbishopric, 121–2

Jesuit college, 118, 184

palatinate, 129

principality/duchy, 26, 39, 50, 54, 74

Poles in exile 316–17

Poles in Lithuania, 55, 67, 85–6, 105, 116, 241–2, 248–52, 259–63, 271–3, 293–4, 300, 302–4, 312–14

   minority since 1945, 8–10, 321, 326–8, 346, 348, 353, 358, 365, 368, 370–1, 379–80, 387, 393–5

Poleshuks, 280

Polish Committee, 254

Polish language, 9–10, 85–6, 120, 181, 188–93, 195–6, 199, 206–9, 212–23, 230–2, 236, 238, 251–2, 254, 261, 269, 275, 294, 328, 342, 348, 392–5

Polish Resettlement Corps, 307

Polish Socialist Party, 224, 239, 246

Polish-Lithuanian Commonwealth (L. *Abiejų Tautų Respublika*, P. *Rzeczpospolita Obojga Narodów*, 1569–1795), 46, 79

   armies, 103–4, 108–11, 124–9, 131–3, 139, 164, 171–5

   civil wars, 112, 119, 129–30, 136

   economic and demographic decline and recovery, 138, 142–5, 159–61

   education, 116–22, 154–6, 162–3, 188

   idea of the *res publica*, 78, 93–4, 101, 169–70, 205

   law and liberty, 64, 123, 140

   magnates, 112–14, 129–33,

INDEX

136–7, 142, 144–5, 151–2, 157, 160, 166, 171
partitions of (1772, 1793, 1795), 6, 50–1, 97, 157–8, 173, 175, 177, 184
religious co-existence and conflicts, 100–1, 104–5, 113, 115–22, 127–8, 130, 145–6, 150, 157, 167–8
royal elections, 100–102, 105–6, 131, 134–5, 151, 155
social transformations, 166–9, 182, 183
supreme tribunals, 105, 152, 166
territorial changes (to 1699), 96, 102, 108, 110–11, 129
vitality of, 98, 170, 176, 383–4
Polish-Lithuanian union (1385–1569) 5–7, 43–46, 49–56, 61–2, 64–5, 67–73, 76–9, 81–3, 86, 88–94
Polish-Lithuanian union (1569–1795), 97–9, 104–7, 125–6, 138, 169–70, 173, 174, 176
Polish-Lithuanian union (idea of after 1795), 185, 191, 195–6, 203–5, 236, 245, 254–6, 263–4, 391
Polonka, Battle of (1660), 128
Poltava, Battle of (1709), 140
Pomerania, 51, 72, see also Prussia (Royal Prussia)
Ponchielli, Amilcare (1834–86), 189
Poniatowska, Konstancja, née Czartoryska (1695–1758), 151–4
Poniatowski, Michał, Archbishop of Gniezno (1736–94), 163
Poniatowski, Stanisław (1676–1762), 140, 150–1, 154
Poniatowski, Stanisław (1732–98), see Stanisław August
Pontic steppes, 17, 20
Possevino, Antonio (1533–1611), 120
Potemkin, Grigorii (1739–91), 163–5
Potemkin, battleship, 233
Potocki, Ignacy (1750–1809), 166
Potocki, Szczęsny (1751–1805), 171
Praga, massacre of (1794), 174
Prague, 24, 62, 287, 375
Prienai (P. Preny), 170
Protasewicz, Walerian, Bishop of Vilnius (B. Valerian Pratasevich, L. Valerijonas Protasevičius, 1505–79), 116–17
Protestant Reformation, 4, 81, 83–5, 88, 91, 114–15, 117–20
Protestantism, 51, 104–5, 116, 120–1, 157, 196, 282, 339, see also Calvinism, Lutheranism
Provisional Basic Law, 353, 363
Provisional Committee of Vilnius Lithuanians, 264
Prunskienė, Kazimira (b. 1943), 353–5
Prussia, 21, 24–5, 328
  Teutonic Ordensstaat (1226–1525), 28–33, 35–7, 40–5, 53, 60–3, 74, 80–1, 88, 350, 379
  Ducal (1525–1701), 81, 84, 87, 113, 115, 120, 124, 126–7
  Royal (Polish, 1454–1772/93), 74, 92, 153, 157–8
  Kingdom of (1701–1918), 144, 152, 156–8, 161, 164–6, 171, 173–5, 179–80, 182–3, 193–4, 248–9

INDEX

East Prussia (1701–1945), 3, 157, 160, 179, 193, 197, 209, 211, 216, 218, 223, 226, 248, 288
(Old) Prussian language, 17, 81, 84, 193
Prut, river, 140
Prypiats', river (P. Prypeć, U. Prypiat'), 18, 22, 238, 279, 344
Pskov, 31–2, 64, 75
Pskov Airborne Division, 356
Ptolemy, Claudius, 21
Pugo, Boris (1937–91), 357, 359
Pukuveras, ruler of Lithuania (d. 1295), 34, 397
Pushkin, Aleksandr (1799–1837), 189
Putin, Vladimir (b. 1952), 360, 363, 377–8, 383–4, 393
Pytheas, 20

Quedlinburg Abbey, 25

Racławice, Battle of (1794), 173
Radvila Astikaitis (d. 1477), 67
Radvila, Albertas, Bishop of Vilnius (P. Wojciech Radziwiłł, 1478–1519), 83
Radziwiłł family (L. Radvila), 10, 67, 113, 120, 132, 152, 153, 160, 394
Radziwiłł, Albrycht Stanisław (L. Albrechtas Stanislovas Radvila, 1593–1656), 118
Radziwiłł, Anna, née Sanguszko (L. Ona Radvilienė, 1676–1746), 152
Radziwiłł, Barbara, see Barbara, née Radziwiłł
Radziwiłł, Bogusław (L. Boguslavas Radvila, 1620–69), 113, 125, 126–7
Radziwiłł, Hieronim Florian (L. Jeronimas Florijonas Radvila, 1705–60), 152
Radziwiłł, Janusz I (L. Jonušas I Radvila, 1579–1620), 112–13
Radziwiłł, Janusz II (L. Jonušas II Radvila, 1612–55), 11, 123, 124–6, 133
Radziwiłł, Jerzy, Cardinal, Bishop of Vilnius and Kraków (L. Jurgis Radvila, 1556–1600), 105, 116
Radziwiłł, Karol Stanisław (L. Karolis Stanislovas Radvila, 1734–90), 152–3, 155
Radziwiłł, Krzysztof I the Thunderbolt (L. Kristupas Radvila Perkūnas, 1547–1603), 103–4
Radziwiłł, Krzysztof II (Kristupas II Radvila, 1585–1640), 110–11
Radziwiłł, Michał (L. Mykolas Radvila, 1702–62), 152
Radziwiłł, Michał Kazimierz (L. Mykolas Kazimieras Radvila, 1635–80), 132
Radziwiłł, Mikołaj the Black (L. Mikalojus Radvila Juodasis, 1515–65), 85–7, 90, 91
Radziwiłł, Mikołaj the Orphan (L. Mikalojus Radvila Našlaitėlis, 1549–1616), 105
Radziwiłł, Mikołaj the Red (L. Mikalojus Radvila Rudasis, c.1515–84), 85–7, 89, 91–3
Radziwiłł, Urszula née Wiśniowiecka (L. Uršulė Radvilienė, 1705–53), 152

INDEX

Rainiai Forest, 303
Rakutis, Valdas (b. 1969), 392
Ramanauskas, Adolfas 'Vanagas' (1918–57), 321
Rava Rus´ka (P. Rawa Ruska), 138
Reagan, Ronald (1911–2004), 342–3, 348
Red Army, 17, 260, 266–7, 290–6, 311–14, 319, 331, 372
Reformed Church, see Calvinism
Reinys, Mečislovas (1884–1953), 338
Reisons, Kārlis (1894–1981), 287–8
Renaissance, 6, 67, 72–73, 81–2, 86–7, 101, 115–16, 153, 336
Repnin, Nikolai (1734–1801), 157
Reytan, Tadeusz (L. Tadas Reitanas, B. Tadevush Reitan, 1742–80), 158
Rhesa, Martin (L. Martynas Rėza, 1776–1840), 193–4
Riazan´, 75
Ribbentrop, Joachim von (1893–1946), 291, see also Molotov-Ribbentrop pact
Riga, 1, 3, 18, 27, 108, 138, 195, 212–13, 262, 287, 345, 347, 355–7, 388
   (Arch)bishopric, 27, 30, 36, 63, 89
   Jesuit college, 118–19
   Treaty of (1921), 267, 279
Rimša, Petras (1881–1961), 214–15
Riurik, 24
Riurikid dynasty, 24, 28–9, 32, 37–8, 66
Roman Catholic Church, see Catholicism

Roman Empire, 22, 39, see also Byzantine Empire
Roman law, 82, 91–2
Romania, 291, 319, 375
Romanians, 181
Rome, 5, 27, 31, 57, 62, 72, 115, 118–20, 123, 183, 254, 315, see also Holy See
   Ancient, 94, 101
Römer, Michał/Mykolas Römeris (1880–1945), 233, 246, 264, 268, 273, 293
Romuva, 389
Roosevelt, Franklin Delano (1882–1945), 315
Ropp, Eduard von der, Bishop of Vilnius (1851–1939), 221
Rosenbaum, Simon, 271
Rowell, S. C. (b. 1964), 39, 42, 57, 63, 83
Roysius, Petrus (Sp. Pedro Ruiz de Moros, c.1505–71), 86
Rus´, 24–6, 29–35, 37–8, 40, 42–5, 50, 53–5, 74–5, 93–4, 106, 123, 205, 239, see also Ruthenia
   Black Rus´, 29
Russia, 4, 11, 35, 50, 74–5, 110, 122, 158, 294, 352, 362
Russian Empire (1721–1917), 6–7, 98, 106, 138, 141, 143–4, 151–2, 154–9, 163–5, 171–250, 253, 255, 269, 313, 383, 395
Russian Soviet Federative Socialist Republic (RSFSR, 1917/22–1991), 245, 255–67, 279, 324, 328, 333, 343, 355, 358–60, see also USSR
Russian Federation (1991–), 3, 363, 369, 373, 377–84, 387, 393–4

471

INDEX

Russian Civil War, 265
Russian Far East Fleet, 225
Russian language, 9–10, 17, 35, 199, 207, 210–14, 238, 240–1, 251–2, 261, 275, 323–5, 328, 330, 341, 348, 365, 370, 385, 387
Russian Social Democratic Workers' Party, 224
Ruszczyc, Ferdynand (1876–1936), 242
Ruthenia (also Roxolania), 35, 38–9, 45, 51, 53–4, 57, 61, 74–5, 86, 91–3, 121, 157, 205, see also Rus'
Duchy of (1658), 127
Red Ruthenia, 53
Ruthenian language (*ruski*), 10, 24, 35, 38, 41, 57–8, 65, 79, 81–2, 106, 128, 174, 191, 237
decline among nobility, 85–6, 135
Ruthenian rite, see Uniate Church
Ruthenians, 34–5, 43, 50–1, 55, 65, 69–71, 75, 76, 79, 82, 93, 112, 121, 128
Ruthenian descent, 114, 156, 185, 207, 237
Rüütel, Arnold (1928–2024), 355, 379
Ryzhkov, Nikolai (1929–2024), 355
Rzewuski, Seweryn (1743–1811), 171

Saakashvili, Mikheil (b. 1967), 379
Saaremaa (G. Ösel), 32–3
Saarland, 290
Sabaliauskaitė, Kristina, 392
Sabbatai Zevi (1626–1676), 150
Sachsenhausen, 294
Sahanovich, Henadz (b. 1961), 129

Saint Petersburg, 139, 154, 171, 175, 207, 212, 225, 233, see also Leningrad
Court of, 141, 151, 157, see also Russian Empire
Lithuanians in, 183, 189, 195, 213, 219, 221, 223, 233
Petrograd (1914–24) 255
university, 199
Sąjūdis (Reform Movement of Lithuania, Lietuvos Persitvarkymo Sąjūdis), 346–7, 351, 353–4, 358, 366–9, 372, 390
Šalčininkai (P. Soleczniki), 394
District, 358, 370, 393
Šalčininkėliai (P. Małe Soleczniki), 327
Saločiai, Battle of (P. Sałaty, 1794), 174
Samogitia (Sam. Žemaitėjė, L. Žemaitija), 29–31, 36–41, 60–1, 63, 84, 125, 175, 184, 208, 230, 231, 242, 269, 337, 370
Bishopric, 63, 115–16, 193, 208–9, 221, 274
cathedral chapter, 86, 115
duchy, 91
chronicles and histories, 81–2, 195, 209
ethnographic region, 2–3, 125, 209
revolts, 60, 66
Samogitian dialect/language, 17, 188, 192–93, 195–6, 212, 238
Samogitians, 17, 28–31, 84, 197
conversion, 63
nobles, 71, 142, 184, 193–4, 203, 215

INDEX

Sanskrit, 18
Sapieha family (B. Sapeha, L. Sapiega), 113, 114, 132–3, 135–7, 139, 140, 165, 167
Sapieha, Benedykt (c.1643–1707), 132, 136
Sapieha, Elżbieta, née Branicka (1734–1800), 165
Sapieha, Kazimierz (c.1642–1720), 132–3, 136
Sapieha, Kazimierz Nestor (1757–98), 165, 167
Sapieha, Lew (B. Leŭ Sapeha, L. Leonas Sapiega, 1557–1633), 114, 118, 119
Sapieha, Michał (1670–1700), 136
Sapieha, Paweł (1606–1665), 128
Šapoka, Adolfas (1902–61), 169, 287
Šapoka, Mindaugas, 141
Sarbiewski, Maciej Kazimierz (Lat. Sarbievius, 1595–1640), 119
Sartre, Jean-Paul (1905–80), 334
Savisaar, Edgar (1950–2022), 351
Saxony, 135–6, 139, 168, 172
Scandinavia, 15, 42
Scandinavians, 23–4, 27
Schengen Zone, 3, 374, 396
Scotland, 307
Scythians, 20
Second World War (1939–45), 10, 245, 272, 286, 291–7, 299–318
  'Great Patriotic War of 1941–45', 50, 350, 390
seimas (parliament), 79, 270, 271, 273–6, 278, 320–1, 366–8, 370, 372–3, 375–6, 379–81, 392
  Great Seimas of Vilnius (1905), 226–8, 231

Constituent Seimas (1920–22), 271, 273
Reconstituent Seimas (1990–92), 353–6, 363, 390
sejm (parliament), 77–9, 89–90, 99–100, 103, 107, 112, 118, 133–4, 147, 151, 155, 167–8,; see also *liberum veto*, soim
  sejms of 1529: 82; 1548: 87, 1562–63: 88; 1563–64: 89–90; 1569: 92–94; 1574: 100; 1578: 102, 105; 1581: 105; 1582: 104, 114; 1588: 106; 1609: 112; 1611: 110; 1652: 133; 1659: 127; 1661: 129; 1664: 130; 1669: 134; 1678–79: 134; 1685: 134; 1688: 134; 1693: 134; 1695: 134; 1701: 137; 1703: 139; 1717: 141; 1719–20: 141; 1736: 151; 1738: 151; 1762: 151; 1764: 148, 155, 157; 1766: 155. 157; 1767–68: 157; 1773–75: 158, 162; 1776: 158, 159; 1778: 159; 1784: 159, 161; 1786: 159; 1788–92 (Great Sejm): 163–70, 172; 1793: 173
sejm in the Republic of Poland, 268, 279
sejmiks, 74, 78, 91, 103, 105, 113–14, 135–7, 140–1, 147, 152, 166, 170, 183
  election of judges, 166, 168
  general sejmiks, 107
  instructions, 121, 134, 166
Sejny (L. Seiniai), 218, 264
  Bishopric, 221, 274
Selonians, 35
Semigallia (G. Semgallen, Latv. Zemgale), 27, 32, 89

INDEX

Semigallians, 35
Šepetys, Lionginas (1926–2017), 332
serfdom, 66, 88, 127, 142–3, 162, 163, 168–9, 172, 173–4, 332
  in the Russian Empire, 182–6, 189, 197, 201–3, 215, 223, 322
Sevastopol, 201
Shenandoah, Pennsylvania, 216
Shenin, Oleg (1937–2009), 358
Shkloŭ (R., Y. Shklov, P. Szkłów), 151
  Battle of (1654), 124
Štromas, Aleksandras (1931–1999), 337
Shvarno (1230–69/70), 32
Siakhnovichy (P. Siechnowicze), 172
Šiauliai (Sam. Šiaulė, Y. Shavel, P. Szawle), 28, 174, 197, 289, 308, 309, 313, 337, 346
Siberia, 198, 205–6, 224, 302, 322, 345, 349–50
Siciński, Władysław (1615–72), 133
Sienkiewicz, Henryk (1846–1916), 125–6, 249
Sierakowski, Zygmunt (1826–63), 203–4
Siestrzeńcewicz, Stanisław Bohusz-, Archbishop of Mahileŭ (B. Stanislaŭ Bohush-Sestrantsevich, 1731–1826), 183–4
Sigismund I the Old, Grand Duke of Lithuania and King of Poland (1467–1548), 72, 78–84, 86–7, 397
Sigismund II Augustus, Grand Duke of Lithuania and King of Poland (1520–72), 6, 81–4, 86–90, 92–3, 98, 102, 115, 196, 397
Sigismund III Vasa, Grand Duke of Lithuania, King of Poland and Sweden (1566–1632), 106, 107–12, 116, 118, 121, 123, 397
Sigismund of Luxemburg, King of Hungary, Germany, and Bohemia (1368–1437), 64–5
Sigismund son of Kęstutis, see Žygimantis Kęstutaitis
Silesia, 51, 72, 126
Šimėnas, Albertas (b. 1950), 355–6
Simeon of Polatsk (1629–80), 122
Šimonytė, Ingrida (b. 1974), 377, 381–2, 393
'Singing Revolutions', 1, 8, 388
Širvydas, Konstantinas (P. Konstanty Szyrwid, 1579–1631), 119
Skalvians, 35
Skarga, Piotr (1536–1612), 118–19
Skirgaila, Grand Duke of Lithuania (P. Skirgiełło, baptised Casimir, 1354/55–1397), 41–2, 44–5, 53–4, 397
Skirmuntt, Konstancja (1851–1934), 263
Škirpa, Kazys (1895–1979), 304
Skvernelis, Saulius (b. 1970), 380
slavery, 21, 23, 29, 54, 66, 88, 172
Slavic languages, 17, 22–5, 29, 35, 54, 122, 238, 287, 336
Slavicisation, 23, 226, 371
Slavs, 1, 22–3, 26–7, 29, 38, 41, 50–1, 57, 65, 226, 248, 304, 358
Šleževičius, Adolfas (1948–2022), 369, 372

INDEX

Sleževičius, Mykolas (1882–1939), 260, 275–6
Slovakia, 375
Slovenia, 375
Slutsk, 120, 147–8, 153, 160, 306
Smetona, Antanas (1874–1944), 223, 230–1, 254–8, 260, 271, 274–5
   President of Lithuania, 276–8, 283, 285, 289–91, 294–7, 315–17, 353
Šmigelskytė-Stukienė, Ramunė (b. 1970), 161, 171
Smolensk, 79, 109–11, 122, 124, 129, 186, 259
   bishopric, 115
   palatinate, 110–11
   principality, 40, 54
Smotryts'kyi, Meletii, Archbishop of Polatsk (c.1577–1633), 122
Śniadecki, Jan (1758–1830), 188–9, 394
Sniečkus, Antanas (1903–74), 297, 303, 318, 323–4, 329, 333, 340
Sniečkus, see Visaginas
Snyder, Timothy (b. 1969), 238–9, 307–8
Sobieski, Jakub (1677–1737), 135
Sobieski, Jan, see John III
Social Democracy of the Kingdom of Poland and Lithuania, 224
Social Democratic Coalition, 373
Social Democratic Party of Lithuania, 374
Social Democratic Workers' Party of Russia, 224
Sodeika, Gintaras (b. 1961), 393
soim (parliament), 79–82, 86, 90–1, see also seimas, sejm
Songaila, Ringaudas (1929–2019), 345–6
Sonka Halshanska, Queen of Poland (1405–61), 64, 69, 397
Sophia Paleologue, Grand Duchess of Muscovy (1455–1503), 75
Sosnowski, Józef (d. 1783), 159
South America, 27, 289
Soviet bloc, 1, 245, 342
Soviet Russia, Soviet Union, see USSR
Sozzini, Fausto (Lat. Faustus Socinus, 1539–1604), 120
Spa, 266
SPQR, 101
SS (Schutzstaffel), 310, 312
Stackelberg, Otto von (1736–1800), 158, 162
Stahlecker, Franz Walter (1900–42), 304–5, 307
Stalin, Iosif Vissarionovich Dzhugashvili (Geo. Ioseb Besarionis dze Jughashvili, 1878–1953), 245, 281, 295, 296, 317, 323–6, 329, 331, 333, 350, 394
Stalinism, 299, 333, 350, 390
Staliūnas, Darius (b. 1970), 50
Staniewicz, Szymon (L. Simonas Stanevičius, 1798–1848), 192–3
Stanislaus, Saint (P. Stanisław, c.1030–79), 3
Stanisław I Leszczyński, Grand Duke of Lithuania and King of Poland, Duke of Lorraine (1677–66), 139–40, 151
Stanisław II August Poniatowski, Grand Duke of Lithuania and King of Poland (1732–98), 140, 149–59, 161, 166, 169, 172, 175

INDEX

Stankevičius, Laurynas (1935–2017), 372
Stavropol region, 344
Stębark (G. Tannenberg), 60
Stephen Báthory, Grand Duke of Lithuania, King of Poland, and Prince of Transylvania (H. Báthory István, P. Stefan Batory, 1533–86), 102–6, 114, 116–17, 284
Stephen the Great, Prince of Moldavia (1433/40–1504), 74
Stockholm, 3, 287
Stolypin, Petr (1862–1911), 229
Stoss, Veit (P. Wit Stwosz, c.1448–1533), 76
Strazdas, Antanas (P. Antoni Drozdowski, 1760–1833), 194
Strupinskas, Andrius (1829–92), 216
Stulginskis, Aleksandras (1885–1969), 271
Stutthof, 309, 11
Supreme National Committee of Poles, 253
Suslov, Mikhail (1902–82), 324
Suvalkija (P. Suwalszczyzna), 14, 217, 227, 242, 264, 266, 268, 289, 311, 383
Suvorov, Aleksandr (1729–1800), 174–5
Suwałki (L. Suvalkai), 265
   'Suwałki gap', 383
   governorate, 217, 227, 229
Švenčionys (P. Święcany), 308, 312
   district, 280
Sviatopolk-Mirskii, Petr (1857–1914), 211
Švitrigaila, Grand Duke of Lithuania (P. Świdrygiełło, baptised Boleslaus, 1370–1452), 68–9, 71, 397
Sweden, 11, 24, 89, 106–8, 175, 256, 344, 354–5, 378, 383
   wars with/in Poland-Lithuania, 107–9, 124–6, 128–9, 138–41
Switzerland, 175, 181, 246, 249, 256, 296
Sword-Brothers, see Livonia (Livonian Order)

Tacitus (c.56–c.120), 21
Taiwan, 382
Tallinn (G. Rewal), 1, 3, 89, 287, 345, 351, 356
Tamkevičius, Sigitas, Archbishop of Kaunas (b. 1938), 339–40
Tannenberg and Masurian Lakes, Battles of (1914), 248
Targowica, Confederation of (U. Torhovytsia, 1792–93), 171
Tartu (G. Dorpat), 119
Tatars, 30, 37–8, 43, 153, 212–13, 317, 332, 389
   Crimean 54, 74–5, 77, 111, 123, 127, 184, 286
   in the service of the Grand Dukes of Lithuania, 54, 55, 60, 66, 285
Tauragė, 277
Tautvilas, 30
Tbilisi, 356–7, 377
Tehran Conference (1943), 317
Telšiai (P. Telsze), 260, 296, 303
   Bishopric, 338
   District, 197
Terleckas, Antanas (1928–2023), 341–2, 345

INDEX

Teutonic Knights/Order, 3–4, 28, 35, 40, 55, 74, 88–9, 189–90, 248, 251, 286, 350, 379, see also Livonia, Prussia
Thatcher, Margaret (1925–2013), 344, 354
Third World War, belief in, 319
Thirteen Years' War (1454–66), 74
Tilsit (L. Tilžė, now R. Sovetsk), 212, 216–17, 305
Tiraspol, 221
Tokhtamish, Khan of the Golden Horde (c.1342–1406), 54
Tollmingkehmen (L. Tolminkiemis, now R. Chistie Prudy), 194
Tomaszewski, Waldemar (L. Valdemar Tomaševski, b. 1965), 379–80
Tomsk, 322
Toruń (G. Thorn), 84, 157–8, 173
Traidenis, ruler of Lithuania (d. 1282), 32–3
Trakai (P./R. Troki), 42, 55, 65, 73
  castle, 69, 333
  Duchy, 40, 42, 53–4, 62, 74
  palatinate, 69, 73, 76, 79
Treniota, ruler of Lithuania (d. 1264), 32
Trent (I. Trento), Council of (1545–63), 114–16
Trianon, Treaty of, 290
Trofimovsk Island, 349
Trump, Donald (b. 1946), 381
Tsikhanouskaia, Sviatlana (b. 1982), 382
Tūbelis, Juozas (1882–1939), 288–9
Turkey, 386
Tverʹ, 40, 41, 75

Tykocin (Y. Tiktin), 126, 147
Tyszkiewicz, Jerzy, Bishop of Vilnius (1596–1656), 125
Tyzenhauz, Antoni (1733–85), 161–2

Ugro–Finnic languages, 2, 4, 19
Ukmergė (P. Wilkomierz), 223
Ukraine, 4, 11, 50, 158, 318, 384
  in the Grand Duchy of Lithuania, 50, 93, see also Rusʹ, Ruthenia, Kyiv
  in the Polish-Lithuanian Commonwealth, 96, 106, 108, 111, 121–3, 125–9, 146–7, 150, 171, 172–3, 383–4
  Cossack Hetmanate, 123–8, 139–40
  in the Russian Empire, 173, 178–9, 188, 198, 205
  Ukrainian People's Republic (1917/18–21), 266
  Ukrainian Soviet Socialist Republic (1918/22–1991), 292, 319, 341, 344, 359–60
  Nazi German-occupied (1941–44), 306
  Republic of (1991–), 65, 79, 127, 138, 205, 343, 360, 362–3, 377, 379, 382–4, 392, 394
Ukrainian Insurgent Army (Ukrainsʹka Povstansʹka Armia) 317, 319
Ukrainian language, 17, 140, 212, 235, 280, 341
Ukrainians, 10, 97, 108, 140, 153, 212, 235, 237–9, 266, 279–80, 292, 310, 317, 387, 389

INDEX

Ula, river, 89
Ulmanis, Guntis (b. 1939), 379
Ulmanis, Kārlis (1877–1942), 278, 296
UNESCO, 287
Uniate Church, 121–2, 128, 144, 184, 198, 204, 238, 281
Union of Poles in Lithuania, 358
United Nations, 342, 360
United Partisan Organisation, 309
United States of America (USA), 97, 167, 175, 225, 254–5, 257, 273–4, 278, 363, 369, 373, 377, 381
    Lithuanian emigration to, 211, 215–16, 220, 222, 227, 272, 288–9, 296, 316–17, 321, 337, 372, 388
    policy towards the Baltic states, 261–2, 314–16, 347–8, 351–6, 359–60, 373–5, 383, 391
    War of American Independence (1775–83), 164, 172
Upytė (P. Upita), 133
Urach, Prince Inigo von (b. 1962), 259
Urach, Prince Wilhelm von, 'Mindaugas II' (1869–1928), 258–9
'Uralic' genomes, 20
Urbanisation, 299, 323, 329, 335
Urbšys, Juozas (1896–1991), 291, 292, 295
Uspaskich, Viktor (b. 1956), 376
    Labour Party, 376, 379
USSR (Union of Soviet Socialist Republics, Soviet Union), 1–2, 9, 114, 131, 144, 175, 233, 245, 266–7, 270, 274–5, 279, 285–8, 291–303, 305, 309–42, 361–2, 373, 386, 395
    Congress of Peoples' Deputies, 351, 354
    downfall, 1, 113, 342–60
    legacy 3, 7, 10, 50, 363, 365, 367, 371, 381, 384–5, 388–91
Utena (P. Uciana, G. Utenen, Y. Utyan), 323
Uvarov, Sergei (1786–1855), 198, 200

Vaad (1919–26) 272
Vaad Arba Aratsot (Council of the Four Lands), 147–9
Vaad medinat Lita (Council of Lithuania), 147–9
Vagnorius, Gediminas (b. 1957), 356, 368, 372–3
Väinameri Sea, 32–3
Vaišvilkas (d. 1267), 32
Vaitkus, Eduardas (b. 1956), 394
Valančius, Motiejus, Bishop of Samogitia (P. Maciej Wołonczewski, 1801–75), 208–9, 380
Valionis, Antanas (b. 1950), 375
Valkininkai (P. Olkieniki), Battle of (1700), 136
'Varangians', 24
Varniai (Medininkai, P. Wornie), 63, 208
Varonka, Iazep (1891–1952), 259–60
Vasiliauskas, Artūras, 113–14
Vasilii I, Grand Duke of Moscow (1371–1425), 63–4, 75
Vasilii II, Grand Duke of Moscow (1415–62), 63–4, 75

INDEX

Vasilii III, Tsar of Muscovy (1479–1533), 76
Vasilii IV Shuiskii, Tsar of Muscovy (c.1552–1612), 109–10
Vatican, the, 294, 301, 315, 338, see also Holy See
  Second Vatican Council (1962–65), 339
Vaŭkavysk district (L. Valkaviskas P. Wołkowysk), 183
Vedrosha, Battle on the (1500), 77
Venclova, Antanas (1906–71), 330, 335
Venclova, Tomas (b. 1937), 242, 335–7, 341, 392
Venice, 36
Versailles, 134–5
Vienna, 254, see also Austria
  Battle of (1683), 133
  Congress of (1814–15), 180, 188
  Court of, 134–5, 141, 151
'Vikings', 23
Vilčinskas, Aleksas, 317
Vilčinskas, Juozas (1909–92), 317
Vileišis, Jonas (1872–1942), 230, 248–1, 256, 275, 287
Vileišis, Petras (1851–1926), 213, 220–1
Vilkaviškis (Y. Vilkovishk, P. Wyłkowyszki), diocese, 274
Vilkutaitis, Antanas (1864–1903), 216
Vilkutaitis, Juozas (1869–1948), 216
Vilnan Baroque and Rococo, 8, 144, 213, 283, 332
Vilnan Courier (Kurier wileński), 233, 282
Vilnan Gazette (Gazeta Wileńska), 233
Vilnan Truth (Vilner emes), 301
Vilnan Weekly (Tygodnik Wileński), 188
Vilnia, river (P. Wilenka), 6
Vilnius (Lat. Vilna, R. Vil´na R., B. Vilnˋia, Y. Vilne, G. Wilna, P. Wilno), 1, 3–10, 34, 42–3, 55–8, 68, 70, 110, 139, 154, 166, 174, 186–7, 197, 223–5, 241–2, 248–9, 260, 280, 282–4, 292–4, 312–13, 331, 358, 371, 375, 388, 393
  Academy, 119, 162, 199, 284, 294, 330
  airport, 9, 388, 394
  Antakalnis (P. Antokol), 131, 187, 213, 321–3, 357, 379
  Avenue: Saint George's, Mickiewicz, Gediminas, Stalin, Lenin, Gediminas, 7, 219, 241, 283, 294, 325–6, 331, 333
  (Arch)bishopric, 58, 115–16, 130, 132, 155, 221, 209, 254, 274–5, 338, 379
  Belarusian nationalism and, 236–8, 250
  Castle Street (L. Pilies gatvė), 8, 73, 257
  Cathedral, 1, 3, 4–5, 31, 58, 72–3, 76, 78, 86, 161, 379
  Cathedral chapter, 83, 86, 115–16, 192
  Cathedral Square, 3, 4–5, 256, 346, 357
  Churches: of the Archangel Michael, 114; Church of the Holy Spirit, 275; Orthodox Church of the Holy Spirit, 144; of St Casimir, 333; of St

INDEX

John and St John, 144; of St Nicholas, 221, 283; Sanctuary of Divine Mercy, 275
Church and seminary of the Priests of the Mission, 144, 161
Civic Committee (1915), 248
City Hall (old), 8, 161
City Hall (new), now Philharmonia, 226
Confederations, 1715: 141; 1792–93: 171
crime, 384
demographics and diversity, 10, 34, 43, 79, 105, 144–6, 160, 212–13, 232, 236, 241–2, 252–3, 280, 283–4, 326–9, 387–8
district, 358, 370–1
Gates of Dawn (L. Aušros vartai)/Sharp Gate (P. Ostra Brama, B. Vostraia Brama), 8, 242
German Street (L. Vokiečių gatvė, Y. Daytshe Gos), 240, 332
governorate, 178, 180, 199, 229
Grand ducal court, 41, 73, 84
Great Street (L. Didžioji gatvė), 8, 73
Holocaust in, 306, 308–9
Great Synagogue, 8, 332, 390
Jews and Judaism, 8, 34, 144–49, 160, 240–1, 262, 283–4, 293, 325–6, 332, 390
Lazdynai, 334
Lithuanian nationalism and (to 1939), 212–13, 215, 219, 220–1, 225–6, 229–32, 249–50, 254–8, 264–70, 272, 282–3, 286, 290–1

Lithuanisation (1939–), 293–4, 300, 317, 328–33
Lower Castle, 6–7, 86–7
Lukiškės Square, 204, 331–2, 391
Monastery of the Holy Trinity, 144
museums, 7, 110, 390–1
Muscovite Occupation (1655–61), 124, 126–8
Neringa café, 333–4
palatinate, 69, 73, 92, 110–11, 126
Parliament Building (Seimas), 77, 79–81, 356, 359–60
parliaments (soims) and assemblies in, 79–81, 86, 91, 93, 101–2, 137
Polish nationalism and, 236, 260, 262–3, 267–8, 282–5, 290–1, 317
protests (1987–91), 1, 345–6, 351, 355–7, 359–60
Protestants, 84, 120, 130, 144
publishing, 117, 188, 191–3, 195–6, 212, 284, 391
railway, 9, 212, 262, 282
Rasos Cemetery (P. Rossa), 9, 283, 285
religious and ethnic conflicts and violence, 128, 130, 262, 283–4, 293–4
seminary, 208
Sovietisation, 329–33
Stock Exchange, 385
Television Tower, 1, 3, 356, 357
University, 116–20, 162–3, 188–9, 192, 194–5, 199, 202, 242, 247, 284, 294, 330–1, 391

INDEX

Upper Castle (Gediminas Hill), 5–6, 204, 231, 293, 312
Užupis (P. Zarzecze), 7
Verkiai (P. Werki), 160
Vingis Park, 7–8, 346
Wróblewski Library (Lietuvos mokslų akademijos Vrublevskių biblioteka), 233–4
Vilnius Liberation Union (Sąjunga Vilniui vaduoti), 269, 291
Vilnius News (Vilniaus žinios), 225–6
Visaginas (Sniečkus, 1975–92), 10, 345, 370, 393–4
Višinskis, Povilas (1875–1906), 215
Vistula, river, 16, 24, 28, 267, 292, 312
Vitkauskas, Vincas (1890–1965), 297
Vitsebsk (R./Y. Vitebsk, P. Witebsk), 58, 89
  governorate, 180, 182, 206
  palatinate, 129
  principality/duchy, 38, 39, 42, 54, 74
Volanus, Andreas (P. Andrzej Wolan, 1530–1610), 120
Voldemaras, Augustinas (1883–1942), 260, 276–7, 282–3
Volga, river, 18
Volhynia (U. Volynʹ, P. Wołyń), 175, 203, 205, 253, 317
  principality, 28–32, 37–9, 41, 68, 71
  incorporated into Polish Crown (1569), 92–3
  annexed by Russia, 175
Volksgeist, 18
Volodymyr the Great, Prince of Kyiv (B. Uladzimir, Norse

Valdamarr, R. Vladimir, c.958–1015), 24–5
Vorskla, Battle by the river (1399), 55, 58
Voŭchin (P. Wołczyn), 150–1, 175
Vyhovsʹkyi, Ivan (d. 1664), 127
Vykintas, 28, 30
Vytautas the Great, Grand Duke of Lithuania (B. Vitaŭt, U. Vitovt, P. Witold, baptised Alexander, c.1354–1430), 5, 11, 42–3, 45, 49–56, 58–69, 70, 75, 397
  'Coronation Tempest' (1429–30), 64–5, 82
  cult, 5–6, 76, 169, 190, 195, 285–6, 320, 333, 379
Vytenis, Grand Duke of Lithuania (c.1260–1316), 33–5, 397

Wałęsa, Lech (b. 1943), 371, 379
Wallenrode, Konrad von (d. 1393), 189
'Wallenrodism', 189
Wars of (Lithuanian) Independence, 269, 286
Warsaw, 137, 156, 160, 172, 192, 207, 218, 223, 230, 232, 234, 253–4, 266–7, 292, 328, 392
  Capital of Poland (1918–), 260, 290, 356
  Confederation of (1573), 99–102, 105, 118
  coronations in, 139, 155
  Duchy of (1807–13/15), 179, 183, 186
  Uprisings, 1794: 173–5; 1830–1: 196–7
  sejms and assemblies in, 90, 110, 129, 133, 140, 165–6, 268

INDEX

University, 199
Washington D.C., 316, 351, 355
Washington, George (1732–99), 159
Weeks, Theodore, 328
'West Russian Volunteer Army', 269
Western Europe, 35, 63, 103, 110, 153, 343, 363, 377
Wilhelm II, Emperor of Germany (1859–1941), 258
William of Austria (c.1370–1406), 45
Williams, Sir Charles Hanbury (1708–59), 154
Wilson, Thomas Woodrow (1856–1924), 257
Witte, Sergei (1849–1915), 226
Wittelsbach dynasty, 72
Władysław I, King of Poland (1260–1333), 37
Władysław III, King of Poland and Hungary (H. I. Ulászló, 1424–1444), 64, 69–70, 397
Władysław IV Vasa, Grand Duke of Lithuania and King of Poland (1595–1648), 107, 109–11, 123, 397
Władysław II Jagiełło, see Jogaila
Władysław Jagiellon, King of Bohemia and Hungary (H. II. Ulászló, Cz. Vladislav I Jagellonský, 1456–1516), 72, 397
Włodkowic, Paweł (Lat. Paulus Vladimiri, 1370/73–1435), 62–3
Wojtyła, Karol, see John Paul II
Woyna, Benedykt, Bishop of Vilnius (d. 1615), 116
Wróblewski, Tadeusz (1858–1925), 233

Wuhan, 381
Wulfstan, 21
Wysocki, Czesław (L. Česlav Vysocki), 370–1

Yad Vashem, 310–12
Yakovlev, Aleksandr (1923–2005), 345–6, 352
Yakutsk, 349
Yale University, 336
Yanaiev, Gennadii (1937–2010), 359
Yaroslav the Wise, Grand Duke of Kyiv (c.978–1054), 24
Yazov, Dmitrii (1924–2020), 359, 381
Yedinstvo (Unity), 347
Yeltsin, Boris (1931–2007), 355–6, 358–60, 369, 377
Yiddish language, 10, 147, 184, 212–13, 240, 261, 262, 271, 275, 280, 284, 301, 325–6, 395
Yosaphat Kuntsevych, Saint (P. Jozafat Kuncewicz, c.1580–1623), 122
Yotvingians, 28, 30, 35
Yuliana of Tver' (c.1325–1391), 41, 397
Yuri II/Bolesław, Prince of Halych and Volhynia (1305/10–40), 37

Zamoyski, Jan (1542–1605), 106, 111–12
Zaporizhian Cossacks, 50, 122, 127, 140, see also Ukraine
Zasztowt, Aleksander (1877–1944), 249
Zatlers, Valdis (b. 1953), 379
Zawadzki, Józef (1781–1838), 188

INDEX

Żeligowski, Lucjan (1865–1947), 267, 394
Žemaitaitis, Remigijus (b. 1982), 392
Žemaitė (Julija Beniuševičiūtė-Žymantienė, 1845–1921), 215, 228, 331
Žemaitija, see Samogitia
Žemaitis, Jonas 'Vytautas' (1909–54), 320–1
Zemeckis, Robert (b. 1952), 316
Zhdanov, Andrei (1896–1948), 325
Zhou Enlai (1898–1976), 361
Zhytomyr (P. Żytomierz), 150
Zikaras, Juozas (1881–1944), 269, 286
Zingeris, Emanuelis (b. 1957), 390
Zionism, 240, 272
Žygimantas Kęstutaitis, Grand Duke of Lithuania (1365–1440), 69, 71, 106, 397
Žymantas, Laurynas (d. 1898), 215